The Politics of Heritage in Afric

Economies, Histories, and Infrastructures

C000048117

Heritage work has had a uniquely wide currency in Africa's politics. Secured within the pages of books, encoded in legal statutes, encased in glass display cases, and enacted in the panoply of court ritual, the artefacts produced by the heritage domain have become a resource for government administration, a library for traditionalists, and a marketable source of value for cultural entrepreneurs.

The Politics of Heritage in Africa draws together disparate fields of study – history, archaeology, linguistics, the performing arts, and cinema – to show how the lifeways of the past were made into capital, a store of authentic knowledge on which political and cultural entrepreneurs could draw. This book shows African heritage to be a mode of political organisation, a means by which the relics of the past are shored up, reconstructed, and revalued – as commodities, as tradition, as morality, or as patrimony.

Derek R. Peterson is Professor of History at the University of Michigan. He has edited several books, including *Recasting the Past: History Writing and Political Work in Modern Africa* (2009), and has authored *Ethnic Patriotism and the East African Revival* (2012).

Kodzo Gavua is Associate Professor of Archaeology and Heritage Studies at the University of Ghana, Legon. He has edited *A Handbook of Eweland: The Northern Ewes in Ghana* (2000) and is co-editor of *Intercultural Perspectives on Ghana* (2005).

Ciraj Rassool is Professor of History and director of the African Programme in Museum and Heritage Studies at the University of the Western Cape. He has co-authored and co-edited several books, including *Recalling Community in Cape Town: Creating and Curating the District Six Museum* (2001) and *Museum Frictions: Public Cultures/Global Transformations* (2006).

London, October 2021

"Heritage is an idea and a movement, and an industry. It engages states, communities, and capital. The work of heritage condenses into common frames both democratic and counterdemocratic impulses. As *The Politics of Heritage in Africa* implies, the contemporary force of heritage may be located in the enravelment of such contradictory effects. The appropriately diverse and engaged essays in this volume affirm that heritage has a history and a politics; moreover, that heritage can be skillfully deconstructed and critiqued, and indeed must be. *The Politics of Heritage in Africa* reflects big changes in the ways that the past of Africa has been and will be represented, known, and used. The volume opens a field of critical examination of heritage as a most influential mode of production of historical and cultural knowledge and meaning."

– David William Cohen, University of Michigan

THE INTERNATIONAL AFRICAN LIBRARY

General Editors

J. D. Y. PEEL, *School of Oriental and African Studies, University of London*
LESLIE BANK, *Fort Hare Institute of Social and Economic Research, South Africa*
HARRI ENGLUND, *University of Cambridge*
DEBORAH JAMES, *London School of Economics and Political Science*
ADELINE MASQUELIER, *Tulane University, Lousiana*

The International African Library is a major monograph series from the International African Institute. Theoretically informed ethnographies, and studies of social relations 'on the ground' which are sensitive to local cultural forms, have long been central to the Institute's publications programme. The IAL maintains this strength and extends it into new areas of contemporary concern, both practical and intellectual. It includes works focused on the linkages between local, national, and global levels of society; writings on political economy and power; studies at the interface of the socio-cultural and the environmental; analyses of the roles of religion, cosmology, and ritual in social organisation; and historical studies, especially those of a social, cultural, or interdisciplinary character.

For a list of titles published in the series, please see the end of the book.

The Politics of Heritage in Africa

Economies, Histories, and Infrastructures

Edited by

Derek R. Peterson
University of Michigan

Kodzo Gavua
University of Ghana

Ciraj Rassool
University of the Western Cape (South Africa)

International African Institute, London

and

CAMBRIDGE
UNIVERSITY PRESS

CAMBRIDGE
UNIVERSITY PRESS

University Printing House, Cambridge CB2 8BS, United Kingdom

One Liberty Plaza, 20th Floor, New York, NY 10006, USA

477 Williamstown Road, Port Melbourne, VIC 3207, Australia

4843/24, 2nd Floor, Ansari Road, Daryaganj, Delhi - 110002, India

79 Anson Road, #06-04/06, Singapore 079906

Cambridge University Press is part of the University of Cambridge.

It furthers the University's mission by disseminating knowledge in the pursuit of
education, learning and research at the highest international levels of excellence.

www.cambridge.org
Information on this title: www.cambridge.org/9781107477476

First published 2015
First paperback edition 2017

A catalogue record for this publication is available from the British Library

Library of Congress Cataloging in Publication data
The politics of heritage in Africa : economies, histories, and infrastructures /
[edited by] Derek Peterson (University of Michigan), Kodzo Gavua (University
of Ghana) Ciraj Rassool (University of the Western Cape (South Africa)).
    pages cm. – (The international African library)
Includes bibliographical references and index.
Papers first presented at a conference held July 2011 at Museum Africa,
Johannesburg.
1. Cultural property – Political aspects – Ghana – Congresses.   2. Cultural
property – Political aspects – South Africa – Congresses.   3. Heritage tourism
– Political aspects – Ghana – Congresses.   4. Heritage tourism – Political
aspects – South Africa – Congresses.   5. Cultural property – Protection –
Ghana – Congresses.   6. Cultural property – Protection – South Africa –
Congresses.   7. Ethnological museums and collections – Political aspects –
Ghana – Congresses.   8. Ethnological museums and collections – Political
aspects – South Africa – Congresses.   I. Peterson, Derek R., 1971– editor of
compilation.   II. Gavua, Kodzo, editor of compilation.   III. Rassool, Ciraj,
editor of compilation.   IV. Series: International African library.
DT510.4.P65   2015
363.69096–dc23   2014038236

ISBN   978-1-107-09485-7   Hardback
ISBN   978-1-107-47747-6   Paperback

Contents

List of Maps and Figures

Notes on Contributors

Mbongiseni Buthelezi is a senior researcher at the Centre for Law and Society, University of Cape Town. His current work focuses on the logics underpinning post-apartheid legislation on customary law and traditional leadership in South Africa. He holds a PhD in English and Comparative Literature from Columbia University and previously taught African literature in the English Department at the University of Cape Town.

Mary Esther Kropp Dakubu received her BA (English and Philosophy) from Queen's University (in Kingston Ontario), MA (Linguistics) from the University of Pennsylvania, and PhD (West African Languages) from the School of Oriental and African Studies, University of London. She joined the staff of the Institute of African Studies of the University of Ghana in 1964, where she is now Emerita Professor of African Studies. She was elected Fellow of the Ghana Academy of Arts and Sciences in 1990.

Kodzo Gavua is Associate Professor of Archaeology and Heritage Studies at the University of Ghana, Legon. He holds a PhD in Archaeology and two MAs, in African Archaeology and International Affairs. His research focus is on cross-cultural interactions and Ghana's cultural, social, and economic development; he also engages in public archaeology and heritage resource management.

Carolyn Hamilton holds a National Research Foundation Chair in Archive and Public Culture at the University of Cape Town. Her research areas include the ethnography and history of the archive, the history of pre-industrial South Africa, and the anthropology of the past in the present. Her publications include *The Cambridge History of South Africa* (2009) (co-editor), *Refiguring the Archive* (2002) (co-editor), *Terrific Majesty: The Powers of Shaka Zulu and the Limits of Invention* (1998), and *The Mfecane Aftermath* (1995).

Daniel Herwitz is Fredrick Huetwell Professor of Comparative Literature, History of Art, and Philosophy at the University of Michigan, where for a decade he directed the Institute for the Humanities. A decade's work in South Africa (at the University of Natal in the 1990s) led to his book *Race and Reconciliation* (2003). Herwitz retains a formal connection with the University of Cape Town, and while an Andrew Mellon Fellow there (in the Archives and Public Culture Seminar, 2010) he wrote the substance of his *Heritage, Culture and Politics in the Postcolony* (2012).

Judith T. Irvine is Edward Sapir Collegiate Professor of Linguistic Anthropology at the University of Michigan. Her research has focused on language and communication in social, cultural, and historical context, with particular attention to how communicative practices both shape and reflect ideology and social hierarchy. She has done ethnographic, linguistic, and sociolinguistic fieldwork in Senegal, as well as research on languages spoken in other parts of the African continent. In addition to publications resulting from those research efforts, and theoretically oriented works on ideologies of language, she is the author of many articles on the colonial history of African linguistics.

Gary Minkley has held the National Research Foundation Chair in Social Change since 2009 and is Professor of History at the University of Fort Hare. One of his major research focus areas is concerned with public histories in South Africa, and with the ways that space, public history, the visual, and the performative produce knowledge about the past and relate to the constituting acts of the social and of social change.

Phindezwa Mnyaka is a senior lecturer in Fine Arts at Rhodes University. She has a PhD in History from the University of Fort Hare. She is particularly interested in photography about Africa in the early twentieth century.

Litheko Modisane is a senior lecturer in Film and Media at the University of Cape Town. He received his Masters and Doctoral degrees at the University of the Witwatersrand. Modisane is the author of *South Africa's Renegade Reels: The Making and Public Lives of Black Centered Films* (2013).

Noëleen Murray is an architect and academic in the Department of Geography and Environmental Studies at the University of the Western Cape. Her research over many years offers a reading of architecture and urban planning under and after apartheid, in which she considers conjunctions between architectural modernism and apartheid modernity. Murray is principal editor of *Desire Lines: Space, Memory and Identity in the Post-apartheid City* and co-editor, with Premesh Lalu, of *Becoming UWC: Reflections, Pathways and Unmaking of Apartheid's Legacy*.

Moses N. Nii-Dortey is a Research Fellow with the 'Music and Dance' section of the Institute of African Studies, University of Ghana, Legon. His research interests are in the music history of Ghana, the development

of folk opera in Ghana, and traditional festivals as integrated perform-
ances. He was one the first cohort of African Presidential Scholars at the
University of Michigan, Ann Arbor, in 2008/9. He received the African
Humanities Dissertation Fellowship of the American Council of Learned
Societies in 2011/12.

Derek R. Peterson teaches African history at the University of
Michigan. He is the author of *Ethnic Patriotism and the East African
Revival: A History of Dissent* (2012), which won the Herskovits Prize and
the Martin Klein Prize, and editor of several books, including *Abolitionism
and Imperialism in Britain, Africa and the Atlantic* (2011) and *Recasting the
Past: History Writing and Political Work in Modern Africa* (2009). With colleagues at Mountains of the Moon University, he coordinates an ongoing
project to organise, preserve, and digitise endangered archival material
in Uganda.

Ciraj Rassool is Professor of History and Director of the African Programme in Museum and Heritage Studies at the University of the Western Cape. He is Chairperson of the board of the District Six Museum and
until 2013 also chaired the council of Iziko Museums of South Africa. He
is also a member of the Human Remains Repatriation Advisory Committee of South Africa's Minister of Arts and Culture. He has co-authored
and co-edited a number of books about museums, collecting, and public
culture including *Skeletons in the Cupboard: South African Museums and
the Trade in Human Remains, 1907–1917* (2000); *Recalling Community in
Cape Town: Creating and Curating the District Six Museum* (2001); *Museum
Frictions: Public Cultures/Global Transformations* (2006); and *Popular Snapshots and Tracks to the Past: Cape Town, Nairobi, Lubumbashi* (2010).

Raymond Silverman is Professor of History of Art, Afroamerican and
African Studies, and Museum Studies at the University of Michigan.
His research has examined the social values associated with creativity
in Ethiopia, the visual cultures of religion in twentieth-century Ethiopia,
and the commodification of art in Ethiopia and Ghana. Most recently Silverman has been exploring 'museum culture' in Africa, specifically how
local knowledge is articulated and translated in national and community-
based cultural institutions.

Leslie Witz is a Professor in the History Department at the University of
the Western Cape and was leader of the Project on Public Pasts and the
Heritage Disciplines Project, funded by the National Research Foundation. His major research centres on how different histories are created
and represented in the public domain through memorials, museums, festivals, and tourism. He is the author of *Write Your Own History* (1988),
Apartheid's Festival: Contesting South Africa's National Pasts (2003) and

co-author, with Ciraj Rassool and Paul Faber, of *South African Family Stories: Reflections on an Experiment in Exhibition Making* (2007).

Kwesi Yankah is a Professor of Linguistics, specialising in ethnography of communication. Educated at the University of Ghana and Indiana University, he is currently President of Central University in Ghana and had previously occupied several positions at the University of Ghana, including Dean, Faculty of Arts, and Pro–Vice Chancellor for Academic and Student Affairs. Yankah has published widely in several international journals, and his book *Speaking for the Chief* (1995) is used in universities worldwide. He has held visiting professorships at the University of Michigan at Ann Arbor, the University of California, Berkeley, and the University of Pennsylvania.

Preface and Acknowledgements

African heritage had never seemed more pertinent than it did at the turn of the second millennium. In South Africa, the end of apartheid occasioned the rapid overhaul of the museum collections, the commissioning of new memorials and monuments, the proliferation of new holidays, and the redeployment of professional scholars. The District Six Museum in Cape Town was opened in 1994. One of the moving spirits within it was Ciraj Rassool of the University of the Western Cape. The Lwandle Migrant Labour Museum opened its doors in the year 2000; on its managing board was Leslie Witz, also of the University of the Western Cape. The Hector Pieterson Museum was opened in Soweto in 2003. Among its core exhibits were a set of oral interviews that the curator, Ali Hlongwane, had conducted with the young participants in the 1976 uprising.[1] The heritage sector in Ghana was likewise occupying new spaces and opening up new sites of memory. There was an increasingly large tourist trade centred around the 'slave castles' on the Ghanaian coast: Elmina received a record 100,000 visitors in 2000; Cape Coast castle received 34,871.[2] In 1994 UNESCO launched the 'Slave Route Project', which encouraged the world's population to 'enhance their awareness of the cultural heritage of the slave trade', and in 2007 Ghana's Ministry of Tourism launched the 'Joseph Project', which aimed to bring together Africans on the continent and in the diaspora to address the legacies of the slave trade. There followed a proliferation of new memorials in upcountry Ghana, as rural people sought to make their localities part of the burgeoning touristic infrastructure. Entrepreneurs in Assin Manso constructed a garden and a 'Wall of Remembrance' at the site of what had once been a slave depot; in Salaga a museum was constructed near the location of a slave market.[3]

---

[1] Described in Ali Khangela Hlongwane, 'The Mapping of the June 16 1976 Soweto Student Uprisings Routes: Past Recollections and Present Reconstructions', *Journal of African Cultural Studies* 19, 1 (2007): 7–36.

[2] Bayo Holsey, *Routes of Remembrance: Refashioning the Slave Trade in Ghana* (Chicago, IL: University of Chicago Press, 2008), 178.

[3] Katharina Schramm, 'Slave Route Projects: Tracing the Heritage of Slavery in Ghana', in Ferdinand de Jong and Michael Rowlands (eds), *Reclaiming Heritage: Alternative Imaginaries of Memory in West Africa* (Walnut Creek, CA: Left Coast Press, 2007), 71–98.

Scholars at the University of Michigan were very much involved in these new articulations of African heritage. Cultural historian Daniel Herwitz was drafting a book about the heritage industry in South Africa.[4] Art historian Ray Silverman was working with local authorities to develop a new museum and cultural centre in Techiman, in central Ghana.[5] Anthropologist Kelly Askew was completing a manuscript about music and national culture in socialist Tanzania.[6] Ethnomusicologist Lester Monts had published a book that classified the instruments and repertoires of Vai musicians in Liberia.[7] Michigan's School of Information had a long-standing relationship with the University of Fort Hare, where Michigan students had been involved in the organisation of the archives of the African National Congress. In 2008 University of Michigan President Mary Sue Coleman paid an official visit to several universities in Ghana and South Africa, and thereafter she opened up a stream of funding to support faculty and student collaborations in the hard sciences, the social sciences, and the humanities. Part of this tranche of funding supported the creation of the 'African Heritage Initiative', an international working group of scholars and practitioners. Since its creation the Heritage Initiative has supported a range of worthy projects: archive preservation work in Uganda and South Sudan; master classes joining opera faculty at Michigan with colleagues in Cape Town; the digitisation of the African music recordings of the Voice of America; the preservation of the video archives of the palace of the Asantehene. Its central task has been to facilitate and sustain collaborations joining faculty in Ann Arbor with colleagues in Ghana and South Africa. There was, first, a seminar about digital records management at Rhodes University; then a large international conference, titled 'Heritage Matters', in Accra in December 2009; and finally, in July 2011, a scholarly meeting held at Museum Africa in Johannesburg.

The present volume grows out of this programme of activity. As editors, we gratefully acknowledge the people who helped to create the infrastructure for our work. We thank, first, President Coleman, whose generous support and capacious vision created the framework for this collaboration. We thank Lester Monts, accomplished ethnomusicologist and Senior Vice Provost for Academic Affairs at Michigan, whose leadership oriented the Heritage Initiative's work. We thank Kelly Askew, founding

---

[4] Since published as Daniel Herwitz, *Heritage, Culture, and Politics in the Postcolony* (New York, NY: Columbia University Press, 2012).

[5] Described in J. Boachie Ansah, 'The Techiman Archaeological Project', *Nyame Akuma* 68 (December 2007): 21–33.

[6] Kelly Askew, *Performing the Nation: Swahili Music and Cultural Politics in Tanzania* (Chicago, IL: University of Chicago Press, 2002).

[7] Lester Monts, *An Annotated Glossary of Vai Musical Language and Its Social Contexts* (Paris: Peeters-Selaf, 1990).

Director of the African Studies Center at Michigan, and Devon Keen, the Center's administrator, whose boundless energy brought coherence and discipline to all of our endeavours. In Accra we were hosted by the Institute of African Studies at the University of Ghana. We thank Brigid Sackey, the Institute's Acting Director, and Kojo Amanor, its Associate Director, for their hospitality. In Johannesburg, where most of the chapters in this volume were discussed, we were hosted by Dr Cynthia Kros and the Division of Arts, Culture, and Heritage Management at the University of the Witwatersrand. Naomi Roux, a postgraduate student at Wits, organised the logistics for the occasion. The conference was held in Museum Africa, where Ali Hlongwane, the museum's director since 2008, generously opened up the vast vaults for us to explore. We thank the several scholars who played a critical role in the Johannesburg conference as discussants or as presenters: Hylton White, Sekepe Matjila, Liz Gunner, Michele Pickover, Peter Lekgoathi, Anthea Josias, and Isabel Hofmeyr.

The International African Institute supported this project in its earliest days, and we particularly thank Mark Horton and Karin Barber, who have been vitally involved in our activities. We are tremendously grateful to Stephanie Kitchen, chair of the Publications Committee of the IAI, who gracefully shepherded this manuscript through the long process of its production. Many thanks.

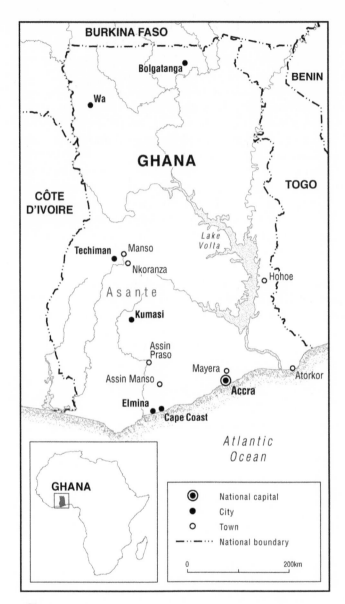

Ghana

South Africa

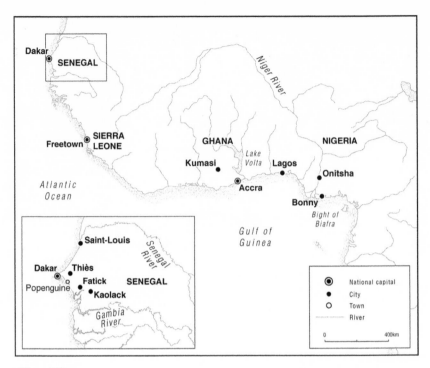

West Africa

1 Introduction

Heritage Management in Colonial and Contemporary Africa

Derek R. Peterson

This book is about the work that the heritage industry does in African political life.[1] Like Barbara Kirshenblatt-Gimblett, we take heritage to be a form of cultural production in the present that has recourse to the past.[2] But unlike her, we argue that the products of heritage work do not always have the museum as their destination. In colonial and post-colonial Africa, the practices of museology – detachment, decontextualisation, display – helped to constitute and organise cultural and political life. Heritage work has had a uniquely wide currency in Africa. In colonial times, administrators organised tribal communities around a supposedly traditional order of law and custom. In the 1960s and 1970s, African politicians sought to build the nation by integrating disparate ethnicities, constituting the basis for unitary national cultures. Today, there is a booming market in heritage products of Africa, and entrepreneurs avidly pursue development by making medicine, art, music, clothing, and other articles into global commodities. A great variety of brokers outside the museum have been involved in the production of heritage. Their work was essential to the construction of regimes of governmentality. Linguists plucked words out of people's mouths, published grammar books and dictionaries, and gave material form to standardised print languages. Ethnographers chose rituals and life practices out of the whole fabric of human life, documented their logic, and created a textual architecture for African religion, kinship, and ethnicity. Administrators looked for the rules that guided human interaction, assembled codes and precedents, and created the infrastructure for customary law. Through these and other documentary practices the routines of human

---

[1] The author gratefully acknowledges comments offered by Andrew State, Neil Kodesh, and participants in the workshop 'Colonial Ruptures and the Politics of Knowledge', held in Ann Arbor in April 2012. Archival collections are abbreviated as follows: BDA: Bundibugyo District Archives; KasDA: Kasese District Archives; KabDA: Kabarole District Archives; Churchill: Churchill College archives, Cambridge; UNA: Uganda National Archives, Entebbe.

[2] Barbara Kirshenblatt-Gimblett, *Destination Culture: Tourism, Museums, and Heritage* (Berkeley, CA: University of California Press, 1998), 149.

life were lifted out of the dynamic real world, placed outside the reach of change and innovation, and rendered anachronistic at the moment of publication. Secure within the pages of the book, encoded in legal statutes, encased in glass display cases, the anachronisms produced by the human sciences became a resource for government administration, a library for traditionalists, and a marketable source of value for cultural entrepreneurs.

All of it was a work of fiction. Africa has always been a place of open frontiers, in which people could move relatively freely across an open terrain.[3] Cultures have always been dynamic and open; pre-colonial states were polyglot and diverse. Prior to the twentieth century, African political leaders did not possess the institutional architecture with which to close their frontiers and impose a monoculture on the disparate people they governed. The notion that any people – whether a tribe, a nation, or any other kind of community – had a settled past is necessarily a fallacy. Almost everyone was an immigrant. There are no purebreds. The diversity and dynamism of Africa's population history has made the work of heritage all the more tendentious. In Africa as elsewhere, heritage work is an act of consolidation, a means of taming cultural diversity and organising diverse rituals, behaviours, and objects into a regimented routine.

The Politics of Heritage in Africa aims to push the study of heritage work outside the domain of museum studies and explore the wider arenas where ideas about tradition, patrimony, and authenticity are debated and defined. The book draws together disparate fields of study to show how the lifeways of the past were made into capital, a store of authentic knowledge on which contemporary political actors could draw. All of the essays take an historical approach to their subject matter. Scholars in the field of museum studies too often orient their research towards the present day, offering prescriptive advice to curators and policy makers about how to reorganise displays and open up heritage sites. This volume, by contrast, explores the changing regimes through which knowledge about the African past was produced, edited, displayed, and made meaningful. The book sheds light on the variety of sites in which this work of editing took place: in linguistics (Irvine and Dakubu); in music (Nii-Dortey); in architecture (Gavua, Silverman); in the building of monuments (Minkley and Mnyaka, Witz and Murray); in poetry (Buthelezi); in cemeteries and laboratories (Rassool). And it brings into view the cultural workers who were involved in the making of African heritage. Here we meet Felicia Obuobie, who conceived a memorial garden for Martin Luther King Jr in the remote Ghanaian town of Manso; Bongani Mgijima, who launched

---

[3] John Iliffe, *Africans: The History of a Continent* (Cambridge: Cambridge University Press, 1995); see also Paul Landau, *Popular Politics in the History of South Africa, 1400 to 1948* (Cambridge: Cambridge University Press, 2010).

an unlikely museum in a disused workers' hostel in Lwandle, in the Western Cape; Sakhile Nxumalo, whose efforts to create a 'Zwide Heritage Day' challenge the coherence of the Zulu ethnic community; and Saka Acquaye, who composed folk operas that linked Ghanaians together in a Nkrumaist vision of national solidarity. Taken together, these chapters show heritage to be a mode of political organisation, a means by which the relics of the past are shored up, reconstructed, and revalued, as commodities, as tradition, as morality, or as a patrimony.

The book grows out of a series of academic exchanges joining scholars at the University of Michigan with colleagues based in the universities of Ghana and South Africa. Over the course of several years – beginning with a workshop on digital records management at Rhodes University, passing through a major conference in Accra, and culminating in a consultation at the University of the Witwatersrand in 2011 – the contributors have been engaged in a comparative conversation about their work. The geographical focus is both exclusive and productive. There are good reasons to study Ghana and South Africa alongside each other. Ghana was the first of Britain's African colonies to claim its political independence; South Africa is the African state that has most recently achieved majority governance. Ghana's first President, Kwame Nkrumah, was an enthusiastic builder of national culture; likewise, South Africa's ruling African National Congress has been remaking its history of struggle into a curriculum for national heritage. Ghana is today a leading destination for African-American tourists, and Ghanaian culture brokers have been active in marketing the historical architecture of the slave trade for the international market. South Africa's entrepreneurs have sought to make history marketable by revaluing the landscape of apartheid's abuses into sites of tourism. By placing Ghana and South Africa alongside each other, we can open up comparisons that productively illuminate the more generalised dynamics of the heritage economy.

This introductory chapter chronicles the history of heritage work in Africa. An historical approach is essential, for it was under colonial governance that both the physical infrastructure and the political rationale for many heritage projects were established. In the early twentieth century colonial states set out to order Africa, developing museum collections, conducting ethnography, and sponsoring linguistic research that uncovered the foundations of Africa's cultural life. Their work made anachronism into a source of authority, herding Africans, both intellectually and politically, into out-of-date regimes. The second section focuses on the work of heritage in independent Africa, showing how sovereign states remade the architecture of colonial governance by rebuilding the museum infrastructure. The chapter ends by reflecting on the dynamics of heritage in contemporary Africa, focusing on the career of the National Resistance Movement government in Uganda. In Uganda as elsewhere in contemporary Africa, the past is a source of marketable value, and an array of entrepreneurs – traditional doctors, chiefs, jewellery makers, philanthropists – are producing heritage commodities. The incorporation of African cultural production is a welcome source of revenue, but it also encourages monopolist practices. There has been a recrudescence of the out-of-date and the anachronistic: new kingdoms are being created, long-forgotten royalist ceremonies are being rehearsed, crowns are being polished. The contemporary heritage economy has encouraged the recreation of profoundly unequal, exclusive government arrangements, giving kings, princes, and other relics a central place in the marketing of history. In this way the heritage economy poses a substantial challenge to the liberal promises of democracy.

Museum Cultures in Colonial Africa

The term 'cultural imperialism' appears to have entered analytical nomenclature in the 1960s.[4] At a time when newly independent African states were establishing the foundations for a sovereign political order, 'cultural imperialism' gave radical intellectuals a lexicon by which to define language, religion, and art as fields of struggle. 'Every colonised people – in other words, every people in whose soul an inferiority complex has been created by the death and burial of its local cultural originality – finds itself face to face with the language of the civilising nation; that is, with the culture of the mother country,' wrote Frantz Fanon in 1967.[5] It was the task of the artist, the novelist, the educator and the musician to 'decolonise the mind', to decouple contemporary life from European influences, to reconnect African culture with the taproot authenticity of the vernacular, the language of the people.[6] The logic of political independence was imported into the field of cultural production, and African artists, musicians, and writers were given a particular vocation: the recovery of a sovereign way of life.

In fact colonial governance was creative, not only destructive, of African cultural systems. Colonial states in Africa were ethnographic states.[7] They valorised African languages, cultures, and institutions, gave them a solid form, put them on the page, so as to make them the grounds of governance. Museums were part of the infrastructure through which

---

[4] John Tomlinson, *Cultural Imperialism* (London: Continuum, 1991), 2–3; see Ryan Dunch, 'Beyond Cultural Imperialism: Cultural Theory, Christian Missions, and Global Modernity', *History and Theory* 41, 3 (October 2002): 301–25.

[5] Frantz Fanon, *Black Skin, White Masks* (New York, NY: Grove, 1967 [1952]), 18.

[6] Argued particularly in Ngũgĩ wa Thiong'o, *Decolonising the Mind: The Politics of Language in African Literature* (Portsmouth, NH: Heinemann Educational Publishers, 1981).

[7] See Nicholas Dirks, *Castes of Mind: Colonialism and the Making of Modern India* (Princeton, NJ: Princeton University Press, 2001), Part Three.

missionaries and other agents of colonialism ordered Africa.[8] The ethnological section at the Uganda Museum originated from the British governor's 1908 order that administrative officers should send in 'curios of all descriptions such as articles of local interest, specimens of native weapons and manufactures, and local products, vegetable and mineral: in fact all articles of historical, ethnological and industrial interest'.[9] For colonial officers, museumisation was a useful way of placing contentious or dangerous objects out of the public domain. On 10 July 1954, the police searched the home of the old woman Magoba, in north-west Uganda, and confiscated five objects that were said to have been used for witchcraft. The objects – a string with cowrie shells, two headbands, a piece of barkcloth – were handed on to the Uganda Museum. They were given numbers E54.58 through E54.62 in the catalogue.[10] Dozens of objects similarly came into the Museum's collection through the operation of the courts, since the law obliged judges to 'order the confiscation and destruction of any article brought before [the court] . . . which the court is satisfied was or might have been used in the commission of [witchcraft]'.[11] Other objects came into the Uganda Museum's collections through military force. In 1963 the Museum was given a collection of artefacts from the mountains of western Uganda – two drums, three spears, flutes, and other articles – by a captain in the police Special Force Unit.[12] He and his men had been fighting to put down a rebellion that people in the mountains had mounted against the Uganda government. Museum collections are the physical remains of practices, institutions, movements, and ideologies that were conquered and dismembered, as governments established their rule over Africa's peoples. Human bodies were similarly disincorporated. In this volume Ciraj Rassool reminds us about the gruesome work by which the collections of physical anthropology museums were constituted. Most famously, the body of Sara Baartman, the 'Hottentot Venus', was upon her demise placed in the Museum of Natural History in Paris, where Georges Cuvier and his students dissected it.[13] A host of other African bodies were likewise dismembered, pickled, placed in barrels, and shipped off to museums, where they became evidence in the enterprise of racial science (Rassool, this volume).

---

[8] See Helen Tilley (ed.), *Ordering Africa: Anthropology, European Imperialism, and the Politics of Knowledge* (Manchester: Manchester University Press, 2007).

[9] Quoted in Valerie Vowles, 'Uganda in the Fifties', *Newsletter (Museum Ethnographers Group)* 12 (October 1981).

[10] Uganda Museum archives, 'Ethnography, 1948–58' catalogue: objects E54.58–E54.62.

[11] UNA CSO Box 105/18373: Uganda Protectorate, 'The Witchcraft Ordinance', 1957.

[12] Uganda Museum archives, 'Ethnography 1958–64' catalogue: objects E63.111–E63.119.

[13] Clifton Crais and Pamela Scully, *Sara Baartman and the Hottentot Venus: A Ghost Story and a Biography* (Princeton, NJ: Princeton University Press, 2009).

The objects that were assembled in ethnographic exhibitions were not, in their conception, destined for the museum. In Africa as elsewhere, museum collections were constituted out of a process of detachment, of dismemberment, as the remains of human and political bodies were pruned, requisitioned, and put on display.[14] In 1919 British officials in southern Uganda managed to kill Ndochibiri, a spirit medium and leader of a long-running rebellion against colonial government. They cut off his distinctive two-fingered hand, dried it, and displayed it for public examination on the District Commissioner's porch. His head was cut off and sent to the British Museum.[15] Other potentially subversive objects were similarly taken out of circulation. The drum Nyakahoza was the voice of the ruling dynasty of Kinkiizi (in southern Uganda). It was an active agent in Kinkiizi's political life: people made offerings to it during times of drought, asking the drum to bring rain on their fields.[16] In the late 1930s two sons of the king converted to Christianity, and they handed the drum to a British missionary as evidence of their sincerity. The missionary deposited it in the Uganda Museum.[17] For the missionary as for the District Commissioner, the museum worked in the service of government. In its halls dangerous objects were stripped of their upsetting powers and naturalised, transformed into subjects of scholarly study and aesthetic admiration. The Uganda Museum opened its ethnography gallery in 1954. The catalogue illuminates the logic that guided the exhibition. Entitled *Tribal Crafts of Uganda*, it categorised objects according to their material form: there were chapters on 'Basketry', on 'Gourd Vessels', and on 'Pottery'. Drums were dealt with in a chapter on 'membranophones'.[18] For the museum's curators, drums were material objects, instruments with which to make music. The political voice of the drum – its coordinating resonance, its power to summon people and punctuate their movements – was rendered inaudible.[19] In the museum, drums became objects of ethnography.

---

[14] Kirshenblatt-Gimblett, *Destination Culture*, Ch. 1.

[15] Yohana Ssebalija, 'Memories of Rukiga and Other Places', in Donald Denoon (ed.), *A History of Kigezi in South-West Uganda* (Kampala: The National Trust, 1972), 195; Rhodes House archive Mss. Afr. s. 1384: J. E. T. Philipps, 'The Nabingi: A Mandwa Secret Society' (typescript, July 1919).

[16] Described in Paulo Ngologoza, *Kigezi and Its People* (Kampala: Fountain, 1998 [1967]), 30.

[17] H. Ahurwendeire, 'Some aspects of the history of Kinkiizi' (BA thesis, Makerere University, 1973).

[18] Margaret Trowell and K. P. Wachsmann, *Tribal Crafts of Uganda* (London: Oxford University Press, 1953).

[19] For drums and political coordination in eastern Africa, see Steven Feierman, 'On Socially Composed Knowledge: Reconstructing a Shambaa Royal Ritual', in Gregory H. Maddox and James L. Giblin (eds), *In Search of a Nation: Histories of Authority and Dissidence in Tanzania* (Athens, OH: Ohio University Press, 2005), 14–32.

The museum was only one among several institutions in which
Africans' bodies, cultures, languages, and institutions were dismembered
and reincorporated as museum pieces. Indirect rule – by which government employed African chiefs, kings, and sultans as lower-level functionaries – was an engine for the production of heritage discourse. It made the
arts of antiquity central to the *realpolitik* of governance. British officials
buttressed the legal authority of their African intermediaries by codifying
apparently ancient traditions, and African intermediaries, in turn, lent
themselves authenticity by emphasising the antique character of their
institutions. The kingdom of Toro, for example, was an administrative
convenience for the British government of colonial Uganda. It had been
constituted in the late nineteenth century by the British conquistadores
who established the colony.[20] But by the mid-twentieth century the kingdom's elites were avidly identifying themselves as legatees of an ancient
civilisation. 'The word LOCAL GOVERNMENT for Toro Government
should not be applied,' wrote the kingdom's prime minister. 'The History
of this country is one of a Kingdom about 2,000 years old.'[21] Royalists
laid on an impressive pageant when a British lawyer visited the court. 'No
one stands in the presence of his sovereign,' the lawyer reported. 'There
is a court Jester who welcomes visitors by leaping about with a spear,
and both sunrise and sunset are heralded with the beating of drums.'[22]
Toro's leaders urged that their king should be given four motorcyclists, a
white-uniformed chauffeur, and a brass band, all clad in blue, to accompany him during state functions. By these means they sought to protect
the 'dignity and conventional prerogatives' of Toro's throne.[23] Royalist
pageantry gave Toro elites means to contrast their kingdom's order with
the uncivil, disordered politics of their neighbours. 'All districts without
a king should be persuaded to elect a hereditary king from among their
noble families,' argued Toro politicians. 'The Kikuyu people have no
hereditary king. . . . If they had kings there would have been no Mau
Mau.'[24] Toro elites were not antiquarians. In archaic rituals, with brass
bands and chauffeurs, they established their kingdom's preeminent place
in history. By their strategic ornamentalism Toro elites made their kingdom worthy of respect in the colonial theatre.

The discourse and practice of colonial governance prized the archaic
and the out-of-date as the foundation of authentic African tradition. The

---

[20] See Edward Steinhart, *Conflict and Collaboration in the Kingdoms of Western Uganda*
(Princeton, NJ: Princeton University Press, 1977).
[21] KabDA Box 122, 'Petitions, Complaints and Enquiries' file: H. Nkojo to Governor,
20 August 1953.
[22] Churchill DGFT 5/8: Dingle Foot, editorial letter, 30 July 1956.
[23] KabDA Box 145, 'Relationship with Rulers in Agreement Countries' file: J. Babiiha
to Katikiros of Toro, Bunyoro and Ankole, 19 July 1958. The District Commissioner
marked this memorandum with the annotation 'Good God!'
[24] Churchill DGFT 5/8: 'Kingdom of Toro, Revised Proposals', n.d. (1956).

enterprise of inventorying, codifying, or inventing traditions was carried out in a number of registers. In linguistics, missionaries and African converts searched out archaic phrases to translate Christian concepts into vernacular languages. African languages were – like all languages – dynamic, full of irregular syntax and loan words. There was much that could not be put into words (Yankah, this volume). Competent speakers had to be creative: they used circumlocution, loan words, and other artifices to avoid bringing controversial or divisive events into discourse. Bible translators regarded loan words and other innovations as corruptions of the authentic vernacular. In their word lists and grammar books, the linguists who first documented African languages sought to uncover the taproots of Africans' intellectual culture, in order to yoke Christian ideas with the basic concepts of African cosmology (Irvine, this volume).[25] In the papers of the Scots missionary who translated the Old Testament into Kenya's Gikuyu language there are dozens of pages titled 'Modernisms' or 'Foreign Words of Comparative Recent Introduction', listing words and phrases that had been imported into the vernacular from English or Swahili.[26] Linguists sought to roll back the clock and compose vernacular texts with anachronistic vocabulary.

Like the linguists, moral reformers looked to uncover the antique foundations of contemporary cultural systems. The mid-twentieth century saw the publication of dozens of history books, written in vernacular languages, that documented the history of the Asante, the Gogo, the Zulu, and other groups. This corpus of homespun history was animated by the need to conserve customary morality against the debilitating threat of amnesia.[27] 'People who have no respect for their society's customs and practices . . . are scattered all over the earth, and people refer to them as *jodak* [vagrants],' wrote Chief Paul Mboya in his 1938 study of Luo culture.[28] One researcher claimed to have traced the history of the Luo people 'as far back as 9,000 BC or thereabout'.[29] In Luo country as elsewhere in colonial Africa, patriotic historians filled volumes with proverbs, folk stories, and legal codes. By this means they sought to protect their people against the rootlessness of ignorance. Historical preservation

---

[25] Paul Landau, ' "Religion" and Christian Conversion in African History: A New Model', *Journal of Religious History* 23, 1 (February 1999): 8–30.

[26] Edinburgh University Library 1785/7: 'Foreign Words of comparatively recent introduction now in use among the Kikuyu', n.d., and 1786/6: 'Modernisms, ndaari na ma tene', n.d.

[27] See Derek R. Peterson and Giacomo Macola, 'Homespun History and the Academic Profession', in Peterson and Macola (eds), *Recasting the Past: History Writing and Political Work in Modern Africa* (Athens, OH: Ohio University Press, 2009).

[28] Paul Mboya, *Luo Kitgi gi Timbegi* (Kisumu: Anyange Press, 1983 [1938]). For a translation, see Jane Achieng, *Paul Mboya's Luo Kitgi gi Timbegi* (Kisumu: Atai Joint, 2001).

[29] The book in question was J. Okinda's *History mar Luo*, described in Kenya National Archives, Kakamega Regional Depot, file NE 9/9: Director of the East African Literature Bureau to Senior Education Officer, Kakamega, 20 February 1951.

helped to buttress the cause of moral reform by giving conservatives a means to contrast the corruptions of the present with the virtues of the past.[30]

The system of apartheid in South Africa was but one expression of this more general valuation of the archaic. The architect of indirect rule in Natal, Theophilus Shepstone, looked to the Zulu state established under Shaka's regime as a model for colonial governance. He surrounded himself with the artefacts and emblems of Zulu royalty – Shepstone had his own snuff-box bearer – and organised local government institutions after Shaka's example.[31] As Mbongiseni Buthelezi reminds us in this volume, the 'Zulu' – like other South African 'native' people – were actually a diverse, polyglot polity, not a coherent cultural unit.[32] But South Africa's heritage industry had no time for nuance. From the 1913 passage of the Native Land Act up through the late twentieth century, millions of Africans were removed from their homes and settled in reserves, called 'homelands', on the basis of their ethnic identity. Ten homelands were established and, eventually, given a nominal political independence. South Africa's tourist industry borrowed the language of separate development, making the archaic into a marketing strategy. The South African Tourism Board – established in 1947 – encouraged tourists to visit 'picturesque Bantu-lands where customs and tribal rites are still practised according to ancient traditions'.[33] A series of cultural villages were established, where visitors were allowed to witness distinctive tribal ceremonies and participate in a daily routine of rituals and ceremonies.

A large and variegated ensemble of entrepreneurs – linguists, moral reformers, missionaries, chiefs and elders, colonial administrators, tour guides – were involved in the invention of tradition in colonial Africa. None of them could adopt a dispassionate view of the past. All of them were preservationists, vigorously defending ways of life that they thought to be endangered by the debilitating passage of time. All of them were conservatives, working to uphold standards of order against the tides of change. All of them regarded culture as a source of moral instruction and a ground for political solidarity. Where did the museum stop and real life

---

[30] Derek R. Peterson, *Ethnic Patriotism and the East African Revival: A History of Dissent, ca. 1935–1972* (Cambridge: Cambridge University Press, 2012).

[31] Carolyn Hamilton, *Terrific Majesty: The Powers of Shaka Zulu and the Limits of Historical Invention* (Cambridge, MA: Harvard University Press, 1998); and Thomas McClendon, *White Chief, Black Lords: Shepstone and the Colonial State in Natal, South Africa, 1845–1878* (Rochester, NY: University of Rochester Press, 2010).

[32] See Michael Mahoney, *The Other Zulus: The Spread of Zulu Ethnicity in Colonial South Africa* (Durham, NC: Duke University Press, 2012).

[33] *The CVR Tourist Guide to South Africa, 1966–67* (Johannesburg: C. van Rensburg Publications, 1966); quoted in Leslie Witz, 'Transforming Museums on Postaparthied Tourist Routes', in Ivan Karp, Corrine A. Kratz, Lynn Szwaja, and Tomás Ybarra-Frausto (eds), *Museum Frictions: Public Cultures/Global Transformations* (Durham, NC: Duke University Press, 2007), 113.

begin? The outmoded, the dead, and the defunct were the foundation of colonial order.

But there were always other lives for the objects of ethnography to live. The drum Nyakahoza was given to missionary Leonard Sharp by its keepers in the late 1930s (above). Sharp had the drum displayed at a local church as evidence of their conversion, then took it to the Uganda Museum. Forty years later, an old man named Baryaruha described the drum's awful revenge in an interview with a Makerere undergraduate.[34] One of the men who had given the drum to the missionary was possessed by a spirit; as he died he cried aloud that Nyakahoza was killing him. Another of the drum keepers was involved in a bicycle accident, and his leg was made lame by his injuries. Baryaruha was reminding his young interviewer that the museum effect had limits, that drums had powers that could not be contained in a glass display case or chronicled in ethnomusicology.

Heritage and Nation Building

The ethnographic order of colonialism was subjected to challenge in the 1960s, during the decade of African independence. In 1964, the only African leaders who did not avowedly embrace socialism were Haile Selassie of Ethiopia, Léon Mba of Gabon, and William Tubman of Liberia.[35] Between the 1950s and the 1980s, no fewer than 35 of 53 African countries declared themselves to be socialist.[36] Their ways of being socialist varied widely: Jomo Kenyatta's regime, which espoused 'African Socialism', actually pursued a decidedly capitalist economic policy; while in Tanzania and Mozambique socialist regimes removed urban dwellers to rural villages and promoted collectivised agriculture as an antidote to capitalism. Regardless of the nature of their commitment, the rhetoric of national governance was Marxist. Fenner Brockway, the famously leftist intellectual of the Labour Party in Britain, once called Africa 'the most comprehensively revolutionary continent', since 'every politically alert African nationalist regards himself as a socialist'.[37]

Africa's authorities thought it their task to free their people from local inequalities and promote an egalitarian society. Nationalists saw tribalism as the leading impediment to unity, and they used the power of the

---

[34] Ahurwendeire, 'History of Kinkiizi'.

[35] Kenneth W. Grundy, 'Mali: The Prospects of Planned Socialism', in William H. Friedland and Carl G. Rosberg, Jr (eds), *African Socialism* (Stanford, CA: Stanford University Press, 1964); cited in Gregory Mann, 'One Party, Several Socialisms: Mali's US-RDA' (African Studies Association annual meeting, 2012).

[36] M. Anne Pitcher and Kelly Askew, 'African Socialisms and Postsocialisms', *Africa: Journal of the International African Institute* 76, 1 (2006): 1–2.

[37] Cited in Joshua Muravchik, *Heaven on Earth: The Rise and Fall of Socialism* (San Francisco, CA: Encounter Books, 2002), 199.

state to re-engineer political identities. In 1966 Ugandan Prime Minister Milton Obote sent an army battalion to destroy the palace of the king of Buganda; the following year he abolished the Toro kingdom and other neo-traditional polities, declaring Uganda to be a unitary state.[38] Uganda's kings were given a few short weeks to vacate their palaces. The accoutrements of their office – ceremonial robes, royal spears, thrones, royal ointments, bells, drums, shoes – were handed over to local government authorities, and the royal chairs that the kings had once occupied in Anglican churches were removed.[39] By 1968, the palace of the Toro king was in a state of dereliction, inhabited by squatters.[40] Royalists decried Obote's destruction of the architecture of kingship. One man wrote to Obote lamenting his 'lack of appreciation of your country's culture, tradition and history.... In almost every civilised country... royal palaces and all that goes with them were preserved even up to now. They are important historical monuments, relics of the past attracting thousand of tourists every year.'[41] But Obote was not interested in preserving the museum cultures of indirect rule. He told an audience at a rally that 'Before 1966 our governmental structure was towards service to particular persons... and these individuals were not all of you but only about five of them throughout Uganda.' But after the events of 1966 and 1967, 'the common men – from top to bottom – are ruling Uganda. They are the rulers in the villages, they are the rulers in the counties, they are the rulers in the districts.'[42] In 1968 Obote's Uganda People's Congress adopted the 'The Common Man's Charter' as its credo. 'The people of Uganda,' it proclaimed, must 'move away from the hold of tribal and other forms of factionalism... and accept that the problems of poverty, development and nation building can and must be tackled on the basis of one Country and one People.'[43]

In Tanzania, too, nation building was conceived as a struggle against the divisive power of tribalism. Tanganyika Territory – formerly under British trusteeship – achieved self-government in 1961 under the

---

[38] Described in vivid detail in Edward Mutesa, *The Desecration of My Kingdom* (London: Constable, 1967); in D. A. Low, *Buganda in Modern History* (London: Littlehampton, 1971); and in Phares Mutibwa, *The Buganda Factor in Uganda Politics* (Kampala: Fountain, 2008).

[39] KabDA box 739, 'Uganda Constitution' file: Permanent Secretary, Minister of Regional Administration, circular letter to all District Commissioners, 12 September 1967; for royal chairs, Minister of Regional Administration to all District Commissioners, 28 November 1967.

[40] KabDA box 739, 'Uganda Constitution' file: F. Rwambarare to Administrative Secretary, Toro, 12 September 1968.

[41] National Archives of Britain DO 213 237: J. Kiggundu to Obote, 17 July 1966.

[42] UNA Office of the President, Confidential Files, Box 63, file S.10482 III: Speech by H.E. the President at a rally in Bombo, 12 December 1968.

[43] Apollo Milton Obote, *The Common Man's Charter* (Entebbe: Government Printer, 1969), articles 7 and 19.

leadership of Julius Nyerere.[44] Nyerere's political aim was clear: he told an audience at the United Nations that he hoped to 'break up . . . tribal consciousness and build up a national consciousness' among Tanganyika's people.[45] In 1967 – the same year that Milton Obote abolished Uganda's kingdoms – President Nyerere announced a campaign to build a socialist state. The aim was both to ensure the country's economic self-reliance and to knit its people together as a national citizenry. 'All human beings are equal,' went the first clause of the Arusha Declaration. 'A truly socialist state is one in which all people are workers and in which neither capitalism nor feudalism exists.'[46] What followed was the largest resettlement effort in the history of Africa: nearly 70 per cent of rural people were uprooted and relocated in collective villages.

As they set about building nations, the leaders of newly independent African states also reworked the architecture of cultural life. It was in the 1960s that the first national museums in Africa were established. They were ordinarily housed on the same premises, and featured essentially the same collections, as their predecessors. Thus the Coryndon Museum became the National Museum of Kenya, the King George V Memorial Museum became the National Museum of Tanzania, the Nyasaland Museum became the Museum of Malawi, and the antiquities collection in Jos became the National Museum of Nigeria.[47] For curators in newly independent states, the museum was an arena where cultural forms that hitherto had represented the authority of colonial-era kingdoms and tribes could be revalued as national culture.[48] In Ghana – the first of Britain's African colonies to achieve independence – President Kwame Nkrumah faced a substantial political challenge from the leaders of regional political parties. The National Liberation Movement threatened to lead the ancient Asante kingdom out of Ghana; while the Togoland Congress, on the eastern border, likewise challenged the coherence of the Nkrumah state.[49] Nkrumah responded by branding Asante and other

---

[44] Described in John Iliffe, 'Breaking the Chain at its Weakest Link: TANU and the Colonial Office', in Gregory H. Maddox and James L. Giblin (eds), *In Search of a Nation: Histories of Authority and Dissidence in Tanzania* (Oxford: James Currey, 2006), 168–97.

[45] Julius Nyerere, *Freedom and Unity* (London: Oxford University Press, 1967), 39.

[46] In Julius Nyerere, *Freedom and Socialism: Uhuru na Ujamaa* (London: Oxford University Press, 1968).

[47] G. D. Hayes, 'The Museum of Malawi', *Society of Malawi Journal* 20, 1 (1967): 49–57; Paul Msemwa, *From King George V Memorial Museum to House of Culture: Royalty to Popularity* (Dar es Salaam: National Museum of Tanzania, 2005).

[48] On museums and national culture, see Carol Duncan, *Civilizing Rituals: Inside Public Art Museums* (London: Routledge, 1995); and Tony Bennett, *The Birth of the Museum: History, Theory, Politics* (London: Routledge, 1995).

[49] Jean Allman, *Quills of the Porcupine: Asante Nationalism in an Emergent Ghana* (Madison, WI: University of Wisconsin Press, 1993); Richard Rathbone, *Nkrumah and the Chiefs: The Politics of Chieftaincy in Ghana, 1951–1960* (Athens, OH: Ohio University Press, 2000).

regional politicians as anachronisms, outdated relics of a former age. 'There should be no reference to Fantis, Ashantis, Ewes, Gas, Dagombas, strangers and so forth, but that we should call ourselves Ghanaians – all brothers and sisters, members of the same community – the state of Ghana,' he argued.[50] After independence Nkrumah's government adopted the 'Avoidance of Discrimination Act', which 'forbade the existence of parties on a regional, tribal or religious basis'.[51] Regional radio stations were proscribed, regional museums were shuttered, and the display of regional flag and emblems was rendered illegal. Nkrumah's regime sought to centre cultural life in Ghana's capital, Accra. The new National Museum was opened in 1957, during the ceremonies that marked Ghana's independence. In the museum's gallery a collection of Asante stools – hitherto regarded as symbols of chiefly authority – were organised in a circle, with portraits of Nkrumah and his colleagues in government displayed above them.[52] Nkrumah likewise appropriated Asante symbolism in his own regalia: his presidential chair was covered with gold, mimicking the Golden Stool of ancient Asante. He employed an Asante linguist, who introduced his speeches with praise poems, and made a point of wearing kente cloth – the symbol of Asante royalty – on state occasions.[53]

In Nkrumah's Ghana as in other parts of post-colonial Africa, nation building had to involve the reconstruction of the heritage industry. The performing arts – like the museums – had to be restaged, recontextualised, and made into platforms for unification.[54] The Ghana Dance Ensemble was established in 1962. The troupe deliberately staged dances from all of the diverse ethnic groups of Ghana. Each member of the troupe was obliged to participate in all of the dances in the repertoire, making the performance into a simulacrum of national unity.[55] In the present volume Moses Nii-Dortey shows how the Ghanaian musician Saka Acquaye pioneered the 'folk opera' as a new performance genre.

---

[50] Kwame Nkrumah, *I Speak of Freedom: A Statement of African Ideology* (Westport, CT: Greenwood, 1976), 168. Quoted in Bayo Holsey, *Routes of Remembrance: Refashioning the Slave Trade in Ghana* (Chicago, IL: University of Chicago Press, 2008), 98.

[51] Quoted in Janet Hess, *Art and Architecture in Postcolonial Africa* (London: McFarland and Company, 2006), 21.

[52] Hess, *Art and Architecture*, 23.

[53] It is said that Nkrumah was so unfamiliar with Asante attire that he had to use a safety pin to hold the cloth in place. Katharina Schramm, 'Senses of Authenticity: Chieftaincy and the Politics of Heritage in Ghana', *Ethnofor* 17, 1/2 (2004): 156–77.

[54] Carola Lentz, 'Local Culture in the National Arena: The Politics of Cultural Festivals in Ghana', *African Studies Review* 44, 3 (December 2001): 47–72.

[55] Katharina Schramm, 'The Politics of Dance: Changing Representations of the Nation in Ghana', *African Spectrum* 35, 3 (2000): 339–58. See also Paul W. Schauert, *Instrumental Nationalism: Dancing Politics and Staging Culture in Ghana* (Bloomington, IN: Indiana University Press, forthcoming). Tanzania's ruling party similarly sought to build the nation through musical performance: see Kelly Askew, *Performing the Nation: Swahili Music and Cultural Politics in Tanzania* (Chicago, IL: University of Chicago Press, 2002).

Acquaye described his objective as being to 'integrate our multi-tribal society in terms of its common reactions, common interests, attitudes and values of various classes. It is to create a basis for the formulation of a common destiny' (quoted in Nii-Dortey, this volume). *The Lost Fishermen*, Acquaye's second composition, was staged in 1965. It incorporated a variety of regional musics, moulding them together within a single framework. The plot drove the political message home: it features a multi-ethnic troupe of fishermen who, ignoring the gods' edict against fishing on a Tuesday, were marooned by a massive storm. The group is rescued only when one of their number – the son of a chief – agrees to sacrifice himself to placate the angered gods. Acquaye's opera was an affirmation of Nkrumah's political vision. It positioned Ghanaians, in all their polyglot complexity, together under divine authority; and it argued that the death of tribal self-interest was a precondition for the welfare of the commonwealth.

It was during this epoch, when African nationalists were busily centralising political structures, opening new museums, and integrating their diverse people in the theatre and in political life, that 'African heritage' surfaced as a subject of discourse. The Library of Congress has catalogued 52 books with this phrase in the title. Among the first was Jacob Drachler's 1963 edited collection *African Heritage: An Anthology of Black African Personality and Culture*.[56] A great variety of literary texts were bundled together on its pages: there were folk tales from Togo, songs from Southern Rhodesia, stories from the Asante kingdom, and excerpts from the published literature of Thomas Mofolo, Jomo Kenyatta, and other authorities. To Melville Herskovits, who wrote the preface, the specific genealogies of the texts – the historical contexts in which they were produced, the ways they resonated within the politics of their own time – were of little interest. The texts were cultural property that belonged to the generality of Africans, an affirmation of 'both the literary resources and literary potential of African cultures'.[57] 'The African . . . whose role was [long thought] to be manipulated by those of presumed superior culture and proven superior power, has suddenly come to life,' Herskovits wrote. The classification of heritage involved the discovery of hitherto unknown aptitudes, literary forms, and accomplishments. There was an urgent need to uncover lost civilisations, republish texts, and write the forgotten histories of Africa's people. In the earliest books 'African heritage' was conceived as a salvage operation; it was something that had to be 'discovered' or 'reclaimed'.[58] In 1967 Edinburgh University Press

---

[56] Jacob Drachler (ed.), *African Heritage: An Anthology of Black African Personality and Culture* (London: Collier, 1963).

[57] The Dahomey text was Frances and Melville Herskovits, *Dahomean Narrative: A Cross Cultural Analysis* (Evanston, IL: Northwestern University Press, 1958).

[58] Basil Davidson, *Discovering Our African Heritage* (Boston: Ginn, 1971); Coy D. Robbins, *Reclaiming African Heritage at Salem, Indiana* (Bowie, MD: Heritage Books, 1995).

launched the 'African Heritage Books' series. Edited by historian George Shepperson – who coined the phrase 'African Diaspora' – the series republished the out-of-print works of Edward Wilmont Blyden and James Africanus Horton.[59] Other hitherto misplaced things could likewise be claimed. In 1975 the Minnesota Museum of Art organised an exhibition, made up of items from its permanent collection, entitled 'African Heritage'.[60]

Heritage work involved the rearrangement of museum collections, the retrieval of outmoded texts, objects, and practices, the assembly of these objects and texts on the pages of the book or on the floor of the museum, and their identification with a particular people. In this way the out-of-print, the lost, and the forgotten could find a new life as ancestral wisdom, a source of instruction and inspiration for the present day. Heritage always involves reclamation. That is why post-colonial states were so eager to retrieve expropriated objects, bodies, and collections for the *patria* (Rassool, this volume). So it was that the regalia of the Ganda war deity Kibuuka was returned, with great pomp, from England to Uganda in 1962, on the eve of the country's independence, by the politician Abubakar Mayanja. The shrine of Kibuuka had been demolished during Buganda's late nineteenth-century wars of religion; afterwards the priest had sold the regalia, together with Kibuuka's embalmed remains, to the missionary ethnographer John Roscoe, who in 1906 deposited them in the Museum of Archaeology and Ethnology at Cambridge University. Abubakar Mayanja must have seen the display in the late 1950s, when he was reading history and law at Cambridge. In 1961, as Minister of Education in the kingdom of Buganda, he wrote to the University's Vice-Chancellor to ask for their return. 'You will appreciate that . . . at the turn of the century when Christianity had just captured the imagination of our people, making them very devout believers who were anxious to forget their pagan past, such things would have been regarded as of little value,' he wrote. But the country's impending independence had caused Ugandans to feel 'great interest' in formerly disposable things. 'We do not have many such things as these which portray our cultural past,' Mayanja told the Vice Chancellor, 'hence our anxiety, if possible, to get back what you are keeping.'[61] The museum's director, Jack Goody, agreed to

[59] Edward Wilmont Blyden, *Christianity, Islam, and the Negro Race* (Edinburgh: Edinburgh University Press, 1967 [1887]); James Africanus Horton, *West African Counties and People* (Edinburgh: Edinburgh University Press, 1969 [1868]). Shepperson's definitional essay was 'The African Abroad or the African Diaspora', in T. O. Ranger (ed.), *Emerging Themes in African History* (Nairobi: East African Publishing House, 1968), 152–76.

[60] Minnesota Museum of Art, *African Heritage: Traditional Sculpture and Crafts from the Permanent Collection of the Minnesota Museum of Art* (Saint Paul, MN: The Museum, 1975).

[61] Museum of Archaeology and Ethnology, University of Cambridge, file AA4/5/15: A. K. Mayanja to Vice-Chancellor, 2 November 1961. Seen courtesy of the museum's director, Prof. Nick Thomas, and archivist Rachel Hand.

repatriate Kibuuka's remains, reasoning that claims for the return of 'particularly sacred objects' would be 'hard to resist'.[62] Abubakar Mayanja spent June 1962 in London, playing a leading part in the conference that hammered out the constitution of the new state of Uganda. On 2 July, having completed his legal work, Mayanja carried Kibuuka's remains with him on his return to Uganda.[63] They were put in an honoured place in the Uganda Museum. The museological work of repatriation and reassembly was contemporaneous with the political work of self-constitution.

In South Africa heritage work has had a different itinerary. While in the mid-twentieth century African nationalists were reorganising cultural infrastructure and incorporating diverse people into an integrated whole, in South Africa white Afrikaners were working to make their history and architecture into the basis for an exclusionary nationalism.[64] When in 1952 the Information Service published *South Africa's Heritage*, the book bore the subtitle 'The Story of White Civilisation in South Africa from the Landing of the First Dutch Settlers with Jan van Riebeeck to the Present Day'.[65] It cast Afrikaners as a racially pure people, 'eighteenth century Europeans born and bred in South African soil'. There followed a series of five illustrated pamphlets, produced by Caltex Africa, which described the homes, furnishings, attire, and education of the country's white minority.[66] The apartheid state built this exclusionary account of South Africa's history in stone and concrete, leaving behind monuments and museum collections for the African National Congress, its successor in government, to re-engineer.[67] Since coming to power in 1994, the ANC has set about renovating the landscape of historical memory. There has been a proliferation of memorials and heritage projects, and museum collections have been overhauled systematically.[68] Much of this heritage work is meant to consecrate the ANC's political history (Herwitz, this volume). Instead of rehearsing the contentious, divisive history of real politics, South Africa's official heritage industry makes the past into a

---

[62] Museum of Archaeology and Ethnology, University of Cambridge, file AA4/5/15: Jack Goody to P. C. Melville, 11 December 1961.

[63] F. B. Welbourn, 'Kibuuka Comes Home', *Transition* 5 (July–August 1962): 15–17; 20; see also Jonathon Earle, 'Political Theologies in Late Colonial Buganda' (PhD dissertation, Cambridge University, 2012), Postscript.

[64] Peter Merrington, 'Cape Dutch Tongaat: A Case Study in "Heritage"', *Journal of Southern African Studies* 32, 4 (December 2006): 683–99.

[65] South African Information Service, *South Africa's Heritage* (Pretoria: South African Information Service, 1952). Quoted in Leslie Witz, 'Making Museums as Heritage in Post-Apartheid South Africa' (unpublished paper, June 2012).

[66] Caltex Africa, *South African Heritage: From Van Riebeeck to Nineteenth Century Times* (Cape Town: Human and Rousseau, 1965).

[67] Shown vividly in Martin Murray, *Commemorating and Forgetting: Challenges for the New South Africa* (Minneapolis, MN: University of Minnesota Press, 2013).

[68] Discussed in Annie F. Coombes, *History after Apartheid: Visual Culture and Public Memory in a Democratic South Africa* (Durham, NC: Duke University Press, 2003).

legacy, a source of inspiration that authenticates the ANC's contemporary policies. The staging of the ANC's history involves the expropriation of local politics, local heroes, and local history into a national narrative of struggle. In August 1985, for example, the diverse residents of Duncan Village outside East London in the Eastern Cape launched a series of protests against the apartheid state's assassination of a local activist. Some 31 of them were shot by the police. Twenty years later, in post-apartheid South Africa, local government erected a memorial to honour the 1985 protests. It featured a warrior, spear aloft, poised and ready to strike an enemy. As Gary Minkley and Phindezwa Mnyaka argue in this volume, the memorial lifts the Duncan Village protests out of their historical and contextual milieu, making them part of the liberatory history of the African National Congress, the 'spear of the nation'.[69]

In post-apartheid South Africa as in Nkrumah's Ghana, the project of nation building demands that local history gets folded into a larger narrative of self-becoming. But in South Africa there are spaces where alternative narratives can be represented and debated. Opened in 1994, the District Six Museum is one of several 'community museums' that operate at the edges of the official heritage industry. The museum honours the experience of the 60,000 people who, in the 1970s and 1980s, were forcibly removed from their homes by apartheid city planners and resettled in a suburb outside Cape Town. Its architects have encouraged ex-residents to compose the museum's collections and work out how to represent their shared experience to a viewing public.[70] The Lwandle Migrant Labour Museum is likewise a work-in-progress. The museum – opened in 2000 – is housed in what was formerly Hostel 33, one of many such buildings erected in the mid-twentieth century to house migrant workers employed in the canning industry in the Western Cape. In the present volume, Leslie Witz and Noëleen Murray bring us into the conflicted work of museum making. The work of historical preservation always involves selection, a set of human decisions concerning what is to be discarded and what is to be preserved, placed in glass display cases, and exhibited. In Lwandle, the curators have made the story of the museum's creation a chief theme of its collections. It is a museum always creating its own subject.

South Africa stands out in today's heritage economy. In no other part of contemporary Africa is national heritage being debated with such vigour, force, and ingenuity. In Ghana and elsewhere, the monumental statuary

---

[69] *Umkhonto we Sizwe*, the 'Spear of the Nation', was the armed wing of the African National Congress.

[70] Ciraj Rassool, 'Community Museums, Memory Politics, and Social Transformation in South Africa: Histories, Possibilities, Limits', in Ivan Karp, Corinne Kratz, Lynn Szwaja, and Tomás Ybarra-Frausto (eds), *Museum Frictions: Public Cultures/Global Transformations* (Durham, NC: Duke University Press, 2006), 286–321.

of nation building has been toppled. After the overthrow of Kwame Nkrumah in 1966, his statue was knocked from its pedestal in the centre of Accra and dismembered, with its head and arms broken away. Other edifices of Ghanaian nation building have been renamed and repurposed (Gavua, this volume). Across the continent, national museums are underfunded and endangered. The institutions that had once defined and upheld the project of nation building are now searching for commodities – expertise, artefacts, cultural products – to sell. In Kampala, the Uganda Museum will soon be replaced with a high-rise commercial building. At the University of Nairobi, the History Department was recently merged with Tourism Studies; it now offers (according to its website) an 'array of market driven diploma and degree programmes', including a BA in Tourism Studies.[71] At the University of Zimbabwe, the History Department has renamed itself the 'Department of Economic History'. At Makerere University, the History Department has been joined with Development Studies.

The institutions that once regulated the production of national culture are now made to answer to the demands of the market. Outmoded ways of life are now enjoying a new birth, not as evidence of national unity, and neither as parts of an ethnographic whole, but as marketing strategies.

Heritage, Inc.

The logic and rhetoric of governance had shifted decisively by the 1990s. Where in a former time African politicians had defined themselves as heralds of a new, egalitarian future, they now began to speak of their economies as 'emerging markets' or as 'market democracies'. Heritage was one of the many areas on which African entrepreneurs sought to capitalise. In a former time nation builders had sought to consolidate diverse local cultures, stitching them together as part of a national whole. By the 1990s, there was an international market for the ethno-commodities of Africa. The local and the authentic can now be sold, purchased, and consumed in a range of media: as medicine, as food, as literature, as art. John and Jean Comaroff have called this industry 'Ethnicity, Inc.', drawing attention to the ways that the commodity form has allowed heritage entrepreneurs to inventory, consolidate, and market their cultures to an international audience.[72] The Comaroffs' work wonderfully illuminates the market logic of contemporary cultural production. But it casts little light on the landscape of politics in contemporary Africa. In Uganda, in Zambia, in Ghana, and in other places chiefs and kings – sidelined or

---

[71] <http://history.uonbi.ac.ke/node>, accessed 14 December 2012.
[72] John L. and Jean Comaroff, *Ethnicity, Inc.* (Chicago, IL: University of Chicago Press, 2009).

ousted by the socialist nation builders of the 1960s and 1970s – have found a new lease of life, and the musty rituals of royalism are again being rehearsed and restaged. The re-articulation of royalism has gone hand-in-hand with the commoditisation of ethnic heritage. The practice of heritage has allowed certain entrepreneurs to trademark culture, claim it as their exclusive property, naturalise behavioural norms, and sideline minorities, dissidents, and other non-conformists.

Uganda is an apposite location from which to survey the contemporary heritage economy. Nowhere are the stakes higher. Colonialism in Uganda was an engine for the production of heritage discourse: under the British protectorate neo-traditional kings exercised a feudal authority over their subjects. After Uganda's independence in 1962, President Milton Obote built the nation by forcibly dismantling tribes and kingdoms. Obote was overthrown by Idi Amin in 1971, and there followed a long period of political turmoil. In 1986 the National Resistance Movement came to power after a bloody guerilla war.[73] Like the nation builders of earlier decades, the new government had little time for traditional culture. The NRM's leader, Yoweri Museveni, was deeply committed to leftist politics: as a student in Dar es Salaam he had been a member of a reading circle that included the West Indian radical Walter Rodney, and he visited the camps that Mozambican revolutionaries had established in southern Tanzania.[74] Museveni and his cohort considered their regime to be the harbinger of a new epoch. An official described the paradigmatic government officer as 'the model of the new man. He is the paragon of talent and good manners, he is the messenger of the new civilisation and the propagandist of the Era of the Wananchi [the People].'[75] NRM authorities thought themselves free from the burdens of history: they were 'completely disencumbered of a shameful past', and were therefore 'free to think and act'. It was the duty of the NRM's enlightened cadres to carry the military struggle into the mundane world. The local government bodies that the NRM organised were titled 'Resistance Councils'. They were led by a 'Secretary of Mass Mobilisation', whose duty was to 'incite the masses to exercise power' by undertaking the most ordinary tasks: building roads and schools, paying taxes, obeying government bylaws. The discursive architecture of guerilla warfare – mobilisation, struggle, resistance – was thereby redeployed, and war became the metaphor guiding the mundane work of governance (see Herwitz, this volume).

---

[73] Nelson Kasfir, 'Guerillas and Civilian Participation: The National Resistance Army in Uganda, 1981–1986', *Journal of Modern African Studies* 43, 2 (2005): 271–96.

[74] Detailed in Andrew Ivaska, *Cultured States: Youth, Gender, and Modern Style in 1960s Dar es Salaam* (Durham, NC: Duke University Press, 2011), Ch. 3.

[75] KasDA 'District Council minutes, political' file: Office of the Resistance Council, Kasese District, 'Good Message to All, Kasese District', n.d.

Ethnic heritage had a strictly limited role to play in the economy of continual revolution. Like other nation builders, NRM authorities had little interest in the ornamentation of neo-traditional government. They thought that self-interested British rulers had imposed chiefs on Ugandans as part of their 'long established... policy of divide and rule'. Because tribalism had thwarted legitimate political thought, 'most Ugandans', wrote an NRM lawyer, 'had not adequately become politically mature' at the time of national independence in 1962.[76] The movement's code of conduct prohibited cadres from engaging in 'tribalism or any form of sectarianism. We must be very stern on this point.'[77] When in 1990 the Directorate of Cultural Affairs launched a literary competition, it defined a limited role for research or writing about history. The competition's purpose was to 'further enlighten Ugandans on the ongoing Revolution in our country'.[78] There was to be no mention of ancestral tradition. Authors were invited to compose their writing around forward-looking themes, such as 'Forward We Go, Backward Never', 'The Era of Resistance Council Democracy: A History in the Making', and 'The Cultural Revolution in Uganda'. The aim, wrote the competition's organisers, was to 'have Uganda's history-in-the-making on permanent record for tomorrow's generations'.

The NRM government of the late 1980s and early 1990s regarded Uganda's conflicted history as a hindrance to progress, and they sought to direct citizens' attention towards a bright and promising future, not towards the benighted past. Government authorities were therefore discomfited when Uganda's people did not, all at once, embrace the new era they announced. In remote Bundibugyo District, on the mountainous border with the Congo, the NRM administrator was surprised to find that the local Amba people feared witches and sorcerers. 'They can recite what they have learned from our cadres with amazing accuracy and clarity,' he noted, but 'the fairly sound knowledge they received from the modern political education has not succeeded to liberate even highly educated men and women from the grip of primitive belief in the power of charms.'[79] Chiefs and other local authorities in Bundibugyo refused to arrest smugglers, fearing they would be killed by witchcraft. 'This primitive belief is holding the entire [population of] natives here the captive of baseless fears,' the official observed. Amba people did indeed possess

---

[76] KasDA 'Constitution' file: 'Why Uganda Needs a New Constitution', n.d. (but 1989).

[77] National Resistance Army, *Code of Conduct for the NRA* (manuscript, 1982), quoted in Kasfir, 'Guerillas and Civilian Participation', 282–3.

[78] KasDA 'Cultural and Information Services Management Committee' file: Press release, Directorate for Cultural Affairs, n.d. (but September 1990).

[79] BDA Box 539, 'Monthly Reports' file: District Administrator to Minister of State, Office of the President, 4 June 1987.

a fearsome reputation: a colonial-era ethnographer argued that 'one cannot progress very far in the understanding of the [Amba] . . . without at least a rudimentary knowledge of their system of witchcraft'.[80] But NRM cadres evinced little interest in the ethnography of the occult, and they had little time for metaphysics. They actively interceded to suppress the social architecture of religion. When in 1989 the residents of Kilembe village collected funds with which to conduct a ritual called *abarimu*, which was meant to allay conflict and encourage sociable relations between people, government authorities banned the ceremony. They thought it to be a distraction from the real, secular work of development. 'It brings poverty and famine to villages, due to the large number of attendants,' one official noted.[81] Such 'backward traditional functions [should] be discouraged . . . [so that a] bright future in development will be realised', argued another official.[82]

The mechanisms of the heritage industry gave NRM authorities instruments with which to naturalise, standardise, and manage the disruptive powers of the occult. In neighbouring Tanzania 'traditional medicine' had been part of the medical school curriculum since the mid-1970s, and Tanzanian researchers had for decades been cataloguing, testing, and marketing herbal remedies for common diseases.[83] With their eye on their neighbour, the NRM authorities agreed in July 1988 to recognise the organisation 'Uganda N'eddagala Lyayo' ('Uganda and its Medicines') as the sole association for traditional healers in the whole of Uganda.[84] Uganda's Director of Medical Services laid out the (gendered) division of labour: traditional healers were to superintend childbirth and treat uncomplicated diseases, but if the healer 'finds a problem in a certain patient let that case be referred to a hospital'. He and other government authorities hoped that Uganda N'eddagala Lyayo would '[promote and preserve] our traditional medicine as well as [uplift] the standards of traditional healers'. They also hoped that that the association would 'protect traditional healers from involving themselves in killing people through spiritual powers and dangerous herbs'. By 1991 the NRM's Minister of

---

[80] Edward Winter, *Bwamba: A Structure-Functional Analysis of a Patrilineal Society* (Cambridge: Heffer and Sons, 1952), 129.

[81] BDA Box 515, 'Bwamba County Reports' file: RC I chairman Kilembe to RC II chairman Bugombwa, 27 August 1989.

[82] BDA Box 515, 'Bwamba County Reports' file: Tom Bakamanyaki, RC II chairman Bugombwa, to RC III chairman Busaru, 30 August 1989.

[83] The configuration of traditional medicine in contemporary Tanzania is described in Stacey Langwick, *Bodies, Politics, and African Healing: The Matter of Maladies in Tanzania* (Bloomington, IN: Indiana University Press, 2011), Chapter 3. As early as 1925 British medical officers in Tanganyika were in correspondence with the Kew Herbarium, sending herbal preparations that they had collected from African healers to London for chemical analysis. The correspondence is in Tanganyika National Archives Acc. 450/207.

[84] BDA Box 526, 'Associations' file: Permanent Secretary, Ministry of Youth, Culture and Sport, to all Culture Officers, 9 August 1988.

Culture and Tourism was encouraging government 'Culture Officers' in Uganda's rural areas to conduct 'serious research in traditional medicines in view of identifying herbs that can be used for curing diseases'.[85] Healers resident in each district were to be registered, and the herbs they used were to be 'identified and recorded together with their botanical names'. 'Witchcraft practices must be discouraged completely,' the Minister wrote, 'and those who practise them must be reported to local authorities.' NRM authorities aimed to make traditional medicine into an auxiliary to biomedicine, folding Amba and other troublesome healers into the medical bureaucracy. By this means they sought to naturalise the metaphysics of the occult.

Traditional healers were notably active participants in the bureaucratisation of their craft. Uganda N'eddagala Lyayo's leaders appointed 'health inspectors' in each district, charging them to ensure that healers worked hygienically. There was also a 'Religion and Traditional Affairs Secretary', who was responsible for 'narrowing or eliminating the differences' between the association and the Christian churches.[86] Uganda N'eddagala Lyayo's leaders promised to 'stamp out and strongly discourage unscrupulous physicians employing activities mistakenly copied or imported from foreign countries for the mere sake of getting money', and planned to organise 'meetings, seminars, visits, [and] full time courses' where healers would be taught to 'use advanced methods and techniques of treatment and healing'.[87] In return for their supervisory work they asked the authorities for access to the infrastructure of local government: for a building to display and sell medicinal herbs; for motorcycles and bicycles with which to undertake their supervisory work; and for a seat on local government councils.

Uganda N'eddagala Lyayo's bureaucrats were engaged in the work of bureaucratic regulation. They were taking herbs and other botanical objects out of their ritual and metaphysical contexts and placing them in the pharmacy. Their work helped to constitute traditional medicine as a credible analogue to Western biomedicine. At the same time it established traditional medicine as cultural property, as part of an assemblage of artefacts that could represent Uganda's culture. Like other heritage organisations, Uganda N'eddagala Lyayo was involved in producing the local for export.[88] For decades Uganda's authorities had been working to capitalise on tradition and culture. The 'Tourist Development

---

[85] BDA Box 527, 'Traditional Healers' file: Permanent Secretary, Ministry of Culture and Tourism, to all District Cultural Officers, 25 June 1991.

[86] KasDA 'Traditional Medicine and Healers' file: Minutes of Uganda N'eddagala Lyayo meeting, Kasese, 15 March 1990.

[87] The preceding quotations come from BDA Box 526, 'Associations' file: President, Uganda N'eddagala Lyayo, to District Administrator, Bundibugyo, n.d. (but July 1988).

[88] See Kirshenblatt-Gimblett, *Destination Culture*, Chapter 3.

Corporation' had been established by President Idi Amin. It organised hospitality for the six hundred tourists who at that time visited Uganda each year.[89] Amin himself barnstormed through the country, laying foundation stones for historical monuments and opening provincial museums for tourists to visit.[90] In 1974 and again in 1976 Amin's regime organised a 'Miss Tourism' beauty pageant as a means of advertising the nascent tourist industry. Competitors were to be 'indigenous Ugandans of African extraction', to possess an 'attractive face and figure without any artificial embellishments', and to adorn themselves in dresses 'made from our local prints'.[91] The winner was chosen at a ballroom dance competition held at Kampala's biggest stadium. The effort to develop a tourist industry foundered in the political turmoil of the late 1970s and early 1980s. By the late 1980s, though, it was possible for organisations like Uganda N'eddagala Lyayo to see a market for the material artefacts of traditional life. The association made explicit connections between the work of pharmaceutical standardisation and the marketing of African heritage. In its constitution the association committed itself to 'preserve [Uganda's] own cultures and traditions which are the prestige and foundation of this part of Africa as a nation'.[92] 'We are fully convinced,' wrote the organisers, that 'if traditions, cultures, and medicines are properly organised, they would not only advertise Uganda abroad but would also be a big earner for foreign currency.' The association's leaders were aiming to realise cultural capital as assets that could be marketed and sold. In their constitution they promised to investigate 'diverse ways of preserving the nation's cultural heritage' by 'encouraging black smithery, bark cloth making, tribal drama and music, and hunting craftmanships'.[93] In this way botanical objects were to take their place alongside locally made cloth, musical instruments, and other objects in the catalogue of the heritage industry.

The heritage industry offered Ugandan authorities an ensemble of techniques – the catalogue, the ethnographic book, the pharmacy, the display case – with which to manage the problematics of culture in benighted hinterlands. In 1987 the NRM posted its first 'Cultural Officer' to Kasese and Bundibuygo districts in western Uganda. His name was Francis Barigye. Shortly after his arrival he assembled a large group of therapists – including some of the Amba healers who troubled the authorities – and

---

[89] 'Tourists and our Culture', *Voice of Uganda* 1 (392).
[90] National Archives of Britain FCO 31 1018: Slater, British High Commission, to East African Department, 5 October 1971.
[91] BDA Box 523, 'National Parks and Tourism' file: Permanent Secretary, Ministry of Culture and Tourism, to all Governors, 21 September 1976.
[92] BDA 'Associations' file: President, Uganda N'eddagala Lyayo, to District Administrator, Bundibugyo, n.d. (but July 1988).
[93] BDA 'Associations' file: Constitution of the Uganda N'eddagala Lyayo Women and Men's Cultural Association, 20 July 1988.

told them that 'those who came as colonists did abuse us calling us witch crafts. But we are African doctors. We are doing the same job as the Bajungu ['whites'] are doing.'[94] In the dawning days of the NRM's government, local authorities were redefining the therapies that western Uganda's people had hitherto practised: not as witchcraft but as traditional medicine, an enterprise that could be pursued alongside biomedicine. Barigye urged his listeners to 'be scientific in the approach of their work and not continue carry on like their ancestors'. Healers were to be hygienic, cooperate with the Ministry of Health, and ensure that their patients were vaccinated against killer diseases.[95] At the same time the heterogeneous processes by which they healed were edited, trimmed, and standardised. Barigye had heard that 'there are some doctors who have different herbs that can even drive away women and kill husbands'. 'We don't want bad herbs,' he declared. 'Those should be driven away.'[96] Herbs that were known to be beneficial were to be registered: Barigye kept a book in his office that listed all the medicinal herbs in the region, together with the diseases that they cured.[97]

Francis Barigye's record book allows us to see the infrastructure of heritage work in its most elemental form. On its pages the leaves, barks, and saps with which Amba healers worked were stripped of their metonymic and metaphysical aspects, detached from the ritual contexts in which they worked, and made to stand in a one-to-one relationship with certain diseases. With Barigye's index in hand it was easy for medical professionals to see herbs as drugs, working biologically to cure the corporeal body. 'Modern medicine [should] intermarry with the old medicine to cure other diseases which attack people,' said an official in a meeting with the 'Native Doctors' of Kasese District.[98] In work like Barigye's, traditional medicine was conceived as an extension of the pharmacy of biomedicine, an expansion of doctors' pharmaceutical repertoire. There was a sense of discovery, of uncovering hitherto untapped potential, about the work of medicinal research. A 1994 pamphlet advertising the 'Rwenzori Medical Herbs' association described how the proprietor – a man named Jacob Mugenyi – had once suffered from an incurable bout of diarrhoea.[99]

---

[94] KasDA 'Traditional Medicine and Healers' file: Cultural meeting, Munkunyu, 11 October 1988.

[95] KasDA 'Traditional Medicine and Healers' file: General meeting of all herbalists from Kasese District, 20 June 1988.

[96] KasDA 'Traditional Medicine and Healers' file: Cultural meeting, Munkunyu, 11 October 1988.

[97] KasDA 'Traditional Medicine and Healers" file: 'African Doctors meeting', 20 June 1988.

[98] KasDA 'Traditional Medicine and Healers' file: Minutes of a meeting with the Native Doctors, Uganda N'eddagala Lyayo, 15 March 1989.

[99] KasDA 'Traditional Medicine and Healers' file: Mugenyi Jacob, 'Rwenzori Medical Herbs' association, n.d. (but 1994).

On the recommendation of a friend he had chewed the hardened gum from a tree, and was immediately cured. 'I realised that there is something we are neglecting, something we are losing than mere burying and mourning over our deceased brothers and sisters,' Mugenyi wrote, 'and this is carrying out research on the local medicinal herbs.' He and his colleagues conducted tests on herbs that healers submitted to them for examination, aiming to 'eliminate the idea of individuals personalising and keeping herbs a secret in order to help the entire community'.

The record book that Francis Barigye kept was a guide to the pharmacy of traditional medicine. It was also an entry in the library of heritage. In their effort to concretise and standardise healers' repertoires, Barigye and his interlocutors were generating cultural capital, articles that could be marketed at a profit to an international audience. For Barigye and other heritage entrepreneurs in western Uganda, tourists were both the financial motor and also the first customers for the products of heritage. Barigye told an audience of 'Native Doctors' that 'When tourists come, in their mind they ask, "What is Uganda?" The first answer they get, as they disboard the plane ladders, they see culture dances, who perform free.' Barigye thought it imperative that Uganda's culture should make a better impression. On the same occasion at which he compared African healers to Western medical doctors, Barigye urged his audience to make 'our African articles, like bags, pots, baskets, emighusu etc. which we can sell to other people abroad. That is our culture.'[100] For Barigye, traditional medicine was one element in a saleable assemblage of crafts, rituals, and repertoires that together constituted heritage.

Rendered in this way, traditional medicine could take its place alongside dance, cuisine, dress, and language as part of the panoply of traditional culture in contemporary Uganda. In 1991, five years after the NRM took power, government authorities organised the inaugural 'Uganda National Cultural Festival' in Kampala's largest stadium. It was the 'first of its kind in Uganda', trumpeted an NRM official, 'bringing together all areas of cultural concern, including visual arts and crafts, traditional foods and drinks, literary works, traditional medicine, traditional games and performing arts'.[101] There was no place for witchcraft in the NRM's theatre. Neither was there room for experimentation or improvisation. Assembled on the stadium grounds, healers took their place alongside artists, authors, cooks, and dancers and other performers in the routinised work of heritage production. The cultural show was a theatre of display, where the alienable artefacts of culture – bottles of

[100] KasDA 'Traditional Medicine and Healers' file: Cultural meeting, Munkunyu, 11 October 1988.
[101] KasDA 'Cultural and Information Services Management Committee' file: Francis Barigye to Treasurer, Kasese District Administration, 24 April 1991.

herbs, drums, baskets, and other gear – could be marketed. On the grounds of heritage, objects, rituals, and performances with disparate genealogies and complicated itineraries could be consolidated in a single arena, packaged, and priced to sell.

Government has thereby sublet the management of culture to entre-preneurs who deal in heritage products. There has been a tendency towards monopolies. Parliament adopted the Restoration of Traditional Rulers Act in 1993. Under the act, the kingdoms of colonial Uganda – abolished in 1967, during the era of nation building – were resuscitated as 'cultural institutions'. According to the 1993 act, the cultural leader's role is to 'promote and preserve the cultural values, norms, and practices which enhance the dignity and well being' of his people. Several king-doms – first Buganda, then Toro, Busoga and Bunyoro, and most recently Rwenzururu – have been recognised under the act. Their architects have been involved in the rebuilding of traditional cultures. A 1947 book on the kings of Bunyoro and a 1955 book on the kings of Ankole were recently republished, and in the past few years new books have appeared on the customary law of the Toro kingdom, on 'The Bakonzo/Banande and Their Culture', on the 'History and Culture' of the kingdom of Ankole, and on 'The People and the Rulers' of the kingdom of Bunyoro-Kitara.[102] Uganda's kingdoms have been using the Internet to expand the audience for their heritage lessons. The Bunyoro kingdom's website, for example, welcomes viewers with a photograph of the king, resplen-dent in a gilt-encrusted robe. It invites readers to "Get an insight into the Kingdom's inspiring history, its rich culture, development projects and what the King . . . and the Royal family are up to lately.'[103]

Uganda's kings have been made the arbiters of custom and the man-agers of tradition. In the contemporary economy of royalism there is little space for cultural pluralism or dissenting politics. Cultural and behavioural norms have been territorialised, and within their particu-lar borders Uganda's kings can dictate on a wide range of affairs. The Rwenzururu kingdom – constituted in law by Uganda's government in 2009 – began life in the 1960s, in a guerilla war fought by Konzo-speaking people against the Ugandan state. By the early 1980s Rwenzururu's king, Charles Wesley Mumbere, was negotiating with the Ugandan govern-ment for the cessation of the war. He used the occasion to dictate terms

---

[102] J. W. Nyakatura, *Abakama of Bunyoro-Kitara* (Kisubi: Marianum Press, 1998 [1947]); Joshua Kamugunguinu, *Abagabe b'Ankole* (Kampala: Fountain, 2005 [1955]); L. T. Rubongoya, *Naaho Nubo: The Ways of our Ancestors* (Köln: Rüdiger Köppe Verlag, 2003); M. W. Magezi, T. E. Nyakango, and M. K. Aganatia, *The People of the Rwenzoris: The Bayira (Bakonzo/Bananade) and Their Culture* (Köln: Rüdiger Köppe Verlag, 2004); G. N. P. Kirindi, *History and Culture of the Kingdom of Ankole* (Kampala: Fountain, 2008); David Kihumuro-Apuli, *A Thousand Years of Bunyoro-Kitara Kingdom: The People and the Rulers* (Kampala: Fountain, 1994).

[103] <http://www.bunyoro-kitara.com>, accessed 17 August 2011.

regarding local administration, demanding that the names of the streets in Kasese town should be changed to honour Rwenzururu, that the Konzo language be used exclusively in government offices, that the city council should resign, and that Rwenzururu partisans should be appointed in their place.[104] He also insisted that the local courts should be barred from pursuing litigation involving Rwenzururu partisans. Some of Kasese's politicians objected when the king named three of his subordinates to serve as the district's representatives in the Uganda Parliament. Rwenzururu's partisans were indignant about the critics' refusal to bend the knee to the royal writ. 'They accuse [the king] of picking people who represent him, and not the people,' explained a Rwenzururu memoirist. 'They say they will elect their genuine members of parliament, and not those representing the view of the king.'[105] Rwenzururu's leaders thought the will of the people to be of little consequence: they demanded that the critics be removed from their government posts, to be replaced by people loyal to the king.

The capitalisation of the heritage industry – the inventorying of assets, the delegation of authority to kings and other cultural entrepreneurs, the marketing of medicine, baskets, beads, and other cultural products – has gone hand in hand with the development of profoundly unequal, undemocratic forms of local government. The trademarking of cultures – as assets to be sold abroad – makes culture into the property of a particular people, and invites brokers to discriminate, to define authentic cultural expression, to treat competition as decadence. Who better to market heritage commodities than a king? Ghana's Asante kingdom has been particularly responsive to the market. In 1984 a lavish exhibition was laid on in New York under the title 'Asante: Kingdom of Gold'. It was opened by Asantehene Opoku Ware II, who processed in state through Central Park and into the Museum of Natural History.[106] African-Americans had long regarded Asante, and Ghana more generally, as a homeland, a place to which they might return: since the late 1950s, Ghana had received more African-American expatriates than any other African nation.[107] The New York exhibition encouraged a further wave of tourism, and invited Asante cultural brokers to elaborate on their royalist credentials. In 2001 a young linguistics graduate published a book in Kumasi entitled

---

104 KasDA 'District Team and Planning Committee' file: Meeting of District Team and District Council, 18 August 1981.
105 KasDA 'Rwenzururu Central Office' file: Baseka Erisa to Establishment Officer, Kasese, 8 March 1981.
106 Described in T. C. McCaskie, 'Asante Origins, Egypt, and the Near East: An Idea and Its Origins', in Derek R. Peterson and Giacomo Macola (eds), Recasting the Past: History Writing and Political Work in Modern Africa (Athens, OH: Ohio University Press, 2009), 125–48.
107 Edward M. Bruner, 'Tourism in Ghana: The Representation of Slavery and the Return of the Black Diaspora', American Anthropologist 98, 2 (1996): 290–304.

The Ancient Egyptians Are Here, which argued that the Asante people had helped to build both the pyramids of Egypt and the city of Jerusalem, and that they had carried the god Yahweh with them to West Africa.[108] In their gilded historiography Asante culture brokers have established a glorious place for themselves in the global history of royalty. It is not by accident that, when Ghana's Parliament established a ministry for cultural affairs, they named it the 'Ministry of Chieftaincy and Culture' (Silverman, this volume). It is the official view that chiefs are the 'custodians of the country's heritage and values', whose role it is to 'preserve their cultural values, which have been weakened or abandoned in the name of so-called modernisation'.

In Ghana, in Uganda, and in other African locales, the heritage industry depends upon the panoply, ceremony, and material culture of kingship. There is no space for a heritage of republicanism, for the marketing of democratic artefacts, for a celebration of the history of acephalous societies. If it is to find a market, cultural heritage has to be centralised. There is much that has to be forgotten, edited out, or suppressed in order to make this account of heritage credible.[109] Rwenzururu's architects can say nothing about the cultural and linguistic minorities who reside within the boundaries of their ostensibly sovereign homeland. Neither can the culture brokers of South Africa's Zulu kingdom. As Mbongiseni Buthelezi shows in this volume, the Zulu polity has been defined in part by the suppression of the Ndwandwe, the Qwabe, and other constituent communities. In poetry and in song history is deliberately edited, and personalities who had once challenged the state builder Shaka's authority are edited out or denigrated. The economy of heritage production cannot allow space for argument over the lessons of history. Conceived as the distinctive property of a particular, unique people, heritage renders political or cultural dissent illegitimate. Heritage work is in many parts of contemporary Africa an instrument of dictatorship.

There are forms of cultural practice that are not conceived within the architecture of the heritage industry. Even as entrepreneurs build the pharmacy of traditional medicine and market heritage products, other healers are engaging in heterodox experiments with bodily and social healing. In the early 1980s a group of a dozen healers calling themselves the 'Apostolic Church' began a medical practice in Misole, high in the mountains of western Uganda. Their chief correspondent, Barnaba Baluku, emphasised the novelty and flexibility of their healing practice.[110] They were 'using their mouths to spray air onto the patient,

---

[108] O. Kwame Osei, *The Ancient Egyptians Are Here* (Kumase, Ghana: Vytall Printing, 2001); cited in McCaskie, 'Asante Origins'.

[109] Bayo Holsey, *Routes of Remembrance: Refashioning the Slave Trade in Ghana* (Chicago, IL: University of Chicago Press, 2008).

[110] KasDA 'Luyira Language' file: Barnaba Baluku to D.C. Kasese, 18 August 1983.

spraying water onto the patient, using sticks with the guidance of the Lord's Holy Spirit to heal the patient in this hospital', he told the District Commissioner. Their techniques could neither be patented nor trademarked. Neither did they make reference to ancestral tradition. The Misole healers made the disciplines of bodily comportment – chastity, probity, asceticism – into a source of healthy living. Baluku described how he and his colleagues 'clean ourselves like the Muslims do. We wear white robes, when entering the House of the Lord we first remove our footwear, we no not treat patients when we are wearing shoes, we do not completely shave our hair, we do not walk proudly, we do not eat meat roasted by another person.' Their practice was extraordinarily broad: Baluku claimed to be able to heal 'madness, epilepsy, dysentery, gonorrhea, leprosy, polio, drunkenness, poisoning, malaria, evil spirits, [and] diarrhoea', while also 'spreading the word of Jesus Christ'. Importantly, no one at Misole claimed to have learned their business from their forefathers. This was not heritage work. They described their therapeutic powers as a gift of revelation, not an ancestral inheritance. 'I was under a tree where I had spent some several days without eating and drinking,' one of them wrote. 'The Lord spoke to me in thunderous voices, in these voices were the words "My child, I have called you in the midst of your brethren to serve me, so don't walk in the arrangements of mankind."'[111]

There was no past in the Misole healers' therapeutic practice, no ancestral tradition to chart, no *longue durée* to reconstruct, no heritage to unearth and celebrate. Neither were there commodities that could be identified, edited, and marketed. The Misole healers worked by aligning bodies and disciplines, by creating a social world, by placing physical bodies in healthy situations. Among their chief clients was Charles Wesley Mumbere, the king of Rwenzururu, the chief architect of the heritage politics of western Uganda.[112] In their labours the Misole healers help us glimpse a space where the ancestral and the archaic have no purchase, where new possibilities can come into the horizon of cultural life.

The Architecture of the Book

This book's opening chapters are about specific places: brick and mortar museums, bronze statues, and granite plinths. But after the concrete opening, the substance of the book becomes progressively more ephemeral. The subject matter of the latter chapters in the book deal with language, bones, film, and music. In the earlier chapters of the book we

---

[111] KasDA file with no cover: Christopher Besweri Kaswabuli to District Executive Secretary, 5 July 1990.
[112] KasDA file with no cover: Y. Kamabu, County Chief Bukonjo, to D.C. Kasese, 3 March 1983.

can see the difficult work of cultural editing as a physical activity. When regimes change – after the fall of apartheid, or after the fall of Kwame Nkrumah – activists take up hammers and chisels, tear down the statuary of the old regime, and erect new monuments that replace older symbols. It is more difficult to glimpse the editorial work of heritage making in the latter part of the book, because the work of revision is not visible. No riotous crowds gather when a dictionary is rewritten. But visible or not, the standardisation of languages and the formalisation of musical forms always involve a process of selection and destruction. Some words gain new definitions; others are labelled as foreign importations and edited out. Some musical styles are labelled as 'traditional' and worthy of investment; others are thought to be derogatory or corrupted. Through this work vernacular idioms are made, and cultural forms become emblems of an authentic tradition.

The book opens with three essays that illuminate the field of debate surrounding the official discourse of heritage in South Africa. As Daniel Herwitz shows in his chapter, the ruling African National Congress has been recounting the events of anti-apartheid resistance in a certain way: as constituent parts of a larger struggle culminating in the ANC's assumption of government in 1994. This teleological reading of history transforms a multifarious assortment of movements, conflicts, and personalities into a singular narrative of national self-becoming. Presented in this way, Herwitz argues, heritage can become a means of distilling a complicated history into political capital, a legacy that has to be carried on. The infrastructure of the heritage industry allows the ANC to claim a continuing role in brokering the struggle for freedom in post-apartheid South Africa.

Gary Minkley and Phindezwa Mnyaka's chapter focuses on the controversies occasioned by the ANC's appropriation of local history. In 2008 government authorities in Duncan Village erected a monument to commemorate a series of protests inspired by the murder of a local anti-apartheid activist in 1985. As mentioned above, it featured a bronze statue of an African warrior, poised in an aggressive stance and holding a spear aloft. Duncan Village residents thought the monument to be out of place, and in the turmoil that followed the unveiling of the statue, some of them proposed that the spear-wielding bronze warrior should be replaced with a statue of a mother carrying her dead child. Neither the spear-carrying warrior nor the bereaved mother accurately represent the events of 1985. But that is not the point, argue Minkley and Mnyaka. Memorials are a means by which political actors recast the past in a particular way, as heroic evidence of resistance or as a pathetic plea for social services and entitlements. Controversies over memorials manifest larger arguments over the relation of the state to its citizenry.

Leslie Witz and Noëleen Murray study an altogether more prosaic structure: the Lwandle Migrant Labour Museum, opened in 2000 on the grounds of what had once been a migrant workers' hostel.[113] The hostel had formerly housed single men, but by the 1990s the buildings were being redeveloped as family housing. The core of the museum was Hostel 33, the last undeveloped hostel in the neighbourhood. Witz and Murray show how the museum developed its collection *en media res*, by transforming outdated bits of infrastructure – signage, crumbling buildings – into the substance of its displays. Lwandle's curators were documenting an outmoded form of sociality even as it was disappearing. They were also involved in the making of a developmentalist narrative, tracking the progressive emergence of a new form of urban sociality. In the museum, argue Witz and Murray, attendees could see how hostels had become homes, how a labour compound had become a township, how racial exclusion had given way (apparently) to multiracial democracy. In contemporary South Africa, museum collections help the architects of a post-apartheid society map the distance travelled, contrast past with present, and chart the arrival of a new era of social life and of politics.

The chapters by Gavua and Silverman move the focus towards Ghana. There are clearly comparisons to be made with the South African material, for in Ghana as in South Africa monuments and museum displays have been edited and remade to suit the state's changing agenda. But where the post-apartheid South African state has been actively building a monumental infrastructure to celebrate its struggle history, Ghana's official monument builders have been more opportunistic in defining a memorial landscape. Kodzo Gavua's chapter highlights the remarkable range of structures that have been made sites of memory. The Ako-Adjei interchange has gone through several name changes: during the Nkrumah regime it was called the Akuafo Roundabout, in honour of Ghana's farmers; after Nkrumah's ouster it became 'National Redemption Circle'. It was named 'Sankara Circle' under the government of Jerry Rawlings, and when in 2001 the New Patriotic Party came to power, it was named after Dr Ebenezer Ako Adjei, an early Gold Coast political leader. It is the faceless character of the transportation infrastructure that allows it to be repurposed in this way. No inconvenient statuary needs to be smuggled out of sight; no names need to be chiselled out of a granite plinth. The anonymity of the transport infrastructure allows it to be rapidly, and

---

[113] Witz has written about the Lwandle museum in his 'Transforming Museums on Postapartheid Tourist Routes', in Ivan Karp, Corinne Kratz, Lynn Szwaja, and Tomás Ybarra-Frausto (eds), *Museum Frictions: Public Cultures/Global Transformations* (Durham, NC: Duke University Press, 2006), 107–34.

repeatedly, renamed in response to the changing political imperatives of Ghana's rulers.

Where Gavua's chapter focuses on the role of government officials in naming and renaming monumental structures, Ray Silverman's chapter focuses on a more marginal set of actors. The town of Manso has an impressive history: it sits atop an older town, Bono Manso, that was the capital of the first centralised state in the Akan region. But Manso's contemporary leaders have little interest in excavating or celebrating this aspect of their history. They have, instead, sought to position their marginal locality as a pilgrimage site for African-American tourists. A bust of the American civil rights leader Martin Luther King Jr was unveiled in 2004, and there are now memorials to Marcus Garvey, Rosa Parks, and Coretta Scott King. As Silverman points out, the evidence of the town's connection with the Atlantic slave trade of the seventeenth and eighteenth centuries is tenuous. But Manso's leaders cannot be dogmatic about historical accuracy. They need to generate a flow of income and attention for their politically and economically disadvantaged region. In their heritage work they overlay the archaeological evidence, making their home region into a site for other people's memories.

Like Silverman, Ciraj Rassool is interested in the ways in which human bodies have been deployed to help the living identify themselves with particular pasts. In Ghana the reburial of expropriated human bodies has transformed localities like Manso into sites of memory for foreign tourists. In South Africa, by contrast, the demand for the return of expropriated human remains is part of a larger effort to define and inventory a national patrimony. Rassool's chapter illuminates the field of contest surrounding human remains in post-apartheid South Africa.[114] In the nineteenth and early twentieth centuries South Africa's museums were built in part from the unethical activities of collectors who stole and smuggled African body parts. It is these collections of human remains – now held in anthropology museums around the world – that are subject to demands for recompense and return. In post-apartheid South Africa, expropriated human remains have been defined as the new nation's property, and their return and reburial has been a dramatic aspect of the inventorying of national heritage.

The nation is not the only political theatre in which the dead are being drafted into a role. Ethnic groups need ancestors, too, and graves at which to venerate them. Mbongiseni Buthelezi's chapter shows how the dead can be marshalled to serve in the construction of a Ndwandwe ethnic community. In the KwaZulu Natal province of South Africa, the Zulu

---

[114] Building on Martin Legassick and Ciraj Rassool, *Skeletons in the Cupboard: South African Museums and the Trade in Human Remains, 1907–1917* (Cape Town: South African Museum, 2000).

king has been given extraordinary powers to define and impose cultural practices on his people. Cultural minorities feel themselves oppressed by this Zulu cultural hegemony. Buthelezi focuses on the uBumbano lwamaZwide, a group of elders and activists who identify themselves as descendants of Zwide, the king of the Ndwandwe polity. In the early nineteenth century the Ndwandwe had been conquered and folded into the Zulu state. In the twenty-first century dissidents are bringing Zwide back to life through the infrastructure of the heritage industry. There is a 'Heritage Day' that honours Zwide; there are praise poems that recount his exploits; there is hymnody that elevates the civility of Ndwandwe ancestors and narrates their tragic overthrow by Shaka. Partisans are reburying their dead, locating deceased parents and grandparents in the precincts of memorials to Ndwandwe heroes. Through this dissident heritage economy, a minority group opens up the possibility for a separate political community.

In the Ndwandwe *patria* as in other projects of its kind, heritage practice demands the discursive expansion of historical facts. The dead do not speak for themselves. Poems need to be written; heroic exploits must be narrated. Material artefacts must likewise be described in labels, placards, and signs. The explanatory work of the commentator, the curator, and the partisan expands the bare chronicle of past events. Not everyone regards this work of curatorial elaboration as positive or enabling. In the kingdom of Asante, the death of a king is not the occasion for discourse. Kwesi Yankah's chapter concerns historical events that cannot be represented, that are hidden from the public eye, that are not subject to elaboration in heritage discourse. In Asante, tragic events are categorised as *ntam*, an unspeakable event, never to be spoken about. Asante subjects' civility – their self-discipline – is measured in part by their ability to keep quiet about political tragedies. Yankah shows how this form of discursive editing is challenged by modern communications technology, in which information and news seems to flow without check. Asante people are critical of the unchecked flow of information: the telephone is called 'the wire that transmits falsehood', for example. By helping us glimpse the limits of the human propensity to narrate the past, Yankah outlines the outer edge of the heritage industry.

The final four chapters of the book are united by their concern with media infrastructure and the heritage economy. The subject matter is transitory: the authors deal with dance, language, and flickering cinematic images. It is this impermanence that animates an impulse towards the concrete, towards the archive. The speakers of hitherto despised languages aspire to a dictionary that can be placed on the library shelves. So do missionaries and linguists, whose professional work depends on the reduction of unwritten tongues to writing. Musicians and dance troupes create scripts and scores that make the subtle dynamics of their art permanent, choreographed, and iterable. Moviemakers likewise aspire towards permanence, using film to capture dying civilisations and chronicle their world. Whether on paper or celluloid, the products of their work are anachronisms at the point of their publication, always outflanked by the innovations and dynamisms of real human life. But in the library or in the archive they live another life, as monuments to past ways of life, chronicles of the past, and source material for heritage work.

Judy Irvine's essay focuses on the role that missionaries and other colonial linguists played in the standardisation of Africa's vernacular languages. Neither the Igbo nor the Serer, nor any other African ethnic community, were actually culturally coherent, linguistically integrated communities. But linguists thought they were, and the texts they created played a central role in the fabrication of ethnic identity. The vocabulary of Nigeria's Igbo language was first defined out of the research that Protestant missionaries conducted in Freetown, in Sierra Leone, among the community of freed slaves living in that city. In French West Africa, the Serer language was rendered distinct from Wolof by French geographers and linguists. Once a particular, geographically bounded people were assigned to a particular language, then a variety of institutions – the school, the law court, the church – obliged them to learn it. In this way, Irvine argues, colonial linguistics helped to overwrite cultural heterodoxy, marshalling Africans as ethnic subjects.

Where Irvine studies the architecture and politics of official languages, Mary Esther Dakubu illuminates the linguistic work that minorities undertake. Dakubu focuses on two cases of linguistic and political innovation. In one instance, she shows how members of a particular lineage, made up of people descended from slave ancestors, have reworked their ritual and religious vocabulary in order to claim membership in a prominent Gã family group. In another instance, Dakubu highlights the work that members of the Farefari minority in northern Ghana have done to redefine their culture. Like the dissident activists of uBumbano lwamaZwide, Farefari people find themselves denigrated by other groups: historically the region was a site of slave raiding, and in colonial times it was a source of servants and workers. In the 1990s, local entrepreneurs established a programme of language development: an orthography was agreed upon and a dictionary was published. Through these efforts the Farefari re-engineered their political position, claiming for themselves a creditable place among Ghana's citizenry.

Like the dictionary, the musical score can be a potent means of convening hitherto divided people as participants in a cultural production. Moses nii-Dortey focuses on the folk operas of the Ghanaian composer Saka Acquaye, particularly on *The Lost Fishermen*, which debuted in 1965. The opera both reflected and advanced the nation-building project of the composer's patron, Ghanaian president Kwame Nkrumah.

Nkrumah sought to create a national culture by deliberately appropriating, synthesising, and recontextualising the symbols of Ghana's disparate regional cultural forms. In the folk opera – as in the National Museum (above) – bits of discourse that had their provenance in one or the other of Ghana's regions were melded together and put on display. *The Lost Fisherman* features Ga, Ewe, and Akan folk songs, a Fante fisherman's song, and dirges of the Ewe people. Acquaye's opera dramatised the project in which Nkrumah and his contemporaries were engaged: they sought to constitute an integrated national culture in which Ghanaians would display their unity in performance.[115]

Acquaye's opera – like the dictionaries that Irvine and Dakubu study – were partisan creations, authored by people who sought to bring a new political community to life. On the page, at least, the authors of these texts could be authoritative: they could associate people with particular properties, put words in their mouths, and urge them to speak, sing, and act in unison. In film, by contrast, the author is never fully in control of his or her medium. Filmic representations of history rely on other people to set a scene, act in character, and provide a sonic landscape. The collaborative character of film, the multiplicity of its participants, the human texture of the scene, make it difficult for any ideologue – however firm in his or her directorial conviction – to control the medium in its totality. In this book's final substantive chapter Litheko Modisane undertakes a study of *African Jim*, a 1949 film made by two British expatriates. The plot is driven by the logic of apartheid: Jim, a rural man, comes to the city of Johannesburg, where he encounters a variety of vices and corruptions for which he is ill-prepared. In the official storyline – voiced by a disembodied narrator – Jim is, like Africans more generally, both culturally and psychologically out of place in the city. But as Modisane shows, *African Jim* offers its viewers 'flashes of modernity' that illuminate the forms of urban culture that Africans created. Extras sing songs in Xhosa or Zulu that are derogatory to their white supervisors; black men play jazz in a setting that evokes Sophiatown's urban culture. Despite the intentions of its producers, the film troubled apartheid definitions of culture that associated Africans with rurality and tradition. No heritage is uncomplicated, Modisane concludes, and no cultural production is fully in the control of its authors.

Taken together, these chapters show that the practices of museology had a pivotal role to play in the territorialisation of political culture. Prior to the twentieth century, the continent's thin topsoil, variegated topography, and relatively sparse human population made it impossible

---

[115] Askew, *Performing the Nation*.

for authorities to settle people in place.[116] The architects of colonial and post-colonial African states had coercive powers that pre-colonial authorities could not command: the census, the identity card, the tax collector, the map. It was therefore possible for authorities to identify Africans with specific localities, to exercise government over bounded tracts of territory, to summon their people as members of tribes or of nations. Cultural practices were territorialised out of this work of political consolidation. In neo-traditional kingdoms and latterly in post-colonial nations, polity builders sought to link the people of a particular place to specific customs, laws, histories, and hierarchies. Here the technologies of the heritage industry proved useful. In museums, the people of a territory – Ghanaians, or the Zulu, or South Africans – regardless of their differences, could learn of a past that they shared. In dictionaries, speakers of a particular language could, notwithstanding differences of dialect, find a vernacular with which to communicate. In monuments they could, despite their particular historical experiences, honour the heroes of the *patria*. Heritage practices helped political authorities identify a particular people with particular *terroir*. That is why the African National Congress appropriated the local history of Duncan Village. That is why the architects of Zulu political community can leave so little space for the Ndwandwe and other ethnic sub-communities. That is why the Farefari and the Serer needed a dictionary. That is why South Africa's dead, so widely dispersed, have to be repatriated. It is through the instruments of heritage discourse that the people of a particular place are attached to ancestors, attributes, history and a homeland. The practice of heritage creates natives.

---

[116] Iliffe, *The Africans*.

2   Heritage and Legacy in the South African State and University

Daniel Herwitz

I

Heritage is that particular reconfiguration of the past that arises in the Europe of the eighteenth and nineteenth centuries. It rescripts a people's past into an exalted set of time-tested and time-honoured values, believed to be of enduring worth and thus to offer the prospect of a unified future.[1] By preaching a common origin it proclaims common destiny. Heritage making is equally central to the rise of the post-colonial nation state. 'Colonialism is not satisfied merely with hiding a people in its grip,' the ever-perspicuous Frantz Fanon wrote. 'By a kind of perverted logic, it turns to the past of the oppressed people and distorts, disfigures and destroys it.'[2] With the rise of the post-colonial state heritage practice enters the domain of reparation, recovery, and acknowledgement of a past always partly alienated under the colonial yoke (while also part of the ongoing texture of contemporary life in the form of tradition). The new state, like its European predecessor of the eighteenth or nineteenth century, deploys heritage institutions and instruments, museums, courts of law, and universities to empower itself with unity, longevity, exaltation of value, origin, and destiny. It can hardly avoid doing this when it takes over the *form* of the nation state from the coloniser, or from an earlier regime. The turning of the past into a heritage is part of the symbolic currency of the nation, defining and driving its common future by marshalling the past into a mythic or religious form, an origin, a set of core values distinctive to the nation, a common destiny. This act of symbolic articulation, or contrivance, tends to favour one version of the nation

[1] I would like to thank Leslie Witz for provocative and useful comments on an earlier draft of this essay, presented to the Archives and Public Culture Seminar at the University of Cape Town in April 2013, where the sparks flew and the essay benefited. I would also like to thank the Anthropology Department of the University of Stellenbosch, where I presented a revised version later that month, and the African Studies Center at Stanford University, where it was presented in June of 2013. Finally I wish to thank Debjani Ganguly and the Humanities Research Centre of the Australian National University, who gave it a platform in August of 2013. I received helpful comments on every occasion.
[2] Frantz Fanon, 'On National Culture', in Patrick Williams and Ian Chrisman (eds), *Colonial and Postcolonial* Theory: A Reader (New York, NY: Columbia University Press, 1994), 37.

37

over others, and may of course be highly contested. The politics of how the past is scripted into a heritage is a window into the divisions between citizens and/or subjects at moments of national formation or transition.

Different kinds of post-colonial states mythologise or otherwise script their pasts into dramatically distinct kinds of heritage. My recent book *Heritage, Culture and Politics in the Postcolony* takes up three cases: India, South Africa, and the United States.[3] This essay is about South Africa, where I lived for a decade during the moment of political transition, the 1990s. At that moment of political negotiation old heritages went into tailspins and new ones hurtled into being. Traditional objects (artefacts of 'indigenous' culture) were being pulled from the 'anthropology sec-tion' of the museum, recontextualised, and given new meaning within contemporary heritage discourses. Performance, so pervasive in African village and town, quickly morphed into a central vehicle for the remaking of identity. Local cultures, some long repressed, began to mourn their dispossessed pasts in city sites razed under apartheid (such as District Six), creating an archive of their lost communities. The struggle against apartheid began to turn to a heritage of the victim, the battle, the brave.

At the national and local levels South Africa National Heritage Policy articulated heritage as redress. Archaeologist Nick Shepherd puts it thus: 'Aspects of this programme include[d] an ongoing public process of renaming of sites, towns, cities, streets and public amenities, and the introduction of the Legacy Projects. At the same time, a decision was made not to expunge the memorials of Afrikaner National History, but rather to retain them as a record of apartheid, and to set them in dialogue with newer, more critically inclusive sites. . . . '[4] Essentially an artefact of transition in the 1990s, this narrative, and policy, stressed a dialogue with the past, wide social engagement in a practice (heritage) that had been exclusionary, and heritage as part of the culture of building human rights. It gravitated towards a de-monumentalising stance in response to the stark power of the colonial and then apartheid monuments.[5] It made no riposte to Rhodes on horseback framed by lions at the highest point on Devil's Peak where it is possible to build, directly above his former estate (designed by Sir Herbert Baker, 1912) where he inhabits a Graeco-Roman amphitheatre in the role of Zeus, lunging towards the fulfilment of his mission of claiming Africa from Cape to Cairo. Nor did it attempt

---

[3] Daniel Herwitz, *Heritage, Culture and Politics in the Postcolony* (New York, NY: Columbia University Press, 2012).

[4] Nick Shepherd, 'Heritage', in Nick Shepherd and Steven Robins (eds), *New South African Keywords* (Athens, OH: Ohio University Press, 2008), 121–2.

[5] This grafting of heritage in the grand style, inherited from the nation building of the European eighteenth and nineteenth centuries, with contemporary neo-liberal and demo-cratic political and economic aspirations, is what I call the live-action remaking of the heritage game by the postcolony in my recent book *Heritage, Culture and Politics in the Postcolony* (Ibid.).

to overfly the Voortrekker Monument (designed by Gerard Moerdyk, 1949) in the suburb of Valhalla outside of Pretoria, turning Afrikaner suffering during the Boer War into a laager for resurgent, indomitable, apartheid power with its stark art-deco walls and its burning cenotaph within, framed by paintings of the 'Great Trek' into the interior and the besting of the Zulu by rifle, ox wagon, and God's will. In response to these difficult inheritances (and the national trauma of history of which they were part), the state and local culture stressed during the moment of transition (the 1990s) a culture of memorialisation, participation, and diversity.

Redress became the moral template of transition, setting a compass towards a better future. In this vein the Constitutional Court building (OMM Architects, 2004) seeks to preserve legal heritage in the form of troubled memory. Within the walls of the court are the ruins of the Old Fort Prison where many anti-apartheid activists were imprisoned without charge – including retired Constitutional Court judge Albie Sachs, impresario for this architectural project. The lobby of the court is constructed around the former part of the prison where prisoners awaited trial (these included Mahatma Gandhi and Sachs himself). And so in deference to apartheid, and before that the colonial heritage, a heritage of injustice stands within the walls of the new South African court as vanquished ruin, but also persistent historical memory. The thought is that judgement and justice require acknowledgement of this memory. The court openly retains the scar of its apartheid prison, and by retaining its crumbling structures the court transforms an old prison into a heritage. The gesture is heritage-creating. It is also *ruin*-creating, since the old prison, torn down, would not have become a living ruin without being subsumed within the court. This dialogue with the past turns that piece of political history into a new heritage form between reminder and ruin.

While redress, dialogue, and participation were the explicit goals of heritage policy at that time, a monumentalising script also entered the South African transitional scene with State President Thabo Mbeki in 1996, and continued through his decade in office beginning in 1998. Mbeki's African Renaissance, articulated in a highfalutin oratory redolent of the first-generation African post-colonial leaders and before them Churchill and Cicero, whose collective heritage hall he wished to enter, proclaimed a new beginning for South Africa/Africa via a return to that mythic once-upon-a-time before the colonial and apartheid struggles. Mbeki sought an origin for South Africa and Africa in 'indigenous' and African peoples, in their knowledge of medicinal plants, ways of surviving in liminal climates, moral communities, patterns of work and sustainability that would set the terms for Africa's twenty-first-century neo-liberal adventure in democracy and long-term economic growth. Having been nearly eradicated, Khoisan peoples were celebrated, their knowledge scrutinised for truth, morality, and dignity, while their know-how (uses of medicinal plants, survival skills in liminal climates) was studied for potential market gain. In accord with the nineteenth-century heritage formula preaching return to origin (usually in Ancient Greece) as the route to national destiny (the Matthew Arnold approach), Mbeki believed Africa should immediately claim its place in the world of global capital and technology transfer by returning to its forgotten storehouse of pre-colonial knowledge and ethics. Old values like *ubuntu*, communalism, work, and patience become in Mbeki's script a heritage source, like the ever-Englishness of green and pleasant fields or the codifications of the Académie Française. In pre-colonial Africa, so mythologised, Mbeki claimed Africa would find origin and futurity: *destiny*.[6]

Heritage tends to denature real politics, turning history into memory or raising it, as litany, to monumentalising mythology. The University of the Western Cape's Heritage Studies programme works closely with Robben Island to promote a similar care for preservation, acknowledgement, and the dignity of place in an increasingly touristic world. It is hard enough for the Island to invite reflection on these values when the Cape tourist rushes from wine farm to Table Mountain to buying mohair scarves at the Waterfront, from where the boat to the Island departs. But in so far as the Island retains its aura of dignified silence, many of the details of history are drained from it, and perhaps should be. For years prisoners on Robben Island fiercely debated the way forward and rifts arose; it is said some refused to speak to others. This is not part of the heritage story a tourist or school child learns, not part of what they want to get from the Island as an artefact of 'heritage', a stark church of remembrance, and perhaps should not be. History becomes for the heritage site a vaguer currency of remembrance, moral reminder, uneasy acknowledgement.

II

Then there is a specific drama played out around the state and its self-legitimation on the basis of heritage: a third way heritage discourse entered the moment of political transition at the level of state policy. It

---

[6] Asserted with all due superiority (no doubt in compensation for decades of unfair castigation in times past), the ideology faltered when Mbeki decided that indigenous knowledge and pre-colonial values existed in contradistinction to the dictates of global medical science with respect to HIV/AIDS. The results were catastrophic for South African public health. In spite of research projects on 'indigenous knowledge research' instituted in universities, museums and the like during the Mbeki years, the project is hopelessly delegitimated by the HIV/AIDS stance. Suffice it to say that whereas the official heritage policy of the transition de-monumentalised heritage construction, Mbeki's goal was to *re-monumentalise* a story of origins, and values for the legitimation of the new state (with him at the helm), and it proved highly attenuated.

is a fundamental need of newly transitional/democratic and often politically weak states that they legitimate their existence on the basis of their
political pasts. Such states often want to take control of the scripting
of their past struggle, proclaim that history from the ramparts, broadcast it in the form of a memoir in which they themselves are the central
players. And this involves a particular grafting of history into heritage.
Heritage tends to denature the nitty-gritty of politics, with its history of
infighting, alliance, and exclusion; gradually it turns the past into a site of
remembrance, moral acknowledgement, ritual, and/or myth. But for the
(South African) state, wanting to broadcast its central role in bringing
about the new political dispensation, heritage must also encode, refer to,
or connote the recent struggle history through which the now-emergent
state played a central role. The past struggle of the new government must
be incanted as heritage myth, but also as *history* – and with it (the new
state) as the central player. And so Thabo Mbeki, then Deputy State
President, proclaimed at the Inauguration of the South African Parliament in May 1996, '... let me begin. I am an African. I am formed of
the migrants who left Europe to find a new home on our native land. ...
In my veins courses the blood of the Cape Malay slaves who came from
the east. ... I am the grandchild of the men and women that Hintsa and
Sekhukhune led. ... My mind and my knowledge of myself is formed by
the victories we earned from Isandhlwana to Khartoum.'[7] And in doing
so he implied the ancient and venerable history of Africa flowed through
him, a heritage of which he is the descendant. A heritage of, for example,
Sekhukhune, the King of the BaPedi, who in 1876 beat off attack by the
Boers under the leadership of President Burghers, and then again by the
British under Shepstone. (It took a third attempt, again by the British,
to rout Sekhukhune, after which he was put in prison in Pretoria.)

In the same speech Mbeki went on to say: 'All of this I know and know
to be true because I am an African! Because of that, I am also able to
state this fundamental truth: that I am born of a people who are heroes
and heroines. I am born of a people who would not tolerate oppression. I
am of a nation that would not allow that.'[8] Here he meant, and everyone
knew he meant, that the people who would not tolerate oppression were
those who resisted apartheid. They are in his speech the substance of
the new nation. Those who went into exile, struggled in the townships
that trained in the training camps, endured the hardships of Robben
Island. Above all the African National Congress. They are his icons of the
nation who 'would not allow that' – they and the young people resisting
in the townships, bravely facing police. And so in the one paragraph
he creates a heritage legacy of those who fought the colonial oppressor

---

[7] Thabo Mbeki, *Africa: The Time Has Come* (Cape Town: Tafelberg, 1998), 31.
[8] Ibid., 32.

(Sekhukhune and Hintsa), in the second he tacitly places the African National Congress at the crown of that heritage legacy, alluding to their history of struggle without referring to it, and so elevating it into the more luminous currency of African heritage. To refer explicitly to the heroes of the African National Congress would have been unworthy of the unifying moment of the opening of Parliament. And so in the first paragraph he creates a heritage of the great heroes of the past (Sekhukune) from whom he is descended; in the next paragraph he tacitly makes it clear that the crowning glory of this heritage is the entire South African nation that 'would not allow' oppression. Of course, the entire South African nation was not against oppression – many were for it, or at least tolerated it – but in Mbeki's unifying heritage moment the entire nation is read back into the past as always having refused oppression, as if the African National Congress and its refusal were the metonym for the whole nation, the national substance or icon. And so, without even referring to it, the ANC is catapulted into standing for all South Africans in a larger heritage of African struggle.

This is myth making at a moment of transition, grafting struggle history into a larger story of heritage, and making the ANC stand in for all South Africans. But a new and weak state must do more if it wishes to legitimate itself. It must also show that the *legacy* of its activist politics continues into the new dispensation, that in its leadership role the new government is carrying on the good fight. Hence the language of *birth* in Mbeki's inauguration of Parliament: I *am born of those who would not tolerate oppression*, which I take to mean: 'I am in my current position as Deputy President of the new state what I was before: a struggle hero. Our struggle continues with me in my new role, and the establishment of Parliament is part of it.'

My argument is thus that a weak or new state, desiring legitimacy from the past, must demonstrate both that its past struggle is now *over* (as the currency of heritage it is a thing of the glorious past) and *not over* (since the new government is born as the child of that past, the old politics of struggle-for-justice continues with it). Together (and only together) these positions marshal the past to legitimate the state. This tension between things being over and not being over defines the difference between what I will call *heritage* and *legacy* in this chapter. *Heritage* is, for my purposes, the granting to something that is finished (that has been completed in 'me') a second life in book, museum, site of memory, grand pronouncement, or ritual, using the institutions and instruments of script, museum, university, court, and the rest. *Legacy* is the ongoing practice of something from the past, a direct inheritance that is still operative – call it politics-as-usual in a new or transformed dispensation, with a genealogy recognisable from days before. This slightly unusual use of 'heritage' and 'legacy' as terms is meant to make a point; for both must be present in order for the state to claim political legitimacy (beyond mere litany or remembrance) from its past. On the one hand the struggle politics of the past, now over and transformed into the new democratic dispensation, must reassert itself as heritage. Once a real-life activity, it must live a second life as a source of value for the new regime. On the other hand, the state must demonstrate that its capacity to struggle remains alive in the present; that it approaches the tasks of instituting the rights contained in the constitution, bringing about socio-economic development and citizenship, with a resolve worthy of its struggle in the past. Otherwise it is simply sitting on its laurels.

At the beginning of the Mandela years this double requirement was well met. For Mandela stood as icon both of the struggle and of its continuation in the new South Africa. He appeared before awestruck crowds in South Africa and world-wide as moral exemplar and political god, while leading the African National Congress through a transition that was widely considered miraculous – and therefore tailor-made to levitate into heritage myth. South Africa's transition to democracy proved the miracle that nobody believed could happen even while it was happening. Apartheid formally ended in 1991. Nelson Mandela and F. W. de Klerk entered a formal state of negotiation/power sharing, to hammer out the terms for a new state. Mandela succeeded in getting his party to drop its demand that the mining industry be nationalised. The talks took place in a climate of fear and conflagration: in the province of Natal, thousands died as Zulu Nationalists (the Inkatha Party), aiming for provincial autonomy, fought the African National Congress. A 'third force' emanating from the South African Security Police aided and abetted the Inkatha combatants. Key African National Congress figures were assassinated. And yet the talks led to an interim constitution (1994) which mandated the first free and democratic elections in the history of the country, the terms of the Truth and Reconciliation Commission, and the pathway to the writing of a final constitution. Mandela – icon, celebrity, god – by demonstrating his ability to forgive and move beyond was praised all the more for humour and humility. When Madiba (Mandela's clan name) was voted the first State President of the new country, an international moral exemplar had assumed power at a moment of Truth and Reconciliation, constitution writing, and the ongoing miracle of the transition.

Mbeki knew he had no Mandela magic and that any state with him at the helm as its President would require a new symbolic currency, a new heritage-speak. He drew on his decolonising instincts, which reached back, as outlined above, to pre-colonial Africa as a new origin for the future. Mbeki's African Renaissance turned heritage into policy. University research centres were established to draw on pre-colonial knowledge and society. Institutions of art and culture illuminated the pre-colonial past as guiding lights for the nation. Heritage was, for Mbeki, the correct form of *legacy*, the way to show that the struggle for African freedom continued in the new democracy, a democracy dedicated to Africanist thinking. Now that the war had been won, the struggle for the future should be shaped by revisiting the past.

As the tenure of his presidency became more problematic he became more adamant in his assertion of this heritage/Renaissance. Almost from the moment Mbeki assumed office in 1998 the government found itself entangled in an infamous crisis of legitimation around its HIV/AIDS policy. Compounding that was a second crisis around human rights delivery in other areas of society, such as housing. The power of the constitution was invoked as corrective to both. In a pair of landmark decisions taken by the Constitutional Court against the government, the rule of law was established and confirmed. The first decision concerned a Mrs Grootboom who had been living in a shack on the Cape Flats, a flimsy lean-to built on sand without electricity, running water, or sewerage. As one among millions in the same condition, she chose to sue for her right to housing in the Constitutional Court. The Court ruled in her favour: that the South African state had failed in its constitutional obligation by not as yet making a 'reasonable effort' to institute her right to housing, meaning the rights of many like her. This decision prompted a programme in which more than two million houses have been built, with electricity introduced into informal settlements, running water, and so on. The results have been as dramatic as they remain inadequate (sadly, Mrs Grootboom died without ever receiving a house).

The second case against the government was brought in 2002 by the Treatment Action Campaign, an HIV/AIDS activist group, which successfully sued in the Constitutional Court on grounds that the government had failed to make the reasonable effort mandated by the constitution to institute the right to health. The government was forced to roll out anti-retroviral drugs, which became affordable after a second lawsuit against two pharmaceutical companies producing the drugs was also won, forcing those corporations to supply the country with affordable drugs.

As the actual legacy of struggle became more and more difficult for the Mbeki presidency to demonstrate, his policy became more and more seeped in heritage – to the point where heritage approached kitsch. Seeking African solutions to African problems, he mandated the finding of a cure for AIDS in the soil of Africa and the substrate of indigenous thinking. Were a new drug to be found which had been cultivated by the Khoi or San (or even by some scientist in Pretoria) he probably would have embraced it, forgetting his position denying the HIV virus as the cause of AIDS. Justice in Africa, whether pertaining to medical cure or economic development, should be home-grown, that is, *heritage*-grown. Heritage, he believed, could cure.

Today, the third South African presidency, with Jacob Zuma at the helm, is increasingly less interested in legitimating itself through any symbolic currency pertaining to the past. The government has become a corporate body with an increasingly greater interest in and links to business, relying (although less and less securely) on the expected support of voters ready to keep it in power whatever it does. The heritage turn, central first to the Mandela, and then to the Mbeki moments, seems to be fading away in a market-oriented state less interested in legitimation. Or is it? For Zuma performs his relationship to *customary culture* regularly, dancing with his Zulu compatriots, trotting out his wives, wearing the occasional leopard skin, suggesting he is the continuation of that ethnicity. Whether he is marketing to voter constituencies, or seeking a new path to heritage is difficult to tell. He seems to look to ethnicity most readily when he is under the gun (the object of rape or corruption charges).

III

The struggle for the future waged over the past has been equally central to civil society in the new South Africa, as is evident in the programmes developed in certain universities, museums, and non-government organisations (NGOs). I turn especially to universities, where heritage practice is robust and contentious, paradoxically because heritage practice deploys a legacy of activist politics formed during the apartheid period. I want to describe this activist legacy of some South African universities.[9] It is hardly the only legacy in the South African university (which has also been a Eurocentric [British] Commonwealth institution, or one with Germanic intellectual roots, and is in many ways part of the regularised world of global knowledge production today). But it is significant.

During apartheid the University of Witwatersrand in Johannesburg had a plaque in the foyer of its Great Hall stating unconditionally that its principled position was in opposition to the government, that it would accept all races, and that it would teach without censorship. Wits of course, followed the law. It had separate residences for students of colour and only admitted students of colour when it was legally possible. The University of Natal was mixed in its liberalism, supporting leftist faculty even when they were 'banned' but also hiring plenty of conservative

---

[9] The next three paragraphs, which outline the template of the South African university, are indebted to an earlier essay written with Professor Ahmed Bawa, whom I thank. Cf. Ahmed Bawa and Daniel Herwitz, 'South African Universities in the Tumult of Change', *Journal of the International Institute* 15, 2 (2009): 1, 12–14.

'collaborators' who would not rock the boat. Students of colour thrived in its black medical school (where the Black Consciousness Movement of Steve Biko was born) but were denied access to many facilities. The Afrikaans universities were all fiercely pro-apartheid, and the University of Pretoria received triple funding from the government because of its allegiance. (These universities are remaking themselves today and have much to offer.) The presence of activist scholars at key universities in South Africa helped to shape their engagement with local communities, and this became being a central feature of the liberal academic profile. In the 1980s and at the early moment of transition in the 1990s, as a way of providing protection to community-based organisations from apartheid's security apparatus, educational institutions created the infrastructure for more than eighty of these organisations. Just prior to the fall of apartheid, the University of the Western Cape was an avowedly Marxist university. The University of Cape Town remained at that time within the ambit of 'white' universities in spite of its liberalism, and against that liberalism the University of the Western Cape arose not only as a university for students and faculty of 'colour' (a so-called coloured university) but with the explicit intention of become a home for the left in the new dispensation, a place where activist models and leftist knowledge production would find synergy not merely at that tumultuous moment of struggle but in the future society to be created.

Activist scholars routinely worked between trade union and treatise, between organising and originating new ideas in economics, history, art criticism, English, archaeology, sociology, public health, or politics. The exchange between field and scholarship was often highly productive. With the collapse of the Soviet Union and the neo-liberal turn in the African National Congress and the new South African state, this dream of housing the left was undercut. Marxist models turned out to be inadequate to the task of thinking the possibility of the new South African democracy in a clearly neo-liberal and globalised world, in spite of their ongoing aptness, and South African universities generally (not simply the University of the Western Cape) were faced with the task of renegotiating epistemologies of activism.

Perhaps the most sustained attempted to bring together theory and praxis was the work of Richard Turner. Writing in the early 1970s when the apartheid state had solidified its grip, Turner, who returned to South Africa from Paris with a PhD in philosophy earned under Jean-Paul Sartre and Raymond Aron, immediately became involved in trade union activism in Durban, leading to his eventual banning and then assassination by the apartheid state. His intellectual project was to bring together his philosophical commitments to existentialist Marxism and Hegelianism with his trade union work in Durban in a way that would understand the political work as part of a general historical dialectic. His philosophical attempt was brilliant, leading to a single published book, *The Eye of the Needle* before he was brutally gunned down. At the time of his early death he left crates full of uncompleted manuscripts, a testament to a noble, if ultimately failed *intellectual* project.

Why the failure? In part Turner's intellectual project failed because there is no general theory of history to be found, Marxist or otherwise. There is no general world-historical dialectic into which South African history can be placed. And there is no general account of the dialectic between theory and praxis to be formulated (in spite of a history of attempts to do so throughout the late nineteenth and twentieth centuries). The South African legacy of engaged commitment highlights *strategic intervention* in its intellectual narratives, and it highlights *particularity of social/historical context* in all its robustness, neither of which is easily generalisable. Facts are hard enough to subsume under a general theory. But here it is not just the depth of facts, the particularity of specific context. It is also that activist knowledge production focuses on the writing of narratives that are critical, interventionist, and strategic. It is this *narrative* tendency, which is about robustness of facts, interpretation of them, and intervention in them, that makes activist epistemology a form of *practical* knowledge, not easily generalised into theory.

This history has given South African universities a particular and important legacy, which stresses social intervention. At the same time there is a commitment to autonomous scholarship, to a kind of writing that analyses, imagines, and contributes to global scholarly norms, including theory-driven norms. The uniqueness of the South African legacy consists in the *tension* between these styles of knowledge production, a tension wholly at one with the larger set of tensions characteristic of a society in transition. It may alternatively be described as a tension between differing kinds of *responsibility:* local culture, history, justice, the global academy, and so on.

It is this South African legacy, which in part motivates the practice of heritage work in universities and other parts of civil society today. The past becomes a living form through which human rights are articulated and unfolded in the public sphere. I personally think battles over the scripting of the *past* (that is, the *role* of the past in the present) are among the last domains open to the intellectual left, since so much of the South African present is, in spite of a progressive constitution, a market generated one. And so heritage fights are regularly engaged when for example the master builders of office mall and hotel unearth slave burial sites opening up the question of what to do given their long invisibility and importance for the signification of the past, given their money already committed to projects with potentially big payoffs. I refer to the debate over 'Prestwich Street' in Cape Town, which took place recently. As has happened before in Cape Town, the digging of a foundation for a new luxury high rise building unearthed skeletal remains of what are known to be Indonesian slaves, prompting fierce argument about whether the project should continue. A compromise was worked out after much protest, that allowed the building to be built (capital always wins), but moved the remains to a brick memorial constructed nearby in downtown Cape Town where they reside in an ossuary. There are commemorating plaques. On the front of the memorial the word 'Truth' prominently appears. Underneath is the word 'coffee'. Here is the condition of the memorial in neo-liberal times, set between the urgency of remembrance and signage advertising lunch.

In a culture where the neo-liberal office mall or hotel has become the new monument of our times, these struggles are in their own way 'monumental'. Here the 'enemy' is neo-liberal erasure of what is or wants to be preserved as heritage, which prevents the dead and buried from emerging and find their post-mortem due. Unchallenged, market imperatives would keep the dead buried, their bones underground, their trauma prevented from surfacing and finding acknowledgement in a way that would interrupt the sleek commerce of Waterfront Mall, vineyard, restaurant, office plaza, and tourism. These battles prove that the naming, defining, and preserving of heritage is in part a battleground where the old legacy of the activist model is marshalled in a neo-liberal, privatised dispensation.

Of course when objects, artefacts, sites of remembrance, and the like become reconceived by a society as 'heritage' this is not simply the work of universities. It is the expression of a particular moment when this shift in consciousness can occur. It is hard to assign a precise date to this shift in the perception of the past, but within a ten-year period Robben Island (for example) changes from prison to site of remembrance. This is partly the work of the Mayibuye Centre, which 'nationalises it', and partly the impact of critical writings of the heritage programme at the University of the Western Cape, which then criticises the work of Mayibuye (in, for example, a conference of 1996 and in its writings and curriculum thereafter). But only in the tidal wave of the moment of transition does the past becomes the object of truth, reconciliation, memory, and moral compass. Later, tourism, profiling, and marketing show their heads, making such sites the object of multiple and conflicting perceptions and uses.

Since the writing/scholarship relevant to these projects (battles) is impelled both by the desire to dignify the past into a heritage, by norms of scholarly contribution to disciplines, and also by activist 'field' engagement, there is a unique tension within the heritage-making field. It is neither merely archival, nor merely about dignity, nor even merely about profiling the past for economic gain. It is also a field where, through the past, the *legacies* of struggle culture reassert themselves. I personally think that part of the obsession with *disciplinary knowledge* in the South African heritage field, derived from the writings of Foucault, is not merely theory-driven background to stage issues of heritage critique, but also an attempt to reign in, contain, or control the contentious near-anarchy that comes from linking these norms into one practice. Foucault's work is part of the intellectual instrumentation of the arts and humanities, used to approach heritage critically, but it is also part of the instrumentation to discipline a fascinating, diverse, and chaotic field of such writings, in a country where heritage practice is equally variegated in genre and purpose. South African universities, I think, try to 'discipline' their knowledge production and interrogate their disciplinary formation because they have a unique template which is so hard to *reign in and keep organised*, which flies off the handle given its grafting of multiple norms to multiple purposes. I rather believe this state of semi-anarchic flux should be celebrated and advertised; it is a special thing when activism and scholarship are organically merged into one thing, when laptop and field are one. One can find similar university formations where knowledge production, politics, and the past go together in parts of the Australian Academy, in Israel/Palestine, and perhaps also in Latin America. This kind of epistemic formation found outside of Europe and America provides a contrast to the 'global North', where it is very difficult for the humanities to link academic study to political action, and where in compensation theory becomes over-politicised, as if it could invest humanistic writing with politics. In America, for example, the critique of representation seems to be as close to politics as the humanities can come.

One cannot know how long this very special legacy will last.

Seeing Beyond the Official and
      the Vernacular
      The Duncan Village Massacre Memorial and
      the Politics of Heritage in South Africa

Gary Minkley and Phindezwa Mnyaka

We begin by suggesting that paying attention to the significance of the visual in heritage construction in South Africa may draw into a single conversation complexities around heritage practice raised by a number of authors in this volume. We orient the discussion around events surrounding the Duncan Village Massacre Memorial constructed in the port city of East London, South Africa, in 2008. In exploring the contestations that emerged following its unveiling, and which were centred on the memorial as image, we engage with Sabine Marschall's recent intervention in articulating the distinction between 'official' and 'vernacular' forms of heritage practice in South Africa, and seek to trouble the 'alternative' possibilities promised by the latter.

It is useful to begin by considering the extent to which this particular memorial conforms to what Herwitz in this volume refers to as the monumentalising script that has characterised heritage practice following then President Thabo Mbeki's ruling African National Congress (hereafter ANC) administration in the late 1990s – a script that almost inevitably invites a celebratory story of indigenous origins and liberatory extension in the articulation of pastness. In that light, it is perhaps not coincidental that the Duncan Village memorial was officially opened in March 2008 by Mbeki, who regarded it as 'a fitting tribute to our heroes and heroines, and a testament to the triumph of justice over the abhorrent system of apartheid'.[1]

The memorial cenotaph, which took the form of a granite plinth and bronze statue, was erected in remembrance of the deaths of approximately 31 people who were killed by state security forces in a climate of antiapartheid activity in Duncan Village in August 1985. Located in Jabavu Street, at the site identified as the central location of the massacre, it images a bronze life-sized African warrior holding a spear aloft.

[1] _Daily Dispatch_, 31 March 2008.

It also bears the inscription 'their blood will nourish the tree of liberty'.[2] For the unveiling, the *Daily Dispatch*, the regional newspaper based in East London, interviewed a number of people who recalled the events of 1985 from memory, as well as recalling evidence submitted to the Truth and Reconciliation Commission (hereafter TRC). The following accounts by Rubushe and Robert Gqeme are only two of many accounts by survivors of the massacre:

We got sick and tired of the restrictions put on us that we should not gather in groups. There was also 'the security' that made our lives hell as well as the undemocratically elected councillors. It was then decided that we do not want the police in the community and the entries to the town were blocked. We would cross the bridge and go to Duncan Village to carry out our work and in the process of doing so, the whites would shoot at us. On the first day a shot narrowly missed [me], hitting an old man who was on his way to the toilet. I took cover on hearing the gunshots. I then moved on, but I thought about the old man who was in pain. I returned and carried him to the road.[3]

We were in the Roman Catholic Church where there was a meeting of the youth. These white people came in a Casper and parked outside and sent someone, a tall man who looked like a Coloured person, and was dressed like a Minister of religion. He said that we were asked to go out of this hall and to disperse by order. The house, the room was full and people were chanting freedom songs and some people did not hear what this man was saying. This white person insisted that we should go out of the hall and disperse and this took about 15 minutes and we went away as people . . . were standing outside, since the hall was packed and we were in fear that these whites were going to shoot us. We walked passed these whites. They followed us in their Casper, leaving the people behind in the hall, following the march. We proceeded and then these policemen started shooting at us, but some of us were not aware until we got next to the cemetery and I could see people running away, people falling and then as I was going up I could see a certain white man in a Casper and he called me, but I ran away and he shot me in the arm. I ran away and he again shot me on the waist and I fell facing upwards and I asked him to pick me up. I struggled trying to stand, though I was aware that I had been shot. Then I could see that I was injured and my legs were feeling very weak. Then this white person came to me, handled me by the collar, pulled me towards the Casper and there were two of these Caspers parked there and he placed me just behind one of them.[4]

This particular series of incidents did not occur in a political vacuum, however, but was largely a response to state repression, and in August 1985 defiance of the security forces in Duncan Village was in part sparked by the assassination of activist Victoria Mxenge. Mxenge's funeral had

---

[2] Which is, of course, 'plagiarising' Thomas Jefferson's address to William Smith in 1787.
[3] *Daily Dispatch*, 31 March 2008.
[4] Evidence from Robert Gqeme to the TRC hearings, East London, <http://sabctrc.saha .org.za/originals/hrvtrans/duncan/gqeme.htm>, accessed 28 August 2014.

been a politically charged affair with a mobilisation effect, characterised by militant addresses to the mourners and the United Democratic Front (UDF) supporters. The returning mourners launched arson attacks on various buildings including the rent hall, schools, and homes of council-lors and policemen suspected of collaborating with the apartheid govern-ment. Yet when 23 years after the series of violent incidents, and in the wake of TRC memorialisation, the Buffalo City Municipality (BCM) – serving the wider East London municipal area – elected to commemor-ate the massacre through a memorial cenotaph designed 'to honour the victims who lost their lives',[5] it was as if this TRC-constituted memory did not exist (see Figure 3.1).

Indeed, soon after its erection, the memorial aroused contestation, revolt, and hostility amongst some residents in Duncan Village on the basis of the visualisation of the massacre through the figure of the warrior (see Figure 3.2) – an example of what Pinney has described as struggle taking place at the level of the visual in envisioning history.[6] In Duncan Village this was expressed overtly when the spear was removed from the statue, and when stones were thrown at the memorial not long after its unveiling (see Figure 3.3).

In related media investigations, residents expressed the following opin-ions:

I think someone carrying a stone and a petrol bomb would have been an appro-priate choice. People who fought in 1985 were not semi-naked like that warrior. It really doesn't reflect what happened back then. We are not satisfied; they must design another sculpture.[7]

The sculpture looks like a Zulu warrior. I don't think they should erect a statue there; a monument with the name of the victims is fine. To have a monument it's a good idea because it will ensure that young people become aware of what their parents have gone through.[8]

To me it doesn't mean anything because this is not what happened in 1985. I was here when those clashed with police; they never used any spears and shields. They were throwing stones at police vehicles. We don't want this statue they must take it back.[9]

We are not satisfied . . . that sculpture portrays Shaka Zulu. The statue . . . must have someone carrying a rock. We used rocks and not spears when we clashed

---

[5] This is quoted in National Heritage Council (NHC), *The Duncan Village Massacre Memorialization Public Hearing Preliminary Report* (hereafter NHC Report), which was released in Buffulo [sic] City on 24 June 2008, 1–38.

[6] See Christopher Pinney, *Photos of the Gods: the Printed Image and Political Struggle in India* (New Delhi: Oxford University Press, 2005).

[7] *Daily Dispatch*, 11 April 2008.

[8] Ibid.

[9] *Daily Dispatch*, 24 June 2008.

Figure 3.1. The Duncan Village Massacre Memorial statue.

with the police. The organising committee never consulted the people, they overlooked us. The sculpture must be removed.[10]

Clearly, there are many directions this discussion could take. It could be read following Herwitz's persuasive argument in this volume, where

[10] Ibid.

Figure 3.2. A close-up of the 'warrior' astride the memorial, a figure of considerable controversy and dispute.

Figure 3.3. Some of the stones thrown at the memorial, signifiers of its contested nature.

the attempt to celebrate and extend state power – to legitimate the new state – was locally seen as a turn to propaganda, a development that further invokes his sense of this event as representing a counter-activist, community-driven model of heritage knowledge production. Equally, it could be read as staging a contestation between what Gavua (this volume) identifies as differing forms of monuments (and particularly forms adopted by ruling political regimes as opposed to those supported by active community organisations), transmitting different kinds of messages of belonging and conservation to different publics. However, we wish to propose a somewhat different reading or, perhaps more accurately, an extended reading of these contests over the monument.

At the centre of the discontent is the memorial as image, and the particular image economies seen as representative of an indigenous amaXhosa past and of 'the struggle' (and thus of 1985). The path that then unfolds is one that partially follows the trajectory outlined by Rassool (in this volume). That is to say, the statue becomes drawn into a debate in which colonial categories of race and ethnicity are invoked, notably around the definition and status of the 'indigenous'. Following the logic that sprang from Mbeki's distinct vision of the African Renaissance, this allows for a turn towards a celebration of Africa's 'mythic' pre-colonial past. In part, this becomes the battleground for contesting 'legitimate' and other more local forms of representation and visuality, but also for asking how these visualities have come to be represented as formed between the official as opposed to the vernacular.

The Official and the Vernacular

Recently Sabine Marschall has argued that in the process of memorialisation in post-apartheid South Africa, memorials, as cultural expressions, manifest the 'intersection of the official or monumental and the vernacular or popular, which . . . always characterises public memory'.[11] Marschall further argues, drawing on the 'Trojan Horse' memorial in Cape Town, that there is an increasing shift away from the vernacular and towards the official, that this is 'paralleled in many other commemorative initiatives in post-apartheid South Africa', and that this shift is 'accompanied, and perhaps defined, by the increasingly significant role accorded to visual images in the design of the memorial marker'.[12] Marschall suggests that the post-1994 heritage sector has seen the rise of a distinct 'post-apartheid memorial aesthetic, in which visual

---

[11] Sabine Marschall, 'Commemorating the "Trojan Horse" Massacre in Cape Town: the Tension between Vernacular and Official Expressions of Memory', *Visual Studies* 25 (2010): 135.

[12] Ibid., 138.

imagery, usually realistically rendered, seems increasingly imperative'. In all cases, the 'new commemorative marker', she argues, 'contains a visual component, usually consisting of a bronze statue or containing bronze relief plaques' with a heroic monumentalised mode of representation and triumphal heroic imagery.[13] In many respects, then, her article provides an important, focused, and synthesised account that integrates much of Minkley, Rassool, and Witz's notion of visual 'spectacle'[14] and Kirshenbaltt-Gimblett's 'agency of display'[15] as the central 'interface' in the particular form and production of heritage in post-apartheid South Africa.

Marschall's elaboration of the processes of memorialisation and the central and changing role of the image and the visual draws together a broader argument (that many have been making) around the ways that heritage is constructed in terms of its narrowing into more dominant 'authorised'[16] versions. The further importance of her contribution lies in her argument that what she calls the vernacular (understood as the public that constitutes the everyday city, the realm of routine activity associated with everyday life) is excluded and marginalised from these more official forms. The latter, according to Marschall, centrally depend on realist and heroic image making and the visual imperatives related to what she calls (after Bodnar) 'dogmatic formalism' and its visual manifestation of the 'triumphalist tone dominating liberation history'.[17] Equally, though, her argument builds on a process in which what she calls countermemories of vernacular popular memory are, in her words, 'encouraged to come to the fore, but also increasingly turned into dominant official memory'. Thus, the 'diversity and ambiguity that is invariably associated with any vernacular cultural expression must necessarily be simplified and synchronised'. Centrally in her argument, this takes place through the ways in which images and the visual economies and display of this post-apartheid memorial aesthetic work.

In the second half of this chapter we want to read the contests around the Trojan Horse memorial in Cape Town and the Duncan Village Massacre Memorial in the light of Marschall's argument about the official and the vernacular, and the centrality of images and the visual in constituting meaning, but also to engage this frame critically as part

---

[13] Ibid., 145.
[14] Gary Minkley, Ciraj Rassool, and Leslie Witz, 'South Africa and the Spectacle of Public Pasts: Heritage, Public Histories and Post Anti-Apartheid South Africa' (unpublished paper, March 2009), 1–32.
[15] Barbara Kirshenblatt-Gimblett, *Destination Culture: Tourism, Museum, Heritage* (Berkeley, CA: University of California Press, 1998), 7.
[16] See Laurajane Smith, *Uses of Heritage* (New York, NY: Routledge, 2006).
[17] Marschall, 'Commemorating', 141.

of a wider critique of heritage practice and disciplinary meaning. The Duncan Village Massacre Memorial provides an opportunity to do this because the contests around this memorial show both the official and the vernacular in play. As opposed to Marschall's arguments, the memorial does not become simply an idealised vernacular that challenges a process that tapers its meaning and representation through an 'official' configuration. Marschall points out that the Trojan Horse memorial is

symptomatic of a wider trend of synthesising the past and appropriating it for the needs of the present. This solidifies hegemonic narratives, invalidates alternative memories, and eclipses other forms of understanding and remembering the past. The question is where this leaves the mothers of the deceased, the other victims and the surrounding community for whom the memorial was supposedly primarily built?[18]

The Duncan Village Massacre Memorial might provide some answers to this question, at least in some ways related to heritage and the notion of the alternative vernacular. Indeed, as we suggest below, invoking the 'forgotten victims' – including the mothers of the deceased and the 'surrounding community' – in contesting such narratives is potentially to re-enter the terrain of official discourse.

The Official and Vernacular in the Duncan Village Massacre Memorial

As we have seen, the Duncan Village Massacre Memorial monument was erected by the BCM and was initiated and implemented by a steering committee made up of councillors and representatives from various organisations. While it is important to note that many aspects of the project came under scrutiny and 'dispute' – the composition, budgets, and tender processes for the design of the statue, its commissioning and construction, the unveiling ceremony and catering, and other matters – we are not concerned to follow this track here. Suffice it to say that questions, allegations, and scenarios featuring the exclusion of people and organisations, leadership contempt, corruption, division, and a lack of consultation strongly marked much of the content of the National Heritage Council (NHC) hearings referred to below.[19]

The BCM steering committee selected Maureen Quin to design the statue as the result of a tender process[20] and with a very particular brief.

---

[18] Ibid., 146.
[19] NHC Report, 3–5.
[20] Maureen Quin has sculpted, amongst others, Jack Nicklaus for the Simola golf estate in Knysna, Cape Minstrels for the Grand Hotel at the Grand West Casino and Entertainment Centre, Mandela for Rhodes University, and other commissioned sculptures.

She described it in the following terms: '[T]he organising committee wanted a warrior that would symbolise the spirit of the ancestors fighting for liberty, rather than portraying people as they were when they died.'[21] More particularly, the steering committee wanted to construct a memorial that drew on scenarios of victory rather than victimhood. According to Basopu, one member of the steering committee, '[A]ll we wanted was a warrior. It doesn't really matter who he was.'[22]

While this statement is illuminating, it is not entirely accurate, for, as the NHC Public Hearing into the 'vandalisation' of the memorial noted in its *Preliminary Report*,[23] the design was chosen on the basis of its depicting not only a historical African symbol of warriorhood and bravery, but also a resonance with the military image of Umkhonto weSizwe (hereafter MK) and the shield and 'Spear of the Nation'. In other words, the memorial was constructed to reverberate with the visual economy of the anti-apartheid struggle. This would, according to the committee, 'endow the memorial with a national appeal' and ensure that it was not too local and particular.[24] Significantly, though, these 'national appeals' turned out to be neither self-evidently national nor appealing. Rather, in terms of both visual economies, focused through the image of the warrior as indigenous ancestor and as liberation figure or subject (as MK soldier), the official view not only blurred, but shifted local recollection of the massacre considerably out of focus.

The most immediate and dramatic loss concerned what we might call the reality effect image of the sculpted warrior and its apparent 'universal symbolism of bravery', which was the way the committee saw it.[25]

The report stated that the 'warrior-like figure does not resonate with the memory of the locals. It is so far removed that it does not capture their recollection of the event'. This loss of focus, though, had most to do with the widespread public reading of the memorial warrior as 'Zulu' rather than as either 'universal' or, more particularly, 'Xhosa'. The terms of this reading are illustrative. On the one hand, Quin, the designer of the

'Her keen observational powers and deep emotional response to her environment enable her to capture the essence of her subject, be it wildlife or realistic studies which in turn form the core of her distinctive expressionistic style, manifesting the rich fusion of her European-African background' is how she is self-described on her website, <http://www .quin-art.co.za/>, accessed 28 August 2014.

21 *Daily Dispatch*, 11 April 2008.
22 Ibid.
23 Following the 'disputes', as they were called, around the Duncan Village Massacre Memorial unveiling, the National Heritage Council appointed a panel to investigate and to report on these matters. We attended the hearings on 20 June 2008, held at the Gompo Welfare Centre, Duncan Village (attended by approximately 300 people), from which notes and observations were drawn; we also draw on the NHC Report.
24 NHC Report, 13.
25 NHC Report, 19.

sculpture, argued – in line with her own self-representational status, concerned with 'capturing the essence' of the subject and with 'realistic studies' – that the warrior was 'Xhosa' and historically accurate, rather than 'universal'. She asserted that she consulted extensively with an authority on amaXhosa history at the Albany Museum in Grahamstown, read the nineteenth-century history of chiefs, studied Xhosa warrior drawings recorded by historians and artists, and that:

Every detail of dress, beads, spears and shields are portrayed accurately in the sculpture as Xhosa and not Zulu. . . . Zulu warriors tie ox tails or something on their spears while the Xhosa ones had thongs at the back of their spears. . . . Xhosa warriors wore beads on their ankles, neck, arms and around their waist, wore bangles on their arm made from elephant tusk, always carried a knobkerrie and wore one oxtail on one leg, while Zulus wore many tails on both legs.[26]

Similarly, in response to the identification of the sculpture as Zulu, a reader wrote a letter to the *Daily Dispatch* that further participated in the battle for origins:

I have discovered that many of our people here in the Eastern Cape associate 'amabeshu', which are aprons made from animal skins and cowhide shields, with the amaZulu warriors only, but they were also part of the amaXhosa warriors' attire. The amaXhosa, like the amaZulu, belong to the Nguni people who moved from the Congo basin area southward to the Eastern Cape. The traditional dress for amaXhosa or Nguni men consisted of animal skins and feathers. Different kinds of skins and feathers indicated the status of a person. The apron worn by them was made from soft calf, goat or any wild animal skin. The traditional weapons of amaXhosa warriors consisted of spears, clubs/knobkerries and shields. A warrior would sometimes carry three to five spears to battle. Traditional amaXhosa shields were cut out of coarse, partly tanned cowhide, and were big enough to cover three-quarters of the body.[27]

On the other hand, the identification of the memorial as Zulu or Shakan perhaps expresses the extent to which a particular ethnographic image of an African male has proliferated and been appropriated as Zuluness. Certainly popular media such as *Shaka Zulu* (1986), a mini-series with an intensely fierce-looking and physically powerful Henry Cele playing the lead role, reconfigured a very particular Africanised image as 'Zulu'. This was an image of a fearless warrior, ready for battle, an image and demeanour that would later be appropriated by the Inkatha Freedom Party, but also implicated, and involved in varying, complex, and extended productions of 'Zuluness' and pastness.[28] It is not necessary to track

---

[26] *Daily Dispatch*, 11 April 2008.
[27] Ibid., 29 April 2008.
[28] For aspects of these debates see Benedict Carton, John Laband, and Jabulani Sithole, *Zulu Identities: Being Zulu, Past And Present* (Scottsville: University of Kwa-Zulu Natal Press, 2008); Carolyn Hamilton, *The Power of Shaka Zulu and the Limits of Invention*

these associations and productions here, since we are proposing a rather more mundane point: that the indigenous warrior image is almost inevitably read/seen as Zulu, and that this image is simultaneously national and particular, exclusive and 'tribal', and not simply universal or 'African' national.

Thus, while the NHC Report and the steering committee read this as simultaneously both 'universal' (a warrior figure symbolising bravery) and as an image of the 'anti-colonial' (which made his depiction as a specifically Xhosa warrior almost incidental, as reflected in Basopu's comment that all they wanted was a warrior, never mind 'who he was'). For them, then, 'the current warrior like figure is a widely known national symbol'[29] of universal African bravery and resistance to colonial rule. However, as already stated, local residents read the image primarily as representing 'Zuluness' and as having 'nothing to do with us'. Their reading marks one emerging limit in the visual translation of 'resistance' into rule, and 'indigenous' into national citizen-subject sovereignty and 'liberty', and thus also a visual limit to the possibilities of heritage. We will return to this below.

But what of the shield and spear? Although residents in the hearing (and as reported in the media) did not readily recognise the insignia of MK in the memorial, for the steering committee this resonance is a clear indication of the memorial as a distinctly anti-apartheid and national image. The committee continually argued, as stated in the NHC Hearings and reported in the NHC Report, that the 'statue is an appropriate symbolism (sic) of the massacre' and that it

symbolises the bravery and warrior-like character of the activists of 1985 . . . and they go on to argue . . . that the current image is not only a historical African symbolism of warriors and bravery, but also resonates with the modern imagery of military resistance waged by the African National Congress's (ANC) military wing, UmKhonto we Sizwe (MK). This refers to the shield and spear that make up the insignia of MK. This similarity, they assert, makes the statue resonates [sic] with the popular and modern imagery of anti-apartheid resistance, and thus is appropriate in its current form. . . . [and] that the variety of names inscribed on the monument also underpin the multi-racial nature of the anti-apartheid struggle.[30]

As the NHC Report further notes, there is consensus 'that the statue was inspired by the MK insignia'. If this was not clear enough, the narrative inscribed on the statue instrumentalises the version that the ANC and

(Massachusetts: Harvard University Press, 1998); Dan Wylie, *Myth of Iron: Shaka in History* (Pietermaritzburg: University Kwa-Zulu Natal Press).

[29] NHC Report, 13.

[30] NHC Hearings, 20 June 2008; NHC Report, 12.

MK led the struggle: 'In the 1980s the people of Duncan Village took up the call of the President of the ANC, Oliver Tambo, that the masses of South Africa had a duty to make the structure and systems of the apartheid government ungovernable.'[31]

Clearly, then, in terms of Marschall's characterisation of current monumentalisation in South Africa, the statue and its visual imagery is meant to be read tightly and narrowly into what she calls these hegemonic official forms: into nation as 'dogmatic formalism' and its visual manifestation of the 'triumphalist tone' claiming local struggles as MK and ANC 'liberation history'. Ultimately, the memorial drew on a romantic narrative notable in current heritage practice in the Eastern Cape, in which anti-colonial history coupled to liberation politics is construed as seamlessly triumphant.[32] Indeed, this is Witz and Murray's insightful summation of the tales of development and museum historiography wherein, typically and problematically, both are committed to a story of triumph over odds (against which Witz and Murray propose a more tragic narrative form). If this romantic memorial visual tale is what is contained in the Duncan Village Massacre memorial, it is little wonder that, in Basopu's words, as long as it images a warrior, 'it doesn't matter who he was'.

This did not reflect Quin's thinking, or her representational strategy and image making – which she saw as being 'authentic Xhosa' – and neither did it resonate with local residents. Here is the NHC Report once more:

But, residents disagreed on this particular image of the monument. Objections against the statue were especially strong among relatives of the deceased victims and survivors of the massacre. . . . One resident noted that the warrior figure contrasts with the contemporary persona of the individuals involved in that political protest, their means of resistance and the modern context within which the struggle was waged. The resident explained that the protesters used modern weaponry, threw stones, and did not look anything like the current statue. Unlike the current statue, protesters were 'not naked, were not carrying spear [sic] and were not even armed' . . . but it does not represent the modern image of ordinary residents who resisted apartheid. . . . Another resident, however, objected to what he thought was politicisation of the symbolism in favour of one political party. He stressed that residents did not participate in the uprising under a political banner nor were the events initiated by any particular organisation. Rather it was a spontaneous community resistance against attempts to relocated [sic] residents to Mdantsane. Ascribing the eruption of the resistance to one particular party, not only distorts the historical record, but also runs the risk of alienating other

---

[31] NHC Report, 13.
[32] Gary Minkley, '"A Fragile Inheritor": the Post-Apartheid Memorial Complex, A. C. Jordan and the Re-Imagining of Cultural Heritage in the Eastern Cape', *Kronos: Southern African Histories* 34 (2008): 16–40.

residents from the monument.... At another level, however, the disagreement over the precise symbolism for the massacre reflects conflicting recollection of the events of that day.... [M]any support the figure of a 'mother carrying a dead baby'.[33]

In Marschall's terms, then, here we have the vernacular reading of the image of the statue, offering an alternative visual economy. In the emphasis on the local, the modern – and the 'spontaneous', localised, internal nature of resistance – the vernacular is read against the official insertion – both instrumental and directive – of traditional, 'anti-colonial' African and MK/ANC national liberation narratives. In particular, there is the counter-visualisation, the emergent counter-image structured according to the need to constitute oneself as a 'modern' subject, and not as either a mythologised pre-colonial warrior or an idealised MK/ANC liberation fighter as the necessary genealogical constituents of sovereignty. Rather, residents assert both a separation from that colonial past – that 'we don't look anything like the current statue' and from imposed politics, which is a 'distortion of the historical record'.[34]

These 'vernacular' articulations were also active in reimagining and reconstituting the statue. Initially, the spear was removed from the statue, prompting the city's municipality to place a fence around it (see Figure 3.4) – thus echoing one of the gestures that Gavua outlines (this volume) of 'gating' castles in Ghana, and ordering in the process certain forms of entry to what is eventually consumed as history.

The fence, however, became a kind of 'notice board' for a series of placards that were placed on it, surrounding the memorial. Statements like 'Remember 1985 we will do it again', 'The blood of the comrades you used will speak', and 'Still victim since 1985'[35] – amongst others – became an unofficial counter-memory and counter-visualisation of the memorial itself.

Additionally, residents littered the space with stones, a powerful reminder of the form of the struggle and of the symbolism of the 'thrown stone' of resistance rather than the now-removed spear in visually and symbolically defining the memorial.

But, what then is the form and content of these apparent 'vernacular' counter-memories and counter-visualisations? Rather than simply reading them as more real, or more accurate, or as more able to articulate a meaningful heritage, perhaps we need to exercise equal critical care

[33] NHC Report, 12–13. We have quoted this at some length in order to get a sense of the NHC Report and the ways that it highlights many issues we wish to address.
[34] NHC Hearings, 20 June 2008.
[35] See *Daily Dispatch*, 28 May 2008, as well as personal photographs and visits to the memorial on the same date, in the period preceding the NHC Hearings.

Figure 3.4. The fencing erected around the memorial.

in interpreting their emergent narrative and its associated notions of the ordinary and the everyday. For, as Witz and Murray argue (this volume), what they call 'making dislocation' entails reading against the easy slide to claiming the local and the community as the oppositional, the authentic, or the vernacular real.

The official memorial, in addition to how it has been elaborated already, also connects the visual image of MK, construed in 'traditional' imagery as equally relying on familiar visual tropes that have been used to represent African men. What is suggested in both the statue and in the intentions of the steering committee and the heritage practitioners, is the sense that if ordinary black people draw on notions of pre-colonial, pre-modern 'power', imagined as militant power, then (again echoing Mbeki's sentiments) they can transcend, albeit only psychologically, the disempowerment that came with the modern warfare technologies of conquest that continues and resulted in the deaths of August 1985. In the memorial, the sense of victory implied in the memorial is thus represented as a hyper-masculine male in the motion of acting upon his environment.

On the other hand, the image of a mother carrying a child is a striking contrast to the current memorial. This might be seen as a feminised statue depicting loss and victimhood. It might also be seen as a localised image unlikely to be subsumed into nationalist and state discourse –

becoming instead an alternative depiction that draws into visibility the less celebratory histories of injury and fatality. It is a visualisation of memory that deploys a familial rather than a national trope. That said, it also constitutes both pasts and presents in a different way, related on the one hand to victimhood, and on the other to what we want to call the 'visual economy of [social] development need'. For, while the NHC Report has a significant amount to say about the 'appalling conditions' in Duncan Village, and varying definitions and discussions of victimhood, it also presents steering committee opinions that attribute the cause of the dispute not to concerns with the forms and meanings of memorialisation, but to underlying grievances that were '*indlala inama nyala*' – 'motivated by hunger'.[36]

While this was clearly politically expedient, it was also vigorously challenged by residents at the NHC Hearings, and this steering committee suggestion was dismissed in the NHC Report as 'shockingly contemptuous'. The broader frame in which the 'vernacular' is constituted, though, was not so readily dismissible. Partly this related to what the NHC Report called 'a renewal of grievance over unresolved issues'; but these 'vernacular' views were also tied into and articulated as the need to visualise, and to connect remembrance to development, 'social improvement', and 'better living standards'.[37] In other words, this apparently vernacular, 'community' view was framed by contemporary social divisions and by the discourses of locally defined and demarcated images to enable poverty alleviation, tourism attraction and job creation, and related service delivery demands. Woman and child, as victim, read as what modern life now is, and as the applicable image for the Massacre memorial – since as an 'enhancement of the significance of remembering' it would both link with the past, and bring 'greater contentment' in the present, because it would be coupled to 'social improvements'.[38]

It seems relatively straightforward, then, to draw a further connection between victim, poverty, and the visual, or an image marker that depicts this. The mother and child idea, while potentially resonant with an imaging of the massacre,[39] relies on two related visual economies that tie victimhood, gender, and poverty together. The first relates to the visual economy of the TRC, and the second to the ways that poverty is related

---

[36] Elsewhere, the NHC Report reflects on this in the following statement: 'To ascribe the dissenting views of residents to their impoverished state, stating that they wanted the funds for themselves instead of using them towards the statue is shockingly contemptuous', 20.

[37] NHC Report, 16–17.

[38] Ibid., 17.

[39] As has been outlined above – while it is disputed whether a mother and child were killed – the overwhelming sense, according to the NHC Report, is that this did take place during the Massacre.

to assembling the sphere of the social as one of social deprivation, need, and improvement for the family.

How does the constitution of 'the victim', or that of 'still victims', remain public, and what might it mean for thinking through the mobilisation of this image as the apparent vernacular counter to the official versions? Fiona Ross is one of a number of writers who have identified how the TRC construed apartheid as a particular violence whose effect was to produce victims. Ross also argued that women's voices were marginalised and taken as 'naturally gendered', in the sense that they were seen as 'secondary witnesses', speaking more often of men's suffering and victimisation than their own.[40] While this is significant, it seems possible to think about a parallel process of visualisation and image making that accompanied this, where the iconic image of the TRC became the 'mourning widow' – the almost personal identification portrait – and the imaging of the 'one left behind', as the 'real' victim of gross human rights violation and loss after apartheid. It is almost inevitably a woman – a mother, wife, heterosexual lover, sister, daughter, child – which allows victimhood visuality, and it is within the personal and the private (and the family) that this image resides.

The TRC (centrally and initially) and thereafter development and service delivery have had major roles as vectors of this image of woman and child (while the role of heritage has been tied into both these dynamics). They have translated this image – through spectacle, or display, or the vernacular – into local collective publics as individual women are individually and cumulatively, and then collectively 'seen'. Normal, ordinary, 'innocent' was how they were depicted and thus how they became victims, and suffered trauma, and it is now this ordinary and everyday woman and child who is the contemporary visual marker of not just the 'injustices of the past', but the image for removing that past and for social well-being. Victimhood and trauma are overcome through the mobilisation of a politics of sentiment as well as of 'liberation' – through the romance of good over evil, from victim to victor, and through social improvement. It is also relocated into the space of the family and revisualised into what we might call 'public sentiment', where these intimate family relations mediate past and present around being victims of state and apartheid violence, and personal and apparently collective 'trauma' and loss; but where this will happen no more.

Thus, one of the key post-apartheid constitutions of the anti-apartheid political subject occurs visually through the TRC, picturing mother and child, and enabling the articulation of these categories to those of social

---

[40] Fiona Rosss, *Women and the TRC*. London: Pluto Press, 2003.

development and 'greater contentment'. In this way, a particular encouragement of a visual bio-politics of the liberated citizen is represented, sustaining the propriety of reconciliation and the acknowledgement of people's victimhood and trauma as memory. Through their portrait of survival and of 'speaking' and 'documenting' and visualising these pasts (as in the case discussed here), however, this is separated out from the present (ironically, given the nature of memory) and is relocated in the victory of community, home, and a secure 'intimacy' of the family, represented through women as ideally and typically 'mother and home maker'. And so these ostensibly 'vernacular' forms, invoked as the counter to the official in relation to the Duncan Village Massacre memorial, are themselves equally located in the constrained governmental politics of post-apartheid heritage.

A Different Direction?

Chris Healy has argued for a broad consideration of heritage as 'a constitutive and organising rhetoric across the field of cultural institutions and practices... [as] the mobilisation of historical understandings of social memory in *institutional* and *citizenly* forms'.[41] He persuasively proposes that this draws attention to the work of heritage in 'not only not just any conjuring of "the past" or evocation of history which falls within the territory of heritage, but specifically the deployment of history in imagining and defining citizenship and governance'. Similarly, as Derek Peterson points out in the introduction to this volume, heritage in Africa needs to be seen not just as a form of museum studies, but as a critical mode of political organisation and governance.

With this significant reminder in place, we propose that it is necessary to rethink the ways that heritage can be thought of as dichotomous – even within the proposed emerging critical discipline, and also when imagining heritage disputes as between the official and the vernacular. In the arena of display around the Duncan Village Massacre Memorial, as this example has sought to demonstrate – and it is worth remarking here that the NHC Report identified 'visual depictions and representations' as central[42] – casting these visible 'disputes' as caught between the official and the vernacular misses the extent to which both are institutional and citizenly visual forms developing visual governmentalities. That is why, following Modisane (Chapter 13) and Witz and Murray (Chapter 4), we

---

[41] Chris Healy, '"Race Portraits" and Vernacular Possibilities: Heritage and Culture', in Tony Bennett and David Carter (eds), *Culture in Australia: Policies, Publics and Programs* (Cambridge: Cambridge University Press, 2001), 278–98.
[42] NHC Report, 8.

equally urge a related broader reading that considers heritage memorialisation in relation to what Modisane calls 'that discontinuous, nonlinear and composite constitution of social and political life called modernity'.

Following Minkley, Rassool, and Witz, however, we want to further invoke the notion of a 'post anti-apartheid heritage complex' in order to propose the co-presence of what we have called the citizenly politics of sentiment (here reimagining what Marschall has called the vernacular) and the politics of liberation (what she calls now the official, hegemonic narrative) as *both*[43] centrally visual deployments in the arena of display where citizenship and governance, and the post-apartheid modern, are mutually composed, imagined, and defined.

Therefore, we are not only arguing that the 'expansion of heritage in southern Africa over the last decade – as mode of cultural production, popular interest, state discourse and international industry' has created an important space and a 'wealth' for academic 'constructive critical engagement'.[44] This may well be so, but we are attempting to say something more. In arguing that a post anti-apartheid heritage complex has become the disciplinary form and institutional apparatus through which *governing* knowledges about pasts are articulated, we argue that this has major implications for how we think and engage heritage, but also history in contemporary South Africa, and more widely. Not only indigeneity and liberation, and their drawing together as the 'official' new imagined nation, but also 'community', home, and belongingness – seemingly as vernacular counters to the official, and invoked from the site of experience and the everyday, and as dispute – are ultimately also articulated in these governing ways. We might want to consider, then, how mobilisations of victims, of trauma, and of memory, and of social well-being or social improvements (articulated to the discourses of development) equally become very narrow and largely governmental ways for negotiating present–past relationships in public. For their limits too, are those of the nation, citizenship, and governance: more responsible, more listening, but ultimately still also constituted on the limited sovereignty of the post anti-apartheid complex.

Constituted in the colonial nexus of 'citizen and subject' and already marked in regional public histories of poverty and dispossession, and of a romantic anti-colonial African nationalism, the 'dispute' over the memorial became rather a matter of 'public hearings' and occasions to remark on 'more consultation' and 'inclusion' and the need for the

---

[43] That is, both of imagined 'mother and child', as much as of liberation MK and the ANC.

[44] See JoAnn McGregor and Lynn Schumaker, 'Heritage in Southern Africa: Imagining and Marketing Public Culture and History,' *Journal of Southern African Studies* 32, (2006): 649–65.

state to deliver on social development through heritage. The other every-day routines of violence and marginality in colonial and apartheid and in post-apartheid governmentality, and the continuities in the political economy of racial capitalism, remain silenced and elided; 'hidden from history', but also from heritage. Rather, new heritage, located in the post anti-apartheid heritage complex of power/knowledge, speaks in this 'one indigenous voice of freedom' for South African pasts, while ration-alising current forms of political governance and citizenship as African and liberated. Needs and social development – building the nation – do not lie beyond this wider nationalism, but rather mark the limits of its inclusivity.[45]

As Tony Bennett reminds us, in this mere fact of placement (and in its determination as local, provincial, or national), local and provin-cial values are separated out, and overdetermined by national ones. The national register and estate, and the 'national heritage vision' become the 'common point of reference', while disputes become 'parochial histories [that] are irretrievably reorganised in being dovetailed to other parochial histories as parts of a wider, nationalised whole'.[46] Most obviously, Bennett continues, these serve as the 'instrument[s] par excellence for both extending and deepening the past while simultaneously organising that past under the sign of the nation'.

Thus, as Patrick Wright has written, making a point that applies to our argument about the post anti-apartheid heritage complex,

This alignment makes it possible to think of historical development as complete, a process which finds its accomplishment in the present. Historical develop-ment is here concealed as a cumulative process which has delivered the nation into the present as its manifest accomplishment. Both celebratory and compla-cent [liberatory and sentimental], it produces a sense that 'we' are the achieve-ment of history and that while the past is thus present as our right it is also something that our narcissism will encourage us to visit, exhibit, write up and discuss.[47]

And, as Bennett remarks, '[t]he future trajectory for the nation which it marks out is *governed* [our emphasis] by the logic of "more of the same"; a never-ending story of development. . . which seems to emerge natur-ally out of the relations between the very land itself and its inhabitants'.[48]

---

[45] For a summary of the 'destination history' of this post anti-apartheid heritage com-plex see Raymond Suttner, 'Talking to the Ancestors: National Heritage, the Freedom Charter and Nation Building in South Africa in 2005', *Development Southern Africa* 23, 1 (2006): 3–27.

[46] Bennett, *Birth of the Museum*, 244.

[47] Patrick Wright, *Formations of Nation and People* (London: Routledge and Kegan Paul, 1984), 52.

[48] Bennett, *Birth of the Museum*, 152.

Thus, we may conclude, appropriating Chakrabarty, that this is a visual-ised heritage complex that makes invisible 'the very structure of its visual forms, its own repressive strategies and practices, [and] the part it plays in collusion with the narratives of citizenship in assimilating to projects of the modern state all other possibilities of human solidarity'.[49]

---

[49] Dipesh Chakrabarty, 'Postcoloniality and the Artifice of History: Who Speaks for 'Indian' Pasts?' *Representations* 32 (1992): 1–26.

4   Fences, Signs, and Property
Heritage, Development, and the Making of Location in Lwandle

Leslie Witz and Noëleen Murray

'Then and Now'

In 2009 the weekend version of the Cape Town newspaper *The Argus* ran a feature entitled 'Then and Now'. Readers were invited to send in photographs of 'old Cape Town, with, if possible the date and any background information' they might have. These were then published alongside a contemporary photograph of the site taken from almost the same vantage point, inviting those who saw the images in the newspaper to make what appeared as legitimate comparisons. It was almost as if claims to history could be made through the attempt to standardise the image of the site over time. On 5 December 2009 the newspaper published a photograph from Dr Piet Claassen coupled with a more recent image (see Figure 4.1). The caption indicated that these were 'two pictures of the Strand beach area looking towards Gordon's Bay'. Claassen's photograph, it said, 'was taken around 1978' and it showed 'the signage that proclaimed the beach for "whites only"'. Almost apologetically it noted that the more recent photograph, alongside, had been 'taken at a different spot because the original position is now home to the municipal pool'. Nonetheless what the new photograph showed was 'an open beach and a much more built up beachfront'.[1] The juxtaposition, where the old appeared as desolate and deserted and the new as bright and populated with a few beachgoers, together with the accompanying caption, confirmed a visual account for the reader that ran from the days of closure and apartheid to openness and development in a post-apartheid present at the seaside.

   That beach sign now appears as a museum piece. Donated by a local beachfront shop owner, Theo Bernhardt, it is on display, a few kilometres away from Strand, in the Lwandle Migrant Labour Museum.[2]

---

[1] 'Then and Now', *Weekend Argus*, 5 December 2009, 12.
[2] Bongani Mgijima, email messages to authors, 3 and 4 September 2012.

THEN & NOW

CHANGING TIMES: Dr Piet Claassen sent in these two pictures taken of the Strand beach area, looking towards Gordon's Bay. The first was taken around 1978 and shows the signage that proclaimed the beach to be for 'whites only'. The recent photo has been taken at a different spot because the original position is now home to the municipal swimming pool. The new photo shows an open beach and a much more built-up beachfront. Send in pictures of old Cape Town with, if possible, the date and any background information you have, to PO Box 56, Cape Town, 8000 or to 122 St George's Mall, Cape Town, 8001 or to argpix@inl.co.za. Please mark them clearly for the Weekend Argus Picture Editor – Then and Now. If you want your picture back, include your address.

Figure 4.1. 'Then and Now', Photographic Weekly Review, *Weekend Argus*, 5 December 2009, 12.

Opened officially on 1 May 2000, the museum is sited in what had been from the late 1950s a 'location' of dormitory accommodation for male migrant workers from areas 600 to 1,000 kilometres to the east. They were recruited as labourers for the municipal services of the seaside resort of Strand and for the fruit and canning industry that was burgeoning in the town of Somerset West at the base of the nearby Helderberg mountain range. When the hostels were converted into family homes in the late 1990s a museum was established 'to commemorate migrancy and hostel life'.[3] The large orange beach sign with its bold black lettering was placed above the stage when the museum was opened and, for many years thereafter, was suspended with chains from a beam below the ceiling near to the entrance. The 'WHITES ONLY' notice that confronted visitors as they entered the Lwandle Migrant Labour Museum subverted the original intention of exclusion, turning it into a memorial to apartheid's pasts and laying claim, through its re-siting, to an anticipated inclusive future. In this 'beach crossing',[4] the very marker that was used to confine and limit possibilities to racially distinct zones had not just been cast away on the rubbish dump of history. Instead, in a move that attempts to avoid both the stasis and fundamentalism of the prescribed word and the reification that emerges from forgetting,[5] it remains on display, reinscribed in a museum that seeks to provide a continual reminder of the very foundation of apartheid, the migrant labour system (see Figure 4.2).

In this chapter we use signs, such as the one that has come to be an identifying emblem of the Lwandle Migrant Labour Museum, not as semiotic markers but to direct our thinking about spaces, heritage, and forms of development. By coupling patently different forms of heritage and development we are able to think about associations, dissociations, and the mobilities of meanings in the remaking of the apartheid city. Sometimes these signs point to newly constructed gated communities that appear as enclaves of segregation that represent themselves as fortresses of a European past. Across the road they guide us into another very different form of development, a 'native location' called Lwandle seeking to open itself up to reconstruction and become a museum of apartheid heritage. The Lwandle Migrant Labour Museum, which emerged at and as one of the first sites of post-apartheid urban experimentation, turned a development project into a museum experience. A scheme of converting single-male barracks into family accommodation, under the rubric

---

[3] This is from a notice, 'The Mission Statement of the Migrant Labour Museum' that was affixed to a board in the museum in 1998. A photograph was taken of the notice by Leslie Witz when he first visited the museum in 1999.

[4] Greg Dening, *Beach Crossings* (Philadelphia, PA: University of Pennsylvania Press, 2004), 18–19.

[5] Dening, *Beach Crossings*, 19.

Figure 4.2. Apartheid Beach Sign, Lwandle Migrant Labour Museum, 26 February 2014. Photo: Noëleen Murray.

Hostels to Homes, was intended to transform the compound landscape into a reprogrammed, reconstructed, and developed future for all.[6] This process anticipated an idealised, hopeful trajectory of community participation and the remaking of urban development in South Africa as sustainable and dignified. Turning the compound into the past, and making homes as the future, enabled the museum to position itself as 'the first township-based museum in the Western Cape' and 'the first museum to commemorate migrancy in South Africa'.[7]

In the story of passage of the 'WHITES ONLY' sign from the beach to the museum, there is an almost seamless nostalgic reversal, where the bad old times are replaced by the present as progressive and the struggles over remaking the space of the past are completely effaced. Instead of simply reading the signs as texts in their own right, we want to trace the movement, positioning, purpose, and transience of signs in and around Lwandle to consider how, instead of being removed, Lwandle was reimagined as a post-apartheid township. We are interested in how these signs appear (and disappear) and in this way disrupt the confident, linear discourses of development and post-apartheid progress. This, we suggest, offers a way into a reading of a more fragmented history of development and heritage in which the signs are notices, fragments in themselves, in a story of rupture rather than repair.

In re-telling that story we draw extensively upon newspaper accounts, documents collected and produced by the Lwandle Migrant Labour Museum, and, most notably, our memories as lecturers to students who were part of the museum's projects, as board members, and as practitioners who participated in the making of the museum. At times we allude to the reflections that we have made in various presentations at conferences, seminars, and in other publications about our involvement in these 'knowledge transactions'.[8] As we said when referring to our 'museum memoirs' at a presentation to the South African History and Humanities Seminar at the University of the Western Cape,

One the one hand our invitation to participate in the Lwandle Museum was because of our disciplinary backgrounds in history and architecture, bringing

---

[6] This is a reference to the Reconstruction and Development Programme (RDP), which was the economic programme developed by the African National Congress (ANC) for a post-apartheid South Africa and used extensively in its 1994 election campaign. According to the ANC the programme recognised 'the need to break down apartheid geography through land reform, more compact cities, decent public transport, and the development of industries and services that use local resources and/or meet local needs'. African National Congress, *The Reconstruction and Development Programme* (Johannesburg: Umanyano Publications, 1994), 83.

[7] Lwandle Migrant Labour Museum (brochure), *Lwandle Migrant Labour Museum and Arts and Crafts Centre* (Somerset West: Lwandle Museum, circa 2000).

[8] Leslie Witz and Ciraj Rassool, 'Making Histories', *Kronos: Southern African Histories*, 34 (2008): 12.

research and design skills to the project. On the other hand, we would like to believe that our cautious approach to the applications of these skills widened and complicated the possibilities for thinking the museum beyond outreach. While, of course, the context of philanthropy and the issue of creating relations of dependency was always present, our hesitations and questionings, and even discomfort... unsettled our involvement as board members, researchers, writers, and exhibition designers.[9]

This is what Murray calls the 'messy in-between space' where one has to negotiate 'difficult histories' where different and competing narratives, claims, and priorities constantly come up against each other.[10] The first memoir we present tells of a museum, some beginnings, and a sign along the motorway.[11]

Heritage Park and a Museum 1999

Leslie Witz had first heard of the possibility of a museum in Lwandle in 1998 when the University of the Western Cape, together with the Robben Island Museum and the University of Cape Town, began offering a Postgraduate Diploma in Museum and Heritage Studies that would extend vocational possibilities in the heritage sector. Importantly the curriculum was structured so that it would not merely involve 'technical process of simply training people for job categories' but would 'emphasise an understanding of the conceptual challenges of transformation'. For students to develop such an understanding, the coordinators of the programme, Ciraj Rassool and Leslie Witz, maintained it was necessary to analyse 'the discursive processes at work in the construction of heritage'.[12]

In the first year of the programme one of the students approached Witz during a break in class, told of where he lived, and spoke of plans to develop a museum of migrant labour around the last remaining hostel. Reflecting on this encounter fourteen years later Witz admitted to being

---

[9] Noëleen Murray and Leslie Witz, 'Dislocation: Making the Lwandle Migrant Labour Museum' (paper presented at the South African Contemporary History and Humanities Seminar, University of the Western Cape, 10 May 2011), 12.

[10] Noëleen Murray, 'Working with Inconsistencies and Discontinuities: Competing Conceptions of Heritage and Urban Design at the Lwandle Migrant Labour Museum', *Architecture South Africa* (March/April 2007), 32.

[11] A first version of this reflection was written for an oral presentation of our paper 'Writing Museum Biography: Displacing Development and Community in Lwandle', presented at The Politics of Heritage conference, University of Michigan/University of the Witwatersrand, Johannesburg, 8–9 July 2011.

[12] Ciraj Rassool and Leslie Witz, 'Transforming Heritage Education in South Africa: a Partnership between the Academy and the Museum' (paper presented at SAMP 2001: Strengthening the Network: a Meeting of African Museums of the Swedish African Museum Programme, 22–27 August 1999), 2, 6.

highly sceptical at the time.[13] Within the boundaries of historical narratives of the Western Cape that he had read and studied over the years, Lwandle did not feature at all. All the histories that were being produced around the social histories and resistance in the settlements designated for people who were racially classified under apartheid as 'native', then later as 'Bantu', were in the more immediate vicinity of Cape Town: Langa, Gugulethu, Nyanga, Crossroads, and Khayelitsha. There were two in-depth ethnographic studies of Lwandle that focused on aspects of daily life placed within a broader narrative of apartheid repression. Sean Jones, who had completed an MA in anthropology at the University of Cape Town, published his thesis on social and family structures of children in Lwandle, showing how the migrant labour system and hostel life had consistently undermined childhood learning and the possibilities of a stable family environment. Similarly, in *Chickens in a Box*, Julia Sloth Nielsen and her co-researchers found that it was the constant fear of being regarded as illegal under apartheid legislation that residents of Lwandle saw as the greatest threat to their security.[14] At the time Witz had not read these studies. In fact he had never even heard of Lwandle before the student mentioned it in class. Nonetheless the student, Bongani Mgijima, seemed bright and enthusiastic – and when he came back to class with a set of somewhat uninspiring and unremarkable photographs of the area, Witz promised to go there to see what was happening and how the envisaged museum was progressing. In 2012 Witz wrote that his 'expectations were not high'.[15]

It was not until almost a year later, in 1999, that he kept his promise to Mgijima, and set off along Settlers Way out of central Cape Town, past the Rondebosch and Mowbray golf courses that create a green belt separating Cape Town from the area designated as the Cape Flats, beyond the townships of Langa and Khayelitsha, Cape Town International Airport, and the wine estates of Stellenbosch, towards Somerset West and Strand. Mgijima had indicated it would be easy to find Lwandle and the museum, as it was just beyond Somerset West off the N2 motorway. Soon after leaving Somerset West, though, Witz saw the large billboard on the left-hand side of the road indicating that he had arrived at a place called Heritage Park. In June 1998 Mgijima had written an article with the title 'Let's talk heritage matters' for the local newspaper, *The District Mail*,

[13] Leslie Witz, 'Observing and Disobeying the Signs: the Lwandle Migrant Labour Museum, a Heritage Park in Cape Town' (paper presented at Norms in the Margins and Margins of the Norm conference, 25–27 October 2012, Royal Museum for Central Africa, Tervuren), 5.

[14] Sean Jones, *Assaulting Childhood* (Johannesburg: Wits University Press, 1993); Julia Sloth-Nielsen, Desiree Hanson, and Colleen Richardson, *Chickens in a Box: a Progressive Participatory Study of Lwandle Hostel Residents' Perceptions of Personal Safety* (Pretoria: HSRC, 1992).

[15] Witz, 'Observing and Disobeying', 6.

and he had given Witz a copy. In the article Migijima pointed to the potential of the buildings of Lwandle as a 'heritage tourism site' that would symbolise 'the struggle of the people'. This aspect combined with the 'hundreds' of 'praise-singers, traditional healers, handcrafts, artists, songs, traditional dancers, art performers and other cultural activists', he maintained, made Lwandle a potential 'showcase . . . of living heritage'.[16] The sign for what was being called 'Heritage Park' seemed not to contain any of the aspects that embraced Mgijima's claims to heritage for Lwandle that were under construction on the opposite side of the N2 motorway.

The heraldic emblem for 'Heritage Park' on the billboard facing the N2 displayed a drawing of a bunch of red grapes and an acorn, signalling a romantic association with a past of leafy European settlement in the Cape winelands. Below the shield inscribed in a scroll of honour were the words: 'Live, work and play in safety'. This was the motto and insignia of a gated community that was being imagined by a private developer. What was being claimed was a notion of the development's future heritage through backward linkages to supposedly gentrified idyllic rural roots and the walled European medieval town bequeathing its security complex through the electrified fences, the 24-hour armed patrols and the marshalled entry/exit booms. Its heritage, as claimed on its website, was a 'medieval past' transposed into the future as a 'whole town fortification to create a crime-free state'.[17]

In the article that Mgijima had written about the planned museum he had described how Lwandle had been sited 'away from the town centre'. Its boundaries were 'the railway line and few strips of farmland, the N2 and Broadlands roads'. A 'corrugated wall' [vibrocrete] separated it from Strand, and the area designated for people classified as coloured, Rusthof, served as 'a buffer zone' between Lwandle and Gordon's Bay, a smaller seaside resort on the False Bay coast.[18] Barely 300 metres after the 'Heritage Park' sign Witz noticed a large open area of land on the right hand side of the motorway. A road sign indicated the correct turn off to Lwandle, which Mgijima had described as the location of the museum project. He turned in, went past a house painted white where a flag with an octagonal decal indicated a police presence, and on to a street named Vulindlela (translated as 'pioneer') where long rows of buildings were all adorned with solar heating panels on their roofs. Opposite what seemed to be a taxi rank there was a small café, and across a stretch of bare dusty

---

[16] Bongani Mgijima, 'Let's talk heritage matters,' *District Mail*, 12 June 1998, 22. The *District Mail* is a small local newspaper largely aimed at a suburban readership in the towns of Strand, Somerset West, and Gordon's Bay.

[17] Rory Carroll, 'Brutal divide: fortified town plays on middle class fear of crime', *The Guardian*, 11 February 2006, <http://www.theguardian.com/world/2006/feb/11/southafrica.rorycarroll>, accessed 15 August 2013.

[18] Mgijima, 'Let's talk'.

ground was a building that bore all the functionality of apartheid design. It was symmetrical, austere, windowless, largely made of face-brick, and had a sloping roof on either side that reached a central apex. According to Witz, 'outside the building' anxiously waiting for him to arrive was Bongani Mgijima, who then 'invited him to enter the Lwandle Migrant Labour Museum'.[19]

What Mgijima had done in the time since graduating with his Post-Graduate Diploma in Museum and Heritage Studies was to begin marking out the space of this unattractive building as a museum. Having few resources at his disposal, he had resorted to affixing notices and photographs to the walls, using A4 sheets, computer-printed and written labels, and malleable removable putty (Prestik) as an adhesive. The content of what he had labelled as an exhibition, 'Raising the curtain: images of hostel life' was largely a series of photographs of contemporary Lwandle street scenes by local photographers who had offered their services without payment. There was also an installation of a curtain behind which there were some photographs of a hostel interior. A notice indicated that the mission of the Lwandle Migrant Labour Museum was: 'To commemorate the migrant labour system and hostel life'.

Contained within this sign of intent the museum's objective was to create a site of conscience that, like similar sites world-wide, would actively use 'history to promote humanitarian and democratic values' and in the process redefine museum practice.[20] None of this entered Witz's mind, though, when driving back to Cape Town. He had thought that Mgijima was either very brave or stupid, and that it would be almost impossible for this so-called museum to survive. But he also had a great deal of admiration for him in trying to initiate this project with almost no resources and with what appeared to be very little support either in Lwandle, from other museums, or from residents of nearby Somerset West. Mgijima and Witz had joked before Witz left about Heritage Park across the motorway – and Mgijima indicated that he had actually approached the property developer, George Hazelden, for assistance, which was not forthcoming.

What was emerging on the opposite sides of the N2 in the late 1990s were two different notions of heritage and development in post-apartheid South Africa. One was the heritage that Heritage Park was seeking to produce. With growing property prices and the suburbanisation of Somerset West, private landowners were beginning to carve out distinct enclaves of privilege around gated communities as spatialised forms of secured development, conceptualising them as heritage. That community heritage harked back to a utopian past where there were supposedly no

---

[19] Witz, 'Observing and Displaying', 7.
[20] International Coalition of Sites of Conscience, <http://www.sitesofconscience.org/wpml_mf_2/about-us>, accessed 30 September 2012.

worries, where 'all followed the rules of cohabitation', in contrast to the time and the space of post-apartheid, which lay beyond the confines of the security zone.[21] In that dystopia beyond there was change, and crime appeared as rampant. Heritage Park thus offered the possibility, according to property developer George Hazelden, of 'living in a safe environment' with a 'much higher quality of life'.[22] Community and development were defined inextricably by the electrified six-foot high fence in 'an attractive palisade style', the security zones, armed guards, monitored entry and exit points, and constant camera surveillance. For Heritage Park it was its separation, its 'closely watched borders rather than its content', that defined the development of the common.[23]

On the opposite side of the N2, beyond the old buffer zone in Lwandle, Bongani Mgijima was drawing upon post-apartheid invocations of heritage that were emerging in policy formulations and discourses of tourism as a passport to development.[24] The claim to inheritance as heritage was contained in the bringing together under the rubric of 'living heritage' of culture projected as tradition and struggles against apartheid.[25] Thus in ideas for the museum as heritage the key imperatives were to imagine and locate sites of resistance struggle in Lwandle that could be presented alongside and with craft and performance. To remake Lwandle into a symbol of resistance Mgijima had started to look for evidence in the material structures of place that could that could 'count' as 'historic'. He identified the temporary police station that used the old farmhouse as a 'local Alcatraz'. Locally known as Withuis [White House], this was where 'those who dared to challenge the pass and other laws . . . in the apartheid heydays' were 'temporarily incarcerated'. The 'infamous beer-hall' he said was another of the 'valuable historic sites'. It 'was used as a drinking spot'. and 'burnt down several years ago' before being made into a craft centre and gymnasium. Hostels were being turned into homes but some of these could be preserved to show the 'cell-like structure' where migrant labourers lived. These were all to be brought together in a Lwandle transformed into heritage for tourists. What Mgijima was envisaging was that all of Lwandle, through its buildings, performances

[21] Zygmunt Bauman, *Liquid Modernity* (Cambridge: Polity Press, 2012), 92.
[22] Jane Flanagan, 'Safe within these walls', *The Telegraph*, 11 September 2002, <http://www .telegraph.co.uk/property/propertyadvice/propertymarket/3306400/Safe-within-these-walls.html>, accessed 15 August 2013.
[23] Bauman, *Liquid Modernity*, 94.
[24] For a critical analysis of this discourse in the early years of post-apartheid South Africa see Ciraj Rassool and Leslie Witz, '"South Africa: a World in One Country": Moments in International Tourist Encounters with Wildlife, the Primitive and the Modern', *Cahiers d'Etudes Africaines*, 143, XXXVI-3 (1996): 335–71.
[25] Gary Minkley, '"A Fragile Inheritor": the Post-Apartheid Memorial Complex, A. C. Jordan and the Re-Imagining of Cultural Heritage in the Eastern Cape', *Kronos: Southern African Histories*, 34 (2008): 16–40.

of arts and crafts, and evidence of post-apartheid construction could link past and present, become heritage as a museum of apartheid, and open up a 'potential tourist route'.[26]

The Residents of Room 33

Although Mgijima presented a set of sites in Lwandle as the home of museumness, what emerged in the 1990s was the identification and conservation of one building as the primary location of the museum. As the hostels were being upgraded into houses for family accommodation, Charmian Plummer, a teacher and resident of Somerset West who had carried out a considerable amount of community work in Lwandle, insisted that one hostel be kept intact 'in order to preserve it for future generations'.[27] Hostel 33, Block 6 was selected for preservation by the Hostels to Homes joint committee, with support from the local Helderberg Municipality, 'for the purpose of the establishment of a museum'.[28] The third sign, presented here, is in a photograph taken by Leslie Witz on the day the museum officially opened on 1 May 2000. Mgijima had taken occupation of the Old Community Hall 50 metres away from the hostel, in order to provide exhibition and office space for the envisaged museum. Following an opening ceremony at the Old Community Hall and a viewing of the exhibition 'Raising the Curtain', guests were divided into small groups and taken on a tour by young residents of Lwandle. The prime destination was Hostel 33. Unbeknown to the organisers, during the festivities some of those living in Hostel 33 had written a makeshift protest notice on the side of a used cardboard box, which was then affixed to the door with packaging tape. When guests arrived at the single entrance to the hostel they were confronted by a notice from its residents claiming that they did not want their rooms turned into a museum until they were provided with alternative accommodation (see Figure 4.3).

The envisaged transformation of a hostel into a museum site, scheduled to culminate on 1 May 2000, emerged from the contests over the future of Lwandle. Lwandle was originally conceived as a temporary encampment in the Helderberg economic region to pre-empt the development of a 'black spot'[29] on the 'landscape of whiteness imagined by

---

[26] Mgijima, 'Let's talk'.

[27] Bongani Mgijima, 'Personal Reflections on Museums and the Promise of Transformation', 30 August 2010, <http://bonganimgijima.blogspot.com/2010/08/personal-reflections-on-museums-and.html>, accessed 22 June 2013.

[28] Helderberg Municipality Memorandum, 1 July 1998, 'Proposed Museum in Lwandle', 17/18/1. All documents which we cite in this article are in the collection of the Lwandle Migrant Labour Museum.

[29] Urban Areas Commissioner, Cape Western Area to Secretary, Divisional Council of Stellenbosch, 21 October 1954.

Figure 4.3. Originally a photographic print, and later digitised, this image of the sign on the door of hostel 33 is the last remaining remnant of the protest at the opening of the museum on 1 May 2000. Above the sign was a 1999 election campaign sticker for the African National Congress. Photo: Leslie Witz.

apartheid's architects'.[30] By the 1980s the 'camp' was showing signs of permanence.[31] With the easing of influx control regulations and increasing poverty in rural areas, families took up residence in the confined hostel setting. For the local authorities of the surrounding towns of Strand, Somerset West, and Gordon's Bay, Lwandle's growth had turned it from a solution to a labour and accommodation shortage in the region into a future that needed to be managed. The limits of Lwandle's present were the subject of 'a stormy future' as different and contested notions of development were proposed. 'Move or improve' were the headlines in the local press. Wanting to 'protect its borders' and affirm the racially designated areas as specified under apartheid, residents of Strand, its town council, and the Hottentots Holland Afrikaanse Sakekamer (Hottentots Holland Chamber of Commerce) saw the removal of Lwandle to Khayelitsha as the appropriate development strategy. Within the Somerset West local municipality a more desirable option was a nearby stable labour force in

[30] Noëleen Murray and Leslie Witz, 'Camp Lwandle: Rehabilitating a Migrant Labour Hostel at the Seaside', *Social Dynamics: A Journal of African Studies*, 39, 1 (2013): 55. For racial planning under apartheid, 'black spots', and forced removals, see also Alan Mabin, 'Comprehensive Segregation: The Origins of the Group Areas Act and Its Planning Apparatuses', *Journal of Southern African Studies* 18, 2 (1992): 405–29.

[31] For an extended discussion on Lwandle as a 'camp' see Murray and Witz, 'Camp Lwandle'.

family accommodation, and they commissioned the Urban Foundation to 'investigate the possible upgrading of Lwandle'.[32] In its report, released the following year, the Urban Foundation maintained that Lwandle was the 'ideal location house for black families in the [Helderberg] basin' and that housing for workers and their families be provided 'together with all the facilities that would be required for the proper social development of the community'.[33] The mayor of Somerset West, Walter Stanford, concurred. Lwandle, he maintained, was 'peaceful and relatively crime-free, providing an essential labour service to the municipalities and factories in the area'. By using available land and keeping the buffer strips in place he was of the opinion that there 'would be adequate room for all facilities to house up to 2,000 Black families on 92 hectares available at Lwandle with all normal amenities'.[34] Development meant creating a stable labour force, and the facilities required to enable this were 'corner shops, a local shopping centre, 1 secondary and 4 primary schools, churches, crèches, a community centre, a post-office, a clinic, a library, a recreational centre, sports fields and playgrounds'.[35] There was no mention of a museum as being a requirement for the development of families in Lwandle.

These struggles over the form and content of development of Lwandle were moving, by the late 1980s, towards the position articulated in the Urban Foundation report. Although in 1987 the government intended to upgrade the hostels but still keep them for single men only, by the following year it had entered into negotiations with major industries in the area, the Somerset West municipality, and the Hostel Dwellers Association (formed in Lwandle in 1987 to fight for family accommodation) over 'plans for Lwandle's future'.[36] Despite vehement opposition from the Strand Town Council, which kept out of the negotiations, Lwandle was declared a township, a local authority and liaison committee was set up, and plans prepared for the construction of family houses as the first phase towards 'town development'.[37] The prospect for a 'new Lwandle' was permanence and stability for a location that was no longer to be a 'temporary camp'.[38]

Reconstituted by government as permanent and legitimate on the eve of Nelson Mandela's release from prison, Lwandle was turned into a site of development aid. A 'Hottentots Holland Mayor's Development

---

[32] 'Lwandle: Move or improve', *District Mail*, 31 October 1986, 1–2; 'Lwandle spectre shakes Strand', *District Mail*, 10 June 1988.

[33] Urban Design Services (report), 'Lwandle: Investigation into the Potential for Black Housing' (Cape Town: Urban Foundation, 1987).

[34] 'Lwandle – This plan won't work', *District Mail*, 17 July 1987.

[35] Urban Design Services, 'Lwandle: Investigation', 66.

[36] 'Lwandle – This plan won't work'; 'The plans for Lwandle's future', *District Mail*, 21 April 1989.

[37] 'Lwandle to develop as a town', *District Mail*, 25 August 1989.

[38] 'The new Lwandle will be no "temporary camp"', *District Mail*, 21 April 1989.

Committee' was formed, that included the mayor of Strand, to coordinate an aid strategy that would enable 'peaceful, happy and positive development and coexistence'. The Committee saw development in Lwandle
as based on government and the private sector providing infrastructure,
and churches and service organisations facilitating social reconstruction.
Whereas the buffer zone had been the mechanism to keep Lwandle
apart, the new developmental agenda was articulated as Somerset West,
Gordon's Bay, and Strand providing 'guidance and input' to Lwandle
that would 'break down' the 'walls of mistrust'. Through working with
the Lwandle Liaison Committee, chaired by Ephraim Nyongwane, the
president of the South African National Civics Organisation branch,
the Development Committee sought to create racial harmony, establish
metaphorical 'bridges of understanding, trust, friendship', and build 'a
better Lwandle'.[39]

Integral to the developmental project of creating a solid, stable citizenry
in Lwandle was the construction and ownership of homes. Stanford, the
mayor of Somerset West in the late 1980s, had insisted that home ownership would create 'an orderly law-abiding community of people' who
were 'needed' and 'vital' to the economy of the Hottentots Holland.[40]
Yet this key element made very little headway in the early 1990s. Finan-
cing the construction of houses was a major problem. A subsidy secured
by the non-profit organisation Cape Utility Homes via the Independent
Development Trust enabled the purchase of sites and setting up of toilet and water services. But both government and banks were unwilling
to take this further and provide loans for the building and purchase of
houses when the risk of default appeared to be high. A photograph that
appeared in the *District Mail* showed '20 toilets at the development site
in Lwandle' and was optimistically entitled 'Lwandle is on the move'.
The photograph was presented as an indication that the next stage, the
construction of houses, was imminent. Another more pessimistic reading of the image was that it indicated that very little had been done and
that there was 'slow development in Lwandle'.[41] Moreover, the residents of Strand were opposed to government making more land available
at heavily subsidised rates for sites and services in Lwandle. 'Whites'
were 'up in arms' as people and pollution were presented as threats to
Strand's future if Lwandle was given the 'green light'.[42] And then there
were reports at the end of 1992 and the beginning of 1993 that Lwandle
was 'up in flames'. Two men, identified in the *District Mail* as 'young'
and 'white' were held hostage in a hostel and almost burnt to death on

---

[39] 'Mayors formulate "Lwandle aid" policy', *District Mail*, 9 February 1990; 'Here's to a
better Lwandle', *District Mail*, 23 February 1990.
[40] 'It's "spruce-up" time for Lwandle', *District Mail*, 31 March 1989.
[41] 'This is Lwandle update', *District Mail*, 4 September 1992.
[42] 'Lwandle green light: whites up in arms', *District Mail*, 3 April 1992.

a Saturday night in Lwandle. Police reported on a necklacing in January 1993 following a verdict passed down in a 'kangaroo court'. On the Easter weekend following the assassination of South African Communist Party leader, Chris Hani, the beerhall and administration block were burnt down, and for a week army troops occupied Lwandle. Portrayed as a 'dark weekend' of violence, this was not the Lwandle that had appeared as the peaceful site for family development and a stable labour force.[43]

The events of 1992/3 and the halting progress of the housing scheme in effect signalled a shift in the focus of development in Lwandle and created the possibilities for a museum. Instead of ownership of property as the site of development, the renovation of hostels from single-dwelling 'bedholds' to units of family occupation became the priority. The Hostels to Homes scheme, which followed upon similar projects undertaken in Cape Town's townships,[44] was more about enabling privacy, providing sustainable energy, and ensuring employment and skills transfer in the construction of rental accommodation. Development was not about a citizenry created out of ownership, but about using local contractors and labourers in the processes of conversion of hostels to the family units, which would be available for rent. The major conflicts which emerged were about tendering, procurement, training, using 'community-based contractors', and the sizes of the refurbished dwellings for individuated families.[45] With development no longer defined primarily through ownership, but rather through 'skills training and capacity building', it was mediation and negotiations over these matters, together with engineering the old to make new, that were the priorities of Brett Myrdal, the project manager for Liebenberg and Stander in Lwandle.[46] By 1998 the first units were ready with water-borne sewerage, showers, hot water provided through solar heaters, individual entrances, ceilings, plastered walls, new doors and windows. New amenities were also built. Out of the remains of the old beerhall a gymnasium and arts and crafts unit were constructed; a town centre with possibilities for shop stalls was developed, inserted into the large open central area surrounded by double-storey hostels; the taxi rank was 'revamped'; and a new library and administrative offices

---

[43] 'Lwandle ontvlam', *District Mail*, 4 December 1992; 'Necklacing in Lwandle', *District Mail*, 15 January 1993; 'Despite Easter "hiccup" Lwandle's on track', *District Mail*, Property section, 18 June 1993; Institute for Housing of South Africa National Housing Awards, 'Housing Person of the Year: Brett Myrdal: Lwandle Hostels-to-Homes', 1999.

[44] Sarah Thurman, 'Umzamo: Improving Hostel Dwellers' Accommodation in South Africa', *Environment and Urbanization*, 9, 2 (1997): 43–62.

[45] Institute for Housing of South Africa: 'Housing Person of the Year'.

[46] Liebenberg and Stander, Consulting Engineers and Project Managers, 'Lwandle Hostels to Homes Project', <http://web.archive.org/web/20050311031334/http://www.engineer.co.za/lwandle.html>, accessed 5 July 2013.

were built.[47] Consultation and engineering had come together to create what appeared to be a development success story in Lwandle.[48]

With some hindsight it can be seen that it also opened up the prospect for an artefactual presence to become a museum that could rent a past and, in return, provide further possibilities for development. That past, as suggested by Charmian Plummer, would take the form of retaining one or two hostels with all their contents. This was to become the foundation of 'a cultural museum', an institutional structure that imbues artefacts with an empirical aura. This collective aura endowed by the remains of objects would then enable development through visits to the museum. According to the Director of the Executive Office of the Helderberg Municipality, an administrative structure which drew together the towns of Somerset West, Strand, and Gordon's Bay, the Lwandle Museum was comparable to the District Six Museum and had the potential to 'become a big drawcard for visitors in the Helderberg'.[49] Indeed this was the primary purpose of the museum, which in June 1998 Mgijima had outlined suggestively in 'Let's talk heritage matters'.[50]

In both respects, the establishment of a museum around Hostel 33, and through its presence a site for development through tourism, was difficult to sustain. It was not only challenging to entice tourists to Lwandle because of its distance from Cape Town, but the museum also found that it was being diverted away from its intention – to tell a story of migrant labour – by the demands of the tourist industry for stereotypes of an African heritage as rural, tribal, and primitive.[51] The form of development implemented through engineering and consultation in the Hostels to Homes project was also unsustainable in terms of making Hostel 33 into a museum. In the newspaper coverage around the decision to establish a museum it was reported that the residents of Hostel 33 had not been informed of plans to make their accommodation into a museum piece and 'would only be told, once alternative accommodation was found'.[52]

---

[47] 'R15 million project sees Lwandle hostels converted into homes', *District Mail*, 20 February 1998, 8; M. Hildebrand and Thubesila Homes, 'Case Studies: Successful Energy Efficient Projects in South Africa: Lessons for Thubelisha Homes' (Joe Slovo 3, N2 Gateway Energy Efficiency Project, commissioned by National Department of Housing, 2008), <http://editorsinc.files.wordpress.com/2012/04/successful-energy-efficient-projects-in-south-africa-for-thubelisha.pdf>, accessed 25 June 2013.

[48] See, for example, Sarah Ward, *The Energy Book for Urban Development in South Africa* (Noordhoek: Sustainable Energy Africa, 2003); William Ruijsch van Dugteren, 'Lwandle Hostels–to–Homes Project: Retrofitting for Sustainability' (paper presented at City Energy Strategies Conference, Cape Town International Convention Centre, 19–21 November 2003).

[49] 'Lwandle hostel to become a cultural museum', *District Mail*, 15 May 1998, 5.

[50] Mgijima, 'Let's talk'.

[51] This is elaborated upon in detail in Leslie Witz, 'Revisualizing Township Tourism in the Western Cape: the Migrant Labour Museum and the Reconstruction of Lwandle', *Journal of Contemporary African Studies*, 29, 4 (2011): 371–88.

[52] 'Lwandle hostel to become a cultural museum'.

The first two curators of the museum, Bongani Mgijima and Vusi Buthelezi, argue that such claims were incorrect. They cite an undated letter from residents of Hostel 33 to the Lwandle Museum Committee:

We, hostel number 33 residents hereby approve our unit be converted to the hostel museum as long as we are still the residents of the hostel and catered for into the hostel to homes project. This idea was clearly explained to us by members of the committee, we are aware that this has the blessings of the community and we also want to fully support the idea of making history of our background and we are also proud that our community is developing gradually and effectively. We also thank you for your care and ambition to make this happen.[53]

Whether Mgijima and Buthelezi are correct in their claims is debatable. Clearly, alternative accommodation for the residents of Hostel 33 had not been found by 1 May 2000 and the opening of the museum was an ideal opportunity for residents to make their point. The consultative model of post-apartheid urban development that was applied in planning building renovations for the transformation of generic hostel space into individual family homes was not an established method in this case, when there were no building works to be done and the hostel was to remain unrenovated as a museum artefact.

So, although the notice disappeared from the hostel door the day after the museum opened, for the staff and the board of the Lwandle Migrant Labour Museum one pressing responsibility was negotiating with local authorities and building contractors to find alternative accommodation for residents of Hostel 33. According to Charmian Plummer she continually phoned and visited the housing board but 'with scant results'. It was a frustrating, 'long and tedious struggle with many broken promises or no response!!'[54] At almost every meeting of the board of the Lwandle Museum from 2000 onwards, Hostel 33 was on the agenda. A partial solution was arrived at when alternative accommodation was found for those who lived on one side of the hostel building, allowing the unoccupied side to be the tourist site. When it seemed the issues would be resolved once alternative accommodation was located for all the residents, a new group of people moved in. The minutes of the museum board dated 29 January 2007 read:

Hostel 33: This still remains a major concern. Some people who were living there have got houses and have moved out, but a new group of people has moved in without the permission of the museum. The museum has no authority to evict them but Lunga [Smile] is to ask Simon [Nehonde] to make a notice indicating that this is museum property.[55]

---

[53] Bongani Mgijima and Vusi Buthelezi, 'Mapping Museum–Community Relations in Lwandle', *Journal of Southern African Studies*, 32, 4 (2006): 800.
[54] Charmian Plummer, email to authors and Lunga Smile, 22 May 2011.
[55] Minutes of meeting of the Board, Lwandle Migrant Labour Museum, 29 January 2007.

A notice assigning Hostel 33 for 'museum purposes only' went up but the following month the issue was once again on the agenda.

Hostel 33: The problems still continue. Mrs Makhabane suggested going to ask the mother of the children in Hostel 33 to come to the museum for a meeting. In the end it was decided that we need to ask Xolani Sotashe (the Lwandle councillor) to assist and to possibly call in the police.[56]

The presence of the past envisaged through Hostel 33 in 1998 was not to come to pass until August 2007. In the interim Mgijima's 'safe guided walk' through the township, which harked back to Lwandle being developed as a place of safety and stability, became the mechanism for holding onto the openness of his intentions for visitors to take in Hostel 33. As a compromise, visitors were taken to the adjacent unoccupied section of the hostel.

In August 2007, when Hostel 33 was finally vacated, the museum was able to take occupation and rehabilitate a past through restoring the hostel to the museum as its primary artefact. With funding from the United States Ambassadors' Fund for Cultural Preservation, the National Lottery Board, and the National Heritage Council, Hostel 33 was rehabilitated to become the museum's Hostel 33.[57] On the wall of the hostel the museum placed a new notice with the name Hostel 33 in a stencil font. This was superimposed on an aerial photograph of Lwandle from the 1980s showing the layout of the migrant labour compound, in effect placing the hostel in a landscape of the past. The sign proclaimed the hostel, its history, and its future formally as the possession of the Lwandle Migrant Labour Museum. In lettering, reminiscent of the anonymous stencilled block numbers, it read: 'HOSTEL 33, LWANDLE MIGRANT LABOUR MUSEUM, OLD COMMUNITY HALL, VULINDLELA ROAD, LWANDLE.' Hostel and Old Community Hall were both developed into a heritage for the museum.

Sign 4: Urban Design

With the idea of a museum primarily located in the apartheid plan of the hostel compound on hold, and while contests over the provision of housing and heritage played themselves out, it was exhibition and activities at the Old Community Hall that constituted the main 'museum effect'.[58] After Mgijima's first exhibition *Raising the Curtain*, the following

---

[56] Minutes of meeting of the Board, Lwandle Migrant Labour Museum, 27 February 2007.

[57] See Murray and Witz, 'Camp Lwandle', for an in-depth account of the restoration process of Hostel 33 between 2008 and 2011.

[58] Barbara Kirshenblatt-Gimblett, 'Objects of Ethnography', in Ivan Karp and Steven D. Lavine (eds), *Exhibiting Cultures* (Washington, DC: Smithsonian Institution, 1991), 410.

Figure 4.4. Two views on arrival at the museum after the City of Cape Town's urban greening project. Photos by Leslie Witz, 2007.

exhibition, *Unayo na Impehu* (Do You Have a Map?), which opened in 2001, drew on documents from the Hostels to Homes Project and the Office of the Surveyor General to show the establishment and growth of Lwandle's urban geography. Using collage and digital graphic methods, a series of panels told stories of buffer zones, the planning of Lwandle, life in the hostels, and the construction, destruction, and reconstruction of the beerhall. Design exhibition panels were affixed to the walls, the floor was marked out with a grid to order the placing of artefacts, and pedestals were installed for the proper display of objects. More than pasting photographs on the wall, *Do You Have a Map?* began a process of making the Old Community Hall into the museum's exhibitionary nexus.

Our next set of signs are sited in and around the entrance to the museum at the Old Community Hall (see Figure 4.4). One image shows a view encountered on arrival at the gate in Vulindlela Road, where a plethora of signs are confusingly juxtaposed against each other. There are two signs announcing the museum. One provides the museum's name, composed into letters using treated timber poles, aesthetically integrated through its positioning at the entrance gate over the surface of a fence in the same material. The other is an information sign, commissioned from a local sign writer, providing the museum's name, addresses, and telephone/fax numbers, and proclaims the museum as a 'Centre of Memory and Hope'. Competing with this museum signage there are a number of branded commercial signs related to the shop next door. The second image shows the museum forecourt transformed through the interventions of an urban design project. An earlier red sign with the museum's name is visible on the wall to the left above the doors to the Old Community Hall, along with a directional notice on the timber door indicating that the entrance to the building was, in fact, around the corner.

These signs on the Old Community Hall and its surrounds stand in contrast to the barren and austere environment that Witz had encountered when he first visited the museum in 1999. In late 2004 a new process had been initiated in Lwandle by the Cape Town Unicity. Whereas Hostels to Homes had concentrated on functionality and the provision of amenities, this new phase was envisioned around the idea of improving the quality and aesthetic of public space in the township. The museum property at the Old Community Hall was identified as a part of this second wave of development, as an area that needed greening and a parking area. A budget of almost one million rand was allocated and, working from a site plan, rather than visiting the museum, a basic landscape layout was quickly drawn up by the civic Urban Design Department based in central Cape Town. Development in Lwandle, which initially had been conceived as home ownership, and had then turned into consultation, skills transference, and self-help, had become beautification.

In an attempt to overturn the allegorical image of the townships as dirty, dusty, overcrowded, ugly, and unsanitary, Cape Town's urban design team invoked models that had been tested recently elsewhere in the city.[59] The premise for the model of beauty and development was that Lwandle had no heritage to speak of. Adopting an approach 'to over-write the existing context', because it was 'unsightly', Lwandle became an empty space, where 'the existing conditions held no value for retention'.[60] In doing so the designers suggested solutions that included using romantic traditionalist spatial ideas. The epicentre of the panoptic layout of the compound was to be turned into a convivial sociable space reminiscent of the publicness of the Medieval Italian town square. At the Old Community Hall the spatial inspiration was drawn from closer to home – invoking the 'werf', the walled working space of a farm in the high Cape Dutch period. Brightly coloured mosaic murals, invoking craft and folklife, were to be used to give the front facade of the ugly hall a facelift. And, finally, there was to be a garden with succulents and flaming aloes, in an essentialised reference to the Eastern Cape as ethnic home. Instead of finding meaning in the dislocated landscape, Lwandle was enthusiastically reimagined and over-designed.

The museum board asserted its public participatory role in this new development and called for a process-based approach before any product was to be accepted from the city's urban designers. After much discussion the museum's board asked one of its members, Noëleen Murray, to assist

---

[59] Noëleen Murray, 'Spatial [Re]Imaginings? Contesting Township Development Post-Apartheid' (paper presented at the Wits Institute for Social and Economic Research Symposium, The Townships Now, 9–11 June 2004).

[60] Noëleen Murray, 'A Campus Apart', in Premesh Lalu and Noëleen Murray (eds), *Becoming UWC: Reflections, Pathways and Unmaking Apartheid's Legacy* (Bellville: UWC, 2012), 75.

with the negotiations. On a very practical level, Murray raised concerns about the planned investment in a dedicated parking area when there was an existing lot in an adjacent parcel of land belonging to the municipality; she expressed doubts about the suggestions to beautify the building with mosaic murals; and raised questions about how money was allocated.[61] As an alternative she suggested that a public precinct be created by the removal of fencing that separated the museum from the adjacent library and the municipal offices, and that creative ways be sought to reuse existing, underutilised buildings and parking areas. Similarly, the city council had to be convinced about preserving elements of the 'ugliness' of the landscape that is so much a part of the story that the museum sets out to tell. Ways had to be found to mark this apartheid character while at the same time improving the environment and making a museum park.

As an architect, Murray was placed in the space of interlocutor between the city authorities and the museum. Acting as an agent of the museum she had to negotiate the often-difficult histories of township intervention, disciplinary authority, and the powerful nature of images of the township that were intact. Throughout she was faced with the prevalence and the persistence of discourses of the township as a space of underdevelopment, in need of upliftment and somehow peopled with an uncritical citizenry. There are histories of distrust in planning processes where objections have often been easily ignored by the council authorities, who have continued in a self-assured policy of spatial intervention through budget spending. Unlike where there are contestations over land in high-yielding land market areas, such contestations often remain unheard. In Lwandle's case the board asserted its right to a voice in the city. The option of being repackaged and beautified as 'township development' was not attractive.

What followed subsequently was a complete reworking of this scheme after discussion between the museum and the city. Instead of turning the museum's surrounds into an Eastern Cape landscape, as the planners envisaged, the development brought together institutions of civil society in Lwandle, combining the museum with a hardly used municipal office and the nearby Hector Peterson library. The spatial intervention was driven in many ways by Murray's specialist intervention, working in association with the urban designers, as well as by the museum's needs. Murray published an article in *Architecture South Africa* in April 2007 profiling the project and the collaborative process. The museum, she wrote, had played a 'proactive role' by suggesting that the fencing between the institutions be removed and a public precinct created. Trees, lawns, and

[61] Achille Mbembe, Grace Khunou, and Nsizwa Dlamini, 'The Township Now: a Conversation,' *WISER in Brief*, 2, 2 (December 2003), 4–7.

a new garden provided the promise of improved public space.[62] Aspirations for a modern museum precinct were accompanied by a whole rearrangement of the internal exhibition space of the museum. When the reoriented museum opened its doors in the new precinct it had a new entrance and the whole space of the old hall had been changed around to undermine the overdetermining symmetry of the building. Although this moment of transforming the Old Community Hall into museum park was limited – a perimeter wire-mesh fence remained, and a treated 'gumpole' fence had been slipped in as a remnant of the city's rural aestheticising ideas to camouflage ugly apartheid – the museum and its board were delighted with the negotiated result of this particular project, and enthusiastic about future possibilities for museum/city collaboration.

Property Signs and Fences

Yet at the moment these words appeared in *Architecture SA*, unbeknown to Murray and the museum staff, the library adjacent to the museum was planning to put up a fence to secure its property. Our final set of images are of signs and fences. We have used these images to help us think of the signs and fences as notes of particular type that appear and disappear from the landscape, narrating the processes of construction outside of the formal script of development. Reading these enable us to revisit the actual spaces of their appearance and disappearance, and to consider their placement and messaging.

In both images there are palisade steel fences. The fence in the first image is below two billboards on the left of the N2 motorway as one leaves Lwandle towards Somerset West and Cape Town. On one billboard is an advertisement enticing potential buyers of new homes in Lwandle Strand that were for sale from R259,000, or from R2,100 per month (see Figure 4.5). 'Don't rent when you can OWN A HOME!' it proclaimed, and only start paying 'once you have moved in'. The second image is the view of the eastern façade of the Old Community Hall (Figure 4.6). In the foreground weeds are prospering in the laterite of the hard surfaces of the new space that has been constructed through the interventions of the city's urban design unit. And, instead of an open precinct leading onto a vegetable garden and the library, there is a brand new palisade steel fence.

Since the creation of the precinct that included the library, museum, and municipal offices in Lwandle, a new librarian, Zoliswa Khanuga, had taken over. She had her own visions for the space surrounding the library.

[62] Murray, 'Working with Inconsistencies', 32.

Figure 4.5. Houses for sale in Lwandle, 27 February 2014. Photo: Noëleen Murray.

Her job demanded that she performed tasks such as risk assessment in order to secure the property. Based on her assessment, the library was at risk and she motivated to receive funds for new physical security measures in the form of burglar bars and gates, and a new industrial steel palisade perimeter fence to be provided through the official coffers. It had become necessary to lock down the library and lessen its exposure to risk. This was in stark contrast with the opening up that was happening next door at the museum, where afternoon homework sessions enticed children into the museum and the education officer devoted his afternoons to attending to the children's needs. Developing permanence was taking on different forms in the two neighbouring institutions that shared the precinct, and when in 2007 a new fence was installed between the museum and the library it caused a stir. Lunga Smile, the museum manager, wrote to us that this was 'the case of the R150,000 fence separating Hector Peterson Library from the Lwandle Migrant Museum'.[63]

The gleaming new steel fence that effectively severed the museum from its prospect onto the library garden surgically followed the strict cadastral lines of property boundaries as it carved up the precinct once again and locked down the museum's vision of open public space. Fences, linked as signs of both private property and development, are perhaps the most pervasive trope of Cape Town's post-apartheid bounding of space.

---

[63] Lunga Smile, email to authors, 12 June 2007.

Figure 4.6. Fence between the entrance to the Lwandle Migrant Labour Museum and the adjacent library. Photo: Noëleen Murray.

Appearing across the landscape of Somerset West and greater Lwandle as markers of 'envelopes and enclaves' of private and securitised space, they in effect recreate Alcatraz-like images of the sort Mgijima referred to in his article in 1998.[64] If Lwandle was in the process of becoming a township from its compound beginnings, the emplotment of the township in becoming could be said to have been completed by the move towards creating a heritage out of the developmental moment of the conversion from hostel bedholds to housing.

As Emaholweni, the place of hostels, became the place of homes, there were indications that a property market was emerging. When the sign advertising new homes in Lwandle first appeared, Leslie Witz recalled a conversation with a first-year history student at UWC. After discussing an essay she had submitted, the conversation turned to the part-time job that she held while completing her studies. She described her work as an estate agent (a realtor) in the townships of Cape Town, selling new houses to first-time prospective owners who were eligible for a government subsidy and thus constituted a lucrative emerging market. Witz mentioned his association with Lwandle over the past years and wondered if that was an area where she was doing any business. 'Oh yes,' she enthused, 'of course. It is one of the main areas in which I work. There are many teachers and nurses who are looking for houses in Lwandle. It is a safe, small, and convenient place to live. It is not like Khayelitsha. There is not so much crime in Lwandle.' I then told her about the museum in Lwandle and she was even more enthusiastic. 'A museum,' she said, 'that's fantastic. I will tell my clients about that. It will most definitely push up the prices of houses.'

The mere existence of an institution called a museum had the potential to transform Lwandle into a type of heritage park that had not been envisaged when Bongani Mgijima had plastered the arbitrary set of photographs onto the walls of the Community Hall some ten years previously. On either side of the national road heritage was underwriting development as a tool for marketing private property. Confidence in these emerging markets was communicated through advertising, proposing on the one side an idealised gated community, and on the other a subsidised suburban bliss in the township. The speculative space of Heritage Park lay on its side of the N2 motorway, behind the booms and electrified fence; on the other, although there were no such physical barriers restricting access, the museum was starting to turn Lwandle into Lwandle Strand.

We started this article thinking about the passage of the 'WHITES ONLY' sign as it travelled from the beach to the Lwandle Migrant Labour Museum, and have ended with a story of the fence as a sign

---

[64] Mgijima, 'Let's talk'; Frederic Jameson interviewed by Michael Speaks, 'Envelopes and Enclaves: The Space of Post-Civil Society', *Assemblage* 17 (1990): 30–7.

of the post-apartheid. We have seen how discourses of private property and development are brought together by the signs and fences we have observed over the years of our association with the museum. As we write this article, the Lwandle Museum continues its work of making the site of development into heritage, with a future seemingly secured as a 'Provincial Aided' museum.[65] In September 2010 it also signed a formal lease for the Old Community Hall and Hostel 33, and is now a legal tenant occupying the City of Cape Town's properties in Lwandle.[66] In this story of emergence from being the 'first township-based museum in the Western Cape' to 'Best Community Tourism Attraction of the Year' (2009) to 'Museum of the Year' (2010) in the province, tracing the narrative thread that runs through the story of the museum, we return to the question of the fence as the museum board has once again been asked to consider this anew. Funds from the local ward councillor's 2013 capital budget allocated by the City of Cape Town were generously allocated to the museum to secure itself against risk. A proposal from the councillor was accepted by the city to replace the fence around the museum with an industrial palisade fence. The risk of this proposal was that it would contain the museum and further reverse its aspirations to the open public precinct and access for communities that it wishes to construct. In correspondence with Councillor Jongudumo Justice Maxheke of Ward 86, the chair of the museum board Leslie Witz argued against the ring fencing of the museum:

The new fence proposed by the City and its service providers, which would be in the same style as that which was constructed between the museum and the library, would therefore be totally unsuitable and merely serve to replicate the problems that have emerged. It would destroy the aesthetic, be alienating and would close down the public space in Lwandle. This style of the fence reinforces the very worst of an apartheid style aesthetic, reminiscent of imprisonment and confinement.[67]

Meanwhile the City of Cape Town's asset of the Old Community Hall property, which is home to the Lwandle Museum's exhibitions and administration, is slowly falling into disrepair without a budget to maintain it. The then blurs with the now.

The convergence of a past with a future of development in Lwandle has always been about both closing spaces and opening them up, of securing and making public, of enabling the commons and institutionalising

---

[65] 'Museum Ordinance: Declaration of the Lwandle Migrant Labour Museum', *Province of Western Cape Provincial Gazette*, 6961 (24 February 2012).

[66] 'Lease of City Land for Museum Purposes Vulindlela and Noxolo Streets, Lwandle, Portion of Erf 13600, Strand, 10 September 2010', File H 142/2/1/2/41 (29447).

[67] Letter from Leslie Witz to Councillor Councillor Jongudumo Justice Maxheke of Ward 86 in the City of Cape Town, 2 August 2013, re: Maintenance Lwandle Migrant Labour Museum.

memory. As indicated in this volume by Minkley and Mnyaka, these are not antithetical processes of the vernacular and the authorised. In the instances of memorialisation in Duncan Village that they describe, tropes of the family as victim, together with the indigenous as the source of healing and heritage, are rendered into a 'visual economy of [social] development need' (Minkley and Mnyaka, this volume). Lwandle, as we argue, is visible through its signs and fences, and more specifically in the institution of a museum that makes claims to the everyday and asserts authorised pasts as heritage. In this simultaneity and convergence the vernacular thread is turned into a parable of development, where the compound becomes a township, hostels become homes, Hostel 33 becomes a museum, and the WHITES ONLY sign crosses the beach to a new location in the museum as an aid to telling the story of 'Memory and Hope' advertised at the entrance gate.

5   Monuments and Negotiations of Power in Ghana

Kodzo Gavua

Ghana arrived at nationhood on 6 March 1957, burdened with many vestiges and entanglements of its pre-colonial and colonial past. Its inherited establishments and facilities were polyglot – it subsumed, and has been presiding over, different polities, traditional authorities, institutions, and interest groups with incongruous aspirations and relationships.[1] As Prime Minister, Dr Kwame Nkrumah led a Convention Peoples Party (CPP) government that was the first to rule the new nation. He and his government failed to dissociate themselves from the Christiansborg Castle, a facility that had served as the seat of the British colonial administration of Gold Coast, and the residence of the Queen of England's representative. Instead, they adopted it as their administrative headquarters and Prime Minister's residence.[2] The castle, on the coast of Accra, Ghana's capital city, was first built in 1652 as a small trading lodge by the Swedish Africa Company, and in 1661 was bought by Danish merchants who refurbished and expanded it into a castle from which they administered their affairs along the Guinea Coast until the British acquired it in 1873. It thus embodies pre-colonial and colonial heritages that relate to the mercantile, political, and other economic interests of Western Europe. Nkrumah and his government's use of the facility was thus a paradox, one officially explained as a 'psychological operation meant to impress upon the people that a new era had dawned'.[3] This suggests Ghanaians were to understand the government's appropriation of the castle as a celebration of their triumph over colonialism.

---

[1] The geopolitical area named Ghana absorbed the Gold Coast colony the British had established, Asante, parts of Togoland, and other territories that were protectorates of the British. It is characterised by a conflation of several chiefdoms, economically powerful communities of Middle Eastern and Indian background, and separate, powerful, political elite groups with conflicting ideological convictions.

[2] See Albert van Dantzig, *Forts and Castles in Ghana* (Accra: Sedco Publishing Limited, 1980) and Robert B. Nunoo, *Christiansborg Castle – Osu* (Accra: Ministry of Information, 1969).

[3] The 18 May 1957 issue of the *Daily Graphic*, the state-owned newspaper, reported the relocation of Nkrumah and his government to the Christiansborg Castle and the rationale for this.

The Nkrumah regime had the task of distinguishing the new nation with an identity that would rid it of its colonial image. Nkrumah's image replaced the Queen of England's on coins and stamps, and in Accra the new government constructed a composite monument it named 'Independence Square'. This monument is characterised by an 'Independence Arch' situated in 'Black Star Square' and other features intended to assert Ghana's independence and to commemorate the struggle that led to it; it also includes facilities for hosting national celebrations. After Ghana adopted a republican constitution in 1960 and elected Nkrumah as President of the first republic, the CPP government – in the midst of active opposition to its machinations – strategically erected statues of the President in front of the country's first Parliament building and at what became 'Kwame Nkrumah Circle', a roundabout at a major road intersection in Accra. In 1961, the government established a 'Kwame Nkrumah Institute of Economics and Political Science' to train civil servants and to promote the nation's sovereignty, Pan-Africanism, socialism, and other ideals of the CPP. Ghanaians have popularly referred to this school as the 'Kwame Nkrumah Ideological Institute'. By an Act of Parliament enacted on 22 August of the same year, the government commissioned the 'Kwame Nkrumah University of Science and Technology' in Kumasi.

The castle, statues, circle, schools, and the square became active voices of Nkrumah's authority as President and of his ideals and strategies. They were also channels for defining and communicating the CPP's version of Ghana's national heritage.[4] Ever since its construction the Independence Square has heralded, irrespective of regime change, Ghana's sovereignty and nationhood, and has been the main venue for celebrations of the nation's independence anniversary and other celebrations of national character. The Christiansborg Castle also remained the seat of government business and 'power house' from where key state policies and directives emanated – until 2013, when the presidency of Ghana relocated to another facility (see below). The statues and schools failed, however, to appeal to a cross-section of Ghanaians. To elements of the opposition to the CPP regime – in the main Dr Kofi Abrefa Busia's National Liberation Movement (NLM) and its successor, the United Party (UP), a union of the NLM and other smaller parties with ethnic and religious affiliations – they were manifestations of Nkrumah's and the CPP's perceived proclivity towards one-man rule and a Marxist-communist dispensation in Ghana.[5] The opposition, hitherto, had

---

[4] See Ahmad Yahaya, 'The Scope and Definitions of Heritage: from Tangible to Intangible', *International Journal of Heritage Studies* 12, 3 (2006): 292–300.

[5] Joseph G. Amamoo, *The Ghanaian Revolution* (London: Jafint Company, 1988), 24–9, discusses the context in which opponents of Nkrumah and the CPP perceived in them a proclivity towards dictatorship.

protested the relocation of Nkrumah to the Christiansborg Castle and his ousting of the Queen on coins and stamps.[6]

On 24 February 1966 a National Liberation Council (NLC) military administration replaced Nkrumah's regime in a coup d'état. This administration worked closely with Dr Busia and other leaders of the opposition in an attempt to override the regime's influence, assert itself, and prosecute a different political agenda. On the day of the coup d'état, irate mobs directed by military officers tore down Nkrumah's statues, one of which lost its head and an arm (see Figure 5.1). Thereafter, the NLC banned the CPP from operating, while 'Flagstaff House', a residential complex the CPP government had built for the President, was seized and converted into Ghana's Armed Forces' headquarters. It decommissioned the Kwame Nkrumah Institute of Economic and Political Science and renamed the Kwame Nkrumah University of Science and Technology and the Kwame Nkrumah Circle, in addition to ordering the public burning of Nkrumah's publications. The university was renamed the 'University of Science and Technology', while the circle became the 'National Liberation Circle'. The NLC also refurbished and renamed the Accra International Airport in honour of General Emmanuel Kwasi Kotoka, leader of the military junta that overthrew the CPP government, who was killed by a group of junior military officers in a short-lived revolt in April 1967. 'Kotoka International Airport', as it was renamed, fronted by a statue of the late General, was thus transformed into a monument of General Kotoka's courage and death, and of Nkrumah's forced exit from power. According to Lieutenant-General Ankrah, who chaired the NLC, renaming the airport after the General was to 'enshrine in the hearts and minds of all Ghanaians, the ideals for which he [Kotoka] sacrificed his life'.[7] The NLC's affront to the supposed invincibility of Nkrumah and his regime promoted the council's authority and image among people and agencies opposed to Nkrumah.

The anti-Nkrumah agenda continued under the democratically elected Progress Party (PP) government, which succeeded the NLC. Under Dr Kofi Busia as Prime Minister, the PP governed from 1969 to 13 January 1972, when another group of military officers overthrew it. This government actualised the agenda partly by naming two roundabouts in Accra

---

[6] Protests against the placement of Nkrumah's head on Ghanaian coins and stamps were reported in the *Daily Graphic*, 17 June 1957.

[7] Eben Quarcoo reported the renaming and dedication of the Kotoka International Airport as a monument, and the rationale for this, in the *Daily Graphic*, 26 February 1969. Lt-General Ankrah is known to have written to President Lyndon Johnson of the United States of America indicating that the agenda of the NLC included the 'task of mentally rehabilitating our people [Ghanaians]', <http://history.state.gov/historicaldocuments/frus1964-68v24/d26>, accessed 21 June 2011.

Figure 5.1. The remains of Kwame Nkrumah's statue, decapitated by an irate mob in support of the 1966 coup d'état.

after Dr Joseph B. Danquah and Mr Obetsebi Lamptey respectively, and by mounting statues of these personalities at the roundabouts. The two men had been instrumental in establishing the United Gold Coast Convention (UGCC), a political movement that agitated against colonial rule in the Gold Coast, and from which Nkrumah defected to form the

CPP in 1948. They had been stalwarts of the anti-Nkrumah opposition, and lost their lives in the course of opposing him.

It would appear, therefore, that the early governments of Ghana manipulated monuments not only to memorialise their heroes but also to define what they saw as Ghana's 'true' political heritage. They saw this idea of the past as a means of bidding for power and a source of their ability to wield authority over citizens and to control and influence their behaviour. By so doing, the governments had established a tradition of monument building, naming, and renaming that has been fraught with subjective definitions of Ghana's heritage. The rest of the discussion covers attempts to show how successful Ghanaian governments after the Progress Party administration have used monuments as channels manifesting discourse, shaping identities, and defining heritage.[8] It explores relationships that may be found between monument building and definitions of heritage to show how various political groups – influenced mainly by the rival ideals of Dr Nkrumah and Dr Danquah/Dr Busia and by particular interests within the society – employed physical constructions to define heritages that objectified their respective ideals and interests in order to legitimise and promote themselves in the process of gaining and sustaining power. In this way the chapter contributes to a wider African conversation in which other chapters in this volume engage (see, for example, Minkley and Mnyaka, this volume).

Monuments and the Nkrumaist Heritage

Following the military coup that removed Dr Busia and his PP government on 13 January 1972, successive governments until 2001 sought to legitimise themselves and gain clout by evoking and objectifying through monument building, naming and renaming the ideals of Nkrumah. The National Redemption Council (NRC) military regime that took over from the PP government, for example, claimed sympathy with Nkrumah's cause as Colonel R. E. A. Kotei, a member of the ruling council, declared.[9] The council expressed this sympathy by restoring the Kwame Nkrumah Circle and organising, in June 1972, a state burial for Nkrumah, who had died in exile. In 1975 it refurbished and named after Nkrumah's mother a house in which she had lived in Accra when the NLC seized it in 1966. The 'Nyaniba House', as the NRC

---

[8] See James Symonds, 'Historical Archaeology and the Recent Urban Past', *International Journal of Heritage Studies* 10, 1 (2004): 33–48, and Daniel Miller, 'Why Some Things Matter', in Daniel Miller (ed.), *Material Cultures: Why Some Things Matter* (London: Routledge, 1998), 3–21.

[9] According to the *Daily Graphic*, 3 May 1975, Colonel Kotei declared that 'The National Redemption Council is devoted to the ideals and aspirations which the late Dr Nkrumah stood for.'

explained in naming the building, was to commemorate Nkrumah's mother. These gestures, in addition to quasi-Nkrumaist programmes the council executed with regard to housing, agriculture, and education, appealed to and won over to it many followers and admirers, including proponents of Nkrumah's political philosophy, programmes, and activities. The NRC, nevertheless, moved a step further to affirming its own identity and presence by renaming after itself a roundabout at the intersection of two major streets in Accra, Ring Road Central and Independence Avenue. 'Akuafo Roundabout', originally named by the Nkrumah regime in honour of Ghanaian farmers, thus became 'National Redemption Circle', a major symbol of the new government's power.

On 4 June 1979 Flight-Lieutenant Jerry John Rawlings led a group of junior military officers to overthrow the 'Supreme Military Council' (SMC) into which the NRC had metamorphosed. The Armed Forces Revolutionary Council (AFRC) – the junta formed by the junior officers at the time of the coup – after a few months organised general elections won by the People's National Party (PNP), which introduced Ghana's third republic under Dr Hilla Limman as President. This republic ended when Flight-Lieutenant Jerry John Rawlings once again headed a Provisional National Defence Council (PNDC) to re-assume power after another coup d'état on 31 December 1981. The PNDC quickly demonstrated its predilection for Nkrumah's Pan-Africanist goals and worldview, which have been dubbed 'Nkrumaism'.[10] For example, it renamed the 'National Redemption Circle' 'Sankara Circle' after Captain Thomas Sankara, a revolutionary and Pan-Africanist head of state of Burkina Faso, previously known as Upper Volta, who had been killed in a palace coup. The council also created and commissioned on 1 July 1992 a 'Kwame Nkrumah Memorial Park'. Located at the old polo grounds where Nkrumah pronounced Ghana's independence in 1957, the park is a composite monument that comprises a bronze statue of Nkrumah, his and his wife's tombs, a museum of his collections, a fountain lined by effigies of indigenous horn blowers, and other features that evoke Pan-Africanist ideals (see Figure 5.2).

This monument has attracted visits from international dignitaries, including Pan-Africanists, and the general public, exercising a symbolic force that earned the PNDC credibility among Pan-Africanists and revolutionaries the world over – and helped to consolidate the administration's influence among Nkrumah's followers.

---

[10] Kwodwo Addison (*Daily Graphic*, 17 March 1964) described 'Nkrumaism' as 'the ideology for the new Africa, independent and absolutely free from imperialism, organised on a continental scale, founded upon the conception of one and united Africa, drawing its strength from modern science and technology and from the traditional African belief that the free development of each is the condition for the free development of all.'

Figure 5.2. A bronze statue of Kwame Nkrumah mounted by the Provisional National Defence Council (PNDC) government at the Kwame Nkrumah Memorial Park.

In the mid-1980s the PNDC embarked upon a World Bank/IMF-prescribed Economic Recovery Programme, ostensibly to boost Ghana's economy. In line with this programme, the administration supported the renovation and transformation of the Cape Coast and Elmina castles into major tourist attractions. These World Heritage Sites were constructed and adapted by early Portuguese and other European merchants from the fifteenth century onwards and have served commercial, religious, educational, political, and other functions.[11] But, in spite of the various heritages these castles embody, the administration converted them into monuments of the trans-Atlantic trade in enslaved people, reflecting the active roles they had played in the trade.[12] It targeted the castles at the global African community and placed them at the centre a 'Pan-African Historical Theatre Festival', dubbed PANAFEST, a biennial cultural event that is meant to bring together peoples of African descent, as prescribed by Pan-Africanism. Thus, the castles became attractions the PNDC utilised to court and develop its relations with diaspora Africans and Pan-Africanists in particular. The administration used the symbolism and heritage of the castles, as it defined these, alongside PANAFEST to lure increasing numbers of African American and other visitors to Ghana. Many people of African descent in the European and American diaspora responded positively and have visited the castles on pilgrimage, with some participating in naming and other ceremonies there.[13] Many of them have relocated to Ghana and formed organisations – such as the African American Association of Ghana, One Africa, Afrikan World Reparations, Repatriation and Truth Commission (AWRRTC) and Fihankra – and have championed and lobbied for the cause of Pan-Africanism and the interests of their members.

The PNDC administration's political and economic development programme was built upon by a National Democratic Congress (NDC) government, which in January 1993 began Ghana's fourth republic with Flight-Lieutenant Jerry John Rawlings as President. By successfully guiding Act 559 of 1998 through Parliament, this government restored the original name of the University of Science and Technology, 'Kwame Nkrumah University of Science and Technology'. It renamed the 'Sankara Circle' 'Sankara Interchange' after developing it into a multi-purpose traffic interchange in 1999, and fostered the Cape Coast and Elmina castles tourism programme. Diaspora African residents and visitors in Ghana continued to identify with the government's Pan-Africanist programme but used it to serve interests that were somewhat at variance

---

[11] See James Kwesi Anquandah, *Castles and Forts of Ghana* (Paris: Atalante, 1999); and van Dantzig, *Forts and Castles in Ghana*.

[12] On the commercial and other activities at the castles, see especially Christopher R. DeCorse, 'Culture Contact, Continuity and Change on the Gold Coast, AD 1400–1900', *The African Archaeological Review* 10 (1992): 163–96; and Christopher R. DeCorse, 'The Danes on the Gold Coast: Culture Change and the European Presence', *The African Archaeological Review* 11 (1993): 149–73.

[13] Naming ceremonies, indigenous music and dance performances, drama, and special prayer sessions are usually staged at the Cape Coast Castle by local and diaspora African groups, the most active of which has been One Africa (www.oneafricaghana.com).

with government's tourism development goals. For example, they exploited the castles' connection with the enslavement and trading of Africans to bargain not only for socio-political recognition in Ghana but also for power to redefine how the castles should function. Many of them contended that the castles were sacred sites for their spiritual development and self-realisation, and for reconnecting to Africa.[14] Such sentiments have been expressed in the following two comments among several recorded in the visitors' book of the Cape Coast Castle: 'This is not a tourist centre only but a place for African-Americans to reconnect with their past. It is a sacred place . . . ' (African-American, 8 January 2000); and 'This was the missing link of my struggle to find my ancestors' (African-American, 8 September 2000). Lobbying and advocacy by some of these 'Africans' for dual citizenship in Ghana culminated in the inclusion of Section 17 (3) in Ghana's Immigration Act, 2000 (Act 573).[15]

The diaspora Africans and other visitors to Ghana have also protested against differential fees at the castles. The Ghana Museums and Monuments Board, which manages the castles, charges foreigners higher entrance fees than Ghanaians pay, with the excuse that this generates additional income towards maintenance of the monuments. Protesters have argued that the higher fees alienated them from the castles and were marks of discrimination. They thus abhorred and strongly objected to the fees in verbal confrontations with castle officials and in written comments found in the Cape Coast Castle visitors' book, such as the following:

'This is a nice place but why do we foreigners have to pay more than Ghanaians if we do this in Europe, they (Ghanaians) call me a racist. Please do something about this form of discrimination' (Dutch, 25 December 1994).

'It is not right that me a slave descendant should have to pay money to see where my ancestors were captured' (African-American, 25 December 1994).

'Having to pay roughly 30 times the entrance fee Ghanaians pay for me is a reason not to visit the castle' (Unspecified visitor, 5 September 2000).

In addition to the above protests, the indigenous people of Cape Coast and Elmina have also felt aversion to entrance fees and security restrictions at the castles, which they consider as unfairly targeting them and inhibiting their patronage of the facilities. An inscription found at the entrance of the Elmina Castle, 'THIS AREA IS RESTRICTED TO ALL

---

[14] See Edward M. Bruner, 'Tourism in Ghana: the Representation of Slavery and the Return of the Black Diaspora', *American Anthropologist* 98, 2 (1996): 290–304 for insights into the activities various groups and organisations stage at the Cape Coast and Elmina castles to target African Americans in particular and to dramatise their perceptions of the sordidness of the trans-Atlantic slave trade.

[15] Section 17 (3) of Ghana Immigration Act 2000 (573) stipulates that 'A person of African descent in the Diaspora qualifies to be considered for the status of a right of abode [in Ghana]' if he meets specified conditions.

PERSONS EXCEPT TOURISTS', for example, implies that people could enter the castles only as tourists and after paying the appropriate fees. The management of the castles claimed protection of tourists from harassment by the local people, maintenance of a relatively clean environment around and within the castles, and income generation as key reasons for the restrictions.

The PNDC/NDC governments may have succeeded in branding and deploying the Elmina and Cape Coast castles to define heritages with which people of African descent and people moved by the waywardness of the enslavement and trading of Africans would identify. They may also have enlisted the monuments to sway Pan-Africanists and to generate revenue. However, government measures in turn provided, among Ghanaians of Elmina and Cape Coast and among diaspora Africans, a stimulus to assertions of belonging and dissent, especially from the tourism agenda, at the sites.

The NDC government not only used monuments to objectify Pan-Africanism, but also employed them to appeal to the indigenous Gã community of Accra, Ghana's capital city, as a means of building a wide support base. In 1997 it renamed the 'Kanda Overpass' in Accra after King Tackie Tawiah I, the twentieth king of the Gã state, to honour his achievements.[16] In June 2000 the government also 'cut the sod' at the Accra central business district for a statue of the king, although it failed to complete the construction before its rule was suspended at the end of that year. The renaming of the overpass after the king and the sod cutting for his statue were politically strategic. The Gã have been formidable and influential in Ghana's political arena and any Ghanaian government would wish to cultivate their support in order to win political elections in their constituencies.

Monuments and the Danquah-Busia Heritage

The PNDC/NDC governments' approaches to consolidating their support bases were disrupted in 2001 when the New Patriotic Party (NPP) – broadly aligned against the Nkrumaist political philosophy and the main opposition to the NDC – won the 2000 general elections and formed a government with John Agyekum Kufuor, who had served as a ministerial secretary in Dr Busia's government, as President. Like its predecessors, the NPP government also embarked on a programme of using monuments to distinguish itself and to demonstrate its resistance to the previous governments' affinity with Nkrumah and his Pan-Africanist

---

[16] King Tackie Tawiah, who assumed the high office of the Gã state in 1862, is known to have fervently sought and defended the interests of the Gã and their neighbours and led them to oppose colonial rule (www.j2nghana.com/kingtackie.html).

philosophies. Thus in 2005 it renamed the Sankara Interchange after Dr Ebenezer Ako Adjei, a founding member of the United Gold Coast Convention (UGCC). Then, as part of Ghana's Golden Jubilee celebrations, which climaxed on 7 March 2007, it refurbished the Obetsebi Lamptey and Danquah Circles, constructed several other monuments in Accra and elsewhere across Ghana to commemorate Dr Busia and other anti-Nkrumah personalities as founding fathers, and pointedly neglected the Kwame Nkrumah Circle. The NPP government also resisted endorsing the Christiansborg Castle as the seat of government, explaining that it had been associated with Ghana's colonial past and with the regime of Flight-Lieutenant Jerry Rawlings, which it despised. President Kufuor refused to relocate to the castle from his private residence and used it only for official assignments. In place of the castle, the government demolished Nkrumah's Flagstaff House residence and constructed on the site a multi-million-dollar presidential edifice it commissioned and named 'Golden Jubilee House' on 9 November 2008. The administration also completed and commissioned the statue of King Tackie Tawiah I, which the NDC government had failed to accomplish. Although this was to honour the king for his achievements, it enhanced the administration's stature among its Gã followers. Earlier, in 2006, a faction of the Gã royal family allegedly affiliated to and supported by the NPP had inaugurated a new king of the Gã state and named him King Tackie Tawiah III.

Restoration of Pro-Nkrumaist Schemes

The NDC returned to power in 2009 with Professor John Evans Atta Mills, who had been Vice-President in the Rawlings-led NDC government, as leader and President of the nation. The new NDC government proceeded to counter the NPP and exert its authority. It re-adopted the castle as presidential residence and maintained it as seat of government, although the NPP had called on the new President to relocate to the Golden Jubilee House, which was available. On 10 October 2010 the government replaced the name 'Golden Jubilee House' with 'Flagstaff House', explaining that the NPP government's naming of the building as 'Golden Jubilee House' was a ploy to 'obliterate the name of Kwame Nkrumah'.[17] It also refurbished and upgraded the Kwame Nkrumah Memorial Park, mounting side by side the headless and one-armed statue of Nkrumah and the head of the statue a private collector had returned to the government in 2009. The two constructions were intended to apprise

---

[17] Alex Segbefia, Deputy Chief of Staff of the NDC government, made these remarks, which were reported by Ghana webmail *General News* on 5 October 2010.

the public of the waywardness of the 1966 coup that ousted Nkrumah, and by implication the CPP government to which the NPP subscribes.

The above actions notwithstanding, President Atta Mills endeavoured to minimise discord between the NDC government and the NPP, its main opposition, by distinguishing himself as 'man of peace' and 'father for all', a tactical manoeuvre that won him admiration and support from a cross-section of Ghanaians. Among other gestures, he named after George Walker Bush, former President of the United States of America, the 14-kilometre N1 highway that was completed in Accra with funds the NPP administration had secured from the Millennium Challenge Account set up by the Bush administration in 2006. This gesture transformed the highway into a monument commemorating cordial relations between both main parties in Ghana and the United States of America.

In the wake of public debate on the appropriateness of the name, 'George Walker Bush Highway', former President Kufuor intimated that the name designation was in line with a promise he had made to President Bush when he visited Ghana in 2008, and an order he had given to that effect in recognition of President Bush's personal contribution to negotiations that yielded Ghana the funds for building the highway.[18] This claim notwithstanding, the Atta Mills government may have decided not to renege on the name in order to foster Ghana's relations with the United States of America and engender other fruitful overtures. President Kufuor's claims about the highway monument could be seen as an attempt to enhance his profile and that of the NPP opposition, while the NDC government may have wanted to place the national interest of Ghana above partisan political interests.

Hailed 'Asondweehene' (King of Peace) by his followers and foes amid contestation between the NPP and NDC over which of them was a violent party, President Atta Mills died on 24 July 2012. The NDC government hurriedly created a presidential mausoleum it named 'Asomdwee Park' (Peace Park), after President Mills's nickname, and buried him there on 10 August 2012. In honour and memory of the late President, the Accra Metropolitan Assembly renamed the Accra High Street 'John Evans Atta Mills High Street' and, in Cape Coast, the paramount chief named a major street in the town 'John Evans Atta Mills Street'. A newly built 'Millennium City School' in Accra was also renamed 'President John Evans Atta Mills Educational Centre of Excellence'. The mausoleum and other facilities that were named after the late President became

---

[18] Peace FM, an Accra-based radio station, broadcast President Kufuor's claims about discussions he had had with President George W. Bush when he visited Ghana about his intentions to name the N1 Highway after him, and an order he had given to that effect following President Bush's acquiescence – see <http://www.peacefmonline.com/politics/201202/95467.php>, accessed 12 June 2011.

monuments that endeared the government to a cross-section of mourners and sympathisers. The NDC capitalised on the euphoria about the monuments and the melancholy around the late President's demise, in addition to his peace making and other legacies, to campaign victoriously in the 2012 general elections. Another attempt by the Accra Metropolitan Assembly, following the elections, to rename after the late President the national hockey pitch in Accra – already named after Madam Theodosia Okoh, designer of Ghana's national flag – was resisted by the public, however, and failed to materialise when government intervened to halt the name change.

Monuments and Community Heritages

On many occasions Ghanaian communities contesting the hegemony of the nation state have also engaged monuments to define heritages that would project their eminence, as the cases discussed below illustrate. The chiefs and people of some communities in the (predominantly Ewe) Volta Region of Ghana had agitated for self-government and actively opposed the incorporation of their territory into Ghana immediately prior to and after the nation's independence.[19] A few recalcitrant leaders of the agitation became political prisoners under the Nkrumah regime and regained their freedom only after the regime was overthrown. As a result, many Ewe people celebrated General E. K. Kotoka, who was Ewe, as a hero for leading the 1966 coup that overthrew the regime. Following his death, the chiefs and people of the Ewe communities of Anlo and Gbi-Bla mounted statues in order to memorialise him in their communities and to signal their support for his action against the Nkrumah regime. Although the monuments were specific to the two communities, they denote Ewe anti-Nkrumah heritage in general.

The Asante kingdom is another entity that had opposed being subsumed under a unitary Ghanaian state over which Nkrumah and his government presided, and has in various ways entrenched its ethnic identity and heritage.[20] At the heart of this heritage is a 'golden stool' that Okomfo Anokye, a legendary priest of the indigenous religion and close friend of the king, Osei Tutu I, who had established the kingdom, allegedly

---

[19] See Edem Adotey, 'The Paradox of Colonialism', in Wazi Apoh and Bea Lundt (eds), *Germany and Its West African Colonies: Excavations of German Colonialism in Post-Colonial Times* (Berlin: Lit Verlag, 2013); and Kosi Kedem, *How Britain Subverted and Betrayed British Togoland* (Accra: Governance and Electoral Systems Agency, 2007).

[20] See Robert Sutherland Rattray, *Religion and Art in Ashanti* (Oxford: AMS Press, 1927), Malcolm D. McLeod, *The Asante* (London: British Museum Publications, 1981), and Ivor Wilks, *The Asante in the Nineteenth Century: the Structure and Evolution of a Political Order* (Cambridge: Cambridge University Press, 1975), which together provide vivid insights into aspects of Asante culture and history to which the people hold fast and guard as their heritage.

conjured as a symbol of Asante unity and invincibility. Agyeman Prempeh II, the Asante king who reigned from 1931 until his death in 1970, in consultation with government gave the name 'Okomfo Anokye Hospital' to the second-largest public hospital in Ghana, located in the Asante capital Kumasi. His immediate successor's administration mounted a statue of the priest holding a stool near the hospital to celebrate and memorialise him and his role in founding the Asante state. The 'golden stool', which the Asante revere and rarely reveal, as well as the statue and the hospital, are therefore monuments that express and perpetuate Asante cultural and political heritage within a national milieu in which the Asante have felt uncomfortable.

Competition for supremacy is common among paramilitary groups, locally referred to as '*Asafo* companies', in coastal communities of Accra and the Central Region of Ghana.[21] Rivalry among the groups relates usually to chieftaincy positions in the communities and occasionally escalates into conflict that draws the attention of public security services. European and African merchants on the Guinea Coast first established many of the *asafo* groups in the eighteenth century to protect their commercial interests and to defend loyal communities against intruders. Each of these groups is organised around a shrine building, *Pobusan*, which it has inherited from its forebears. The shrine, elaborately decorated with colours, images, and flags peculiar to the founders of a company, serves as a monument representing the company's heritage and acts as a spiritual nerve-centre that inspires the members and refreshes public knowledge of the company's prowess and fortitude. Such monumental shrines are regularly refurbished and maintained in communities where they are found, as *Asafo* companies continually compete among themselves.

Reflections

The discussion in this chapter has focused on the roles monuments have played in the definition of heritage at national and community levels in Ghana. It has attempted to show that governments and communities with varying political interests, aspirations, and motivations have deliberately engaged monuments to memorialise personalities, ideals, events, and actions. In this way they have distinguished essential components of their heritage as a means of cultivating public support in their bid to attain power and supremacy. Apart from structures that have been built to serve as monuments, physical constructions originally intended

---

[21] Nii-Adziri H. Wellington, *Stones Tell Stories at Osu: Memories of a Host Community of the Danish Trans-Atlantic Slave Trade* (Accra: Sub Saharan Publishers, 2011) provides narratives of how early paramilitary groups, *Asafo*, worked with Danish and local merchants to procure, store, and export human cargo, and to defend their superiors against rival groups.

to be utilitarian have also been transformed opportunely into memorabilia of the heritages of rival establishments. Thus the particular heritages
monuments have commemorated and propagated have been factional
and moot – and therefore susceptible to transformation within changing
contexts.[22] The Ghanaian situation is not unique and may be common
to other African nations and to the United States of America. It brings
into focus questions about who defines national heritage and the heritage
of communities within a nation, what kinds of heritages such agencies
define, and under what typical circumstances heritages are defined, contested, and redefined or (re)created.

The Ghanaian context suggests that the definition of national heritage
has been the preserve of agencies that have political power and ability,
including ruling governments and well-established traditional authorities. The subjective voices of these entities have been proclaimed publicly as national heritages to inspire the nation's citizenry in line with
the aspirations of the defining agencies. Heritages, so defined, have per-
tained to identities through which governments have sought to set the
nation apart from its colonial past; and also to identities, political ideals,
and aspirations that polities inherited by the nation from its colonial
past have sought to uphold. The CPP government and subsequent governments that Nkrumah inspired affiliated with Nkrumah and his Pan-
Africanist and other ideals to define a national heritage that has been
skewed towards his image, vision, and activities. Other governments
opposed to Nkrumah and his ideals made efforts to obliterate the Nkrumaist heritage but failed to deviate from the CPP's approach to defining
heritage by having recourse to images of their own favourite personalities.

The discussion suggests that heritages are defined, refined, or redefined
when ruling authorities are actively opposed and, as a consequence,
wish to strengthen their positions of power. The heritages defined under
such circumstances, and the monuments utilised to convey them, assume
national character when they evoke the collective memories and interests
of a cross-section of Ghanaians, or are able to withstand regime change
and contestation. Monuments that portray national heritage are important bases for public assessment of government's performance; their neglect could publicly indict a government for being insensitive to the
national interest, while proper management of them may enhance the

---

[22] On the malleability of meanings material objects convey, and how these meanings transform in relation to changing conditions and circumstances, see Carl R. Lounsbury,
'Architectural and Cultural History', in Dan Hicks and Mary C. Beaudry (eds), *The
Oxford Handbook of Material Culture Studies* (Oxford and New York, NY: Oxford University Press, 2010), 484–501; and Arjun Appadurai, 'Introduction: Commodities and
the Politics of Value' in Arjun Appadurai (ed.), *The Social Life of Things: Commodities in
Cultural Perspective* (Cambridge: Cambridge University Press, 1986), 3–63.

government's public image. It is in this light that 'Independence Square', 'Kwame Nkrumah Memorial Park', and the Cape Coast and Elmina castles, for example, have not been renamed, nor deliberately neglected, by any government of Ghana. On the contrary, heritages that are overly factional, and monuments that express them, are controversial and ephemeral; they may risk public resistance and eventual rejection, as the cases of Nkrumah's pre-1966 statues and the abortive renaming of the Accra hockey pitch illustrate.

I would posit, therefore, that except those which clearly define national interests, heritages created and recreated at national and community levels in Ghana, South Africa, and other African nations would remain relative, irrespective of the medium through which they are expressed, as the interests, aspirations, and motivations of communities and polities that comprise the nations vary in relation to pre-colonial, colonial and post-colonial political and socio-economic influences. There would be convergence of thought among contesting parties only when heritages mutually benefit them. There seems to have been consensus among the different parties and interests contesting political power in Ghana about the monumental status of the Cape Coast and Elmina castles, Christiansborg Castle, Flagstaff House, and the George Walker Bush Highway, for example, because the parties and interests, irrespective of their philosophical differences, can make capital out of the heritages these facilities symbolise.

6   Of Chiefs, Tourists, and Culture

Heritage Production in Contemporary Ghana

Raymond Silverman

Many people travelling by road to the northern parts of Ghana pass through the community of Manso, located 17 kilometres north-east of Techiman. Today, Manso is a modest village of roughly 3,000 people.[1] It is a community that one could easily drive through without noticing anything exceptional if it were not for a couple of road signs suggesting that Manso is a special place. One sign, now heavily weathered, reads 'Bono Manso, The Capital of Ancient Bono Kingdom and Historic Slave Market', the other signals that Manso is the site of the 'Martin Luther King Jr Village' (Figure 6.1).[2] Ten years ago, neither of these signs existed. Their presence is associated with a number of related projects that have been pursued at Manso over the last decade, an attempt to establish this small rural community as a site of commemoration associated with local and global heritage traditions.

Manso is the site of the capital of the ancient Bono state commonly referred to as Bono Manso, believed to have been founded in the thirteenth or fourteenth century and to have been a significant political presence in the region until the early eighteenth century, when it was conquered by the Asante nation.[3] Despite the site's considerable historical significance, it has received little attention from historians and archaeologists. Recently, Manso's importance was augmented with its identification as the site of a major slave market associated with the Atlantic slave trade. Manso is a place with many histories, some of them

---

[1] The 2000 Ghana Census records 2,780 people living in Manso. Ghana Statistical Service, *2000 Population and Housing Census: Special Reports on 20 Largest Localities* (Accra: Ghana Statistical Service, 2002), 58.

[2] The full text of the second sign reads, 'Dr Martin Luther King Jr Village (1929–1968), A Pivotal Figure in African American Civil Right [sic] Movement, "non-violence is the way of life," Centre for Savana Art and Civilization.'

[3] Bono Manso, the name encountered in the literature to denote the capital of the ancient state of Bono, is also used to signify the state itself. The state might more accurately be referred to as Bonoman (lit. the Bono state or nation). The name Bono Manso may be glossed as, literally, 'place of the Bono state' or 'the place at which the Bono state is located'. In this essay, I shall use the term 'Bono Manso' to signify the ancient Bono state, and 'Manso' for the contemporary community that rests upon the ruins of the abandoned capital of Bono Manso.

Figure 6.1. Roadside sign for the Martin Luther King Jr Village, Manso, Brong Ahafo. Photo: Raymond Silverman, October 2008.

grounded in well-established local traditions, while others are constructions derived from recently resuscitated or invented traditions.

At the heart of this essay is a story that begins in 2001 in Manso. Here chiefs have been integral to the transformation of this small rural community into an international tourist destination associated with remembering the Atlantic slave trade and celebrating the contributions of pivotal figures in the African diaspora. The story offers a compelling example of how heritage works in contemporary Ghana and the important role that chiefs play in this process.

The essay begins with a recounting of the various strategies that have been pursued by a diverse group of actors – chiefs, members of Ghana's repatriate community, heritage tourism professionals, representatives of the Ministry of Tourism (formerly the Ministry of Tourism and Diasporan Relations), and tourists – to transform Manso into a commemorative site and tourist destination. This is followed by a consideration of the role that chiefs have played in this process. My particular interest in what has been going on in Manso and in other places in Ghana concerns the considerable costs associated with the presentation and marketing of tangible and intangible 'objects of heritage', specifically the costs associated with the consumption of irreplaceable fragments of the past – here I am referring to the archaeological record and to radical revisions of local histories. My argument is primarily directed at Ghana's chiefs, who actively participate in the country's development efforts and who have been charged with exploiting their unique position in Ghanaian society to conserve the nation's distinctive cultural traditions.[4]

Of Chiefs, Tourists, and Culture: Memorialising Diaspora in a Ghanaian Village

In 2001, I returned to the town of Techiman in central Ghana where I had lived twenty years earlier while pursuing research for my PhD dissertation.[5] I had not been to Techiman since 1988. One of the people I met was Nana Emmanuel Asare, the Techiman Adontenhene, a high-ranking chief in Techiman's traditional political structure.[6] Like many of today's chiefs, Nana Asare is university-educated. He has earned diplomas in community development and social administration, a Bachelor's degree in psychology and sociology, and, in 2007, a postgraduate diploma in museum and heritage studies from the African Programme in Museum and Heritage Studies in Cape Town, South Africa. He is dedicated to his community and actively involved in a host of development projects directed at improving the lives of Techiman's citizens.

Part of my agenda for the 2001 visit to Techiman was to return to some of the sites at which I had conducted research twenty years earlier. Nana Asare has a keen interest in local history and accompanied me on a number of trips to villages around Techiman, one of which was Manso. As mentioned above, Manso is of considerable historical importance as the site of the capital of the earliest Akan centralised state, Bono Manso. In its heyday, during the sixteenth century, 10,000 people are believed to have lived in the capital, which covered roughly 2.3 square kilometres.[7] After it was conquered in the early eighteenth century by Asante, Manso was abandoned and the capital later relocated to Techiman – the chiefs of Techiman are the descendants of Bono Manso's leaders. However, despite its import, only a single scholar, the archaeologist Emmanuel Kwaku Effah-Gyamfi, has studied Manso in any depth. In the 1970s he collected oral histories and excavated at a number of sites associated with the ancient state. Significantly, though Nana Asare had visited Manso to attend funerals, he had never spoken with any of the chiefs or elders of

---

[4] I would like to express my gratitude to Nana Emmanuel Asare for sharing his thoughts about the heritage project at Manso and for his comments on an earlier draft of this essay. I also wish to thank Professor Kwesi Yankah for his careful reading of the essay.

[5] The following is a brief chronicle of the heritage project at Manso constructed from articles appearing in the Ghanaian news media over the last eight years, as well as from an informal account, 'Recounting the Memorial Gardens at Manso', written in 2008 by Nana Emmanuel Asare, the chief responsible for initiating the Manso heritage project.

[6] His stool name is Nana Baffour Asare Twi Brempong II; in this essay I shall refer to him as Nana Asare.

[7] Emmanuel K. Effah-Gyamfi, *Bono Manso: An Archaeological Investigation into Early Akan Urbanism* (Calgary: The University of Calgary Press, 1985), 29, 213.

Manso regarding its considerable historical importance for the Techiman Bono.[8]

A few weeks later, I left Techiman, and did not return until 2005. Soon after I left, Nana Asare visited Nana Kwabena Mensah, the chief shrine priest of the Techiman Bono state. In the course of their conversation, Nana Asare spoke about our visit to Manso, and Nana Kwabena Mensah commented on the significance of the site as Techiman's ancestral capital, offering some additional information about the ancient capital:

These days, who would dare to say that someone is the descendant of a slave. There is a big baobab tree that stands a little ways from the community. According to my ancestors, the site of the tree was located in front of the Bono King's palace. During the days of the slave trade, captured slaves who were on their journey to the coast used the place as a stopover to rest. At times the weaker ones who were considered unhealthy to continue the journey were left in the community. Some of them survived and their descendants still live in the community. For the sake of social cohesion you cannot say certain things that might denigrate members in society.[9]

Nana Asare, thinking about Techiman's interest in participating in Ghana's heritage tourist market, saw an opportunity. He returned to Manso to corroborate the information about the slave trade and the baobab. He spoke with many people; most of them denied knowing anything about slavery in ancient Bono Manso. However, one elderly man mentioned that he had heard the story of 'slave raiders' passing through Manso on their way to the coast.[10] When Nana Asare asked about the baobab, he was directed to a large tree located roughly half a kilometre north-west of the village, as well as to two sites that Effah-Gyamfi had excavated near the tree. Nana Asare then approached the village chief to inquire about developing the baobab site as a tourist attraction, a site of memory and commemoration. The Techiman Tourist Centre, which had been founded in 2000, in collaboration with the Regional Tourist Board, began to seek Manso's recognition by the architects of Ghana's Slave Route Project, part of the international Slave Route Project organised and funded by UNESCO.[11] Since the early 1990s and the rise

---

[8] During the 2001 trip, as well as several subsequent trips to Techiman, I learned that virtually none of Techiman's current chiefs had visited the sites associated with the ancient Bono state, places such as Manso, Amowi, Pinihi, and Yefri. This is due in part to the political geography of the area; these sites are now located in the Nkoranza Traditional Area, not Techiman.

[9] Asare, 'Recounting the Memorial Gardens'.

[10] Ibid.

[11] For an overview of the UNESCO Slave Route Project and its implications for Ghana's project see Katrina Schramm, 'Slave Route Projects: Tracing the Heritage of Slavery in Ghana', in Ferdinand de Jong and Michael Rowlands (eds), *Reclaiming Heritage: Alternative Imaginaries of Memory in West Africa* (Walnut Creek, CA: Left Coast Press, 2007), 77–80. See the UNESCO website devoted to the project, <http://www.unesco.org/new/en/culture/themes/dialogue/the-slave-route>, accessed 7 June 2011.

of heritage tourism in Ghana, numerous sites of memory have been developed as nodes in what has become a pilgrimage route associated with remembering slavery in Ghana.[12]

Nana Asare recalls various impediments to the initiative, perhaps the most significant being the long history of enmity between Techiman and its neighbour Nkoranza. Despite its historical ties with Techiman, since the early eighteenth century Manso has been situated within the borders of the Nkoranza Traditional Area. Most of the core communities associated with the ancient Bono state were given to the chief of Nkoranza after Bono's defeat in the Bono–Asante war of 1722–3. Nana Asare and the Techiman Tourist Centre's initiative in Manso was perceived as a threat to Nkoranza authority, and the people of Manso were unable to obtain the support of the Nkoranzahene, the paramount chief of the Nkoranza state.

In early 2003, Nana Asare met Felicia Obuobie, Executive Director of the Centre for Savana Art and Civilisation (now the Centre for African Art and Civilisation), an NGO that works closely with the Ministry of Tourism, the Ghana Tourist Board, and the repatriate community in Ghana. She has played an important role in realising the Slave Route Project and in organising Panafest and Emancipation Day events, as well as celebrations associated with Black History Month in Ghana.[13] The Manso initiative was similar to projects in which Ms Obuobie had been involved in other parts of Ghana, so she welcomed the opportunity to assist. She was perceived as a neutral party and her intervention eventually cleared the air and the way for the project to proceed. Later that year, in time for Panafest and Emancipation Day, a monument of concrete was placed at the baobab with an inscription that formally implicates the Bono state in the trafficking of slaves destined for the Americas and establishes the tree as a site of memory commemorating the Atlantic slave trade (Figure 6.2). The inscription reads:

IN HONOUR OF THE MEMORY OF OUR ANCESTORS
Bono Manso marks the site where captured African Ancestors were first
   chained for onward enslavement in the North Atlantic Slave Trade.
Bono Manso, Brong Ahafo Region Ghana.
REMEMBERED THIS DAY 23RD. JULY, 2003

---

[12] Much has been written on this new tradition. See for example the *Guidebook to the Major Pilgrimage Routes in Ghana*, published by the Ghana Ministry of Tourism and Diasporan Relations in 2008. There are a good number of scholarly critiques of the tradition, among them Schramm, 'Slave Routes Project'. See Minkley and Mnyaka as well as Gavua in this volume for discussions concerning the social and political implications of memorial projects.

[13] Panafest is the biennial Pan African Festival of Performing Arts, first organised in 1992. Emancipation Day is an annual event held in late July or early August that originated in the Caribbean to commemorate the abolition of the Atlantic slave trade. Similarly, Black History Month, celebrated in February, is borrowed from the United States.

Figure 6.2. Monument marking the site of the 'ancient slave market' and commemorating the Atlantic slave trade, Manso, Brong Ahafo. Photo: Raymond Silverman, June 2009.

CENTRE FOR SAVANA ART AND CIVILISATION
PANAFEST/EMANCIPATION 2003
This monument was unveiled by:
Mr. Kohain Nathanyah Halevi Rabbi – Panafest/Emancipation
Assisted by:
Katakyie Agyeman Kodom IV – Omanhene Nkoranza Trad. Area.
Osabarima Dotobibi Takyia Ameyaw II – Omanhene Techiman Traditional
Area.

An unveiling ceremony was held on 23 July, presided over by Kohain
Nathanyah Halevi, Executive Secretary of the Panafest Foundation and
a leader in Ghana's repatriate community, and the paramount chiefs of
the Nkoranza and Techiman Traditional Areas.

Later that year, Felicia Obuobie asked the leaders of Manso and the
Nkoranza Traditional Area for land in Manso to create a memorial garden
dedicated to Dr Martin Luther King Jr. On 13 January 2004, Nana Okofo
Agyapong III, Adontenhene of Nkoranza, announced that the Nkoranza Traditional Council would donate two hectares of land for the
establishment of a 'village' in honour of Dr King.[14] On 16 January, a
durbar (a festival presided over by chiefs) organised and sponsored by
the Centre for Savana Art and Civilisation was held in Manso to celebrate the seventy-fifth birthday of Dr King.[15] A bronze bust of the civil
rights leader was commissioned and installed, and on 24 July 2004 it
was unveiled at a ceremony attended by Ghana's Minister of Tourism
and Diasporan Relations, Jake Obetsebi Lamptey (Figure 6.3). There
was a large turnout of local residents as well as members of the repatriate community and tourists who had travelled to Manso from the coast.
A number of speeches were delivered addressing the slave trade in the
Gold Coast as well as the life and legacy of Dr King. This was the first
of several memorial gardens established at Manso to commemorate key
figures in the twentieth-century black struggle for freedom and equality
in the US and Caribbean.

Dr King's seventy-sixth birthday was remembered in January 2005 at
another durbar in Manso organised by Felicia Obuobie and presided
over by Nana Okofo Agyapong III. In his speech, the chief urged
those in attendance to 'take good care of the Village to boost its tourist attraction'.[16] Over the course of the following year, members of
the Caribbean and Muslim repatriate communities working with and
through Ms Obuobie sought to establish separate memorial gardens to

---

[14] <http://pub10.bravenet.com/forum/852978379/fetch/233603>, accessed 1 August 2005.
[15] <http://www.ghanaweb.com/GhanaHomePage/economy/artikel.php?ID=50011>,
accessed 1 August 2005.
[16] <http://www.modernghana.com/news/70423/1/centre-celebrates-martin-luther-kings-
birthday.html>, accessed 1 August 2005.

Figure 6.3. Monument to Martin Luther King Jr, centre, with flanking monuments (covered in cloth) to Coretta Scott King and Rosa Parks. Manso, Brong Ahafo. Photo: Raymond Silverman, October 2008.

commemorate Marcus Garvey and Malcolm X. She once again negotiated with the leaders in Manso and Nkoranza, and in 2005 a memorial was erected to Marcus Garvey; the following year, across the road, a monument to Malcolm X was completed. At the July 2007 Emancipation Day/Panafest ceremonies in Manso, two more monuments flanking Dr Martin Luther King's monument, one dedicated to Rosa Parks and the other to Coretta Scott King, were unveiled by Pamela E. Bridgewater, the then US Ambassador to Ghana, in association with the Ministry of Tourism and Diasporan Relations' Joseph Project, an initiative designed to encourage Africans in the diaspora to return to Ghana.[17]

In January 2008, a ceremony celebrating the birthday of Dr King was held at Manso, organised by Felicia Obuobie. And a few months later, on 30 April, Ambassador Bridgewater returned to Manso to unveil a plaque commemorating the 40th anniversary of the civil rights leader's death.[18] The paramount chiefs of Techiman and Nkoranza, as well as a good number of district chiefs and regional and local government officials, were in attendance at the ceremony.

Further engagement with the repatriate community has involved the enstoolment of Mahar Cooke, the son of Ambassador Dr Erieka Bennett,

---

[17] For a discussion of the Joseph Project see Schramm, 'Slave Routes Project', 80–90.
[18] Personal communication, Nana Asare, 2 November 2011.

the Convening Founder and Head of Mission of the African Union's Diaspora African Forum. Cooke was enstooled as the Nkosuohene of Manso in 2008 and given the stool name Nana Kweku Brempong Katakyira II after one of the kings of ancient Bono Manso. The *nkosuo* stool, commonly referred to as the 'development' stool, is often occupied by foreigners. It is a recent invention created in the mid-1980s as a strategy for stimulating economic development in Ghanaian communities.[19] References to Nana Kweku Brempong Katakyira II on the Internet refer to him not as the Nkosuohene but as Bono Manso's 'Diaspora Chief'.[20]

That same year, the Universal Negro Improvement Association and African Communities League (UNIA and ACL) High Commissioner, Nana Kwabena Prempeh, reported in a newspaper article that

On Sunday August 17th, 2008 the UNIA and ACL in conjunction with the Caribbean Association and the Rastafarian Association along with the African American Association of Ghana – will have a 'Great Garvey Day' celebration at [sic] Bono Manso site. At that time we will raise the 'Red, Black, and Green' flag of the UNIA and the Ghanaian national flag with the Black Star of Garvey, since this is the only site in Ghana with a monument to the Rt Excellent Marcus Garvey.[21]

He also spoke of plans to build a museum, library, gift shop, and restaurant at the site, and to erect monuments to Amy Ashwood Garvey and Amy Jacques Garvey, Marcus Garvey's first and second wives.[22]

The Krontihene of Manso, Nana Asante Nyarko, possesses considerable knowledge of the history of Bono Manso as well as an understanding of the heritage work that has been going on in Manso over the last ten years. He believes that remembering slavery and the slave trade is important, and that remembering slavery in the context of heritage tourism and engaging Ghana's repatriate community will potentially benefit Manso. But, so far, Manso has not seen much of a return on its investment in this project.[23]

---

[19] There have been a number of analyses of this recent tradition, for example George M. Bob-Milliar, 'Chieftaincy, Diaspora, and Development: The Institution of Nkosuohene in Ghana', *African Affairs* 108, 433 (2009); Susan Benson, 'Connecting with the Past, Building the Future: African Americans and Chieftaincy in Southern Ghana', *Ghana Studies* 6 (2003): 109–33.

[20] For instance, see the 2009 annual report of the AU Diaspora African Forum at <http://diasporaafricanforum.webscom/annualreport.htm>, accessed 20 March 2011. The Manso Krontihene, Nana Asante Nyarko, indicated that Kohain Nathanyah Halevi, mentioned above, had been enstooled as Manso's 'Diasporahene'. Interview, Nana Asante Nyarko, 23 June 2011.

[21] Originally published in *The Negro World* 43 (29 June 2008), <http://www.angelfire.com/electronic/negroworld/>, accessed 20 March 2011.

[22] Ibid. The Universal Negro Improvement Association and African Communities League is a black nationalist fraternal organisation founded by Marcus Garvey in the late 1920s.

[23] Interview, Nana Asante Nyarko, 23 June 2011.

New freshwater wells and a school have been promised but so far the village has seen neither. The first sign of assistance appeared in 2011 when a water storage tank was donated to the community by the AU Diaspora African Forum in the name of Nana Kweku Brempong Katakyira II. Throughout Ghana, communities like Manso see tourism as a panacea – if tourists come, they will bring money.[24] In Manso, visitors come for Emancipation Day/Panafest festivities; they come to remember those who made the Middle Passage and to celebrate the lives of the 'diasporans' who are commemorated at Manso. A few people who make the slave route pilgrimage on their own occasionally visit. But, to date, Manso has not seen many visitors.[25] Even with the road signs mentioned at the beginning of this essay, few people stop to visit the King, Garvey, and Malcolm X memorial gardens, and there is little interest in experiencing the site of the capital of the earliest Akan state.[26] When people visit, they usually stay for one to three hours, before moving on to their next destination. They spend very little, if any, money in the community.[27]

In 2008, the following description of Manso appeared in a *Guidebook to the Major Pilgrimage Routes in Ghana*, published in conjunction with the National Slave Routes Project by the Ministry of Tourism and Diasporan Relations:

Bono Manso is one of the oldest continuously inhabited settlements in Ghana. Archaeological digs have shown that the old town was one mile square during the 14th century, rivalling Kumasi in size. The town was an important textile, mining, and trading centre. Slave trading started in this village in the 16th century. It is the most centrally located slave market in the country.

The ancient slave market was centred at a giant Baobab tree to the west of the town. This tree was the resting point for slaves and their masters. This was one of the oldest slave transition points in the Gold Coast and existed before the town of Hani Badu was founded. Slaves were brought in from the north through Salaga, Kintampo, and beyond. It is alleged there are still descendants of these slaves at Bono Manso but it is a taboo to call a person 'slave' in these parts.

Bono Manso was the seat of the Bono kingdom which includes Techiman and Nkoranza. If Assin Manso in the Central region was the last slave post, Bono Manso was its largest supply source for slaves. Most of the elderly remember the

24 Alexander Yao Segbefia, for example, suggests that community-based tourism offers a viable 'poverty reduction strategy'. Alexander Yao Segbefia, 'Community Approach to Tourism Development in Ghana', in Oheneba Akyeampong and Alex Boakye Asiedu (eds), *Tourism in Ghana: A Modern Synthesis* (Accra: Assemblies of God Literature Centre Ltd, 2008), 64–6.

25 Nana Asante Nyarko, who often serves as a guide to visitors at Manso, indicated that roughly 100 people have been coming to Manso annually. Interview, 23 June 2011.

26 It seems that Manso may not yet be on the 'tourist map'. The fifth edition of the popular Bradt guide, *Ghana*, published in 2010, makes no reference to Manso. Philip Briggs, *Ghana*, 5th edn (Chalfont St Peter: Bradt Travel Guides, 2010).

27 Interview, Nana Asante Nyarko, 23 June 2011.

role Bono Manso played in the slave trade. The chiefs and community want to immortalise the memory and remains of the slave market story with the present-ation of male and female bones excavated in 1974 at the Dwisabirim tree.[28]

The fragment of evidence that sparked the developments at Manso in 2001 was greatly elaborated – to describe Bono Manso as 'the largest supply source for slaves' borders on the absurd.

It is beyond the scope of this essay to critique the evidence for Bono Manso's involvement in the Atlantic slave trade. Suffice it to point out that no one so far has critically examined the evidence of slavery in the ancient Bono state, nor specifically at the site of its capital. Effah-Gyamfi's archaeological and ethno-historical work is often cited as providing evid-ence of the slave trade at Bono Manso, yet nowhere in his published or unpublished writing does he mention a slave market at Manso; in fact, he has very little to say about slavery in the ancient Bono state. Recent popular accounts, such as the one cited above, reference Effah-Gyamfi's 1974 discovery of the remains of a male and female slave. Effah-Gyamfi did not carry out excavations in 1974. Nor did he excavate male and female bones at the site of the baobab. Effah-Gyamfi did report that his excavations at Manso in 1973 and 1976 produced the remains of three female adults and an infant, but he makes no reference to any of them being slaves.[29]

The assertion that Bono Manso was a major slave market has made its way into scholarly writing. Recently, Ghanaian historian Akosua Adoma Perbi wrote in her book, *A History of Indigenous Slavery in Ghana from the 15th to the 19th Century*, that Bono Manso was 'involved in slave trading, slave owning and slave dealing'.[30] She offers no source for this statement. In fact, the scholarship that has examined the Middle Passage suggests that it is unlikely that Bono Manso played a noteworthy role in the Atlantic slave trade. Commercial documents indicate that between the fifteenth and the seventeenth centuries gold was the focus of trade on the Gold Coast, and that slaves being transported to the south by Dyula merchants may have passed through Manso, but they were not destined for the Atlantic slave trade. They were purchased in the south to support the local gold mining industry. Documents from this period reveal that slaves from other parts of West Africa were in fact being

[28] Ghana Ministry of Tourism, *Guidebook to the Major Pilgrimage Routes*, 9.

[29] Emmanuel K. Effah-Gyamfi, 'Bono-Manso: An Archaeological Investigation into Early Akan Urbanism' (PhD thesis, University of Ghana, 1978), 146–51; Effah-Gyamfi, *Bono Manso*, 65–7. See Rassool in this volume for a discussion of the use of human remains in memorial strategies in South Africa.

[30] Akosua Adoma Perbi, *A History of Indigenous Slavery in Ghana from the 15th to the 19th Century* (Legon: Sub-Saharan Publishers, 2004), 20. Perbi indicates that Bono Manso was situated on one of the major routes associated with the slave trade, specifically the one that brought slaves from north-west (Wa, Bole, and Banda) to Asante, and ultimately to the coast. Ibid., Map 3, 40.

imported on the Gold Coast to work in the Akan goldfields.[31] It was not until the late seventeenth century that slaves began to be exported from the Gold Coast – it was at this time that those polities involved in the trafficking of human beings became involved in the Atlantic slave trade. Since the state of Bono Manso was conquered by Asante in the early eighteenth century and Manso no longer functioned as its capital, it is unlikely that the ancient Bono state played a conspicuous role in the Atlantic slave trade – there simply is no evidence to support the claim that Manso was the 'largest supply source for slaves'.

That said, it is possible that there *may* have been a slave market associated with Bono Manso, though it is unlikely that it would have been situated in the capital. Oral traditions collected by Effah-Gyamfi and the archaeological excavations of James Anquandah indicate that the market associated with the ancient Bono state was located 17 kilometres southwest of Manso, near the current city of Techiman.[32] If, as alluded to in Nana Kwabena Mensah's 2001 observation cited above, the Bono king's palace was situated near the baobab that now serves as a site of commemoration, it is highly unlikely that there would have been a slave market in front of it. But it is possible that after the fall of Bono Manso in the early eighteenth century, the site of the baobab may have been a resting spot for slaves being taken to the coast. And though Effah-Gyamfi does not report on any material evidence of slavery, this does not mean the institution did not exist in Bono Manso. As Nana Kwabena Mensah suggested, slavery is not a topic that people speak about openly. Indeed, it has been only recently, with the growth of a heritage tourist industry built on remembering and commemorating the history of slavery in Ghana, that the subject has emerged as a common theme in public discourse.

It may seem as though I am contradicting myself. I am not. Since there is considerable indirect evidence for slavery in this part of Africa during the time of Bono Manso it is quite likely that the state was involved in the trafficking of human beings, either importing them to work in gold-mining operations or exporting them to work in gold fields to the south. The point I wish to make is that there is little if any evidence that implicates Bono Manso in the Atlantic slave trade.

---

[31] A number of scholars writing on Gold Coast trade during this period have made this observation. See, for example, Christopher R. DeCorse, 'Introduction', in Christopher R. DeCorse (ed.), *West Africa During the Atlantic Slave Trade* (London: Leicester University Press, 2001), 7; Ray A. Kea, *Settlements, Trade, and Polities in the Seventeenth-Century Gold Coast* (Baltimore, MA: Johns Hopkins University Press, 1982), 197–201; Ivor Wilks, 'The State of the Akan and the Akan States: A Discursion', *Cahiers d'Études Africaines* 22, 3–4 (1982): 231–49.

[32] Emmanuel K. Effah-Gyamfi, 'Oral Traditions and Archaeology: A Case Study of the Bono State' (MA thesis, University of Ghana, 1974), 91; James Anquandah, 'An Archaeological Survey of the Takyiman-Wenchi Area', in Jack Goody and Kwame Arhin (eds), *Ashanti and the Northwest* (Legon: Institute of African Studies, University of Ghana, 1965), 116.

Nana Asare, the Techiman chief responsible for launching the Manso initiative, has expressed concern about the revision of history that has occurred at Manso – he wonders when and how the site was transformed from a resting place along a slave route to a market 'where people were captured and sold into slavery in ancient Bono Manso'.[33] He notes that what has happened at Manso has led to 'history being distorted and forgotten'.[34] Through a process of conflation and inflation, a single fragment of evidence has been used to rationalise a heritage project that has little to do with the local community but instead involves the producers and consumers of a heritage commodity.

Though there are nominal references to the ancient Bono kingdom in narratives offered to Manso visitors, most of that history has been eclipsed by accounts of the slave trade and new traditions commemorating the lives of key figures in the African diaspora. In effect, Ghanaians involved in the tourist industry and the repatriate community have appropriated the site. But in Nana Asare's words, 'The move to create a vibrant tourist industry should not undermine the historic narrative of the Bono kingdom and the cultural heritage of the people.'[35]

Historical traditions associated with ancient Bono Manso and those associated with slavery are not necessarily competing narratives. Indeed, they are part of a larger metanarrative. The crux of the issue concerns which narratives are foregrounded and what becomes of those that are suppressed.

This is a situation not unlike initiatives being pursued in other parts of Ghana. Various authors have critiqued what is happening at sites that, like Manso, are spaces where various narratives, some well established, others recently invented, converge and compete. Indeed, since Edward Bruner's seminal 1996 essay, 'Tourism in Ghana: The Representation of Slavery and the Return of the Black Diaspora', heritage tourism in Ghana has received considerable attention from scholars.[36] Much of this work has considered the contested nature of producing and performing heritage in Ghana, reconciling new global narratives with long-standing local traditions. These 'heritage wars' or conflicts between constituencies with discordant agendas have been situated, for the most part, on or near the coast at well-known historical sites such as Cape Coast Castle and São Jorge da Mina Castle at Elmina, and at recently established sites of memory such as Assin Manso and Assin Praso.

Today, precedence is given to remembering the Atlantic slave trade and the desire on the part of Ghanaians to welcome Africans in the diaspora,

---

[33] Asare, 'Recounting the Memorial Gardens'.
[34] Personal communication, Nana Emmanuel Asare, 2 November 2011.
[35] Asare, 'Recounting the Memorial Gardens'.
[36] The most comprehensive writing on the subject to date is the recent book by Katharina Schramm, *African Homecoming: Pan-African Ideology and Contested Heritage* (Walnut Creek, CA: Left Coast Press, 2010).

especially those who are descendants of former slaves, back to Africa, to reconcile 'difficult histories' and to invite them to play an active role in Ghana's future. The heritage narratives that are being forged in this context involve revisions to Ghana's remembered past to accommodate the remembered pasts of people who are either visiting Ghana or who have joined Ghanaian society as repatriates. The rhetoric surrounding this rewriting focuses not so much on the *invention* of new traditions, but on *remembering* forgotten or suppressed memories. However, there is ample evidence that many of the local traditions that have recently resurfaced as part of the slave trade metanarrative are in fact invented.[37] The individuals and groups who are participating in these debates are grappling with a now familiar question centred on the notion of culture as heritage, *who in fact owns the past?*[38]

As we have seen at Manso, this is a dynamic process that engages actors representing a number of interests, including tourists, primarily Africans in the diaspora, members of Ghana's repatriate community, representatives of the tourist industry, including the Ministry of Tourism, and chiefs. Recognised as the country's custodians of culture, chiefs are participating in the production of heritage that is developed for and consumed by tourists.

Chiefs and the Future of Ghana's Past

Today, chiefs, the traditional leaders of the communities that comprise the country's citizenry, possess a rather ambivalent status in Ghana – they are at one and the same time respected bastions of core social values and advocates for development, but they also are seen as impediments to the nation's progress. Ghana, like many modern nations that continue to support pre-democratic political structures (such as monarchies), has created a system that recognises the benefits of supporting traditional leaders, but it also struggles with the tensions that emerge from an institution that is slowly evolving so that it might effectively function in a democracy.

Chiefs continue to play a significant role in the communities over which they preside, particularly outside Ghana's large urban centres. In this short essay it is not possible to offer a comprehensive overview of the institution of chieftaincy in Ghana today. A good deal has been

---

[37] An example of this is presented in Benson and McCaskie's critique of recent events at Assin Praso, a site of remembrance modelled after Assin Manso, a major tourist site developed by chiefs and the Ministry of Tourism and Diasporan Relations. Susan Benson and T. C. McCaskie, 'Asen Praso in History and Memory', *Ghana Studies* 7 (2004), 93–113.

[38] Variations of this question have been posed using the terms 'heritage', 'history', and 'culture'.

written on the subject, especially in the last ten years.[39] My intention here is to focus on two of their most important roles – as proponents of economic and social development and as custodians of culture. In many communities, as we have observed at Manso, it is possible to see chiefs attempting to bridge these two arenas in efforts to exploit local culture as a commodity that can be marketed to yield economic and social benefits for the community.

Perhaps more than any other African nation, Ghana is devoted to and invested in its chiefs. The country's constitution recognises and guarantees the institution of chieftaincy, but sentiments regarding the institution are mixed. Donald Ray points out that the

simultaneous existence of loyalties for many Ghanaians by being both citizens of the state and subjects of the chief reflects the political realities of the Ghanaian state. Ghana is not just a state but a post-colonial state containing political structures known as chieftaincies that are rooted in the period of pre-colonial states and other polities.[40]

Despite the constitution's recognition, there are many who see chieftaincy as an anachronistic institution.[41] But most Ghanaians believe that chieftaincy is still of considerable relevance, that chiefs play an important social role in their rapidly changing society. This sentiment was expressed in the comments of the Minister of the Brong Ahafo Region reported in a 2000 newspaper article:

as custodians of the country's heritage and values, they [chiefs] have a great responsibility to lead their traditional areas in the effort to preserve their cultural values, which have been weakened or abandoned in the name of so-called modernisation. He noted that it is this 'modernisation' which has brought a breakdown in moral values in the society.[42]

---

[39] There is a considerable body of writing on the subject. See, for example, Arhin Brempong, *Transformations in Traditional Rule in Ghana 1951–1996*, 2nd edn (Legon: Institute of African Studies, University of Ghana, 2007); Irene K. Odotei and Albert K. Awedoba (eds), *Chieftaincy in Ghana: Culture, Governance and Development* (Legon: Sub-Saharan Publishers, 2006); and Donald Iain Ray, 'Chiefs in Their Millennium Sandals: Traditional Authority in Ghana – Relevance, Challenges and Prospects', in Wisdom Tettey, Korbla P. Puplampu, and Bruce Berman (eds), *Critical Perspectives in Politics and Socio-Economic Development in Ghana* (Leiden: Brill, 2003), 241–71.

[40] Ray, 'Chiefs in Their Millennium Sandals', 242.

[41] Ray (ibid., 243) identifies three major challenges to chieftaincy: (1) chieftaincy's fundamental relationship to the post-colonial state and chieftaincy disputes; (2) the economic and political challenges of globalisation (especially those associated with ownership of land); and (3) gender issues concerning the position of women as chiefs.

[42] *The Daily Graphic*, 29 April 2000. Quoted in Christian Owusu-Sarpong, 'Setting the Ghanaian Context of Rural Local Government: Traditional Authority Values', in Donald Iain Ray and P. S. Reddy (eds), *Grassroots Governance? Chiefs in Africa and the Afro-Caribbean* (Calgary: University of Calgary Press, 2003), 51.

Similarly, in a recent book on the future of chieftaincy in Ghana, the paramount chief of the Akuapem Traditional Area, Oseadeeyo Addo Dankwa III, commented:

In their societies, chiefs constitute sources of hope, inspiration and trust to their people. Chiefs also, in situations of stress and strain, act as fathers of the people who can rise to the occasion and be stabilising forces capable of bringing peace and unity among the people. It is quite clear that the institution of chieftaincy will continue to provide crucial social services to provide the needed stability to a society in transition.[43]

Kwame Nkrumah, Ghana's first President, cognisant of the considerable social and economic power held by chiefs, as well as the influence they exercised in national, regional, and especially local politics, attempted to limit their authority. However the British colonial legacy of indirect rule left him with a considerable challenge.[44] In addition, the founding of the nation in 1957 brought with it the recognition that 80–90 per cent of the land within Ghana's borders is stool or skin property, with chiefs serving as the stewards of these lands.[45] Over the last fifty years their roles in society have changed considerably.[46] Since this early period in the nation's history, the position of chiefs has coalesced into serving as arbitrators of civil disputes, as custodians of tradition, and as champions of social and economic development.

In the context of this essay, what we are most interested in is the fundamental perception that chiefs are the nation's primary stewards of tradition, who embody the nation's culture. This is perhaps most clearly demonstrated in the name given to the ministry responsible for cultural affairs by the government of President John Kufuor, the Ministry of Chieftaincy and Culture.

In 2004, after several years of work, Ghana's Commission on Culture published *The Cultural Policy of Ghana* – an agenda for creating and managing a national culture.[47] Almost ten years later, most of the initiatives

---

[43] Oseadeeyo Addo Dankwa III, *The Institution of Chieftaincy in Ghana – the Future* (Accra: Konrad Adenauer Foundation, 2004), 124.

[44] See Richard Rathbone, *Nkrumah and the Chiefs: The Politics of Chieftaincy in Ghana 1951–1960* (Oxford: James Currey, 2000).

[45] In Ghana, the traditional state is often characterised as the 'seat' upon which the chief sits – in the central and southern states, a stool, and, in the north, an animal skin. Thus, for example, one speaks of 'stool (or skin) property' or 'skin (or stool) land'.

[46] A good number of authors have commented on the institution's ability to respond and adapt to shifting political and social landscapes during the colonial and post-colonial periods. See, for example, A. Kodzo Paaku KIudze, 'The Future of Chieftaincy in Modern Ghana', in *Chieftaincy in Ghana* (Lanham, MD: Austin and Winfield, 2000), 529–71; Kwame Boafo-Arthur, 'Chieftaincy in Ghana: Challenges and Prospects in the 21st Century', *African and Asian Affairs* 2, 2 (2003): 126–53; Dankwa, *The Institution of Chieftaincy in Ghana*; and Brempong, *Transformations in Traditional Rule in Ghana*.

[47] National Commission on Culture, *The Cultural Policy of Ghana* (Accra: National Commission on Culture, 2004).

outlined in this impressive document have yet to be implemented. With the exception of activities associated with tourism, the government of Ghana has failed to allocate the resources for their implementation. The *Policy* clearly expresses the national government's view that chiefs are the primary custodians and proponents of the traditions and cultural values that underpin Ghanaian society.[48] A fundamental question that lies beyond the purview of this essay is, *whose culture is it that chiefs represent?*[49]

In theory, chiefs and the government are both striving for the same goals of improving the quality of life for Ghana's citizens; both are dedicated to the political, economic, and social development of the nation. But significant tensions exist between values and practices associated with the institution of chieftaincy and those of a young, democratic nation state. The media – radio, television, newspapers – are rife with stories about chiefs – stories that either commend or condemn.

Despite these tensions, it is apparent that chiefs are still perceived by most Ghanaians as vital members of contemporary society. A recent study by Johannes Knierzinger comparing perceptions of chiefs versus Members of Parliament revealed that chiefs are regarded as more invested in their community's well-being, more interested in their community's everyday life, more inclined to seek the consent of their communities, more trustworthy, and more powerful.[50] Let us now return to Manso.

In the context of this essay my primary interest has been thinking about two of the primary roles that chiefs are playing in contemporary Ghanaian society, serving as agents for social and economic development, specifically associated with tourism, and as custodians of culture. Currently, at sites such as Manso, the former is taking precedence over the latter. Traditions that have been suppressed in the past, specifically those associated with slavery, are being brought to the fore and further elaborated to conform to a narrative tailored to the perceived expectations of an audience comprised of heritage tourists and the repatriate community. In fact what is going on at Manso and other sites in Ghana fits an archetypical heritage tourism model succinctly articulated by G. J. Ashworth, who writes, 'The successful tourism product is . . . an interpretation of the local historical experience in so far as it can be related to, and incorporated in, the historical experience of the visitor. Thus a successful foreign heritage tourism industry is dependent not on the sale of the heritage of the destination country to visitors from the consumer country but, on

---

[48] See in particular pages 13 and 14 of the *Cultural Policy*.
[49] I deal with this question at length in Raymond Silverman, 'Locating Culture with/in a Ghanaian Community', in Raymond Silverman (ed.), *Museum as Process: Translating Local and Global Knowledges* (London: Routledge, 2015), 208–27.
[50] Johannes Knierzinger, 'Chieftaincy and Development in Ghana: From Political Intermediaries to Neotraditional Development Brokers', *Working Papers, Institut für Ethnologie und Afrikastudien* (Mainz: Johannes Gutenberg Universität, 2011), 34.

the contrary, on the resale in a different guise of the consumers' own heritage in an unexpected context within the destination country.'[51] In addition, with the invention of the *nkosuo* stool, chieftaincy, an institution that formerly was purely hereditary, has been adapted to accommodate foreigners as well as new citizens of Ghana who demonstrate a potential for contributing to the well-being of the communities with which they have become involved. What we observe in Manso is representative of the dynamic nature of tradition in contemporary Ghana. Such changes are indicative of a vibrant, evolving society. However, one needs to take into account the costs associated with the production of heritage. What is happening to the fragments of evidence used to access the past? At places such as Manso oral histories are being radically rewritten and the archaeological record consumed. Many of these cultural resources are not renewable.

Oral traditions, by nature, are susceptible to the vicissitudes of political and social circumstances. And as mentioned above, the contemporary village of Manso and the farms that surround it sit on top of the ruins of the ancient capital of Bono Manso – the archaeological record is constantly under threat from the everyday activities of the community. Discussing the challenges of mitigating such threats is beyond the purview of this essay.[52] However, in the context of heritage projects, like those being pursued at Manso under the patronage of chiefs, doesn't it seem reasonable to expect these chiefs – who have been charged with and who have accepted the responsibility for serving as stewards of the nation's cultures – to ensure that such fragile remnants of the past are preserved and protected?

At Manso, chiefs are among the key actors shaping heritage. It was Nana Asare, the Adontenhene of Techiman, who in 2001 started thinking about exploiting Manso as a tourist destination. It is the Nkoranzahene who donated land for the establishment of the memorial gardens. It is chiefs who preside over the dedication of new monuments as well as many of the commemorative events that have been organised over the last ten years. It is the recently enstooled Nkosuohene or Diasporan Chief who is expected to contribute to the development of Manso. But these chiefs are not providing the oversight that might mitigate the negative effects that heritage production has brought to Manso. Instead, they have ceded

---

[51] G. J. Ashworth, 'From History to Heritage – from Heritage to Identity', in G. J. Ashworth and P. J. Larkham (eds), *Building a New Heritage: Tourism, Culture and Identity in the New Europe* (London: Routledge, 1994), 24.

[52] For a discussion of the toll that development is taking on Ghana's past see Benjamin W. Kankpeyeng and Christopher R. DeCorse, 'Ghana's Vanishing Past: Development, Antiquities, and the Destruction of the Archaeological Record', *African Archaeological Review* 21, 2 (2004): 89–128.

that responsibility to representatives of the Ministry of Tourism and to culture brokers such as Felicia Obuobie, whose priorities involve creating experiences that conform to the expectations of tourists and the repatriate community.

At the moment, development strategies focused on the tourist industry are taking a considerable toll on Ghana's past. What is going on at places such as Manso underscores the necessity for dialogue among the various stakeholders involved in the production and consumption of heritage.[53] As mentioned above, it is important to point out that the present stakeholders include chiefs, representatives of the tourist industry, tourists, and members of the repatriate community. A group that is noticeably absent is non-royal members of the Manso community. One might argue that all citizens of a community, not just its leaders, should assume some responsibility for and voice in (re)presenting culture.

Preserving an archaeological site and celebrating local and global heritages are not necessarily conflicting projects. There is no reason why a more conscientious stewardship of this important site – attempting to preserve its multi-layered histories and protect the archaeological record – cannot exist alongside the commemoration and celebration of the African diaspora. The challenge, of course, is developing strategies for creating and sustaining a dialogue in which the voices of all stakeholders may be heard. Ultimately, such a dialogue could open a space in which multiple narratives might coexist – thinking about heritage sites as dialogical spaces in which competing narratives can be mediated.[54]

Perhaps it is useful to think of sites such as Manso as contact zones, not as Mary Louise Pratt originally characterised them, as spaces 'in which peoples geographically and historically separated come into contact with each other and establish ongoing relations, usually involving conditions of coercion, radical inequality, and intractable conflict', but as spaces in which such disparities might be reconciled.[55] Chiefs in Ghana seem to be

---

[53] This is a challenge facing many communities around the world; it is also a major concern of the international development community. There is a considerable literature on the subject of 'culture and development' or 'sustainable heritage'. See for example, Danida, *Culture and Development: Strategy and Guidelines* (Copenhagen: Danida, Ministry of Foreign Affairs, 2002). It also is one of the central themes articulated in UNESCO's mission. See the UNESCO website: <http://www.unesco.org/new/en/culture/themes/culture-and-development/>, accessed 11 September 2013. See Witz and Murray in this volume for a discussion of the use of heritage in the context of development.

[54] T. C. McCaskie does an excellent job of setting this sort of discourse in a historical perspective. See T. C. McCaskie, 'Asante Origins, Egypt, and the near East: An Idea and Its History', in Derek Peterson and Giacomo Macola (eds), *Recasting the Past: History Writing and Political Work in Modern Africa* (Athens, OH: Ohio University Press, 2009), 125–48.

[55] Mary Louise Pratt, *Imperial Eyes: Travel Writing and Transculturation* (London: Routledge, 1992), 7.

ideally positioned to create and sustain such spaces and assume responsibility for mediating dialogues that would allow for a better-informed and more effective stewarding of culture, as well as the coexistence of multiple heritage agendas. They are also uniquely situated to play an important role in protecting what remains of Ghana's past, while at the same time encouraging the positive shaping of the country's future.

7   Human Remains, the Disciplines of the Dead, and the South African Memorial Complex

Ciraj Rassool

Since the advent of democracy in South Africa in 1994, human remains and body parts have featured significantly in debates and disputes over how aspects of the country's traumatic history should be remembered, and how these pasts should be expressed in the institutions and spaces of public culture. Human remains have been the subject of claims and demands for repatriation, restitution, and reburial, as part of attempts to address legacies of colonial ethnography and racial science in the representation of South African people in museums in South Africa and Europe. Bodies and body parts of dead soldiers of the South African liberation movement have also been repatriated to South Africa, while the subject of repatriation of the remains of fallen cadres has featured in debates over national heritage, memorial practices, and the 'postwars of the dead'.[1] In the same period and with similar concerns, the Missing Person's Task Team of South Africa's National Prosecuting Authority (MPTT) set about locating remains of murdered or executed cadres, as an aspect of the work of symbolic reparation, national healing, and transitional justice.[2] These issues had emerged quite powerfully from the start of the proceedings of the Truth and Reconciliation Commission (TRC). In Cape Town, the remains of slaves were the subject of a 'heritage war' at Prestwich Place, where the imperatives of development and the demands of memory collided at the site of a colonial slave burial ground.[3]

---

[1] Richard Werbner, 'Smoke from the Barrel of a Gun: Postwars of the Dead, Memory and Reinscription in Zimbabwe', in Richard Werbner (ed.), *Memory and the Postcolony: African Anthropology and the Critique of Power* (London and New York, NY: Zed Books, 1998), 71.

[2] Emily Dugan, 'Digging up bones to find the truth', *Sunday Argus*, 23 January 2011; Polly Dewhirst, 'The Establishment of the South African Disappearance Task Team: the Roots for a Regional Network?' *Linking Solidarity Newsletter* 2005, <http://www.csvr.org .za/wits/articles/artdew.htm>, accessed 20 March 2011.

[3] This subject is beyond the scope of this chapter but see the following excellent analyses: Nick Shepherd and Christian Ernsten, 'The World Below: Post-Apartheid Urban Imaginaries and the Bones of the Prestwich Street Dead', in Noëleen Murray, Nick Shepherd, and Martin Hall (eds), *Desire Lines: Space, Memory and Identity in the Post-Apartheid City* (London and New York, NY: Routledge 2007) and Heidi Grunebaum, 'Unburying the

These cases of bones and South African memory have drawn connections between museum curators, families of the dead, and activist NGOs,
as well as national heritage bodies, a national prosecuting authority, and
researchers of the dead. As doubt increases about the value of continued
retention of racialised human remains in collections of museums of culture and natural history,[4] questions have been raised about the validity
and suitability of physical anthropology as a discipline of the dead in a
post-colonial world. This has occurred because of its historic association
with racial research and a repressive anthropometry, expressed in the
academy and the museum in its methods of research and data gathering,
and in legacies of collection and image production, even though these
may have been conducted at the time in the name of science.

These doubts have escalated in spite of the claims made by physical
anthropologists, now renamed as human biologists, that in the early
twenty-first century their research on bones and bodies enables them
to recover histories of health, disease, and demography, and even to
restore the social histories of those who have suffered repression, among
them the slaves of Prestwich.[5] While physical anthropology continues to
have difficulty reinventing itself and its relationship with the dead in a
democratic South Africa, through a connection with forensic science the
discipline has acquired new meaning in a relationship between the MPTT
and the Argentine Forensic Anthropology Team/Equipo Argentino de
Antropologia Forense (EAAF). In laying claim to be able to recover and
identify remains of apartheid's murdered and executed, and to participate
in resolving traumatic histories of human rights violations and open up
the possibilities of transitional justice, physical anthropology – under the
name of forensic anthropology – has sought to shake off its associations
in South Africa with a legacy of racial research and violations of the dead.

Sara Baartman, the Nation and Science

After a lengthy campaign that included the participation of political groups rallying around a rediscovered indigeneity and Khoesan

Dead in the 'Mother City': Urban Topographies of Erasure', *PMLA* 122, 1 (January
2010).
[4] Cressida Fforde, Jane Hubert, and Paul Turnbull (eds), *The Dead and Their Possessions:
Repatriation in Principle, Policy and Practice*, One World Archaeology 43 (London and
New York, NY: Routledge, 2002); Martin Legassick and Ciraj Rassool, *Skeletons in the
Cupboard: South African Museums and the Trade in Human Remains, 1907–1917* (Cape
Town and Kimberley: South African Museum and McGregor Museum, 2000); David
van Duuren with Mischa ten Kate, Micaela Pereira, Steven Vink, and Susan Legêne,
Physical Anthropology Reconsidered: Human Remains at the Tropenmuseum (Amsterdam:
KIT Publishers, 2007).
[5] Judith Sealy, 'Managing collections of human remains in South African museums and
universities: ethical policy-making and scientific value', *South African Journal of Science*,
99 (2003); Alan Morris, *Inaugural Lecture: The Politics of Old Bones* (Cape Town: University of Cape Town, 2008).

'revivalism', the year 2002 saw the return of the remains of Sara Baart-man to South Africa from the Musée de l'Homme after a protrac-ted period of negotiations with the French government. Put on show between 1810 and 1815 in the pleasure fairs and display spaces of Britain and France, Baartman had acquired fame as the embodiment of the 'Hottentot Venus' before her body entered the world of the science of comparative anatomy in the Museum of Natural History in Paris. Here her body had been studied by Georges Cuvier and his assistant Henri de Blainville in March 1815, and after her death – once a full body cast had been made, later to be adorned with artist's paint, hair, and animal skin – her corpse was dissected by Cuvier in his laboratory near the amphitheatre of the *Jardin des Plantes*, with careful attention to her buttocks and genitalia. Suitably preserved, her brain, sex organs, and skeleton, together with the cast, entered the institutions of collection and display as the Hottenot Venus first in the Jardin, and, after 1937, in the Musée de l'Homme.[6]

Between then and 2002, according to Crais and Scully, while Sara Baartman 'had disappeared from history', so as 'to become nameless', the figure of the Hottentot Venus had come to feature significantly in the culture wars over race and gender, especially in the United States, when popular writers, poets, playwrights, and artists 'adopted' it as a means of challenging 'negative stereotypes of black women'. Later, following a play written by Susan-Lori Parks in 1996, Sara Baartman had been 'brought to life' in a biographical treatment that opened the question of her participation in the objectified portrayal of her otherness – in other words, of her agency and choice, challenging her presentation as 'uncom-prehending victim'.[7] While Parks was taken to task for making Baartman a participant in her oppression, this debate over victimhood and agency had been one of the disputed issues in Baartman studies, in which a range of arguments had been put forward about her complicity, victimisation, racialisation, and even enslavement, with one of the foremost scholars of race and sexuality, Sander Gilman, criticised for allegedly perpetuating the sins of science.[8] The work of Zoe Strother, on the other hand, shif-ted away from an emphasis on Cuvier's dissection of Baartman's body,

---

[6] Clifton C. Crais and Pamela Scully, *Sarah Baartman and the Hottentot Venus: A Ghost Story and a Biography* (Princeton, NJ: Princeton University Press, 2009).

[7] Ibid., 148–9. See also Suzan-Lori Parks, *Venus: A Play* (New York, NY: Theatre Com-munications Group, 1997).

[8] Stephen Jay Gould, 'The Hottentot Venus', *Natural History* 10 (1982); Sander Gilman, 'Black Bodies, White Bodies: Toward an Iconography of Female Sexuality in Late Nine-teenth Century Art, Medicine and Literature', *Critical Enquiry* 12, 1 (1985); Yvette Abrahams, 'Images of Sara Bartman: Sexuality, Race and Gender in Early Nineteenth-Century Britain', in Ruth Roach Pierson and Nupur Chaudhuri (eds), *Nation, Empire, Colony: Historicising Gender and Race* (Bloomington, IN: Indiana University Press, 1998).

dignifying her through a focus on her extraordinary language skills, eloquently demonstrated during her court case.[9]

Amid the upsurge in Khoesan political and cultural 'revivalism' after 1994, and the re-emergence of Griqua political and constitutional claims on the new democratic polity through the Griqua National Conference (GNC), Sara Baartman had been turned into an 'indigenous people's issue', and the subject of a campaign to 'bring [her] home', following the intervention of GNC legal adviser Mansell Upham. Spurred by appeals to Nelson Mandela and the French Embassy in Pretoria that drew on the United Nations' Declaration of Human Rights and the Draft Declaration on the Rights of Indigenous People, the French and South African governments held discussions between 1996 and 1998 about the return of Baartman's remains to South Africa. These culminated in formal negotiations conducted on behalf of the Department of Arts and Culture, Science, and Technology (DACST) by Phillip Tobias, professor emeritus of human biology and anatomy at the University of the Witwatersrand (Wits) with his colleagues at the Musée de l'Homme.[10]

In 2002, after the French National Assembly had passed a bill instructing the Musée to return Baartman's remains, Tobias again found himself a member of a DAC Reference Group created to oversee issues of 'return, burial, and memorialisation'.[11] Baartman's skeleton and soft tissue remains, along with her full body cast, were returned to South Africa in a coffin, and received at Cape Town Airport by a formal reception committee on 3 May 2002. Once internal disputes among various Khoesan groups about questions of belonging, ceremonial matters, and the location of interment had been resolved by the Reference Group, Sara Baartman's burial occurred over two days with an enrobement ceremony in Cape Town, and her interment into a memorial grave at Hankey in the Eastern Cape in a national ceremony of state, held on Women's Day, 9 August 2002, and broadcast live on TV. The official speech by former President Thabo Mbeki set out a complex colonial history of the racialised and gendered body and the complicities of science.

The funereal ceremonies, memorial rituals, and state burial of Sara Baartman sought to perform a symbolic healing of the new nation and a

---

[9] Z. S. Strother, 'Display of the Body Hottentot' in Bernth Lindfors (ed.), *Africans on Stage: Studies in Ethnological Show Business* (Bloomington, IN: Indiana University Press, 1999).

[10] Crais and Scully, *Sarah Baartman and the Hottentot Venus*: 152–4; Michael Besten, 'Transformation and the Reconstitution of Khoe-San Identities: A. A. S. le Fleur I, Griqua Identities and Post-Apartheid Khoe-San Revivalism (1894–2004)' (PhD thesis, Leiden University, 2006), 309–43; Phillip V. Tobias, with Goran Štrkalj and Jane Dugard, *Tobias in Conversation: Genes, Fossils and Anthropology* (Johannesburg; Wits University Press 2008): 267–83.

[11] Crais and Scully, *Sarah Baartman and the Hottentot Venus*: 155.

settlement of the past, after centuries of colonial violence, colonial racism, and atrocity, especially in the 'scientific' treatment of the racialised female body. In some ways, the return and reburial of Sara Baartman in solemn ceremonies of state came to stand for the settlement of all colonial atrocity and racial museum collections, with the state having been seen to deliver on this demand. This delivery has gone further with Baartman's grave on Vergaderingkop in Hankey declared a national heritage site, and a Sarah Baartman Centre of Memory, planned to become a national heritage institution, that will provide public education, heritage interpretation, and visitor management. In part the symbolism of Baartman's return and reburial served to obscure wider legacies of gendered racial science in South Africa,[12] as well as of human remains collections from South Africa in museum collections at home and overseas. The South African state was also slow to consider further cases of return from European museums, even where research on provenance had been completed, and where those museums had proclaimed their readiness to cooperate in de-accession and repatriation.[13]

Phillip Tobias featured prominently in these processes, as the appointed negotiator, part of the Sara Baartman reception committee, and a member of the Reference Group. The group itself was composed of a mix of academics, human rights and gender commission representatives, members of government, and Khoesan representatives. Tobias had been a protégé of physical anthropologist and racial scientist Raymond Dart, and had become Dart's successor as professor and Chair of Anatomy at the Wits Medical School in 1959. While he later distanced himself from Dart's typological thinking, Tobias framed his career very much in relation to Dart's legacies of expeditions, excavations, and discovery, and fell seamlessly into a heroic paradigm of pioneering international scientific achievement in a magnificent legacy that began with Dart and the Taung skull, and continued through research at Sterkfontein, in a history of the South Africanisation of science, where the fossil record of hominids was compared to the human anatomy of the Khoesan.[14]

Building on Dart's legacy, Tobias was positioned as the director, mentor, and facilitator of the South African field of palaeoanthropology, which continued to feed South Africa's need for a scientised modernity

---

[12] Ciraj Rassool and Patricia Hayes, 'Science and the Spectacle: /Khanako's South Africa, 1936–1937', in Wendy Woodward, Patricia Hayes, and Gary Minkley (eds), *Deep hiStories: Gender and Colonialism in Southern Africa* (Amsterdam: Rodopi, 2002).

[13] Martin Legassick and Ciraj Rassool, 'South African Human Remains, Viennese Museums, and the Politics of Repatriation: Reconsidering the Legacy of Rudolf Pöch' (unpublished paper presented to the Symposium on The Life of the Corpse, WISER, University of Witwatersrand, 25–26 August 2008).

[14] Saul Dubow, *Scientific Racism in Modern South Africa* (Cambridge: Cambridge University Press, 1995); Rassool and Hayes, 'Science and the Spectacle'.

after apartheid. 'Discoveries' of 'Little Foot' and Australopithecus sediba by Tobias's rival protégés, Ron Clarke and Lee Berger respectively, each announced with careful choreography in 1995 and 2010, served to confirm the greatness of the scientific empire started by Dart, but built by Tobias. This seamless narrative of continuity has culminated in a discourse of science, discovery, and origins, replete with its academic disciplines, institutional edifices, world heritage sites, and sites of popular education, display, and wonder, with Tobias and his legacy (and his association with the Leakeys in Kenya) positioned at its epicentre, enabling it to rest on the shoulders of its legendary men (and sometimes, women).

It is indeed ironic that it was Tobias, excavator of Griqua human remains and successor to racial scientist, Raymond Dart, who was a deliverer of the 'human dignity' of Sara Baartman's return to South Africa. Moreover, in the proceedings of the Sara Baartman Reference Group, among the questions deliberated were her name, the site of the burial and the nature of the funereal practices. And as Crais and Scully have noted, 'the politics of science was never very far away from the claims of indigeneity'. Tobias and his Wits geneticist colleague, Trefor Jenkins, had raised the interests of science, in asking for a DNA sampling of the remains, which would not only provide 'crucial information' connecting her to living kin, but also shed light on the 'complicated and rich history' of 'exceptionally diverse' community interaction over 'hundreds of years'. It was as if, Crais and Scully write, 'biology might tell us who, in fact, Sara Baartman was and how she stood in relation to South Africa's complicated racial histories'.[15]

In spite of Tobias's inability to appreciate the view that this research would have constituted a repetition of the violations of science, their wish for a science repositioned as 'knowledge in the service of humanity' lost out in the Reference Group's deliberations in favour of an argument that genetic research would have dishonoured and infringed the dead Sara Baartman's human rights. As much as enlightenment science and evolutionary biology (stretching from Cuvier to Tobias) may have been part of the constitution of modernity, so were the concepts of personhood and human rights, which seemed to attach themselves to the living and the dead. And as Sara Baartman's body entered into the public rituals of the constitution of the post-apartheid nation, to be laid to rest, she was not only spoken of as 'our great Foremother', who symbolised 'the great and enduring disgraces of Western civilisation', she was also turned into a 'human rights icon'.[16]

[15] Crais and Scully, *Sarah Baartman and the Hottentot Venus*: 158–63.
[16] Ibid., 161–5.

Human Rights, Transitional Justice and the Dead

As with the remains of Sara Baartman, it was also through the operation of the Truth and Reconciliation Commission (TRC) and its objective of settling the past of gross violations of human rights committed and experienced under apartheid – as well as through the TRC's afterlives – that the desire to recover, restore, and possibly rebury the dead or missing body of the freedom fighter emerged with equal power. At the visual core of the hearings of the Truth and Reconciliation Commission had been descriptions, representations, and conflicts around bodies in various states of mutilation, dismemberment, and secret burial within the terror of the past. Again and again, witnesses made claims in respect of body parts and human remains, making their visibility, recovery, and repossession a metaphor for the settlement of the pasts of apartheid. Amanda Eunice Magwaca told the TRC: 'I lost my husband, I want his remains, his bones, and I want to know what they did to him.' Ncediwe Mfeti demanded to know about the fate of her husband: 'Even if it is his remains, if he was burnt to death, even if we can get his ashes, the bones belonging to his body, because no person can disappear without trace. If I could bury him, I am sure I could be reconciled.'[17]

The physical markings of violence and trauma on each dismembered body that was identified, held up, and displayed provided tangible evidence of the individualised acts of history. 'That hand that is said to be in the bottle in Port Elizabeth, I would like it back.' This utterance, repeated again and again in other cases within the TRC, identified body parts into the site of torture, seeking physically to recover and re-member the hidden past and to uncover and establish its location. Joyce Mthimkulu brought the physical remains of her son – 'scraps of [his] hair attached to parts of his scalp' – to a TRC hearing and held them up to be seen.[18] It was the physicality of mutilation that embodied the materiality of apartheid. Heads and burials, bodies and returns, seeking to settle the landscape and finalise the unresolved past, were powerful reminders of different histories; they provided an inventory of human rights violations and an archive of symbolic reparations.

From the late 1990s, there were individualised instances of repatriations of the dead bodies of resistance leaders and ordinary fighters from the Southern African region and further afield – largely through private means, as the state showed its reluctance to facilitate individual

---

[17] Ciraj Rassool, Leslie Witz, and Gary Minkley, 'Burying and Memorialising the Body of Truth: The TRC and National Heritage', in Wilmot James and Linda van de Vijver (eds), *After the TRC: Reflections on Truth and Reconciliation in South Africa* (Cape Town: David Philip, 2000), 125.

[18] Rassool, Witz, and Minkley, 'Burying and Memorialising the Body of Truth', 126.

repatriations. From about 2005, in the wake of the TRC's findings on apartheid's death squads, the MPTT in partnership with the EAAF began the tasks of locating burial sites (often at places of apartheid torture), identifying the dead, returning corpses or body parts, and making arrangements for family and state participation in funerals. In 1998, at the request of the TRC, the EAAF had conducted forensic analyses on exhumed corpses (in 1996 it had advised the TRC on the application of forensic sciences to human rights investigations). Here, the skills of physical anthropological research, notwithstanding its powerful historical associations with discredited racial science and anthropometric studies, were put to use in the forensic identification of the remains of cadres who died as political prisoners, or who had been executed or murdered by the apartheid state.[19] At the same time, from about 2000, sites associated with 'victims of conflict' became one of the categories of heritage site recognised by new heritage legislation, in an updating of South Africa's modern 'memorial complex', which earlier had protected South African War and World War graves as monuments.[20]

Established in 1984 to investigate the cases of 9,000 people who had 'disappeared' at the hands of the Argentine dictatorship, the EAAF went on to work in 30 countries on four continents – Latin America, Asia, Europe, and Africa – to investigate cases of dead or missing people following on from cases of gross violations of human rights as well as war crimes. In countries of Latin America and elsewhere, these efforts to recover missing bodies usually operated as an element of memory work, often as part of a range of memory programmes to address legacies of violence, including attention to the creation of memorial museums, with places of violence or resistance turned into *lieux de memoire*.[21]

In Latin America, the widespread experience of violence and attempts at post-conflict social reconstruction had also seen the emergence of a radical archaeological practice of researching sites of torture, imprisonment, and violence, with archaeological methods employed alongside those of forensic anthropology. In the process, archaeological and forensic anthropological research have been placed on an ethical footing. The

---

[19] Emily Dugan, 'Digging up bones'; Argentine Forensic Anthropology Team/Equipo Argentino de Antropología Forense, 'Annual Report (Covering the Period January to December 2006)', 2007, <http://eaaf.typepad.com/eaaf/An07_Report.pdf>, accessed 20 March 2011.

[20] Werbner, 'Smoke from the Barrel of a Gun', 72; Thomas Laqueur, 'Memory and Naming in the Great War', in John R. Gillis (ed.), *Commemorations* (Princeton, NJ: Princeton University Press, 1994).

[21] <http://eaaf.typepad.com/>, accessed 15 March 2011. In one of the best-known cases, Barcelona's Castell de Montjuïc, an 'execution ground of hundreds' was turned into a site of memory, space of culture, and international peace centre, as new memory laws passed in the state of Catalunya and in Spain more generally saw Spain's 'unfinished business' of fascism turned into a field of heritage proclamation. This also became a site for ICTJ courses on transitional justice.

'guiding principle' for the EAAF was 'to maintain the utmost respect for the wishes of victim's relatives and communities', and to 'work closely with them through all stages of exhumation and identification'.[22]

Building partly on experiences of truth commissions in Latin America, the activities, procedures, and rituals of the TRC began to put in place a model of transitional justice involving truth seeking and amnesty. In South Africa, reconciliation was never a condition to be achieved and assessed, but was always a discourse about the society to be created through the language and knowledge systems of political and civic institutions as well as disciplines. The afterlives of the TRC emerged in work done in a range of national and international NGOs such as the Institute for Justice and Reconciliation (IJR), the Foundation for Human Rights (FHR) and the International Centre for Transitional Justice (ICTJ). These gave rise to a discourse of transitional justice that expressed itself in South Africa and overseas. In this discursive space, a professionalised toolkit was created to be applied to traumatised parts of the world deemed to be 'in transition' from violence and repression to peace and reconciliation. In some ways building on the South African experience, but also those of Latin America and Eastern Europe, the ICTJ was established in 2001 as an international NGO with offices in different parts of the world and its headquarters in New York. In its mission, the ICTJ sought to 'redress and prevent the most severe violations of human rights by confronting legacies of mass abuse', to find 'holistic solutions to promote accountability' and 'create just and peaceful societies'.[23]

In this 'multidisciplinary field' of law, history, politics, social work, and sometimes even medical sciences and religion – and involving technologies of political transition and forms of human rights activism – in order to be effective, transitional justice was implemented through a range of complementary strategies and approaches, with criminal trials and judicial measures understood to be ineffective. As well as efforts at memorialisation, these approaches included truth commissions and forums of truth telling, reparations programmes, and the reform of security systems. Geared towards building 'a bulwark' against the 'recurrence' of 'past abuse', memorialisation programmes included 'museums and memorials that preserve[d] public memory of victims' and 'raise[d] moral consciousness' about human rights violations.[24]

As a toolkit, the ICTJ has turned transitional justice into a range of education and training possibilities, with courses and fellowship programmes offered in different countries on four continents on human rights, truth seeking, and democratisation processes. As part of the

---

[22] <http://www.eaaf.org/founding_of_eaaf/>, accessed 15 March 2011.
[23] <http://www.ictj.org/en/index.html>, accessed 15 March 2011.
[24] <http://www.ictj.org/en/tj/>, accessed 15 March 2011.

toolkit, the ICTJ's Memory, Memorials and Museums (MMM) programme sought to 'strengthen the potential of public memorials to contribute to justice by expanding democratic space and prompting civic
dialogue about the past'. Focusing on the 'communicative and educat-
ive power of public memorials', the MMM programme was 'committed
to experiential learning for an informed citizenry' and to promoting 'a
healthy and democratic dialogue about the past'. Working with victims'
groups, human rights bodies, and government agencies, through the
MMM programme the ICTJ sought to mediate discussions with artists
and designers, 'providing advice on memorial design, consultation, and
commissioning processes'.[25]

While this may not have involved top-down methods of work, nevertheless, through these approaches and strategies, transitional justice
became a discourse to be implemented through technical application and
professionalised procedures. And the memorialising element of transitional justice mistakenly understood its professionalising methodologies
of working with stakeholders as similar to the museum-as-process and
new memorial museologies in which museums were understood to be
constituted out of the processes and transactions of knowledge rather
than collections, exhibitions, or edifices.

Located in this democratising discourse of transitional justice, human
rights, and personhood, physical anthropology – now figured as forensic
anthropology – offered respect for the victim and missing body, promising to return the dead to personhood, and to extend the biography of
the dead person through procedures of recovery and identification. The
techniques of recovery, identification, DNA analysis, and return, conducted in close association with relatives of the dead and other interested
parties, followed on from procedures of truth recovery and reparations,
and were part of the process of memorial and remembrance of violence.
As a recovered person with a biography, which saw violence narrated
into democratic reconstruction, the bones of the dead one were offered
dignified closure through burial in a grave, in many ways the primary
memorial. The material edifice of the grave, its headstone and the story
of its creation, would be incorporated into a narrative of the making of
democracy, whose telling might be part of a public history geared towards
citizen formation.

In the early years of the operations of the MPTT/EAAF work on the
recovery and identification of missing persons, use was made of conventional spaces of anatomical analysis in South Africa, such as the laboratories of the African Cultural History Museum in Pretoria and the University of Pretoria (UP), and work was done on training graduate anatomy
students from the University of Cape Town (UCT) working under Alan

---

[25] <http://ictj.org/en/tj/785.html>, accessed 15 March 2011.

Morris, former student of Phillip Tobias. While the EAAF needed to attend to country-based capacity building in forensic anthropology, as part of its international mandate within the frame of transitional justice, it found itself utilising the inherited infrastructure of anatomical studies and physical anthropology, which had been marked by past associations with racial science. And it seems that in Pretoria, while some scientists were enthusiastic about engaging in this work with the MPTT, and even later created a forensic anthropology research centre, some of its leading scientists displayed a measure of hostility. Part of the solution was to switch the forensic laboratory analyses to the University of the Western Cape (UWC), which had opened a Human Identification Laboratory in its Biochemistry Department.[26] In the last two decades of apartheid, UWC had styled itself as the 'university of the left' and as a historically black university without a medical school, it had no direct background in racial science.

While there was every possibility that the forensic anthropology work of MPTT/EAAF might merely have been the implementation of an element of transitional justice in a professionalised way through utilising existing infrastructures, there was some recognition of how controversial these might be. After all, these spaces and institutions might exist within gene-alogies and histories of race and apartheid that might compromise the ethical basis of the work of recovery and identification that needed to be done. Moreover, in order to configure this research as part of the process of public history and citizen formation that was not part of the invoca-tion of authority, forensic anthropology needed to take place alongside other disciplines and genres of expression, as part of a multidisciplinary approach to explaining the history of violence and recovery, and as part of the brokerage of different knowledge forms. With forensic anthropology standing alongside other disciplines and genres of expression, it might have been able to participate in fostering a critical citizenship.

Because they were dealing with sites associated with 'victims of con-flict', the work of MPTT/EAAF always occurred with due regard to permits from South African Heritage Resources Agency (SAHRA), as part of the management of the 'national estate', after applications to its Burial Sites Unit, which had replaced the older War Graves Unit of the old National Monuments Council. Nevertheless, it was through the creation of the Freedom Park legacy project that the most significant strides occurred in deliberations about the dead or missing body of the freedom fighter. Built on Salvokop in Pretoria, opposite the Voortrekker Monument and within sight of the Union Buildings, Freedom Park was South Africa's official national memorial about human rights violations,

---

[26] Argentine Forensic Anthropology Team, 'Annual Report'; Madeleine Fullard, personal communication, 2011.

reconciliation, and freedom. This was created as the site where South Africans would experience symbolic reparations that were recommended by the TRC. This multidimensional commemorative institution, which aimed to 'tell the history of South Africa from pre-colonial times up to the present' and to celebrate 'the attainment of freedom and democracy', would also 'commemorate those who fell in the struggle for liberation'. With a walled memorial of names, an experiential exhibition, and a memorial garden, its creation needs to be understood with some reference to the history of the modern memorial complex and the tomb of the Unknown Soldier, as well as to the debate over the Heroes' Acre model from Zimbabwe and Namibia.[27]

As a memorial to the dead, Freedom Park deliberately avoided becoming a cemetery, as happened with the Heroes' Acres of Zimbabwe and Namibia. Rather, it concentrated on the symbolic return of the spirits of the dead freedom fighters from the African and international locations of their death and burial through the transfer of soil, rocks, plants, and trees to the memorial garden, *Isivivane*, after the performance of national and international healing and cleansing ceremonies. These memorial methods may have sought authority in indigenous knowledge of ancestral relations as part of intangible heritage. Yet, for some families of the dead, and formations of ex-guerrillas, this symbolic approach confirmed the failure on the part of the state to facilitate the physical return of the corpses of dead South African soldiers for reburial at the locations of their birth.

In this memorial model, the new discipline of the dead was rooted in 'indigenous knowledge systems' through a modernisation of tradition – with heritage managers, struggle intellectuals, and retired soldiers trained as *sangomas* and *inyangas*, and with some participation by cultural anthropologists. What had previously been concentrated in the hands of the anthropometric and forensic sciences of the body – with their demands for the evidence of measurement and genetics, tied to practices of disinterment/exhumation, forensic identification, and reburial – was now channelled into a spiritual memorial framework of ancestors and indigenous knowledge. This model also served to recognise that South African cadres died across the region and further afield, and that their deaths and their resting places formed part of a transnational landscape of exile, political mobilisation, and resistance to apartheid.

While Freedom Park added a new, large-scale, centralised, national heritage institution to the South African memorial landscape, and some conventional memorial strategies such as an expanded Wall of Names

---

[27] Werbner, 'Smoke from the Barrel of a Gun'; Thomas Laqueur, 'Memory and Naming in the Great War'.

known as *Sikhumbuto*, it also opened up discussion on new memorial methods through which to remember the dead and missing body. Certainly *Sikhumbuto*, and especially *Isivivane*, may have reproduced elements of the modern memorial complex in creating 'self-conscious and sacralised oblivion' through commemorating 'the presence of absence', as in the empty tomb of the cenotaph and the tomb of the Unknown Soldier.[28]

With the emergence of modern memorialism after the First World War, except for the 'unknown warrior' for the British and 'other imperial dead', no remains of any soldier were allowed to return home from the battlefields of Europe. Likewise, Freedom Park would be a national memorial to the South African dead who died in the cause of freedom without the presence of the remains of the dead. Their names on a wall would be 'traces of bones'.[29] Its methods of memorialism were new, incorporating indigenous practices of remembering the dead into a modern institution of national memory, thereby turning the missing dead into the ancestors of the nation. The idea of identifying and repatriating the bones of a dead soldier, albeit through the assistance of the MPTT and other state institutions, belonged to the family and to the private cemetery, and not to the framework of memory as national heritage. Sara Baartman's remains in her national heritage site grave on Vergaderingkop in Hankey were perhaps the only remains that had been 'buried' into the South African memorial complex. But the grave was also deemed to be in a local area, managed by the Kouga municipality, and needing to reflect indigenous history and culture.

While forensic anthropology was the discipline of the murdered or executed cadre, whose remains were missing, waiting to be recovered, identified and returned, it took the new national memorial complex expressed through Freedom Park to shift the discipline, with the public historian/inventorist/names verifier as the deliverer of names to be chiselled into granite, and the *sangoma* and *inyanga* as the deliverers and keepers of the spirits of the dead. While historical research may have been reduced to names verification based on simplified dichotomies of resister/collaborator, the work of recovering the spirits of the dead carried all the ambiguities of indigenous knowledge and its concepts of Africanness. In some ways the dead of South Africa's liberation struggle became ancestral heroes of the nation. In other ways, they were drawn into a post-apartheid politics of African indigeneity rooted in familiar colonial categories of tribe and sometimes even race. It was as if colonial categories were never too far away in rethinking the bones of South Africa's dead.

---

[28] Laqueur, 'Memory and Naming in the Great War,' 155–64.
[29] Ibid., 162–4.

The Skeletons of Physical Anthropology

The challenge of rethinking colonial categories was part of the remaking of museums in South Africa as part of the reconstitution of heritage. Questions began to be posed about the future of the ethnographic museum (or of ethnography in the natural history museum) in a new democracy. Although the record is uneven across national, provincial, and local museums, one of the routes to museum renovation has been the unification and potential integration of previously segregated collections of cultural history and anthropology in a new collections division of social history, like that which occurred at Iziko Museums of Cape Town.[30] The controversial diorama of a nineteenth-century San Camp made in 1959–60 out of painted body casts, and on display since then, was shut by the South African Museum in 2001, after the museum had been incorporated into a Smithsonian-like flagship museum called Iziko Museums of Cape Town. In essence, the diorama was 'archived' while its future was decided upon. The casts, produced as racial studies in the early twentieth century, had been placed in an invented scene of cultural anthropology, where, as 'the diorama', it had been subjected to criticism by scholars, and become the subject of intense debate and contestation through the exhibition 'Miscast' in 1996.[31]

Moreover, beyond the presence of body casts in the collection, as artefacts of anthropometric study and racial science – which had somehow been little questioned – more challenges were posed around settling the future of human remains collections in a reconstituted national museum. Here they remained under the purview of science, but sat uncomfortably between archaeology, social history, and natural history in their separate storage space as 'sensitive collections' in a manner that 'show[ed] respect for the dead, and accord[ed] with the wishes of descendant communities'. After 2005, they became subject to an approved management policy, which included oversight by an advisory committee comprising members drawn from 'descendant communities, scientific communities, and other concerned groups' as stakeholders. The advisory committee would 'guide Iziko in making decisions regarding the management of human remains in its collections'.[32]

---

[30] Patricia Davison, 'Redressing the Past: Integrating Social History Collections at Iziko', *South African Museums Association Bulletin* (2005).

[31] Leslie Witz, 'Transforming Museums on Postapartheid Tourist Routes', in Ivan Karp, Corinne A. Kratz, Lynn Szwaja, and Tomás Ybarra-Frausto (eds), with Gustavo Buntinx, Barbara Kirshenblatt-Gimblett, and Ciraj Rassool, *Museum Frictions: Global Transformations/Public Cultures* (Durham, NC: Duke University Press, 2006); Pippa Skotnes, 'The Politics of Bushman Representations', in Paul S. Landau and Deborah D. Kaspin (eds), *Images and Empires: Visuality in Colonial and Postcolonial Africa* (Berkeley, CA: University of California Press, 2002).

[32] Iziko Museums, 'Policy on the Management of Human Remains in Iziko Collections' (approved by Iziko Council, 29 September), 2005.

While notions of descendant communities ('related by established or recognised lines of descent') held the danger of an ethnic framework, this was a body of stakeholders imagined to work through a process of compromise and 'sufficient consensus', but where scientists would still be able to negotiate the possibility of future research access.[33] The management policy asserted that 'no research access to unethically acquired human remains' would be granted, 'except in terms of agreements negotiated with descendant communities'. Yet, this seemingly enlightened and ethical policy remained burdened by the assertion of the possibility of the scientific value of continued retention and research access. Moreover, any possibility of repatriation rested on the onus of identification of 'descendant communities', and was understood as belonging to the relationship between the museum and specific descendant communities.[34] What was missing was a framework of community interest that avoided ethnicity, but focused instead on communities of a specific location, such as the idea of a 'source community', whose composition might even have undergone significant change.[35] What was also missing was a proactive approach that also appreciated the disruptive consequences of colonialism in South Africa, the difficulties of ethnic continuity, as well as long, complex, and hybrid histories of ethnic and racial formation and reconstitution.

Five years before this policy had been made, 'in the absence of national policy guidelines', pressure had begun to mount through the publication of a book I wrote in 2000 with a colleague, Martin Legassick, *Skeletons in the Cupboard*, in which we revealed how significant numbers of skeletons had entered the South African Museum and McGregor Museum at the beginning of the twentieth century through unethical deals with gravediggers and body traders who dealt in 'freshly dead corpses'. South African museums also competed with scientists in Britain and elsewhere in Europe for access to the bushman body for the purposes of racial research. Previously, South African scientists sent skeletons to Britain for analysis, and Europeans like the Austrian anthropologist, Rudolf Pöch, undertook field excursions across Southern Africa. In these circumstances, the Bushman Relics Act was passed in 1911, seeking to prohibit the export of rock art as well as Khoesan human remains. At this time, when the institutions of the new nation of the Union of South Africa were being established, the Bushman Relics Act became the original document of South Africa's law on heritage. And, as part of the South Africanisation of science, anatomists and museums in South Africa

---

[33] Ibid.
[34] Ibid.
[35] Laura Lynn Peers and Alison Kay Brown (eds), *Museums and Source Communities* (London: Routledge, 2002).

began to lay claim to their own collections of skeletons, casts, and other biological data about the Bushmen as primitive type. And, as Legassick and I argued, human remains, including those 'unethically collected', were central to the origins of the modern museum in South Africa.[36]

When our research was first presented there was some debate with curators and scientists on the issues of repatriation and reburial. In many quarters, there was general defensiveness and a marked desire to retain possession of bones, even a sense of scientific entitlement. Already at that stage, Alan Morris had argued that bones continued to tell us about the 'trials and tribulations of disease' in the first decades of the twentieth century. Archaeologists from the McGregor Museum in Kimberley, David Morris and Leon Jacobson, suggested that human remains of differing age and context could yield significant and unique historical insights on gene flow and health, and provided 'testimony to the very origins of humanity in Africa'. Iziko's Graham Avery raised the possibility of continued retention, but in special areas with restricted access. These could be designated museums or special buildings in communities ('keeping places'), with attention paid to appropriate cultural ceremonies and community elders.[37]

One of the most noteworthy responses was from the eminent archaeologist Tim Maggs, who, at a Consultation with Curators of Significant Collections convened by SAHRA at the South African Museum on 18 May 2000, was haunted by the spectre of his bones being taken away from him. This he likened to the act of burning the archive.[38] Some of the debate even took place in the national press, and, in one contribution, the archaeologist Sven Ouzman made a key point in response to these claims. He wrote that he did not think any of these scientists would claim continued research access to remains if they had been found to belong to dead victims of the Holocaust.[39]

Skeletons in the Cupboard put forward an understanding of the history of colonial collecting and museum anthropology as violent and appropriative. South African museums have been reluctant to address these aspects of their history, choosing rather to portray the museum as benevolent, and to produce exhibitions about Khoesan material culture by rendering Khoesan people as 'harmless' and in need of salvation, without any fundamental epistemological reassessment of the blood of colonial history.

---

[36] Legassick and Rassool, *Skeletons in the Cupboard*; Saul Dubow, 'White South Africa and the South Africanisation of Science: Humankind or Kinds of Humans?', in Philip Bonner, Amanda Esterhuysen, and Trefor Jenkins (eds), *A Search for Origins: Science, History and South Africa's 'Cradle of Humankind'* (Johannesburg: Wits University Press, 2007).

[37] Legassick and Rassool, *Skeletons in the Cupboard*: 73–84.

[38] Ibid., 102.

[39] *Sunday Independent*, 18 July; 1, 8, 15 August 1999.

This is a stewardship model of the museum, whose benevolence exists within a genealogy of paternalism and atonement through which heritage is understood as the magnanimous recovery and salvation of lost pasts of indigenous people.[40]

Skeletons in the Cupboard, with its demands that museums examine their blood-stained complicity with colonialism, unsettled this fuzzy view of history. While the SA Museum was under pressure to co-publish the book in 2000, its relationship with the book was uneasy from the start, and it only saw fit to hold a formal book launch in 2002, as part of an event held to discuss the imminent reburial of Sarah Baartman. The other co-publisher, McGregor Museum, located in Kimberley and closer in some ways to the unfolding politics of indigeneity, launched the book on 10 September 2001 as part of the events of a special workshop on 'Human Remains in the Museum'. This workshop was attended by anatomists, palaeoanthropologists, archaeologists, heritage officials, and representatives of Khoisan political groups. Amid difficult discussions, the McGregor Museum undertook to embark on a process of research and preparation for the de-accessioning and restitution of human remains nefariously collected, or collected for racial research.

This workshop followed on from the conference of the South African Museums Association (SAMA) of that year, held in Port Elizabeth, where members committed themselves and their institutions to restitution and/or repatriation. In his address to the 2001 SAMA conference, Mike Raath, then of the Bernard Price Institute at Wits, and Francis Thackeray, then of the Northern Flagship Institute's Transvaal Museum, expressed the desire of their institutions to engage in a process of restitution and repatriation.[41] With reference to the research and the arguments contained in *Skeletons in the Cupboard*, they had conducted fresh audits of the skeletal collections inside their institutions, and discovered that a significant percentage of their bones were also 'ill-begotten'.

Thus while the Iziko policy proceeded from some critique of racial theory, from an appreciation of the Vermillion Accord of the World Archaeological Congress, and from the arguments outlined in *Skeletons in the Cupboard*, it seemed stuck in older notions of ethnic continuity and the possibility of scientific interest. Even in Britain, a Working Group on Human Remains set up by the Department of Culture, Media, and Sport had expressed concerns about the presence in British collections of human remains obtained without consent, and had recommended that

---

[40] Ciraj Rassool, 'Beyond the Cult of "Salvation" and "Remarkable Equality": A New Paradigm for the Bleek-Lloyd Collection', *Kronos* 32 (2006).
[41] Mike Raath, address to South African Museums Association conference, 2001; Francis Thackeray, personal communication.

laws preventing the repatriation of human remains be rescinded.[42] And in the Netherlands, the Tropenmuseum seemed to go even further, to assert that it wanted to repatriate its entire human remains collection, and initiated a process that would also culminate in 'the restitution of authority over these remains'.[43]

There seemed to be some progress around the Mapungubwe landscape, which had been declared a national and world heritage site, and in respect of which the issue of repatriation of cultural artefacts to an appropriate site museum within the landscape had run into political difficulty. Following claims from surrounding Limpopo communities, 143 sets of Iron Age human remains were returned and reinterred at the site, after direct intervention by President Thabo Mbeki. After SAHRA had developed draft regulations, so that the repatriation clause of the National Heritage Resources Act (1999) could be implemented, the reburial went ahead, seemingly 'confounded' by the involvement of government officials and politicians who participated in the Steering Committee, also made up of claimant communities, holding institutions, and conservation officials. While no sampling or destructive analysis of the remains were allowed before reburial, the nature of the interment reflected compromises between the demands of science and memory. Almost all the remains were carefully documented, and all were placed in sealed plastic set in high density foam in individual PVC containers, which were then welded and sealed. While the main holding institution, the University of Pretoria, was able to develop a repatriation policy and come to an understanding of the value of a proactive approach, the reinterments took place in a manner that allowed for the possibility of future research by anatomists, with the remains placed in 'graves' constructed of brick walls, with concrete floor and roof.[44] It was as if the reinterments took place into a new underground collections store within the Mapungubwe landscape, like an Australian 'keeping place', subject to ongoing negotiation and co-management. These reinterments were thus not reburials into the post-apartheid memorial complex.

There was a glimmer of initiative, when in 2009, after a few years of research, deliberation, and some foot-dragging within Iziko, its council took a decision to 'be proactive in de-accessioning those human remains that were unethically collected in South Africa, as a first step towards

---

[42] Department of Culture, Media, and Sport (UK), *Guidance for the Treatment of Human Remains in Museums* (London, October 2005): 23–30.

[43] van Duuren, with ten Kate, Pereira, Vink, and Legêne, *Physical Anthropology Reconsidered*, 83–93.

[44] Willem C. Nienaber, Natalie Keough, and Maryna Steyn, 'Repatriation of the Mapungubwe Human Remains: An Overview of the Process and Procedure' (Poster), Forensic Anthropology Research Centre, University of Pretoria, 2008, <http://repository.up.ac.za/bitstream/handle/2263/7390/nienaber_repatriation_poster .pdf?sequence=1>, accessed 15 March 2011.

their eventual reburial or return to their communities of origin'. These included remains collected 'solely for the purposes of racial study', those collected 'without appropriate consent', and those 'from recent graves of individuals who were known in life, or were from known communities'. It may have taken four years of negotiation and compromise within the Advisory Committee. Along the way, some Advisory Committee members certainly felt they were being incorporated into a bureaucratic procedure that was driven by 'scientific interest'. Was this step a strategy of finding a new moral order to govern the future of scientific research on human remains? All that would remain in the collection would be remains 'accidentally discovered on private or public property', and from burials deemed to be at risk, after a community request.[45] Or was this a moment of Iziko rethinking its complicity with racial science and seeking to remake a museum appropriate for a post-apartheid, post-racial society? This may have been the first major sign from a national museum that they were ready to take the next step in their decolonisation process.

While the influence of *Skeletons in the Cupboard* on human remains collections management principles and procedures in South African museums may have been episodic and uneven, its impact on museums and collecting institutions in Vienna, Austria was very slow indeed. Our book had examined the research and collecting expedition made by Dr Rudolf Pöch to the Kalahari in 1907–9, and the relationships he entered into in order to achieve his purpose of collecting San remains principally for the measurement of skulls in order to understand the 'racial' classification of human 'types' and their 'primitive' or even 'pre-human' ancestors. These he collected with a sense of 'thoroughness and tenacity' alongside cultural objects, while he also made ethnographic photographs of assembled Khoesan people, field sound recordings on wax disc, and ethnographic film. Far from being a 'lone heroic researcher', as is suggested by his image within the history of Austrian anthropology, Pöch 'surrounded himself with . . . "assistants" whose help he enlisted for the acquisition of skeletal remains of Bushman "relics"'. His record of 'collecting' human remains was indeed one of '*systematic* grave robbery, and of clandestine deals for newly dead corpses in the name of science'.[46]

Pöch's expedition, following on from his research in New Guinea, Indonesia, and Australia, was significant in the development of a range of scientific and collecting institutions in Vienna and was an important moment in the emergence of anthropology in German-speaking Europe. Pöch died young, in 1921, after conducting physical anthropology

---

[45] Iziko Museums, 'Policy on the Management of Human Remains in Iziko Collections', 29 September 2005; Iziko Museums, 'Minutes of the Meeting of the Council of Iziko Museums of Cape Town', 31 July 2009.
[46] Legassick and Rassool, *Skeletons in the Cupboard*, 9–13.

research in prisoner-of-war camps during the First World War. As the 'founding father' of Austrian anthropology, and holder of Austria's first anthropology chair, Pöch's scholarly and collecting legacy was the focus of commemorative activity in Vienna in the late 2000s. One of the projects was an attempt to develop an understanding of his legacy by creating a 'digital database' of 'important objects and media formats' now 'scattered across' five Austrian institutions into a digital research database, with the intention 'to repatriate this material by way of digital restitution' to groups studied by Pöch. The project involved the Natural History Museum, the Film Archive, the Phonogramme Archive, the Academy of Science, and the Department of Anthropology at the University of Vienna, all institutions holding Pöch collections, and the South African San Institute was named as one of the repatriation recipients.[47] In reply to criticism of this digital project that it may include the unauthorised digitisation of human remains and their records, Maria Teschler-Nicola, director of Anthropology at the Natural History Museum in Vienna, one of the partners on the digital project, denied this, maintaining that it was a 'discipline-historical project' and was never intended to include physical anthropology.[48]

In May 2008, as part of the development of the digital project and the Pöch commemorations, Teschler-Nicola organised a workshop in Vienna entitled 'Archival Horizons: Landscapes of knowledge and borders of perspective within the multimedia estate of anthropologist and explorer Rudolf Pöch'. In the previous year, Austrian historian, human rights activist, and former head of the Austrian Anti-Apartheid Movement, Walter Sauer, had published a review of *Skeletons in the Cupboard* in *Indaba*, a journal attached to the Southern African Documentation and Cooperation Centre (SADOCC) in Vienna, and had passed on a copy of the book to Teschler-Nicola.[49] As a result of this connection, Martin Legassick and I were invited to present our findings to the workshop. Much of the workshop focused on Pöch's legacy as a pioneering technological one, with his work understood as foundational for field photographic and film documentation as well as field sound recording. In this celebratory frame, Pöch was seen as the first person 'to combine the roles of explorer and archivist', and his anatomical and anthropometric studies were understood in an aestheticised way. The fact

[47] 'Rudolf Pöch – Anthropologist, Explorer, Media Pioneer', <http//poech.fox.co.at/en/>, accessed 11 February 2009.

[48] Tony Scully, 'Online Anthropology Draws Protest from Aboriginal Group', *Nature* 453, 1155 (2008), <http://www.nature.com/news/2008/080625/full/4531155a.html>, accessed 15 March 2011; Maria Teschler-Nicola, 'Letter to General Director of the Natural History Museum, Ministry of Education and Cultural Affairs, the General Secretary of the Austrian Academy of Sciences, the Head of the Department of Anthropology at the University of Vienna, and the South African Embassy, Vienna', 2 July 2008.

[49] *Indaba: Das SADOCC-Magazin für Südliche Afrika* 54 (2007).

that Pöch's research seemed always to have been conducted in spaces of confinement or colonial authority was never raised.[50]

On the second day of the workshop, drawing on his notebooks, Teschler-Nicola outlined Pöch's collecting methods in South Africa. Pöch had seemingly collected 80 skeletons and 150 skulls, and made 50 casts. He saw 1,000 Bushmen who spoke 10 different languages, and measured 300 bodies. Pöch's widow, Hella, who tried to promote Pöch's legacy after his death, had held on to a range of significant artefacts and documents that did not find their way into any collecting institution. In 1927, Teschler-Nicola revealed, Hella Pöch had published a paper discussing two corpses of Bushmen, one male and one female, which had been imported from South Africa.[51] Legassick and I knew these must have been the bodies disinterred illegally by one of Pöch's assistants, Mehnarto, about whom we had written; he had acquired them from Gamopedi, where the man and the woman had died after suffering from fever. They had been sent out of South Africa as corpses in barrels, with the head of the woman kept separately.[52] They had been taken by sea to Europe, where they entered the world of racial science as artefacts of a primitive type. The collecting processes and classificatory systems of modernity had denied them any biography or personhood other than what was granted through typology.

In our presentation, which was met with shock, embarrassment, and silence, amid a description of the gruesome details of Pöch's work, we were able to name the dead as Klaas and Trooi Pienaar, colonial subjects of Gamopedi, whose corpses had entered the Natural History Museum as types. We also spoke about the circumstances of their deaths, and the ways in which their bodies had been 'collected'. This had been the work of Pöch's assistant Mehnarto, who had organised for their remains to be exhumed 3 and 4 months after their respective deaths. We know from archival records that after the disinterment of the 'well preserved' corpses, these were 'wound [with] white linen', and after their knee joints were cut, were 'forced . . . into a large barrel', with 'two sacks of salt'.[53]

In his presentation to the discussion session on digital restitution, Walter Sauer expressed sentiments that his Austrian colleagues were not able to voice. He suggested that Pöch had systematically degraded and humiliated people, and that he should no longer be regarded merely as

---

[50] Legassick and Rassool, 'South African Human Remains, Viennese Museums, and the Politics of Repatriation'.

[51] Hella Pöch, 'Beitrag zur Kenntnis des Muskelsystems und einiger Rassenmerkmale der Buschmänner', *Mitteilungen der Anthropologischen Gesellschaft* 57 (1927): 108–12; Legassick and Rassool, 'South African Human Remains, Viennese Museums, and the Politics of Repatriation'.

[52] Legassick and Rassool, *Skeletons in the Cupboard*, 21–4.

[53] Ibid., 22–3.

a scientist and researcher. To digitise the collection and to return it in digital form did not help at all in dealing with the legacy of Pöch, who had violated the 'human rights of families and social networks'. This was also in the immediate aftermath of the German war of extermination against the Herero and Nama. Sauer recommended that the corpses be reburied in the areas from which they had been taken in the presence of the Austrian and South African Presidents. Repatriation, it was argued, did not necessarily bring closure, but European museums needed to comprehend what they had done, and to pass this knowledge on to future generations.[54]

Immediately after the workshop, a colleague of Teschler-Nicola revealed that the Pienaars' corpses been macerated, possibly in the 1930s after they had deteriorated extensively. Teschler-Nicola then located the macerated corpses at the Natural History Museum in the 'private collection' of Emil Breitinger, the former head of the Institute for Human Biology (now Institute for Anthropology) at the University of Vienna, who was known to have had Nazi sympathies. As objects, the corpses had been passed down a research chain from Pöch to his wife Hella, who in turn had passed them on to Breitlinger. From our research and from the presentation by Teschler-Nicola, it was clear, in retrospect, that the nature of the 'acquisition' of these remains, their journey from Gamopedi to Vienna, and their further journey through the disciplines of physical anthropology and racial science at the Natural History Museum and the University of Vienna, posed serious ethical challenges for collections management in a twenty-first-century museum.[55]

These challenges occurred amid a wider debate in the museum sector internationally about the future of museum collections in a post-colonial world. Some museums had begun describing themselves as universal museums as a defence against the threat of having to return artefacts to their source societies.[56] Elsewhere, new approaches to museums had begun to emerge, with a post-colonial turn in some anthropology museums in Europe, reordering their museum methods with more careful attention to the history of collecting. Some also began advocating de-accessioning as an active collections management strategy. And, amid these debates, human remains in museum collections were a matter of serious contention, with cases of repatriation occurring to communities in New Zealand, Australia, Botswana, and Greenland, among others. In 2009 and 2011, the Natural History Museum in Vienna repatriated

---

[54] Legassick and Rassool, 'South African Human Remains, Viennese Museums, and the Politics of Repatriation'.

[55] Ibid.

[56] James Cuno, *Who Owns Antiquity? Museums and the Battle over Our Ancient Heritage* (Princeton, NJ: Princeton University Press, 2008).

remains of indigenous Australians as a result of a claim.[57] Also, the Natural History Museum had gone through a painful experience a few years before, with the repatriation to Vienna's Jewish community of remains of Jewish children that had been discovered in their collection, part of the museum's legacy of Nazi racial research.

After the workshop, Maria Teschler-Nicola expressed the wish on the part of the Natural History Museum to repatriate the remains of Klaas and Trooi Pienaar as soon as possible. Indeed, shortly after the workshop the Austrian Natural History Museum formally offered the repatriation of two sets of skeletons, those of Klaas and Trooi Pienaar from Gamopedi, near Kuruman. This matter was brought before the governments of Austria and South Africa, and, despite delays and complex negotiations, during 2012 the remains of the Pienaars were returned to South Africa and reburied at Kuruman in a ceremony addressed by the President. With the emphasis on return as rehumanisation and even a sense of post-mortem citizenship, the matter of Klaas and Trooi Pienaar represented the first case of remains de-accessioned and returned from the patrimony of a European state as those of human beings and not museum objects. A full audit of human skeletal material as well as of associated cultural artefacts and museum documentation across Viennese museums and institutions remains to be conducted in order to determine further returns and repatriations. Moreover, Iziko South African Museum has also made proactive strides to identify unethically acquired remains in its collection, to place these in a special temporary depot, awaiting return and reburial in their areas of origin, particularly the Northern Cape and Namibia, South Africa's former colony. With a national human remains policy being prepared, the reburial of the skeletons of racial science holds the promise of decolonising and deracialising museums in South Africa. This would address multidirectional legacies of colonialism, of South Africa as colonial victim and perpetrator.

Bone Memory

This chapter has tried to bring together different fields in which the dead body – either as part of physical anthropology or natural history collection, or as recovered from its secret disposal after state-sanctioned murder – has featured in debates about the constitution of the new nation of South Africa. Since the First World War, one of the ways in which new nations have been formed has been through the presence of the absent body configured within the modern memorial complex. As the post-apartheid memorial complex was being made at Freedom Park with

---

[57] Walter Sauer, 'Österreich – Südafrika: Die Geschichte von Klaas und Trooi Pienaar', *Indaba: Das SADOCC-Magazin für Südliche Afrika* 74 (2012): 8.

the presence of its absent and missing bodies, the bones of the dead were being recovered by the MPTT/EAAF through the discourse of transitional justice, but returned to families for burial in private cemeteries.

In the formation of the new nation of South Africa out of the multiple deaths of colonialism and apartheid, questions have been raised about the history and value of the disciplines of the dead. These have concerned the complicities of physical anthropology and human biology with predatory colonial collecting and with unethical racial science in consigning the racialised, typologised Khoesan body to museums of anthropology and natural history. Notice has been taken of the difficulties of physical anthropology and archaeology to shake off its associations with race and typology, even where it has marshalled a discourse of origins, science, and discovery to reinvent itself alongside palaeoanthropology in the quest to reveal the nation's earliest heritage. But it is interesting how physical anthropology, reframed as forensic anthropology, has been able to present itself as able to deliver the missing body from its history of violation and death and to humanise it through identification, disinterment, and reburial in family cemeteries. In the South African case, the work of MPTT/EAAF has taken place as part of a multidisciplinary process including readings of the TRC record, and reading the archival evidence of atrocity. And, from time to time, the critics of physical anthropology suggest that history is a more appropriate discipline of the dead in the twenty-first century.

While the post-apartheid South African memorial complex has for the most part excluded physical anthropology from its disciplinary regimes, it is rather the discipline of history that has been called upon to provide evidence and verification for the nation's dead. While Sara Baartman's physical remains have been incorporated into a site of the new memorial complex, with few exceptions, the skeletons of racial science have yet to be de-accessioned and repatriated. Until then, notwithstanding attempts at transformation and reform, the museum will remain fundamentally a colonial institution. While new national heritage policy seeks to draw together the cases studied here into a single, all-encompassing policy on human remains as part of wider policy on the repatriation of heritage resources,[58] post-apartheid South Africa continues to be marked by the unfinished business of the dead.

---

[58] National Heritage Council, 'Position Paper on a Proposed Policy Framework on the Repatriation of Heritage Resources' (National Heritage Council, Pretoria, January 2011).

8   Heritage vs Heritage

Reaching for Pre-Zulu Identities in KwaZulu-Natal, South Africa[1]

Mbongiseni Buthelezi

Ababoni kodwa abantu ukuthi singamakhos' impel' uqobo lwawo! Imizi yethu thina, imizi yenkosi yakhiwe izinkantolo. Muphi nje owakwaZulu nje, eyoShaka, ngaphandle kweStanger nje esesinedolobha?

– Sakhile Nxumalo

People don't see that we are real kings! Our homes, the homes of our king are made up of magistrates' courts. Where are those of the Zulu, of Shaka, except in Stanger where there is now a town?

I interviewed Sakhile[2] Nxumalo on 4 April 2008 in Nongoma, a rural town in KwaZulu-Natal Province in the north-eastern corner of South Africa. Until his death in 2012, Sakhile[3] lived in a village about 5 kilometres from one of the residences of the Zulu king Zwelithini kaBhekuzulu. A few days earlier he had taken my co-researcher and I to a site near his home where, he maintains, once stood one of the homesteads of Zwide kaLanga, the last ruler of the Ndwandwe kingdom before it was routed by the Zulu. He identified himself as a Ndwandwe descendant and revivalist who wanted everybody to know that the Ndwandwe and their last ruler were, and are, important – despite the long shadow cast by Shaka kaSenzangakhona, the famed king of the Zulu.

Nongoma has been home to Zulu kings since the 1840s. The history of Ndwandwe rule under Zwide kaLanga is largely forgotten in public histories of the area, even though it is present when one begins to listen more carefully to people's daily speech, as well as to songs and poetry performed on family ceremonial occasions. So, who was Zwide and who were, and are, the Ndwandwe? What did he have to do with the founder of the Zulu kingdom, Shaka?

[1] I acknowledge the financial support of the Wenner-Gren Foundation and the National Research Foundation for different phases of my research. Opinions expressed and findings reached are those of the author and not be be attributed to either of these Foundations.
[2] Not his real name. I have given my sources pseudonyms to protect their identities.
[3] I use first names or nicknames for my interviewees after first introducing them by their full names because most of them have the same family names: Ndwandwe and Nxumalo.

The Ndwandwe kingdom was one of the three most powerful polities in the east of Southern Africa in the early nineteenth century. From a base in the area between Nongoma and Magudu, it competed with the Mabhudu-Tembe, centred south of today's Maputo, and the Mthethwa, who lived around today's Richard's Bay-Empangeni.[4] Zwide was the last ruler of the kingdom before its collapse following a series of wars with the expanding Zulu kingdom under Shaka. As I show in this essay, Zwide kaLanga is being given more prominence by a group of Ndwandwe revivalists whose project is to overcome almost two hundred years of what they perceive to be the public silencing of their history. Like the uBumbano lwamaZwide – the association I discuss below, formed by various groupings of these Ndwandwe revivalists – Sakhile blamed Shaka and the Zulu for the Ndwandwe's historical and contemporary woes. In the interview, he went off on a facetious tangent about present Zulu authority over Ndwandwe descendants:

Awu, kodwa bakithi, la masimba la kudlala ngathi lokhu! Uyazi la manyala la! Kuhamba kuthi kuphethe lelizwe lokhu. Ayi. Ayi. Ayi, yazi ngithathe nami ngit-hukuthele!... [ahleke] Ake kubanjwe yena okungcono. [Kuthiwe] [l]o Shaka lo ke nimvuse; mina ke ngimthathelele ngedwa. ... Ngisho lokhu engiyaye ngithi amacala athethelwa la. Kuyadlala nje; kunamuph' umlando khona?[5]

Awu, but really, this shit is messing with us! You know, this disgusting thing! It goes around saying it is in charge of this land this thing. No, no, no, I just get angry!... [laughs] He should be caught [in the place of those who defeated and displaced the Ndwandwe]. [It should be said,] Bring this Shaka back to life; I want to take him on on my own... I am talking about this thing where [court] cases are heard. This thing is just playing; what history does it have?

In the above extract Sakhile disparages the local leader as a nonentity who does not have the long history in the area that the Ndwandwe have. He rhetorically reduces the Zulu polity to the minor chiefdom it was before Shaka started building it into a larger state after 1815. He calls up the memory of Ndwandwe rule in the Nongoma-Magudu area to question Zulu authority under present democratic governance. He challenges the incessant celebration of Shaka's conquests that brought many previously independent polities under Zulu control. He suggests that, if it were possible, he would demand of the Zulu royal elite that it raises Shaka, on whose suspect success its position rests today, so that he could take him on, toe to toe.

Sakhile went further in his invocation of the Ndwandwe past. Asked which land he was referring to when he said we were on Ndwandwe

---

[4] John Wright and Carolyn Hamilton, 'Traditions and Transformations: the Phongolo-Mzimkhulu Region in the Late Eighteenth and Early Nineteenth Centuries' in Andrew Duminy and Bill Guest (eds), *Natal and Zululand from Earliest Times to 1910: A New History* (Pietermaritzburg: University of Natal Press, 1989), 59–63.

[5] Mbongiseni Buthelezi and Antony Ndwandwe, Interview with Sakhile Ndwandwe, Nongoma, 4 April 2008.

territory, his response was: '*ElakwaNdwandwe leli, lonke leli. Izwe lak-waNdwandwe nje. ElakwaZulu liseStanger lapho kukhona khon' uShaka. Izwe lakwaNdwandwe nje kusukela nganeno koThukela.*' (This is the land of kwaNdwandwe[6] all here. This is simply land of kwaNdwandwe. The land of KwaZulu is in Stanger where Shaka is. It's kwaNdwandwe land from the near side of the Thukela River.) For Sakhile, then, the land of the Zulu is in and around KwaDukuza, where Shaka eventually died and lies buried, and where an annual celebration in his honour has been carried out since 1970.[7] This celebration was initiated by the leadership of the KwaZulu government under Inkatha, the Zulu nationalist organisation which governed KwaZulu under the apartheid government. It celebrated Zulu Heritage with Shaka, the founding hero, as its centre. The celebration was continued after the end of apartheid as part of the annual national Heritage Day on 24 September by the provincial government, first under the leadership of the renamed Inkatha Freedom Party (IFP) and then under the African National Congress (ANC). The ANC took over the annual celebration once, by 2004, it had secured political control of the province through, among other things, wresting the control and use of Zulu symbols from the IFP.[8] Key to this capture of Zulu symbols formerly mobilised by Inkatha was the defection of the Zulu king, who aligned himself with the ANC in 1994.[9]

Quoting from Shaka's *izibongo* (praises) – central to commemorating Shaka and to this essay – Sakhile spoke of the Ndwandwe as continuing to be suppressed by the Zulu to this day:

Akaze babuye banikwe [abakwaNdwandwe] isiqephu [sezwe ukuthi basiphathe] ngoba kwakusentweni yabo, ngoba uma benganikwa isiqephu njena uzovuka lomlilo. Njoba beze babong' uShaka kuthiwe 'umxoshi womunt' amxoshele futhi nje' kwakusholwo khon' ukuthi uyobaxosha njal' abakwaNdwandwe ngoba uma babuye banikwe [izwe] nje kuyoba khon... uyovuk' umlilo.[10]

They [the people of kwaNdwandwe] were never again given a piece of land [to rule over] because this was their land. Shaka is praised saying, 'the pursuer of a person who chases him ceaselessly' – it was meant that he will forever chase

---

[6] I translate Sakhile's '*elakwaNdwandwe*' as 'the land of kwaNdwandwe' to keep in view the locative prefix 'kwa-'. This prefix suggests that the land belongs to a place called kwaNdwandwe, that is, the place of the putative ancestor called Ndwandwe.

[7] Nsizwa Dlamini, 'Monuments of Division: Apartheid and Post-Apartheid Struggles over Zulu Nationalist Heritage Sites' in B. Carton, J. Laband, and J. Sithole (eds), *Zulu Identities: Being Zulu, Past and Present* (Pietermaritzburg: University of KwaZulu-Natal Press, 2008), 383.

[8] Sandra Klopper, '"He Is My King, but He Is Also My Child": Inkatha, the African National Congress and the Struggle for Control over Zulu Cultural Symbols', *Oxford Art Journal* 19, 1 (1996): 59.

[9] Wonder Hlongwa, 'Buthelezi and Zwelithini at loggerheads,' <http://www.citypress.co .za/SouthAfrica/News/Buthelezi-and-Zwelithini-at-loggerheads-20100614>, accessed 28 December 2011.

[10] Mbongiseni Buthelezi and Antony Ndwandwe, Interview with Sakhile Ndwandwe.

the abakwaNdwandwe because if they were ever given [land], the fire would reignite.[11]

Sakhile interprets the public silence on the Ndwandwe past and the absence of any prominent Ndwandwe 'traditional leader' in Zululand as the continuing pursuit of Zwide by Shaka. Indeed Shaka's symbolic presence and that of Zulu royalty is inescapable in KwaZulu-Natal: from the King Shaka International Airport built in time for the 2010 Fifa Soccer World Cup, through the province being marketed as the kingdom of the Zulu, to the king's residences dotted throughout the Ulundi-Nongoma-Magudu areas. What is more, Shaka's *izibongo* are ubiquitous, excerpted by singers of the popular *maskanda* form, such as Mfaz' omnyama, in their songs and in widely used greetings of 'Zulu' people as '*nina beLembe*' (you people of the axe). The greeting is an excerpt from the praise '*ilemb' eleq' amany' amalembe ngokukhalipha*' (axe that surpasses other axes in sharpness).[12]

In the ongoing transition from apartheid to democratic rule, many people in KwaZulu-Natal (and elsewhere in South Africa) are probing their identities and confronting what the Zulu kingdom and Zuluness mean to them. As a consequence of the renovation of Shaka and the making the Zulu past as the heritage of the province, people who trace their history to KwaZulu-Natal have to (circum)navigate this symbolic centrality of the Zulu kingdom and Zuluness when seeking to understand their pasts. The probing of identities that is in progress has a range of motivations: from claiming land through the state's Land Restitution Programme to jostling for control of tourism revenues on land alienated under British colonial rule and apartheid once this land is restored to descendants of earlier inhabitants. Some are merely attempting to restore dignity stripped away from their forebears under white rule by claiming chieftainship through the Commission on Traditional Leadership Disputes and Claims.[13] In order to determine their forebears' experiences that have shaped the present, most people who have inherited a Zulu identity have to make sense of how the Zulu kingdom and Zuluness have gone into the making of who they are today. The many groups currently attempting these engagements with their pasts include Mbatha, Qwabe,

---

[11] Somaphunga fled with Zwide when the Ndwandwe kingdom collapsed. After Zwide's death, he was embroiled in a succession dispute with Sikhunyana, his brother, over the new kingdom that Zwide had built. Somaphunga returned to pay allegiance to Shaka. See John Wright, 'Rediscovering the Ndwandwe Kingdom', in N. Swanepoel, A. Esterhuysen, and P. Bonner (eds), *Five Hundred Years Rediscovered: Southern African Precedents and Prospects* (Johannesburg: Wits University Press, 2008), 232.

[12] Trevor Cope, *Izibongo: Zulu Oral Literature* (London: Clarendon Press 1968), 88, 89.

[13] Jabulani Sithole, 'Preface – Zuluness in South Africa: from "Struggle" Debate to Democratic Transformation', in B. Carton, J. Laband, and J. Sithole (eds), *Zulu Identities: Being Zulu, Past and Present* (Pietermaritzburg: University of KwaZulu-Natal Press, 2008): xiv–vi.

Buthelezi, and Mkhize.[14] They are calling up identities coterminous with pre-Zulu polities. Among the Ndwandwe, the uBumbano lwamaZwide, an association inaugurated in 2006, is attempting to mobilise people like Sakhile and Thokozani to engage with their Ndwandwe pasts. How then did the forebears of these groupings become Zulu?

In her MA thesis, 'Ideology, Oral Traditions and the Struggle for Power in the Early Zulu Kingdom', Carolyn Hamilton argues that, in contrast to the Mthethwa and Qwabe as well as to its earlier defensive tactics, the later Zulu state maintained cohesion through more pronounced manipulation of kinship as an ideology of state. While 'the pre-state societies of south-east Africa were essentially lineage-based',[15] these lineage identities were progressively subsumed under Zuluness. In my view, this process accelerated with the arrival of Boer trekkers from the Cape Colony in the late 1830s. For some inside and on the margins of the Zulu kingdom, Zulu identity became a shield against the humiliation of defeat and dispossession by European invaders in the mid- to late-nineteenth centuries. It subsequently came to be passed down and inherited without question, even among groups that had been recalcitrant to Zulu control at first, such as the Qwabe. However, pre-Zulu identities were simultaneously maintained through lineage group symbols in the form of three genres of oral art: each kinship group's *ihubo lesizwe* ('national' hymn), *izithakazelo* (kinship group address names), and the *izibongo* (personal praises) of important people in the group's past.[16] These forms are used in a range of settings: from the *izithakazelo* as polite address in daily speech to all three forms being deployed to address the group's ancestors during family rituals. Increasingly, they are now being put to use in mobilising for the re(dis)covery of lineage-based pre-Zulu identities as heritage in KwaZulu-Natal and elsewhere.

In this chapter, focusing on the uBumbano and the Ndwandwe more broadly, I argue that the mobilisation of pre-Zulu identities in part takes its cue from the promotion of Zulu Heritage. Heritage has become the domain in which the struggle over public history is being waged. The chapter investigates the paradoxical operation of heritage discourse in KwaZulu-Natal. On one hand the promotion of Zulu heritage, or

---

[14] For coverage of some of these projects, see the work of the Archival Platform's Ancestral Stories initiative at <www.archivalplatform.org.za>, accessed 27 December 2011. In addition to groups of older people who hold face-to-face meetings, younger people are using social networking websites, especially Facebook, extensively to discuss their identities and arrange social gatherings of groups of 'kin'.

[15] Carolyn Hamilton, 'Ideology, Oral Traditions and the Struggle for Power in the Early Zulu Kingdom' (Master of Arts thesis, University of the Witwatersrand, 1985): 10.

[16] To be sure, kinship appears to have been, and to continue to be, used as an ideological tool. Groupings that are identified as Ndwandwe through kinship are likely to have been conquered and suppressed in much the same way that the Ndwandwe revivalists see their forebears as having been suppressed under Zulu authority.

Heritage with a capital 'H', has continued to hold in place the iteration of the past of KwaZulu-Natal as singularly Zulu with Shaka as the central character.[17] The promotion of this Heritage has transported into the present, in renovated form, Shaka- and Zulu-centric versions of the past of north-eastern South Africa that have prevailed for close on two centuries. On the other hand, this Heritage has given people who are attempting to question the position of the Zulu establishment in the present a language with which to articulate their projects. Heritage discourse has opened the space to question Zuluness in ways that are unprecedented by articulating projects that put pressure on Zuluness as celebrating these groups' heritages, or what I shall term heritage with a small 'h'. It has made possible the reconstructing of the histories of groups that were incorporated into the Zulu kingdom in ways that seem not to threaten Zulu identity and the position of the Zulu monarchy as promoted by the state and the heritage and tourism industries. Focusing first on the making of Shaka and the Zulu kingdom as Heritage in KwaZulu-Natal, and then on the response of the uBumbano lwamaZwide, which was formed in 2006, I explore how the centrality of Heritage is being (circum)navigated against the odds of its iteration.

Making KwaZulu-Natal Zulu, or the Making of Heritage with a Capital 'H'

Ciraj Rassool accurately points out that 'it is [in the domain of heritage and public history] that attempts are being made to fashion the categories and images of the post-apartheid nation. It is also in the domain of historical production that important contests are unfolding over the South African past.'[18] A major concern has been how, after liberation, to reverse colonial and apartheid representations of Africans as without history. To overcome racist stereotypes about black South Africans and to give the South African nation, especially Africans, a past in which to take pride, heritage rapidly became a key domain. The re-engineering of the nation's past entailed renovating and magnifying to the level of national heroes figures in whom South Africans were exhorted collectively to take pride, especially in then-president Thabo Mbeki's African Renaissance.[19] Among these figures was Shaka.

On the part of the ruling ANC at national level, the post-apartheid renovation and foregrounding of Zuluness and Shaka has also been a

---

[17] What we see at play in this process is the correlation between language and ethnic identity that Irvine and Dakubu discuss in their respective chapters in this volume.

[18] Ciraj Rassool, 'The Rise of Heritage and the Reconstruction of History in South Africa', *Kronos* 26 (2000): 1. See also Herwitz in this volume.

[19] See Mbeki's 1998 African Renaissance Statement, <http://www.dfa.gov.za/docs/speeches/1998/mbek0813.htm>, accessed 26 December 2011.

pragmatic political response to the martial Zuluness promoted by intellectuals tied to the Zulu-nationalist organisation Inkatha since the 1970s.
This renovation and emphasis then became part of the state's job creation efforts for purposes of poverty alleviation by developing a tourism
economy that built on the easy identification of the province with the
Zulu. The province thus came to be marketed as 'the Zulu kingdom'.
These processes have yielded Zulu heritage or Heritage with a capital 'H'
as the dominant mode of official public history in the province. Rassool
refers to 'capital "H" history' to criticise the dismissal of heritage by guild
historians who see it as a lesser form of history than their practice.[20] Here
I use Rassool's implicit reference to heritage as small 'h' history and apply
the terms to heritage in the case of KwaZulu-Natal, referring to state-
promoted heritage as Heritage with a capital 'H', whereas the deployment
of the same heritage discourse to counter the dominant version has man-
ufactured small 'h' heritage. To trace the making of images of Shaka and
the Zulu that created Heritage for use in post-apartheid South Africa, I
turn to John Wright's periodisation of these images.

Wright offers a comprehensive but succinct genealogy of portrayals of
Shaka. Essentially, he demonstrates,

From the 1820s to the 1990s, images of Shaka were a product of what can be
characterised as colonial-type conflicts, in which white people in southern Africa
and Europe sought to establish political, economic and cultural domination over
the indigenous black people, and in which black people sought first to resist
and subsequently to throw off white domination. . . . In important senses this
era of conflict came to an end in South Africa with the establishment of its
first democratically elected government in 1994. The upshot was the startlingly
rapid depoliticisation of the process in which images of Shaka were made, and the
rendering of the figure of Shaka the Mighty as increasingly an anachronism in the
New South Africa. Hollowed-out versions of this figure lived on in appropriations
of it made by interests in business and in the heritage industry. . . . [21]

Wright identifies four phases in the period from the 1820s to the 1990s as
the different political contexts in which images of Shaka were produced.
The first of these phases was before the late 1870s, when there were still
a number of black societies in Southern Africa that were independent of
white rule. The second phase, from the late 1870s to the early twentieth
century, saw the subjugation of black societies by European imperial
and local settler interests. Lasting from the early twentieth century to the
1950s, the third phase was a period of no serious challenge to white settler
domination. Finally, the late 1950s onward saw more militant African

---

[20] Rassool, 'The Rise of Heritage', 4–6.
[21] John Wright, 'Reconstituting Shaka Zulu for the Twenty-First Century', *Southern African Humanities* 18, 2 (2006): 140.

nationalism and decolonisation.[22] The discourses of each of these phases has its own dominant Shakas, as Wright demonstrates.

In the first place, while early Cape colonial records contain reports of Shaka, Zwide of the Ndwandwe, and Mzilikazi (then still identified as Ndwandwe by settler writers) as powerful chiefs responsible for the wars and migrations that were destabilising the interior of Southern Africa, by the late 1820s Shaka had come to be credited with being the main reason for the instability. In the 1840s, the migration in the 1820s and 1830s of other successful raiders and conquerors – Mzilikazi, Sebetwane of the Kololo, Zwangendaba of the Ngoni and Soshangane of the Gaza – further north into Southern Africa, focused attention on Shaka as the motor for the upheavals in the 1820s.[23]

The images of Shaka among black populations in this phase can be divided into two: on one hand, in the Zulu kingdom he increasingly came to be remembered as a powerful ruler and conqueror as anxiety grew about white expansion. On the other hand, Wright speculates, it is most likely that in colonial Natal Africans were ambivalent about Shaka, seeing him as the destroyer of the old order when people lived in their own independent chiefdoms.[24] The inhabitants of this region are likely to have adopted a more positive view of Shaka only in the 1870s and 1880s, as colonial rule bore down more and more heavily on them.[25]

The Shaka stereotype that had been building up since the 1840s finally solidified in the second phase of Wright's periodisation, the 1880s to the 1920s. The victory of Zulu over British forces at the battle of iSandlwana in the early stages of the Anglo-Zulu War set in circulation a world-wide reputation of the Zulu as warlike, a stereotype that was traced back to Shaka. And as the last black societies in Southern Africa were being brought under white control, popular writers like George Theal and Henry Rider Haggard further entrenched this stereotype of the Zulu and Shaka. Theal's sweeping representation of Southern Africa was later taken up in the early twentieth century by various authors, all either colonial officials or missionaries, who were 'experts' on more localised areas – among them A. T. Bryant, the author of *Olden Times in Zululand and Natal* (1929).[26]

Wright further states that in rural black communities memories of the period of Shaka's rule were dying out, some of the last being collected by

---

[22] Ibid.
[23] Ibid., 141–2.
[24] In Shaka's day, the chiefdoms south of the Thukela River were exploited for tribute but never integrated into the Zulu kingdom (Carolyn Hamilton and John Wright), 'The Making of the AmaLala: Ethnicity, Ideology and Relations of Subordination in a Precolonial Context', *South African Historical Journal* 22, 1 (1990): 3–23.
[25] Wright, 'Reconstituting Shaka Zulu', 142.
[26] Ibid., 143.

James Stuart between 1897 and 1922 and finding their way into works like Magema Fuze's *Abantu Abamnyama Lapa Bavela Ngakona* (1922). The dying out of such memories led to a narrowing of views on Shaka, stereotypes of Shaka the Mighty becoming more generally normative. In the third phase, Wright demonstrates, there was a similar narrowing of views among black intellectuals writing in the 1940s and 1950s. At this point nationalist resistance against white domination was on the rise as it became clearer that racial segregation was going to be strictly enforced. Shaka was increasingly recast as an African hero.[27]

In the final phase of Wright's schema, in the era of decolonisation academic discourses revamped the previous stereotype of Shaka the bloody tyrant and began describing him as 'a great statesman'.[28] It was in this period that Shaka's conquests were viewed as part of the processes of 'state formation' and 'nation building' and the term *mfecane*, which from the 1980s would come to be the focus of intense debate, was adopted in the historiography. Over the next two decades from the late 1970s, the making of images of Shaka in academic and public discourses came under critical scrutiny, eventually yielding works such as Hamilton's *Terrific Majesty: The Powers of Shaka and the Limits of Historical Invention* (1998) and Dan Wylie's *Savage Delight: White Myths of Shaka* (2000). In contrast to the revision of representations of the Southern African past and of Shaka conducted in academic discourses, black writers such as C. L. S. Nyembezi, Jordan Ngubane, and Mazisi Kunene have continued to produce views of Shaka that are informed by the early twentieth-century literature of liberal writers like Bryant and Stuart.[29]

In this chapter I focus on a key component of the making of images of Shaka for Zulu-speaking societies throughout the period discussed by Wright – the rhetorical monumentalisation of Shaka through his *izibongo* (praise poem). Today these *izibongo* are indeed the centrepiece of the province's Heritage. Less widely used than in the nineteenth century, when Zulu-speaking society was still a relatively cohesive polity, *izibongo* are nevertheless a widely understood and admired genre of praise poetry. A person's *izibongo* is a series of epithets or praise names given to him by parents (often), other relations, and neighbours, or self-composed. They build up the person's greatness by praising the subject's deeds as heroic. To build up this greatness, the *izibongo* use metaphor, allusion, and parallelism profusely.[30] The *izibongo* of leaders are much more extensive

---

[27] Ibid., 144.
[28] Ibid., 145.
[29] Ibid., 147.
[30] See Duncan Brown, *Voicing the Text: South African Oral Poetry and Performance* (Cape Town: Oxford University Press, 1998): 102–4; and Liz Gunner and Mafika Gwala, *Musho!: Zulu Popular Praises* (East Lansing, MI: Michigan State University Press, 1991), 1–7.

and are composed by *izimbongi*, praise poets, who are often the leader's followers. Shaka's *izibongo* were composed in his lifetime and have come down to us through repeated performance and recording.

For almost two hundred years, Shaka's *izibongo* have been repeated at Zulu 'national' festivals, used in greeting 'Zulu' people, published in books, analysed by scholars, and memorised by students in Zulu language classes. As far as the Ndwandwe are represented, the *izibongo* celebrate the defeat of their putative ancestor, Zwide kaLanga, and the resulting end of their autonomy. Shaka is effusively celebrated in relation to Zwide in five places in the version of his *izibongo* James Stuart compiled:

> *UBholokoqa bazalukanisile,*
> *Zalukaniswe uNoju noNgqengenye,*
> *EyakwaNtombazi neyakwaNandi;*
> *Yayikhiph' eshoba libomvu,*
> *Ikhishwa elimhlophe lakwaNandi...*

> The open-handed one, they have matched the regiments,
> They were matched by Noju and Ngqengenye,
> The one belonging to Ntombazi and the other to Nandi,
> He brought out the one with the red bush,
> Brought out by the white one of Nandi...[31]

The above lines celebrate Shaka's triumph over Zwide. Zwide and Shaka are likened to two bulls, erroneously translated as regiments, being 'matched' to fight. Noju and Ngqengenye, who are said to have matched the contenders, were, respectively, Zwide's and Shaka's counsellors. Noju defected to Shaka's side and was involved in devising the strategy to defeat the Ndwandwe.[32] The two bulls are identified as belonging to Ntombazi and Nandi, Zwide's and Shaka's mothers respectively, hence they are Zwide and Shaka. In the end it is the one belonging to Nandi – Shaka – who triumphs. The *izibongo* continue:

> *Umxoshi womuntu amxoshele futhi;*
> *Ngimthand' exosh' uZwide ozalwa uLanga,*
> *Emthabatha lapha liphuma khona,*
> *Emsingisa lapha lishona khona;*
> *UZwide wampheq' amahlonjan' omabili.*

> Pursuer of a person and he pursues him unceasingly;
> I liked him when he pursued Zwide son of Langa,
> Taking him from where the sun rises
> And sending him to where it sets;
> As for Zwide, he folded his two little shoulders together.[33]

---

[31] Cope, *Izibongo: Zulu Oral Literature*, lines 16–19.
[32] Ibid., 89.
[33] Ibid., lines 100–4.

These are often-repeated lines today – evident in how readily Sakhile deployed them as evidence of continuing Ndwandwe humiliation – that refer to Zwide's escape from Shaka's invading force. After a protracted war in which the Zulu army overcame the Ndwandwe, Zwide fled north, first into Swazi territory, before settling in today's Mpumalanga Province where he re-established his kingdom.[34] This is a painful memory for most of those involved in organising the uBumbano. Moreover, Ntombazi is said to have been burned to death in her house, compounding the sense of injury felt today.

Ntombazi is remembered as having been a major influence on Zwide through her counsel and her use of witchcraft. Shaka's *izibongo* confirm this when the subject of the praise is said to have been cooked (strengthened) in Ntombazi's (witch's) pot:

UMagongobala!
Ophekwe ngembiz' ende yakwaNtombazi
Waphekwa wagongobala.

He who gets stiff!
He was cooked in the deep pot of Ntombazi,
He was cooked and got stiff.[35]

A further reference to Ntombazi comes later in the poem:

Inkonyan' ekhwele phezu kwendlu kwaNtombazi,
Bathi iyahlola,
Kanti yibo bezaz' ukuhlola...

Calf that climbed on top of a hut at Ntombazi's kraal,
They said it was scouting,
But it was they who prided themselves on scouting...[36]

The epithet suggests that Shaka completely dominated Zwide, even climbing on Zwide's mother's house. The term '*ukuhlola*' is mistranslated in Cope's English version to assert that Shaka was scouting, whereas the praise suggests Shaka was said by the unnamed (seemingly Ndwandwe) observers to be foretelling disaster when they were the ones doing so.

Shaka is further eulogised for his defeat of Zwide:

UMaswezisela wakithi kwaBulawayo,
Oswezisel' uZwide ngamagqanqula.
Izulu elimagwagwaba likaMageba,
Elidume phezulu kuNomangci,
Laduma' emva kwomuzi eKuqhobokeni laqanda,
Lazithath' izihlangu zaMaphela naMankayiya,
Amabheqan' ezimpaka asal' ezihlahleni...

---

[34] John Wright, 'Rediscovering the Ndwandwe Kingdom', 231–2.
[35] Cope, *Izibongo: Zulu Oral Literature*, lines 171–3.
[36] Ibid., lines 208–10.

Our own bringer of poverty [of] Bulawayo,
Who made Zwide destitute by great strides.
The sky that rumbled, the sky of Mageba,
That thundered above Nomangci mountain,
It thundered behind the kraal at Kuqhobokeni and struck,
It took the shields of the Maphela and the Mankayiya,
And the little melons of the Zimpaka were left on the vines . . . [37]

The praise mocks Ndwandwe warriors: their *amabheqe* (decorative tassels made of animal skins worn hanging on the side of the head), mistranslated as melons above, are reduced to the diminutive form, *amabheqana*. These tassels are said to have snagged and been left hanging off trees as the warriors fled. This humiliation is bolstered by the cataloguing that follows of Zwide's sons and adherents who were killed in the war: Nomahlanjana, Mphepha, Nombengula, Dayingubo, Sonsukwana, Mtimona, Mpondo-phumela-kwezinye, Ndengezi-mashumi, Sikloloba-singamabele, Sihlala-mthini-munye and Nqangube.[38] Shaka is then given a rhetorical pat on the back in the form of 'advice' to leave the Ndwandwe alone, having turned Zwide into a homeless criminal and subdued his son, Sikhun-yana (who had tried to launch an attack on the Zulu in 1826 but was comprehensively defeated with the help of white mercenaries from Port Natal):

Buya Mgengi phela indaba usuyenzile,
UZwide umphendul' isigcwelegcwele,
Namuhla futhi usuphendul' indodana.
USikhunyana uyintombi ukuganile
Ekufunyanis' uhlez' enkundlen' esibayen' eNkandla,
Engaz' ukuth' amabuth' akho anomgombolozelo.

Return, Trickster, you have finished this matter,
As for Zwide, you have made him into a homeless criminal,
And now today you have done the same to the son,
Sikhunyana is a girl and he has married you,
He found you sitting in council in the cattle-fold at Nkandla,
Not knowing that your soldiers had a cross-questioning.[39]

It is this boast, this ideologically charged reminder of the Ndwandwes' domination by the Zulu, that the uBumbano must (circum)navigate if it hopes to make sense of the past. How then are they going about attempting this project?

[37] Ibid., lines 178–84.
[38] Ibid., lines 185–96.
[39] Ibid., lines 198–204.

Becoming Less Zulu: Heritage against Heritage

On 13 November 2010 the uBumbano lwamaZwide held its first annual Zwide Heritage Celebration in the Mabaso area of Mbazwana in the far north-east of KwaZulu-Natal. Hosted by *inkosi* (chief) Justice Nxumalo, the organisation of the event was led by savvy politicians and business owners from Durban, Pietermaritzburg, and Empangeni, and included activists from Nongoma. The event was billed as an occasion to recall Zwide kaLanga. On 6 August 2011, the uBumbano convened its second annual event, this time named the Zwide Heritage Day. Moving closer in name to the annual national holiday on 24 September called Heritage Day, the uBumbano seemed finally to have found a language to position its project publicly.

These events recall the caution Rassool urges when considering the formulation and contestation of the dominant narrations of national identity and the past through heritage, tourism, and memorialisation in South Africa after apartheid:

> it must be recognised that these dominant discursive forms have not been uncontested. In significant cases, particularly in community museums and local cultural projects, certain initiatives have begun to push beyond these dominant narrations, contesting the constitutive elements of the nation, the cultural politics of tourism, as well as the signage systems and forms of memorialisation attached to urban and rural landscapes.[40]

The uBumbano's project can be seen as a cultural project that contests the dominant narrative of the Zulu element of the nation. The association turned to heritage in part as a result of attempts by the Zulu royal establishment to stop what it perceived as a move to unseat the king. Because of the inherited sense that Zwelithini is king of all 'Zulus' and the upholding of Heritage, openly calling into question one's Zuluness or anything to do with the Zulu king is almost impossible in KwaZulu-Natal. It quickly gets interpreted as *ukuvukela umbuso* (attempting to overthrow the monarchy) by the political underwriters and media upholders of Zuluness and by members of the public who unquestioningly subscribe to a Zulu identity. Thus the project of Ndwandwe self-reconstruction has had to proceed in very subtle ways, especially given the symbolic importance of the Ndwandwe as Shaka's adversaries. This caution is the result of previous experience after the launch of the association in 2006.

The uBumbano was launched after years of mobilisation by Ndwandwe, Nxumalo, and Madlobha people in KwaZulu-Natal, a process led from about 1990 by activists in various parts of the province and in Johannesburg.[41] In Johannesburg, a group of migrant workers

---

[40] Rassool, 'The Rise of Heritage', 1.
[41] Mbongiseni Buthelezi, Interview with Nkanyiso Ndwandwe, Durban, 12 May 2008.

of Ndwandwe descent had been meeting in Thokoza township since 1986.[42] Efforts elsewhere have yielded similar results – small groups of people energetically attempting to learn about their Ndwandwe past and to mobilise others. Today the association comprises a number of relatively autonomous groupings with different geneses and trajectories in Intshanga between Pietermaritzburg and Durban, Durban itself, Empangeni, Nongoma, and Johannesburg. After 20 years of disparate efforts and intensifying networking, the 2006 event was to mark the coming together of all these groups into one association. However, the momentum of the association was slowed drastically by the intervention of the Zulu king.

Perceiving Ndwandwe organisation as a threat, the king became uneasy with the uBumbano. This followed reports reaching him that the Ndwandwe were making moves to reclaim the former Ndwandwe territory of Magudu-Nongoma. Hence he quickly suspended one of the leaders of a section of the Nongoma uBumbano who was on the staff at one of the king's residences. He also summoned the Ndwandwe administrator he identifies as the legitimate leader of the Ndwandwe to explain the meeting. None of those involved in these events will go on record about the events. I have pieced them together from conversations in and outside of meetings of the association I have attended since 2008 in Nongoma, Johannesburg, and Durban. Moreover, none of them will speak about the submissions a branch of the uBumbano made to the Land Claims Commission and to the Commission on Traditional Leadership Disputes and Claims. It was a report in a daily newspaper on the Ndwandwe claiming land from Nongoma to Magudu, the former Ndwandwe heartland, that appears to have triggered the Zulu king's response. Those who had submitted the claim had approached the leader from the lineage that sought refuge under Shaka to sign the claim, which he did without understanding the implications. The newspaper's interpretation was that he wanted to unseat the Zulu king. His response upon being questioned by the king was to attempt suicide.

The perception remains that the king is keeping an eye on Ndwandwe activities because, as Sakhile put it, he does not trust them. In recent years, he has increasingly emphasised his Ndwandwe roots, going as far as having his Ndwandwe mother's remains exhumed and reburied on 7 May 2011 in a heritage site that is being developed in Durban.[43] These events reinforce Sakhile's words about the Zulu king being suspicious of the Ndwandwe because of their symbolic power:

[42] Mbongiseni Buthelezi, Interview with Sifiso Ndwandwe, Johannesburg, 14 September 2009.
[43] Bongani Mthethwa, 'Fitting send-off for king's mother', <http://www.timeslive.co.za/local/article1055682.ece/Fitting-send-off-for-kings-mother#, accessed 22 December 2011.

[Kusukela koSomaphunga kuze kuzofika manje] kwaqhubeka ngokuthi siyazaz'
ukuthi siyini, nabakwaZulu bayasaz' ukuthi siyini . . . Basaz' ukuthi la mhlampe
singahle siphinde esikaMbopha. Nayo ingonyama sihleli nayo ayisethembile, iyazi
ukuthi singahle siphinde esikaMbopha, ukuthi, 'Nawe Mbopha nduna yami uyangibu-
lala?' . . . Yikho-ke kungekho nduna yakwaNdwandwe, kungekho nkosi yakwa-
Ndwandwe, ngoba ingaba khon' inkosi phela kuyobe sekuphelile.

[From Somaphunga and others – his contemporaries – until now] things have
continued in such a way that we know what we are [royalty], and those of kwaZulu
know what we are. . . . They still know that here what happened with Mbopha
might repeat itself. Even the lion [Zulu king] we live with him but he doesn't
trust us, he knows that what happened with Mbopha might repeat itself, that,
'Even you Mbopha, my counsellor, you are killing me?' . . . That's why there is
no Ndwandwe counsellor, no Ndwandwe chief, because if there is a chief then
it'll be over.

Sakhile likens what could happen if the Ndwandwe were allowed freely to
coalesce to Shaka's experience with Mbopha kaSithayi. A trusted counsellor, Mbopha became one of Shaka's assassins to whom Shaka is said
to have uttered the words Sakhile quotes as he was dying, hence the Zulu
royal establishment's surveillance of the Ndwandwe.

In my view, the Ndwandwe events have been called Heritage Day in
order to blunt the political force of such gatherings of the symbolically
powerful Ndwandwe. For those leaders of the uBumbano whose involvement in the association could have had significant implications, 'Heritage
Day' offers the best means to make the annual event politically innocu-
ous. Yet thus naming the commemoration is also a subversive move. To
call the event a Heritage Day is to identify it with the annual national
holiday. It is to place the two events on an equal footing. However, to
qualify the name of the Ndwandwe commemoration by adding 'Zwide'
in front at once posits the event as just a minor Ndwandwe affair, but
at the same time insists on putting Zwide upfront as the figure through
whom Ndwandweness is again being mediated today. The modification
goes one step further than the official commemoration of Shaka. Shaka
is submerged in the annual Heritage Day, albeit as the centre-piece of
this most high-profile of provincial commemorations. On the contrary,
the Ndwandwe explicitly tie their search for heritage, and therefore for a
past, to Zwide, Shaka's one-time adversary. For anybody learning about
the Ndwandwe event, which is announced on radio and in newspapers,
especially for those who are not Ndwandwe, this emphasis on Zwide begs
the question, 'Who was or is Zwide?' Those familiar with Ndwandwe
and Nxumalo *izithakazelo* immediately recognise the name as the main
Ndwandwe *isithakazelo*.

The naming of the event after Zwide thus inaugurates the potential for
the past to be narrated differently to the current Zulu-centric norm, and
for heritage to contest Heritage in the province. To be sure, an answer

to who Zwide is/was begins with his forces' war against Shaka's army. But potentially the narrative eventually displaces Shaka as it gets beyond Zwide's defeat to who he was before the confrontation with Shaka. In this way, heritage opens the path to narrations of the past that could overturn the current status quo. Heritage with a small 'h' thus minimises the subversive nature of the Ndwandwe reach for a pre-Zulu identity. This heritage begins to give a new edge to the symbolic power of the Ndwandwe that the Zulu royal establishment has tried to keep in check for almost two hundred years. This symbolic power of the Ndwandwe has lived on in Shaka's *izibongo* (praises) since the defeat of the Ndwandwe, and has been maintained in Ndwandwe oral artistic forms. It opens up political space to recall pasts and reconstruct in more public ways identities other than the singular 'Zulu' that had been inherited by the African inhabitants of the region that is now KwaZulu-Natal.

As evident from the Ndwandwe case, the attempt to (re)construct identities over which Zuluness has been emphasised takes the form of mobilising along the now-faint contours of the pre-Zulu polities by promoting the extant notion that people of the same family name historically belonged together in a chiefdom understood as an extended family unit. It is these identities that are now being increasingly emphasised over Zuluness. As suggested earlier, Ndwandweness has been retained in everyday language as well as in the oral art. In all this, how has a Ndwandwe identity been maintained over almost two centuries to be available to be mobilised today?

Being a 'Nation' within a Nation within the Nation

The concept of nation in the Zulu language is unstable. The term '*isizwe*' works on at least three levels. On one level is the South African Nation, under formation since the end of apartheid. On the second level, the Zulu ethnic group continues to be called an *isizwe* even as its stability and sustainability come under pressure. Finally, a group that shares a family name such as Ndwandwe – and related names like Nxumalo, Madlobha, and others – is called '*isizwe samaNdwandwe/sakwaNdwandwe*' (the Ndwandwe 'nation').[44] The Ndwandwe are thus considered a 'nation' within the Zulu nation within the South African Nation. However, they also exceed both the Zulu nation and the South African Nation: the Ndwandwe diaspora that has been drawn into the uBumbano is descended from people who, in the 1820s, relocated outside today's KwaZulu-Natal and what was to become South Africa. This 'nation', though

---

[44] A fourth use of the term, which does not relate to my analysis here, is in referring to a territorially based 'community' under a chief.

disjointed for almost two hundred years, is able to be constituted – rhetorically for now – by the uBumbano because language has kept the notion of this nation alive.

Evidence suggests that groups who were incorporated into the Zulu kingdom continued to refer to themselves as *izizwe* (nations, sing. *isizwe*).[45] The Ndwandwe have continued to call themselves an *isizwe* ('nation'). When the Ndwandwe kingdom collapsed in the 1820s, indications are that the Ndwandwe who submitted and were incorporated into the Zulu kingdom were allowed to continue calling themselves an *isizwe* ('nation') even as they were being integrated into the expanding Zulu *isizwe* (nation). But the term would have referred to the totality of Ndwandwe, both those incorporated into the Zulu kingdom and those in the diaspora who settled in other polities such as the Swazi or went on to found new polities – such as the Gaza – as they moved through Southern Africa. In the Zulu kingdom, integration entailed the careful management of politically dangerous memories of the past. This process saw forced forgetting alongside the natural atrophy of recalling the past. Hence, by the beginning of the twentieth century, effectively, sustained narrations of the Ndwandwe past had ceased. As John Wright puts it, 'The overall effect [of suppression of the public narration of the histories of incorporated groups] was that by the beginning of the twentieth century, at least, "officially" sustained telling of the history of the Ndwandwe kingdom had effectively come to an end.'[46] Yet the memory of belonging to a Ndwandwe nation of sorts has been carried forward into the present among people of Ndwandwe descent through the repeated invocation of ancestors.

The notion of being an *isizwe* has been transmitted in the Ndwandwe *ihubo lesizwe* ('national' hymn) at events such as weddings and funerals when the ancestors of the *isizwe* are addressed and the *izithakazelo* are used to address the ancestors as well as the living. The *ihubo* and the *izithakazelo* maintain the memory of, and rhetorically reconstitute, the Ndwandwe *isizwe* in each present moment of their utterance. The term *ihubo lesizwe* carries forward the notion of Ndwandweness contained by the kinship group name Ndwandwe. It calls up all the *oNdwandwe* or *abakwaNdwandwe* (Ndwandwe people) who are now the *amathongo* (ancestors) who have ever lived to be present at the event where they are used. The leader sings, '*Inj' emnyama*' and the rest of the crowd responds, '*Hhiya hho, hhiya hho, hhiya hho.*' The singing only stops when the man leading the ceremony calls out the first *isithakazelo*, '*Zwide!*' and

[45] Colin Webb and John Wright, *The James Stuart Archive of Recorded Oral Evidence Relating to the History of the Zulu and Neighbouring Peoples*, Volume 4 (Durban: Killie Campbell Africana Library and University of Natal Press, 1986), 297.
[46] Wright, 'Rediscovering the Ndwandwe Kingdom', 217.

the crowd has to respond. It is a hymn with which many are familiar as it is sung at all Ndwandwe, Nxumalo, and other *imizi* (homes) where ritual observances are practised. Each time a Ndwandwe hears it, it is a reminder that s/he is part of the Ndwandwe 'nation'.[47]

In ceremonial usage, other names of putative ancestors of the Ndwandwe 'nation' follow 'Zwide'. The *izithakazelo* of the Ndwandwe can thus be used for all Ndwandwe people. These generic *izithakazelo* – Zwide, Mkhatshwa, Nkabanhle, wena waseGudunkomo, wena kaKhokhel' abantu bahlatshwe, Sidinane – are all names of Ndwandwe and Nxumalo ancestors who are presumed to have been leaders in the past. According to Hamilton, 'The ostensible function of *izithakazelo* seems to have been preservation of the memory of a clan's wider genealogical connections. People claim genealogical connections and tend to observe marriage prohibitions with groups who share the same *izithakazelo*, even where the circumstances of their connection are not (or no longer) known. It is widely asserted that a group 'must' be related to whosoever their *izithakazelo* (or *tinanatelo*) conjoin with.'[48] What is notable in the genealogical connections maintained by Ndwandwe *izithakazelo* today is that the names of people who came after Zwide – Somaphunga and Mgojana, who lived in the Zulu kingdom in this case – do not feature in the *izithakazelo*. This suggests that the *isizwe* that is recalled is that which existed up to Zwide's defeat.

Ndwandwe *izithakazelo* as used in polite address and family rituals thus maintain and recall the Ndwandwe *isizwe* up to the moment of its collapse – that is, the defeat of the Ndwandwe by the Zulu in approximately 1820 – in the way they name notables up to Zwide. It is thus little wonder that founders of the uBumbano hold on strongly to the idea of the defeat of the Ndwandwe as the moment that chartered Ndwandwe loss of status that persists to this day. This memory lies dormant in the *izithakazelo*. It is activated each time a Ndwandwe ceremony is performed and the ancestors hailed with the *izithakazelo*.

Conclusion

Since the end of apartheid heritage has been made a central arena of the re-narration of the South African past, as Daniel Herwitz demonstrates in his chapter in this volume. However, it is far from settled which version of the past will prevail as the nation's foundational narrative. As Rassool argues, the same arena of heritage is a terrain of struggle as different versions of the past jostle for dominance. The Ndwandwe case I

---

[47] Mbongiseni Buthelezi and Antony Ndwandwe, Interview with Gabisa and Mathanda Ndwandwe, Nongoma, 21 May 2008.
[48] Hamilton, 'Ideology, Oral Traditions and the Struggle for Power', 66–7.

have discussed in this essay is an example of what the state's attempt at initiating a post-apartheid national narrative through Heritage has activated. By positioning Shaka and Zulu history as the dominant Heritage of KwaZulu-Natal province, marketing the province through this version, and encouraging members of the public to take pride in their heritage, the state's efforts have simultaneously encouraged the reach for heritages that contest the very narrative being propagated by the state. The ubiquitous discourse of heritage has opened the path for the public assertion of histories that do not sit easily with singular notions of national heroes and identity that would fit into the nation-building project. These alternative histories and the inheritances they port with them are being positioned in the public domain as heritage, the very thing the state is encouraging.

What is of note in the Ndwandwe case is that whereas Zulu Heritage is currency in the tourism market, what impels elders like Sakhile and the activists who have formed the uBumbano lwamaZwide is not (yet) the currency of heritage in tourism. Rather, they are interested in claiming back for themselves a past that was denied Ndwandwe descendants for almost two hundred years. Heritage is thus a terrain of struggle over and for the past in post-apartheid society. The struggle puts various players with divergent interests in heritage – some invested in singular versions of the province's heritage and others seeking ways around these singular versions – on a collision course. Minor heritages threaten to unravel the grand narrative of the Zulu kingdom and its leader Shaka, on whom so much rests today.

9   9/11 and the Painful Death of an Asante King

National Tragedies in Comparative Perspective[1]

Kwesi Yankah

In presenting this chapter I claim no expertise on the 9/11 tragedy, a topic
Americans are better placed to examine. Neither do I seek to make an
unfair comparison between 'apples' and 'oranges' in a way that prioritises
or valorises one national calamity over the other, or uncritically trivialises
other cultures or peoples. Instead, the chapter seeks to use an event like
9–11 as a frame of reference to highlight national catastrophes in some
predominantly oral cultures – such as those in Africa – that over time have
been integrated within the regulatory institutions of the contemporary
nation state. I refer specifically to the Asante people who occupy the
most populous region of Ghana, a nation with a population of 25 million
in which there are close to 50 ethnic groups and languages.

I saw the World Trade Centre in 1999, when I visited New York from
Philadelphia with my family, weeks before I wound up a visiting profess-
orship position at the University of Pennsylvania. During this visit we
saw a great many American monuments and historic sites virtually at a
glance, in the course of a boat ride on the Hudson River. These included
the World Trade Centre, the Twin Towers.

On 11 September 2001 when the tragedy occurred I was in Ghana, on
official business at the seat of government in Accra, when video footage of
the event started emerging on CNN: terrified throngs of people running
helter skelter in alleys and streets, screaming, utterly devastated by a
calamity that was only just starting. The final outcome is now known
the world over: nearly 3,000 people were killed, including emergency
workers trying to rescue people and fight fires, police personnel, and
paramedics; more than 6,000 were injured. This is besides considerable
structural damage to several nearby buildings and offices. The tragedy
had happened after four coordinated attacks aimed at New York and
Washington, DC. Two hijacked passenger jets were crashed into the
World Trade Centre, reducing the Twin Towers to rubble, and a third
into the west wall of the Pentagon, inflicting major damage and loss of

---

[1] This chapter was originally delivered as a paper in a distinguished lecture series organised
by the African Studies Center of the University of Michigan, Ann Arbor, in November
2011, when the author was on sabbatical leave from the University of Ghana.

life. The fourth passenger jet crashed in a field in Pennsylvania after a struggle between passengers and hijackers, killing all aboard.

The wounds from the tragedy are still festering, and the scars are self-evident. The tragedy is considered as perhaps the single most devastating blow suffered by citizens in the recent history of America. But America remembers, and quickly rises to mark the tragedy through annual commemorative events and memorial services throughout the country; annual roll calls of the heroes; and ongoing reconstruction of a twin tower, a National September 11 Memorial and Museum in New York, the Pentagon Memorial, the Flight 93 National Memorial, and other monuments.

In all such cases, monuments are built out of fear of the rapid disappearance of the event from memory, possibilities of its reinvention or transformation, or of a simple collapse of the act of public memory itself.[2] Additionally, America is not just saying 'We mourn', 'We remember', 'We salute', but also 'Never Again'. On the occasion of anniversaries, the Internet and airwaves throughout the world are saturated with media discussions, personal 'Where were you?' narratives, recollections through personal videos, and the work of professional and amateur cameramen, displaying various slices of the tragedy in vivid, sometimes gory pictures.

If there is one single incident in recent times over which America has united to mourn and commemorate with a singleness of purpose, it is the tragedy of 11 September 2001. The tragedy is perhaps the one event in connection with which jokes have not been fully acceptable in America's rich repertoire of disaster jokes, ten years or more after the national calamity.[3] This in itself points to the deep dent the tragedy has made in American history, and the resolve to preserve the pain and misery it has unleashed, as an auspicious way of commemorating the tragedy, and honouring those who sacrificed their lives.

But world history has observed other calamities for which various commemorative monuments have been built: the Hiroshima memorial in Japan, which celebrated the 65th anniversary of the tragedy in August 2010; and the several holocaust museums in various parts of the world would be listed early in a long list.

The United Nations recently approved the construction of a Permanent memorial at the United Nations Headquarters in New York to honour victims of slavery and the transatlantic slave trade. The monument aims to bring the international community to perpetual acknowledgement of what has been one of the worst chapters in human history, and

---

[2] Pierre Nora, 'Between Memory and History: Les Lieux de Memoire', *Representations* 26 (1989): 7–25.
[3] Bill Ellis, 'A Model for Collecting and Interpreting World Trade Centre Disaster Jokes', *New Directions in Folklore* 5 (October 2011).

a reminder that millions of Africans, over a period of over five hundred years, were violently removed from their homelands, abused, and robbed of their dignity. Although the actual design has yet to be announced, the goal will be to complete a memorial that reflects each region affected by the transatlantic slave trade.

These monuments are built to represent sites or flashpoints of pain, to mark tragedies in world history, and, with some irony, to build peace in the hearts and minds of men. They do constitute a Lest we Forget, but also a Never Again: historical incidents that evoke painful memories but are too important, indeed too risky, to forget. To forget these incidents is to further expose the world to higher levels of insecurity.

But have we thought of possibilities for other modes of commemoration, where past calamities are remembered not through material manifestations, but paradoxically through acts of denial, acts of negation – where avoidance, rather than physical expression, is deemed a most appropriate mode of anchoring memory?

The theoretical possibilities of this cannot be ruled out considering the significant role silence and silent spaces as a whole play in the preservation of memory and in an integrated theory of communication.[4] I refer here to the delicate balance between speech and silence, and to the structural function of silence in communication: ritual-based silences,[5] and several other situations where major statements are made not in verbal expression, but in audible silences.[6] I refer to situations where individuals or groups may consciously foreground silence or void spaces in memory to convey propositional content. Here the message conveyed may not necessarily be interpreted as 'I have nothing to say', but, indeed, may be read as 'Purposeful silence is my statement.'

Such palpable voids do not occur in isolation; they are often part of whole systems of communication, and of memory preservation. In predominantly oral cultures where avoidance, indirection, and silences may be construed as strategic responses to uncertainty, ambiguity, and crisis, this calls for the exploration of the speakable and the unspeakable, the sayable and the unsayable, and indeed a whole ethnography of silence.[7]

In several African cultures, proverbs and wise saws point to such ethnographies, and draw attention to differential – or strategic – attitudes to

---

[4] Muriel Saville-Troike, 'The Place of Silence in an Integrated Theory of Communication', in Deborah Tannen and Muriel Saville-Troike (eds), *Perspectives on Silence* (Norwood, NJ: Ablex, 1983), 3–18.

[5] Bohdan Szuchewyez, 'Silence in Ritual Communication', in Adam Jaworski (ed.), *Silence: Interdisciplinary Perspectives* (Berlin: Mouton de Gruyter, 1997), 63–84.

[6] Kofi Agyekum, 'Ntam "Reminiscential Oath" Taboo in Akan', *Language in Society* 33 (2004): 317–34.

[7] Kofi Agyekum, *Akan Verbal Taboos in the Context of Ethnography of Communication* (Accra: Ghana Universities Press, 2010).

communication and silence. For example, important traits in the cat and the dog, two pets considered as partly nocturnal, have drawn interesting observations in Africa about tenuous links between experience and its ventilation in speech. Several cultures have proverbs to the effect that 'The cat only blinks over night events that would provoke the dog to bark.' Africans closely associated with hunters' lore are aware that 'The hunter does not speak of horrors he sees in the forest.' And, when the climber of the coconut tree has climbed to the tree top, and seen a poisonous snake coiled around the targeted bunch of coconuts, he quietly descends to safety.

The situations above advocate the exercise of restraint in volatile situations where indiscretion, verbal or attitudinal, may exacerbate a crisis. The Akan would say, *Opanyin due mante mante*, 'The wise elder strategically feigns deafness' or 'The elder expresses indifference in situations where a hasty intervention may lead to a crisis.'

Perhaps the most dramatic example of audible silences within the Ghanaian society is the unusual name one of Ghana's rich industrial magnates decided to give to a hotel he owned in the 1980s. Mese Hmm Hotel means simply, 'I say – silence,' or 'I say nothing.' There is no doubt that the name indexes a whole unspoken narration, which the hotel proprietor philosophically decided to reference with a simple sigh under his breath. The sigh then encapsulates a whole narrative, creatively deformed into a loud silence.[8]

In significant moments, then, communication may cease to be an unbroken sequence of words and sentences. Silence becomes markedly communicative; and avoidance of words may not signal insensitivity, ignorance, disability, or a felt lack of verbal remedies or resources, but a strategic verbal retreat, which in a sense may constitute a speech act in itself.

It is indeed significant that, despite its impact on world and local history, slavery does not appear to have left visible traces in African oral traditions. Were Africans oblivious to the significance of slavery? If the oral traditions and folklore of a people normally reflect a people's culture and experiences, why are there few or no folktales on slavery? Is this a case of collective amnesia, a conscious attempt to avoid grief and stress, a negative heritage? Remarkably, even though the Akan of Ghana are very sensitive to the past, they would paradoxically point to the proverb, *wonkyere obi ase* 'One does not reveal another's origins.' Much as accounts of origins are important, indiscreet investigation of individuals' or a people's origins, may evoke tragic memories should the past reveal a stigma, such as traces of slave ancestry. This may lead to selective

---

[8] Kwesi Yankah, *Free Speech in Traditional Society: The Cultural Foundations of Communication in Contemporary Ghana* (Accra: Ghana Universities Press, 1998).

persecution, social exclusion, xenophobia, and needless paranoia (see the chapters by Dakubu and Silverman in this volume).

How would a calamity like 9/11 have been perceived or marked in Africa? There is no simple answer to this. The truth is that post-colonial Africa poses dilemmas, compounded by intrusive Western norms and multiple channels of expression, that have enormously compromised pristine cultural norms.

Africa's Contemporary Monuments

Without making generalisations, I would like take you to one such culture in Africa: the Asante of Ghana, and discuss a notable way of incorporating such calamities within the norms of indigenous communication.

Indeed one might begin by drawing attention to the existence of conspicuous monuments in general within contemporary nation states in Africa. In Ghana, specifically, one cannot ignore imposing sculptures commemorating the life of the nation's charismatic founder and first President, Kwame Nkrumah, who led a formidable team of nationalists to bring independence to Ghana in 1957, and was overthrown by a military coup in 1966.

Contemporary Ghana has reached back into pre-colonial history to honour past heroes through various memorials and sculptures dotted throughout the country. The Asante have built museums and memorials to preserve their history and honour past warriors, including Yaa Asantewa, the great Queen Mother of Ejisu in Asante, who led a large Asante army to confront the British in 1900. And they built a monument to honour the legendary priest of the eighteenth century who planted an immutable sword in the Asante capital that, to this day, has not been lifted. The immovable sword is now a monument around which a regional hospital, named after him, has been constructed.

While physical sites of memory are common, certain severe calamities are considered to belong to a higher order of history, and may be admitted to a rare category of historical incidents that, unlike 9/11, are Unspeakable, Unmentionable, virtually Verbal Taboos.[9] These are catastrophes that are not to be referenced verbally, or made subjects of public or private discussion. Even though origins of this practice can be traced to the pre-colonial era, it should not be assumed that the modern nation state of Ghana has found it inconsistent with the tenets of Ghana's modern-day constitution.

The difference, perhaps, could be traced to differential attitudes of various cultures to the spoken word. The Asante, like many African societies, believe in the potency of the spoken word and its capacity to make

[9] Agyekum, *Akan Verbal Taboos.*

or break, and thus have established institutions to control references to marked tragedies in their past. The spoken word, even though having no permanence, is believed capable of unleashing forces that can destabilise the state. Cultures therefore have instituted procedures and institutions ostensibly meant to curb or control the potency of the spoken word, to ensure national integrity, cohesion, and stability.[10]

The most important among such institutions is *ntam*, literally in Asante, 'a burden which cannot be lifted', 'that which is too heavy to be carried'. It denotes a historical incident or calamity, a grievous national incident that is a taboo to recall verbally, evoke, or reference. It may be a catastrophe, a major disease outbreak, a major earthquake, a painful defeat in war. Such incidents are considered weighty or burdensome historical events that should be left alone. When they are evoked, not only are national grief and pain intensely aroused, but the society is exposed to the risk of suffering a devastating recurrence.

In recognition of its importance to the state, *ntam* – the unspeakable calamity – is protected and indeed owned by the king, who holds it in trust for the people. The king is the sole custodian of *ntam*, and makes it an instrument for adjudication in the traditional court. Since it is the king's duty to maintain peace and national stability, it is also his responsibility to pre-empt or forestall acts that have the potential of unleashing destabilising forces, or disturbing the integrity or cohesion of state. Any person who carelessly utters *ntam* is therefore liable to instant arrest (*kye dadua*), and presentation before the aggrieved king, who holds court and officially opens hearing.

Unlike other historical incidents that are contested, the decision to categorise an incident as *ntam* was a unanimous decision of the past, one that is binding on the people as well as future generations in so far as they owe allegiance to the Asante state. *Ntam* evokes solemnity and is a source of national cohesion; it is an instrument of justice, and a commemoration of heritage, but of a different character from that of Shaka among the Zulu of South Africa (see Buthelezi, this volume). It is therefore expected that in handling *ntam*-related cases, the king himself does not undermine confidence in the institution through the abuse or misapplication of justice.

Historical Memory

The Asante state was the most powerful traditional state before Ghana became a modern nation state in 1957. It extended its sovereignty over almost the entirety of present-day Ghana through wars of expansion

---

[10] Kwesi Yankah, *Speaking for the Chief: Okyeame and the Politics of Akan Royal Oratory* (Bloomington, IN: Indiana University Press, 1995).

from the eighteenth into the early part of the twentieth century. A typical conservative state, the Asante empire was famed for its military prowess and enduring cultural institutions. Indeed to this day the Asante state, which was the last to yield to colonial rule in 1900, has preserved most of its customary institutions within the modern nation state of Ghana. *Ntam* among the Asante is still a potent force. It commands loyalty to the traditional Asante state, and is an effective tool for arbitration in the traditional courts.

Largely, the Asante have codified one particular important historical calamity into what is called *ntam kɛse*, the Great Unspeakable Oath. This specifically refers to one particular incident in the eighteenth century, when the great founder of the Asante state, King Osei Tutu, lost his life in a surprise ambush by enemy forces while crossing the Prah River, which divides the Ashanti and neighbouring Fante states. According to oral tradition, just as King Osei Tutu and the royal party were about to cross the Prah, the army of the Akim people, belonging to a neighbouring state, opened fire in a surprise attack. Caught unawares, the warrior king Osei Tutu was killed, drowning in the river. Taking advantage of the confusion, the Akim forces charged, killing the whole residue party of 300, including 60 wives of the king and his nobles.

Osei Tutu's body was never found but his memory did not perish. He died on a Saturday and, in commemoration, his people instituted their most sacred oath after the sad event: *Coromantee Memenda* (the sacred Coromantee Saturday). The oath taken on this day was considered so solemn and binding that it was hardly ever mentioned by name, and was only spoken of as 'the great oath of the dreadful day'.

When the Asante army returned to the capital Kumasi after the incident, it became a taboo to mention what happened in that war. So when returning warriors were asked what exactly happened in the encounter, they responded *Mekoo bi, nanso mante hwee*. In everyday Asante dialect, it became 'Kormante', translated into English as 'Well, I was present at the battlefield, but I did not hear anything, I was not privy to the incident. I never saw it, never heard it, and never will I speak to it.' Witnesses simply refused to admit to what happened at the battlefield (mainly, the claim that Asantehene Osei Tutu, founder of the formidable Asante state, was no more). It was a taboo to narrate the event verbally or admit its occurrence, or else, in those days, one could lose one's head.

This type of verbal taboo, driven by belief or superstition and based on the unquestioned potency of the spoken word, should be distinguished from indiscreet or indecent expressions, often avoided or skirted in verbal interactions, and for which cultures have acceptable euphemisms. *Ntam*, however, is not the type of verbal taboo for which there are euphemistic alternatives.

To date, not only is there a codified reference to the event in *Ntam Kɛse*, the Great Unspeakable Oath of Asante; it is a verbal taboo to make literal references to the death of a king. Only euphemisms are permissible when it comes to referring to any king's death. Instead of 'The king has died,' one would rather euphemistically say, *odupɔn atutu*, 'A great tree has fallen,' or *Nana kɔ akuraa*, 'The king has gone to the village.'

Such euphemisms, where certain words and events are skirted, are so important that direct references to a great king's ill health are verbal taboos. In the Asante state, it is often not the King who is said to be ill; it is his close confidante or orator, to which the king's ill health is verbally associated: *'ɔkyeame* the orator is indisposed' is the permissible utterance, in Asante socio-linguistic normative use.

Other traditional states have their own *ntam*, but Asante are exceptionally notable in their adherence to and reverence for *ntam*. Though *ntam* may belong to a traditional state, lesser groups in the social hierarchy may have their own *ntam*, based on their respective histories – whether these are towns, lineages, families, or individuals. Each may have set aside a special day or incident in history, whose recall normally produces unbearable grief and stress, and in respect of which restraint is exercised. Thus one may have *abusua ntam*, unspoken oath or incident within a lineage; *kuro ntam*, unspeakable oath or incident within the history of a town; or personal *ntam*, a grievous incident in an individual's life, to which verbal references should rather not be made, or else that individual, family, or lineage breaks down, or is overwhelmed with grief.[11] *Ntam* belonging to lesser units may have weaker judicial force, and may or may not be used for the arbitration of cases.

Because it is revered and collectively binding, *ntam* may be utilised only sparingly, to support a statement of fact or contest ownership of property. Its use denotes seriousness of intent, gravity of claim, or an unalloyed commitment to truth on the part of the speaker. One does not support one's claim with *ntam*, if one is unsure of the basis of the claim; if the matter in hand is frivolous; or if one's claim is a palpable falsehood.

Indeed, *ntam* is a rare judicial instrument for the preservation of desirable virtues. It is considered heavy, weighty, indeed a state burden. Its potency paradoxically derives from its perception as a burden, a burden that can only be lifted sparingly, to propel the wheels of justice.

But *ntam* is also an abstract symbol of unity. Like the Golden Stool of Asante in which the united soul of Asante people is enshrined, it is a sacred institution whose purity must not be compromised, or contested. To evoke *ntam* by speech, or word of mouth, is to lift a sacred and immutable institution of state. Contravention of its terms amounts to an

---

[11] Agyekum, *Akan Verbal Taboos.*

act of subversion, indeed an attempt to undermine trust and confidence in institutions responsible for state cohesion.

Let me give an example of such sparing uses to support a claim:

I hereby evoke the Great Unspeakable Calamity in the King's custody, to support my claim that this piece of land belongs to my forefathers . . . and none other.

Evoking this great unspeakable, I declare that our forefathers settled here before your great grandfather, and that your claims to the said property are false.

It is implied that, by the speaker's evocation of the unspeakable calamity, he is committed to truth telling, and that by speaking the king's unspeakable, he makes himself liable to judicial proceedings, which in any case would give him the opportunity to prove or elaborate his case before the king. Indeed the use of the unspeakable, by default, signals a breach of the law, a potential breach of peace; and it is often the civic duty of any third party present to immediately cause the speaker's arrest, and put him before the king.

In any case, the one contesting the claims may, on hearing the Great Oath evoked, wisely retract his earlier claims if he thinks he would have a weak defence before the king; or he may confront the evocation, by challenging or contesting the unspeakable with the same unspeakable calamity: virtually breaking the law, to challenge a breach of the law. He would imply that 'I hereby contest your claims with the support of the same unspeakable calamity.' Such a counter-claim (in making which one would say, *ode aboso*) is often the climax of a keen litigation. The speaker challenges, confronts or rejoins the evocation, paving the way for intense, sometimes protracted hearings over which the aggrieved king presides. Regardless of the final verdict, both litigants are fined for evoking the unspeakable *ntam*, and the one proven guilty in the substantive case pays a much higher fine. The fines imposed on both litigants are ostensibly for the recall of the unspeakable calamity; but it is understandably lighter for the litigant whose evocation of the calamity was more justifiable, or preserves its potency.

Thus while it is a verbal taboo, *ntam* may be used sparingly to support rightful claims, and deter or fend off tale bearers, generally in ways that safeguard desired values. Most importantly, *ntam* may be made available by the king, as custodian of the institution, to elicit serious commitment to duty and other national causes. Here the use of *ntam* is compelling, in accordance with tradition, and indeed constitutes no violation in itself. This may happen during ceremonies to install a new chief, where he pledges allegiance to a superior chief or king. Pointing a sword at the king, the newly installed may evoke the unspeakable calamity, to swear loyalty and allegiance to the king, as well as commitment to duty. He pledges to rise to the occasion whenever duty calls – at all times, whether in the morning, at noon, or night – and proclaims his awareness that a violation of the unspeakable would occur if he should default. To support one's pledge of loyalty and dedication with an unspeakable *ntam* is indeed the utmost expression of commitment to national cause within a traditional state. In accordance with standard formula, the new king may say,

> If I don't respond to your call, morning, noon, or night, except under conditions of ill health, I shall be deemed to have violated the terms governing evocation of the Great Unspeakable Calamity.

To date, all newly appointed chiefs and other officers about to occupy key traditional positions within the royal domain are considered appointed only after evoking the Unspeakable to support their pledge of commitment to duty.

The Post-Colonial State Apparatus

My discussion of *ntam* is not meant to locate its significance exclusively within pre-colonial Asante. It is still potent in Asante in the twenty-first century, and indeed constitutes a good proportion of cases currently pending before the king. But in the twentieth and twenty-first centuries, the potential for a clash with the forces of modernity has loomed (see Silverman, this volume). A looming crisis has to do with (1) its accommodation within the modern nation state, where free speech is enshrined within the national constitution; and (2) the penetration of sovereign boundaries by the global media, which are bound to undermine strict adherence to norms governing the spoken word.

The issue is that the traditional Asante state is part of modern Ghana, which operates under a national constitution, most recently promulgated in 1992. But, as is well known, the traditional states in several African countries still operate in the shadows of the modern nation states, where there is a President, an executive and a modern legislature.

But the national constitution of Ghana recognises chiefs as well as customary laws that do not infringe on individual rights and liberties as defined by the constitution. There is thus a National House of Chiefs and Regional Houses of chiefs that adjudicate over chieftaincy and custom-related issues. These of course are all subject to the deliberations of an Appeal Court, and the Supreme Court.

How do matters related to the spoken word, and its potential to create instability, operate in a modern world of free speech, free press, freedom of association – a modern world of cosmopolitan townships, cities, the media, the Internet?

Within the modern nation state, a clash of conflicting norms can be detected in a major incident in July 1996, which threw the Asante state into crisis. The Regional Minister, appointed by government, was reported by a newspaper to have made the sacrilegious statement, *Mensuro Otumfuɔ* – literally meaning, 'I do not fear Otumfuor, the King of Asante' – during a heated discussion with a section of the people in Kumasi, the capital. Following this major violation, the Kumasi Traditional Council gave an ultimatum to the government to remove the Regional Minister, otherwise the chiefs and elders of Asante should not be held responsible if any mishap befell him. Based on the gravity of the verbal breach, the elders, wrapped in mourning clothes, held a meeting and slaughtered a sheep to pacify the gods. They then invited the Minister to proceed to explain himself, since he appeared to have taken advantage of his executive powers derived from the modern nation state to denigrate a sacred traditional institution.

When it was his turn to speak at the meeting, the Minister flatly denied the allegations, and, to support his claim of innocence, declared his readiness to evoke the unspeakable calamity if the need arose. This serious statement led to a prolonged moment of silence. He then went further to dare any of his accusers, present at the meeting, to join him in evoking the calamity if they desired to contest issues.

The challenge thrown by the Minister was a clear signal of his intention to petition a judicial hearing, but it also indexed the gravity of his concern that he was a victim of conspiracy. Only then were his accusers silenced; for the unspeakable *ntam* is also deemed to be a lie detector. One does not evoke the unspeakable to support a false claim. The resultant silence after the Minister's open challenge meant that the matter was heading towards closure, and that he might be innocent after all.

The inability of his accusers to respond to the challenge was proof that the allegations were frivolous, and that they were afraid to stand trial and support a falsehood with the unspeakable calamity, which would have amounted to a willful attempt to compromise the integrity of state.

A Royal Death and the BBC

Three years after this crisis, in 1999, a greater crisis was in the offing, a bigger test of the resilience of customary institutions. Late in February 1999, the King of Asante, Otumfuor Opoku Ware II, passed away. Under Asante customary law, it is a verbal taboo to announce the death of a king or chief until all necessary custom has been observed. That normally takes months, or sometimes years. Whenever such tragedies occur, word is passed around only in whispers and sometimes communicative silences, for as long as an official declaration has not been made. And as I indicated earlier, references to a royal death would normally be couched in euphemisms.

When that tragedy occurred in 1999, I happened to be in the US, at the University of Pennsylvania as mentioned earlier, where I was a visiting professor on sabbatical leave. I heard the news from a close friend in Ghana who sent me an email, but I respectfully refused to pass it on to Ghanaian colleagues in the US.

In Ghana itself, the entire Asante state was thrown in a state of crisis, partly by the royal death, but largely by a greater tragedy: that this had been announced instantly by the BBC. A BBC correspondent, a Ghanaian, who was in Kumasi at the time, on hearing the news or rumour of the royal death, instantly sent a report to London, which was broadcast by the BBC world-wide. In compliance with contemporary broadcast tradition, he was openly and proudly credited with what was considered a journalistic scoop.

Unbeknown to the BBC, a major verbal taboo in Asante had been breached, and the Asante state had been thrown into a state of crisis within a crisis: the death of the king who had ruled for 28 years, but also the premature and undignified announcement of the death in the modern media. The elders of Asante would not accept this. A state of emergency was declared, and Asante chiefs, clad in mourning clothes due to the breach, had to convene to deliberate on the tragic development. The BBC reporter, himself an Asante, had to run for cover over an indefinite period. The great Asante state had been disrespected by a brazen violation of norms associated with the spoken word. And this breach had been committed by a reporter who was an Asante himself, and should have prioritised traditional norms over modern or global provisions of free speech. The Asante would say, 'If bird of the forest can be pardoned for not knowing that rice is edible grain, bird of the grassland has no excuse.'

Significantly, the usually outspoken Ghanaian press, even though it had learned of the death, had chosen to be silent on the tragedy, in deference to Asante norms! Indeed, during the raging controversy over the BBC report, an official statement released by the Ghana Journalists Association joined the condemnation of the BBC, and advocated compliance with Asante custom.

Perhaps unaware of a potential violation, the *New York Times* on 4 March, within days of the tragedy, also came up with a full-page article on its obituary pages titled: 'Otumfuor Opoku Ware, the King of Asante, is dead at 89'. The *New York Times* in turn attributed its source as the Agence France Press, which was reported as saying, 'Officials confirmed his death but did not give a date, and that an announcement was being withheld pending consultations on burial arrangements.' This apparent violation, perhaps, did not come to the attention of traditional authorities in Asante, for the *New York Times* is not in circulation in Ghana.

Significantly, the *New York Times* of 5 March 1999, a day after its story, published a correction of factual errors in their report. These had to do with the king's age, which was not 89 as reported, but 79; and the attainment of Ghana's independence from colonial rule, which was not 1960 as stated, but 1957. What would an apology of this sort really mean to the Asante? They would most likely respond with the proverb, 'The child does not pluck all feathers of a strange bird, before asking the elder to name it.' The harm had already been caused. It was like a string of precious beads carelessly broken; the fragments were scattered, scattered beyond retrieval.

The general mistrust of Western technologies of communication, when these were serially introduced in Africa, can be inferred from the indigenous names parts of Africa gave to the radio, the telephone, and the newspaper. Radio in parts of Nigeria was considered a new type of tyranny, and was called 'the machine that speaks but accepts no reply'. And the telephone in Ghana was *ahomatrofo*, the wire that transmits falsehood, or rather 'the string that conveys lies'. Here was a wire, the telephone, that speedily transmitted hearsays, sometimes unverified allegations, over long distances. As for the newspaper, the Akan, including the Asante, still refer to it as *koowaa krataa*, literally 'the paper that speaks frivolities'.

Precisely that is what Asante would have said happened: the *New York Times*, true to its name as *koowaa krataa*, had rushed to report a grievous tragedy, in a frivolous manner that made factual errors unavoidable. The corrections of course are normally for the records only. Not only are they often buried in an obscure corner of the newspaper; very few people ever read corrigenda, much less the Asante in Ghana, who are dealing with a newspaper unknown to most readers.

Indeed the errors or anomalies arising from the publication would appear to justify cultural restraint exercised in announcing a royal death; for what if Nana was not dead, after all, but in a coma? In Asante, to declare a living person dead (referred to as *bo owuto*), which occasionally happens, is a grievous abomination, and could as well betray ill motives on the part of the perpetrator. It's much worse if the subject is a king, no less.

By custom the Asante, like other Akans, would normally require a protracted period of waiting to ensure that a death has truly occurred, but also that all relevant customary rites have been observed, before an official announcement is made. In most cases, the successor is nominated and charged with the responsibility of organising the royal funeral, before the death is announced officially. But it is also to avoid an unnecessary stampede for succession, and a possible scramble for royal property in the aftermath of a royal death that has been announced prematurely.

It is important to note that on the Ghanaweb page of the Internet, during the media crisis in 1999, there was ironically another news item, announcing the death of yet another chief in Ghana: the King or Oman-hene of another traditional state, Akim Kotoku. He had died on 17 June 1998, but his death was being announced officially on 22 March 1999, nine months after the fact. That was when all customary rites had been duly performed, and his burial date made known.

This is not to say that the Akan or Asante do not believe in free speech. The Asante believe in and indeed encourage freedom of speech and expression. The therapeutic functions of speech are well known and observed in various ways. Festivals are observed where free speech is cel-ebrated to demonstrate its crucial significance to national development. But free speech, to the Asante, should be exercised with responsibility, and in ways that do not compromise the stability, integrity, and cohesion of state. To evoke *ntam* or utter a verbal taboo is considered an abuse of free speech, in so far as it has consequences for national cohesion and stability.

Significantly, the limits of free speech here have been marked by a major site of pain, a national covenant to which there is undivided loy-alty and commitment. In the covenant is enshrined all ingredients that collectively constitute state security and cohesion. Any attempt to breach the covenant is an attempt to tinker with the state security apparatus, which could put the entire state in needless jeopardy.

Conclusion

Are events associated with 9/11 the complete opposite of how the Asante would have responded, or how they responded in the past to major national disasters? In conclusion, let me say that the calamity of 9/11 and the commemorative monuments constructed to mark the tragedy are not necessarily at the other end of the scale. Muted reactions of families who lost loved ones and relatives, and are still at a loss for words, or would rather not verbalise their devastation, partly index a kind of 'unspeak-able', even if not institutionalised. The very euphemistic reference to the calamity in numbers, representing the day or date of the catastrophe, marks an attempt to codify and avoid gory details. The same can be said of codified references to devastating natural disasters – hurricanes and the like – that have attracted human nomenclatures, perhaps to skirt direct reference.

But nations of the West have risen to occasions to construct national, sometimes international monuments to mark major tragedies. These monuments nevertheless are stress-inducing memorabilia; they are nationally certified sites of pain and memory, in which are sown the seeds of hope and relief. That also explains their ready submission to the new media that virtually take over respective anniversaries through world-wide discussion.

It is remarkable, however, to observe in all this the puzzling paradox that – despite the permeation of the global media with narratives of 9/11, discussions, video coverage, and various recollections and horror stories during its anniversaries, despite the widespread verbal and visual narratives – one never saw a single dead body, on video or in still picture, pulled from the rubble. Where were the bodies of the victims, the dead, the mutilated remains? Are these America's version of silences, voids in visual memory? Does carnage dismantle the apparatus of free speech? Is the seal of silence broken only in fragments; is that an exercise in visual self-censorship, visual euphemism? Are images of carnage only otherised? This paradox still puzzles me, and it would take American scholars themselves to fill in the blank spaces I have left.

But I can speak more authoritatively about Africa, the Akan, and indeed the Asante who, on the other hand, revere the potency of the spoken word, and have sought to suppress frivolous allusions to key national catastrophes by enshrining these in state laws that enjoin caution in the evocation of security-sensitive events.

The Asante remember their great heroes in ritual observances, and other commemorative structures, but certain past calamities are commemorated in marked, or pronounced silences, indeed in acts of negation and avoidance. Such silences are not meant to suppress historical memory, or induce memory collapse or collective amnesia. They are communicative silences and void spaces that preserve the purity of institutions that drive state cohesion. Avoidances strengthen the potency of the judicial instrument, and help to perpetuate desirable social values.

More importantly, the Asante and other African cultures have sought to harness their belief systems, unalloyed commitment to state cohesion, and absolute reverence for the monarch, to strengthen their judicial system several years into the post-colonial era. After nearly four hundred years of the Asante empire – despite the existence of an overarching modern nation state of Ghana as well as widespread literacy – belief in the supremacy of the spoken word, and the executive control of the unspeakable, is still paramount.

Only time will tell how far this resilience can continue to survive the tenacity of the new media, with their remorseless penetration of cultural and sovereign boundaries.

10 Language as Cultural 'Heritage'

Visions of Ethnicity in Nineteenth-Century African Linguistics

Judith T. Irvine

The idea that 'peoples' are identifiable by the languages they speak is widespread and tenacious. It is a simple – though often misleading – way to try to make sense of a complex social world. A version of it, prominent among many post-enlightenment scholars and people influenced by them, goes like this: a language both represents and embodies a social group's exclusive cultural heritage; that group is mainly monolingual; and the language is largely homogeneous, with only minor variations, within that group's boundaries. It is as if language were a kind of natural social and cultural glue, creating community and homogeneity as against outsiders. This view persists despite decades of sociolinguistic research showing that what is taken to be a single language is often highly variable, and that the majority of the world's population is multilingual or multidialectal. We know, too, that languages can influence one another intensively, and that people in the past must have shifted among the languages they spoke, just as people do today.

Nevertheless, much scholarship in the social sciences, even when it questions the 'naturalness' of ethnicity, still does not problematise the language aspect – the identification of languages or the nature of the connections between a language and some set of its putative speakers, an 'ethnolinguistic group' (so called).[1] Outside of the disciplines specifically

---

[1] But see David Zeitlyn and Bruce Connell, 'Ethnogenesis and Fractal History on an African Frontier: Mambila – Njerep – Mandulu', *Journal of African History* 44 (2003), 117–38; Patrick Harries, 'The Roots of Ethnicity: Discourse and the Politics of Language Construction in South-East Africa', *African Affairs* 87, 346 (1998), 25–52; Patrick Harries, 'Discovering Languages: The Historical Origins of Standard Tsonga in Southern Africa', in R. Mesthrie (ed.), *Language and Social History: Studies in South African Sociolinguistics* (Cape Town: David Philip, 1995), 154–75; Sinfree Makoni, 'From Misinvention to Disinvention of Language: Multilingualism and the South African Constitution', in Sinfree Makoni, Geneva Smitherman, Arnetha F. Ball, and Arthur K. Spears (eds), *Black Linguistics: Language, Society, and Politics in Africa and the Americas* (London and New York, NY: Routledge, 2003), 132–51; Judith T. Irvine, 'Subjected Words: African Linguistics and the Colonial Encounter', *Language and Communication* 28 (2008), 323–43; and Judith T. Irvine and Susan Gal, 'Language Ideology and Linguistic Differentiation', in Paul Kroskrity (ed.), *Regimes of Language: Language Ideologies and the Discursive*

concerned with them, languages are often treated as givens – potential badges in an ethnic politics of language, and bases for ethnic identification, yet somehow, as objects, unquestioned. Notions of 'mother tongue' and, in educational settings, 'heritage language learners' – common expressions in contemporary parlance – reflect those assumptions about language: that a person has a natural connection to a language, acquired at the mother's knee, and that even if one cannot actually speak the language of one's maternal ancestors it remains somehow one's own, as an essential linguistic-*cum*-cultural heritage.

I take the linguistic side of 'ethnolinguistic' categorisations to be as questionable and problematisable as the ethnic side – equally rooted in historical settings that make some kinds of linguistic differentiations salient, and make those differentiations interpretable as signs of ethnic affiliation.[2] Language, then, offers useful terrain for interrogating conceptions of 'heritage'.

To begin with, there is a kind of heritage in the very fact of acquiring language in childhood. All human beings who grow up in a language-using social environment acquire, from that environment in conjunction with inherent cognitive abilities, competence in at least one language. Such a language is not constructed *de novo*; in this sense it is a kind of heritage, as are some of the historically and socially particular ideas embedded in it. Yet – even holding multilingualisms aside – all such languages are variable, with varieties that differ to greater or lesser degree according to differences among speakers and among social activities.[3] That variation is suppressed in projects of language standardisation, which – especially when attached to institutional regimentations (state, church, educational establishments) – create linguistic forms that may differ substantially from what anyone thus regimented actually speaks. 'Heritage learners' must study a language in school exactly because of their inadequate knowledge of the language that is supposedly their own. The ways of speaking these people actually did acquire as children (or by some other oral/aural route outside of any large-scale institutions) can

Construction of Power and Identity (Santa Fe, NM: School of American Research Press, 2000), 35–83, among other works. See also Terence Ranger, 'Missionaries, Migrants and the Manyika: The Invention of Ethnicity in Zimbabwe', in Leroy Vail (ed.), *The Creation of Tribalism in Southern Africa* (Berkeley and Los Angeles, CA: University of California Press, 1991), 151–92; and Herbert Chimhundu, 'Early Missionaries and the Ethnolinguistic Factor during the "Invention of Tribalism" in Zimbabwe', *Journal of African History* 33 (1992), 87–109.

2 Yet enterprises like 'Ethnologue', a catalogue of languages produced by the Summer Institute of Linguistics, a missionary organisation, have institutionalised a list of the world's languages – and therefore of 'ethnolinguistic groups' – that is taken to be a stable, objective fact independent of the cataloguers.

3 Multilingualism cannot actually be distinguished from multidialectism on linguistic grounds alone. Nevertheless, the point for the moment is that even where the varieties grouped together under the umbrella of a single 'language' are fairly similar, that language is still variable.

seem to be 'broken', 'bad', or perhaps 'quaintly provincial'. Those ways of speaking may, however, become the basis for contesting the standard-isation project or its institutional venues. If so, the contestation pits a relatively local, or minority, linguistic 'heritage' against a more centrist, institutionalised one.

In his chapter in this volume, Mbongiseni Buthelezi distinguishes between heritage (lower-case h) and Heritage (upper-case H), as between localist modes of historical discourse and centrist modes promoted by the state and by national-level heritage industries.[4] A similar distinc-tion between the relatively local and the relatively central is pertinent for language too. The language situation in Africa includes many cases of contested standardisation, as well as cases in which minority languages are giving way – their very existence possibly unacknowledged by the state – to languages with larger speaker populations, or to globally prom-inent languages (mainly English, French, or Arabic). Moreover, as Mary Esther Dakubu's chapter shows, the ethnic connotations of linguistic affiliation – never as clear-cut in life as they may be in ideology – can be influenced or even altered by refashioning or reinterpreting their putative linguistic basis. One of her cases shows that a new standardisation project can promote a minority language at the level of the state, thus elevating its speakers ideologically to a position of parity with other ethnicities. Her other case shows how a new interpretation of etymologies and lin-guistic sources can bring a previously unrecognised ethnic heritage to light. Though seldom as closely described as in her chapter, such cases are not rare. The continent is full of sites in which linguistic heritage and ethnic belonging offer grounds, potential or already exploited, for contestation and for creative action by local, regional, and (in the past) colonial agents.

The present chapter explores issues of language and ethnic group-ing in the early history of Africanist linguistics, a field of study that emerged in the nineteenth century along with European colonial pro-jects. It is a field that was dominated by outsiders, mainly Europeans (and some Americans) but also some missionised Africans – although other African perspectives were influential in various ways. I focus on the visions of ethnicity held by the people who identified and described African languages, and I consider the ways their linguistic descriptions related to some population of speakers taken to be an ethnic unit. (Since 'ethnic' as a term is largely of later vintage, it is not what such units were generally called, before the 1950s or 1960s. Instead, the social groupings later called 'ethnic' were referred to by such terms as 'tribes',

---

[4] Buthelezi cites Ciraaj Rassool's discussions of contestations over the South African past, with their efforts at fashioning the terms and images through which the contemporary nation is to be understood. Ciraj Rassool, 'The Rise of Heritage and the Reconstruction of History in South Africa', *Kronos* 26 (2000): 1–21.

'peoples', 'nations', or 'races', or their equivalents in other European languages.)

As background, recall that at the beginning of the nineteenth century, political and intellectual developments in Europe itself had gone far towards creating an ideologised vision of distinct 'peoples' whose essential 'spirit' or mentality was to be found in their languages. As the expression of the spiritual or cognitive (and even, some scholars thought, biological) essences of particular human collectivities, languages were regarded as natural entities out there to be discovered – 'natural' in the sense that they were consequences of a variable human nature, not the creations of any self-conscious human intervention. Since languages were deemed to be independent of, or ontologically prior to, human political activity, they could then serve as its warrant. In this view, languages identified separate populations and territories that could be treated as political unities, whether these were self-governing nation states as in the case of the European powers, or units for colonial administration. As the German nationalist J. G. Fichte wrote in 1808, 'wherever a separate language is found, there is also a separate nation which has the right to manage its affairs . . . and rule itself'.[5]

The model for envisioning the groupings later termed 'ethnolinguistic', in short, was the European nation state with bounded territory, single standardised language, and supposed national character or culture. There were even colonial territories in Africa known as 'Little Germany' and the like, because their African residents seemed German-like in character compared to their neighbours, or because of some perceived similarity of landscape. Since this model was so well accepted by Europeans, Euro-Americans, and people influenced by them, it permitted an observer to infer that if some part of the model could be found, the rest must also be there. That is, if it were true that all these factors – homogeneous language, bounded territory, and culture and/or political unity – went together 'naturally' (as in the model), it would be possible to take any one of these factors as the observational starting point, and the rest must fall into place. Of course, this vision does not easily accommodate multilingualism, linguistic variation, territorial discontinuities, and cultural differences internal to a linguistic grouping – inconvenient facts which, where they were found, had to be explained away.

There was more than one way to explain away language distributions and usages that failed to correspond to a model of ethnicity as proto-nation. To illustrate these processes I will discuss two cases, one from the world of French colonial West Africa and one from British dominions, also in West Africa. They contrast partly according to which factor they

---

[5] In Johann Gottlieb Fichte, *Reden an die Deutsche Nation* (Berlin: Realschulbuchhandlung, 1808). My translation. All translations in this chapter are mine, except where otherwise noted.

took as starting-point – language (actually, only *supposed* linguistic unity) or culture (also, only supposed unity). Finally, in the conclusion to the chapter, I will add a few comments on analogous processes in Southern Africa.

Language and Ethnicity in Colonial South-Eastern Nigeria: Igbo

On the British side, consider the linguistic research that was undertaken in the colony of liberated slaves in Freetown, Sierra Leone. Freetown was the site where the first grammatical descriptions and dictionaries of many African languages, not only from Freetown's hinterland but also from other parts of the continent, were developed. The authors of these studies were missionaries working with speakers liberated from slave ships or former slaves brought back to Africa from the New World. An interesting example is Igbo (or, 'Ibo'), a term that can be found in eighteenth-century sources as a label for a category of African slaves in the Americas. Its first unambiguous application to an African language and 'nation' comes from the Caribbean, where slaves captured from south-eastern regions of Nigeria called themselves 'Ibos' in comparison with fellow slaves from other parts of Africa.[6] Apparently, in Nigeria itself the term *igbo* had been a geographical term, meaning 'upland' regions as opposed to the

---

[6] Oldendorp's survey of the origins and languages of African slaves in the Virgin Islands, from his stay there in 1767–9, is detailed and careful, compared with other sources at the time. He cites interviews and provides linguistic examples. Christian Georg Andreas Oldendorp, *History of the Mission of the Evangelical Brethren on the Caribbean Islands of St Thomas, St Croix, and St John*, ed. Johann Jakob Bossard, trans. A. R. Highfield and V. Barac (Ann Arbor, MI: Karoma, 1987 [1777]). Before Oldendorp, there are earlier references to 'Eboes' and 'Eboe country', for example in notices describing missing slaves in South Carolina. Michael Gomez, 'A Quality of Anguish: The Igbo Response to Enslavement in the Americas', in Paul Lovejoy and David Trotman (eds), *Transatlantic Dimensions of Ethnicity in the African Diaspora* (London and New York, NY: Continuum, 2003), 82–95. However, whether such usages as 'Eboe' identify anything like today's ethnic group or language is unclear. Northrup argues that they do not represent the transportation of an already-established African cultural identity across the Atlantic, although there has been debate on this point. See David Northrup, 'Igbo and Myth Igbo: Culture and Ethnicity in the Atlantic World, 1600–1850', *Slavery and Abolition* 21, 3 (2000), 1–20; Douglas B. Chambers, 'Rejoinder – The Significance of Igbo in the Bight of Biafra Slave-Trade: A Rejoinder to Northrup's "Myth Igbo"', *Slavery and Abolition* 23, 1 (2002), 101–20; Gwendolyn Midlo Hall, *Slavery and African Ethnicities in the Americas: Restoring the Links* (Chapel Hill, NC: University of North Carolina Press, 2005); David Northrup, 'Becoming African: Identity Formation among Liberated Slaves in Nineteenth-Century Sierra Leone', *Slavery and Abolition* 27, 1 (2006), 1–21. It seems to me that some of the early usages – especially those attributable to African-origin authors – are consistent with a primarily geographical sense, rather than a linguistic one; for a famous example, see Equiano, whose usage of 'Eboe' could be interpreted as primarily geographical, although it has been assumed to be ethnic. Olaudah Equiano, *The Interesting Narrative of Olaudah Equiano, or Gustavus Vasa, the African*, in Philip D. Curtin, *Africa Remembered: Narratives by West Africans from the Era of the Slave Trade* (Madison, WI: University of Wisconsin Press, 1967 [1789]), 69–98.

lower-lying areas along the Niger River and the coast.[7] These upland regions were overpopulated and an important source of slaves, but the geographical designation did not correspond to a pre-colonial Igbo polity or distinct, homogeneous cultural unit. Although there is much debate on the extent to which African cultural particulars were retained on the other side of the Atlantic, as well as debates concerning the cultural prehistory of south-eastern Nigeria, it is clear enough that labels such as 'Ibo' in the New World cannot be assumed to represent 'tribes' or self-conscious ethnic identities in the African region of origin.

So it was in a diasporan setting, where identities and differences were reconfigured under conditions of vast distance and the overwhelming social changes brought by the Middle Passage and plantation slavery, that the geographical term became a cover term for people called 'Ibo'. Slippages of identifications from geography, or from coastal port of embarkation, to social categories seem to have been common as Africans were brought across the ocean in the seventeenth and eighteenth centuries. Subsequently, in the early nineteenth century this particular identification, 'Ibo', became solidified as a label for people – and language – of a category of liberated slaves in Freetown, where the first linguistic descriptions of it were undertaken under the auspices of the (Anglican) Church Missionary Society (CMS).

The 'Ibo' ex-slaves in Sierra Leone came from various parts of south-eastern Nigeria and there was initially much variety in their speech. The great linguistic survey of Freetown residents in 1854, the *Polyglotta Africana*, describes at least five languages, or linguistic varieties, that are taken to be dialects of 'Ibo', and the survey's author, the missionary Sigismund Koelle, suggests that there are many more. However, within Freetown, one particular variety, Isuama (or 'Isoama'), seems to have become dominant – sufficiently, at least, for the missionary linguists to declare it the proper candidate for linguistic research and Bible translations, which, they supposed, would be easily understood in eastern Nigeria itself, all over 'Iboland'. The linguistic researchers in Freetown confidently wrote about 'the Ibo' and their ('Ibo') language, as if about the homogeneous language of a monolingual nation. As Koelle – despite having identified the several varieties, and having described them as rather different from one another – wrote:

In Sierra Leone certain natives who have come from the Bight [of Biafra, in eastern Nigeria] are called Ibos. In speaking to some of them respecting this

---

[7]   Elizabeth Isichei, *A History of the Igbo People* (New York, NY: St Martin's Press, 1976), 19; Richard Henderson, *The King in Every Man: Evolutionary Trends in Onitsha Ibo Society and Culture* (New Haven, CT: Yale University Press, 1972), 37, 41; Kenneth Onwuka Dike and Felicia Ekejiuba, *The Aro of Southeastern Nigeria, 1650–1980: A Study of Socio-Economic Formation and Transformation in Nigeria* (Ibadan: University Press, 1990), 6.

name, I learned that they never had heard it till they came to Sierra Leone. In their own country they seem to have lost their general national name, like the Akus [Yorubas], and know only the names of their respective districts or countries.[8]

Evidently, Koelle assumed that if these populations within Nigeria had no name to refer to their whole 'nation', there must nevertheless have been such a name in the past. It had simply been lost.

But when missionary linguists actually went to 'Iboland', the linguistic situation turned out to be far different, and far more diverse, than what they had seen in Freetown. Nigerian 'Ibos' failed to recognise the missionaries' language, or to agree that they belonged to any sort of national unity. The missionary J. C. Taylor – himself an 'Ibo' born in that community in Freetown – experienced great difficulties when stationed in Onitsha, in eastern Nigeria, in 1857. Although he was equipped with a vocabulary, primer, and other start-up materials that had been developed for Ibo in Freetown, Taylor's linguistic work in Onitsha did not go smoothly. From a later vantage point we can see that Isuama, the language predominating among 'Ibo' in Sierra Leone, would have been quite different from what was spoken at Onitsha.[9] This would be the case if Freetown Isuama resembled the 'Isuama' described in Nigeria more recently, or if the Freetown version was a creolised variety, influenced by other languages including English. Perhaps it is not surprising, then, that when Taylor travelled to England in 1859 to see his Igbo Bible translations edited for publication, his rendering of Igbo was found to be chaotic. The problem was blamed on Taylor. When he quarrelled about the translations with one of the European missionaries who had worked on Igbo in Freetown and was now living in London, the CMS authorities said Taylor lacked linguistic talent and was a stubborn and difficult person. The bishop even attributed those personality characteristics to his Ibo mission personnel in general.[10]

[8] Sigismund W. Koelle, *Polyglotta Africana* (London: Church Missionary House, 1854), 7–8.
[9] Today, the Onitsha dialects are classified within Northern Igboid, while the Ụlụ dialect cluster, which is probably closest to the missionaries' 'Isuama', falls within the Central branch of Southern Igboid. See Victor Manfredi, 'Àgbọ and Éhụgbò: Ìgbo Linguistic Consciousness, Its Origins and Limits' (PhD thesis, Harvard University, 1991), 32. For the connection between 'Isuama' and Ụlụ, see Daryll Forde and G. J. Jones, *The Ibo and Ibibio-speaking Peoples of South-Eastern Nigeria* (London: International African Institute, 1950), 37. Forde and Jones use the label 'Isu-Ama' to describe one of several 'tribal' groupings within Southern Ibo, and locate Isu-Ama in Orlu (= Ụlụ) District in Owerri Province. The label 'Isu-Ama' is less common in more recent literature than in works of the colonial period.
[10] For more detail see Irvine, 'Stance in a Colonial Encounter: How Mr Taylor Lost His Footing', in Alexandra Jaffe (ed.), *Stance: Sociolinguistic Perspectives* (Oxford: Oxford University Press, 2009), 53–71. Note that the bishop (Samuel Ajayi Crowther) was

So certain were the missionaries that 'the Ibo' were a nation, which must have a particular 'spirit' or character and which ought to be homogeneously monolingual, that they interpreted the Igbo linguistic variation as an essentialised dimension of Igbo national character or psychology. In 1874, Bishop Crowther lamented that 'One common disadvantage which characterises the Ibo country is, Want of a king, who is supreme head of the nation, or even of a tribe. . . . Like disunion in their government, the dialects of the Ibos . . . are multifarious.'[11] A characterisation of Igbo as essentially unruly and individualistic lasted well into the colonial period – the period in which 'tribal' groups were concretised through censuses and administrative policies that treated them as separate legal entities.

I have drawn on this case to illustrate how the Anglican missionaries took what they thought was a 'national' (that is, ethnic) language and then assumed there must be a nation/ethnic group, and cultural unity with a particular psychology, to go along with it – a nation that must occupy a specific territorial homeland. Actually the slippage among geographical territory, language, and nation goes back earlier, with the coalescence of 'Ibo' Africans from the Bight of Biafra who formed a collectivity in the Americas and identified with a name they had not called themselves in Africa. Yet, the mismatch between these assumptions and the linguistic situation in Nigeria could only lead to trouble, and not only for Mr Taylor. During the many decades after Taylor was removed from his post, there were several efforts to standardise and unify Igbo language; yet, even when the standardisations were not based on Isuama, these efforts continually came up against the problem that large numbers of the 'Ibo' population found them too unfamiliar to use. Rivalries between Protestant and Catholic missions compounded the difficulty, since these missions used different orthographies, based their translations on different varieties of 'Igbo', and had different attitudes towards indigenous-language education.[12] As a result, none of the standardisations of Igbo have been very successful in attracting large numbers of adherents willing to embrace that version as their linguistic heritage and acquire it in school. Instead, people who self-identify as Igbo ethnics

himself a mission-educated African, born in a region near the capital of old Oyo. See also the CMS archives on the Niger Mission.

[11] CMS A3/04 A: Crowther, 'A Charge Delivered at Onitsha', October 1874.

[12] For more detail on linguistic contestations and mission differences, see, for example, A. E. Afigbo, 'The Place of the Igbo Language in Our Schools: A Historical Explanation', in F. Chidozie Ogbalu and E. Nolue Emenanjo (eds), *Igbo Language and Culture*, Vol. 1 (Ibadan: Oxford University Press, 1975), 70–84; E. Nolue Emenanjo, 'Central Igbo – An Objective Appraisal' in F. Chidozie Ogbalu and E. Nolue Emenanjo (eds), *Igbo Language and Culture*, Vol. 1 (Ibadan: Oxford University Press, 1975), 114–37; Francis Arinze, 'Christianity and Igbo Culture', in F. Chidozie Ogbalu and E. Nolue Emenanjo (eds), *Igbo Language and Culture*, Vol. 2 (Ibadan: University Press, 1982), 181–97; and P. Nwachukwu, *Towards an Igbo Literary Standard* (London: Kegan Paul International for the International African Institute, 1983).

maintain their local variety for local oral purposes and tend to turn to English for everything else. (Arguably, it was their alacrity in learning English, rather than any shared indigenous language, that 'Ibo' people had in common throughout the colonial period.)

In addition to contestations based on differences between some officially sanctioned 'Ibo' and a local variety, the archive reveals efforts by some of the indigenous population to be ethnically reclassified on the basis of language. For example, A. E. Afigbo has traced the record of disputes from the 1920s to the 1950s concerning the ethnic categorisation of a village cluster called Ika-na-Anang.[13] The residents, or at least some of the residents, of these villages were ethnically either Igbo or Ibibio, depending on how you looked at it and what was at stake. The residents of the Ika-na-anang villages were almost all bilingual or multilingual; their genealogies linked them to Ibibio clans, but they had also intermarried with people from nearby villages identified as Ndoki Igbo, with whom they had trade and property relations. They seldom met with their 'parent' Ibibio clans for traditional rituals or anything else.

In a British colonial administrative system mandating that indigenous peoples should be grouped along ethnic lines – understood as linguistic lines – for the jurisdictions of Native Courts and for participation in Native Councils, there were continual problems in establishing what villages actually belonged to which units. The effort of matching local administration to language and ethnicity proved very difficult. Populations seemed to be intermingled and multilingual, and they had their own notions as to which court and which District Officer they preferred.

Ika-na-anang had been assigned since early in the twentieth century to an administrative unit serving primarily Ndoki Igbo, but there were continual disputes over the assignment. In 1931, following a broader reorganisation in which many district lines were redrawn, a British officer investigating the case acknowledged the problems attending Ika-na-Anang's case, but nevertheless assigned the villages to a 'Ndoki Ibo' administrative district. In 1939 a group of elders petitioned to be removed from that Igbo district and placed in an Ibibio jurisdiction in neighbouring Calabar Province.[14] Among other grievances the elders claimed that, as Ibibios, they could not speak the Igbo language of the Ndoki Igbo council. The District Officer at the time found against the petitioners, however – partly because one of the elders discussed the case with him in Igbo. Still, a new set of petitions in 1953–4 made the same argument: that the villages should be reassigned, on linguistic grounds. This time the

---

[13] A. E. Afigbo, *The Igbo and Their Neighbours: Intergroup Relations in Southeastern Nigeria to 1953* (Ibadan: University Press, 1987).

[14] A compromise ruling earlier that year had accorded Ika-na-anang its own separate, Ibibio-language Native Court, but still assigned the villages to an Igbo district's Clan Council for other purposes.

colonial administrators were more willing to ignore the villagers' (multi-lingual) competence in Igbo and focus, instead, on their competence in the Ibibios' language. Now subdividing the region administratively, the British authorities transferred some eleven villages in the cluster to an Ibibio jurisdiction in April 1953. But as for the remaining villages, a visit to the area changed the District Officer's mind. The local subdivisions would have had to be so tiny and geographically complicated that he seems to have decided the issues could not really be about ethnicity at all.[15] In short, he threw out the case, not the model of language-ethnicity-territory it failed to match.

The many tensions surrounding Igbo ethnicity – tensions that include the Nigerian Civil War in the late 1960s – do not owe all their bases to linguistic diversity or to the misguided ideas of some British administrators. A fuller historical account would need to consider many other factors. My purpose in this chapter has not been to offer that account, but to illustrate how the complexities of language, culture, ethnicity, and genealogy in south-eastern Nigeria make any language-based notion of ethnic heritage or of cultural unity a problematic matter.

Language and Ethnicity in Colonial Senegal: 'Serer'

For a second case, I turn to the French colonial domain, in the colony of Senegal. This case concerns the populations and ways of speaking identified as 'Serer' (and Wolof). The French colonisers and linguists took cultural unity, or what they thought was unity, as their starting point for ethnic classification, a categorisation that entailed a putative linguistic unity along with the cultural. The result is similar to the Nigerian case, in that the categorisation masks sharp linguistic differences. More clearly than in Nigeria, however, the ethnic/linguistic classification derives less from the efforts of the French colonisers themselves than from the terms used by neighbouring Africans.

In lists of Senegal's ethnic groups one will find the term 'Serer'.[16] It groups together people whose linguistic practices, from a modern linguistic perspective, are very disparate. There are two sets of 'Serer' populations in Senegal. One set inhabits a region south of the Cap Vert and extending towards the Gambian border (see Map of West Africa, p. xx); this region, surrounding the town of Fatick and including a pop-ulation numbering in the hundreds of thousands, is south and west of the main 'Wolof' population areas. Another set of 'Serer' lives in small village enclaves within an otherwise mostly Wolof region east of Dakar.

---

[15] See Afigbo, *The Igbo and their Neighbours* for documents relating to the case.
[16] 'Serer' in many English-language publications; 'Sérère' in Francophone works; 'Sereer' in Senegalese official orthography.

North-west of the first set of Serer, these enclave villages are scattered around the city of Thiès, although one of the clusters of enclave villages extends as far south as the coastal town of Popenguine. The southern 'Serer' varieties are clearly related, linguistically, to Wolof, while the languages spoken by the northern 'Serer' are very different from both (the southern set of Serer varieties, and Wolof). Nevertheless, the two 'Serer' populations and their languages were and are lumped together, identified as 'Serer' by neighbouring Africans – Wolof people – to whom it is decidedly preferable *not* to be 'Serer'.[17]

That is, people who self-identify as Wolof, the largest ethnic group in Senegal and the coastal population with whom European colonisers had first and most intense contact, apply the term Serer indiscriminately to both sets of populations (as do most maps of language or of ethnicity in Senegal). To Wolof people such as those I worked with in a rural area north of Dakar, 'Serer' seems to refer, somewhat vaguely, to non-Muslim people to their south who don't speak Wolof, or to those people's descendants, and to their language(s). Linguistic differences within such populations do not particularly interest most Wolof, who are unlikely to learn to speak any of the languages they have lumped together as Serer. Wolof is a lingua franca in much of Senegal. It is speakers of other languages who acquire Wolof, not the other way around.[18]

Opposition between 'Wolof' and 'Serer' was highly salient in the mid-nineteenth century when the French, who already held a fairly well-established small colony at the mouth of the Senegal River and another on Gorée Island, embarked on an effort to control the interior. The opposition rested on the then-recent history of the slave trade and on differing relations with Islam. The 'Serer' were people who had sought refuge from slave raiding, while Wolof were people who pursued it (though Wolof populations were vulnerable to raiding, too). At the time, many Serer tended to resist conversion to Islam, while Wolof had accepted an Islamic presence, to greater or lesser degree, since the eleventh century.

However, there were also factors that undermine any simple opposition between Serer and Wolof. In an earlier period (fifteenth century), the

---

[17] In fieldwork in the 1970s I heard Wolof people make comments more disparaging about people they identify as Serer than about any other ethnicity: jokes about their stupidity or big feet; throwaway remarks suggesting Serer are all just escaped slaves; a warning that I should not mention the word 'Serer' around a local family reputed to be of Serer origin, because it would embarrass or anger them. Such comments were not frequent, but they did focus more on 'Serer' than on others, and without any distinction among the populations so labelled.

[18] See Louis-Jean Calvet, *Les Voix de la ville: Introduction à la sociolinguistique urbaine* (Paris: Payot et Rivages, 1994) for a discussion of sociolinguistic surveys and census figures. Although figures vary, it is clear that over 70 per cent of the population of Senegal speaks Wolof, and at least a third of these have acquired it as a second language. Meanwhile, very few people who claim Wolof ethnicity acquire any other African language.

whole area, including the part where the southern 'Serer' populations live, had been ruled by a single Wolof state, the Jolof Empire. Even after the Jolof state dissolved (in the mid-sixteenth century), its former provinces shared in a political sphere where the leadership spoke Wolof as the language of politics and used Wolof terms for many political titles.[19] Some of these former provinces – now separate kingdoms – especially the two southernmost ones, Siin (the area around Fatick) and Saluum (from Kaolack to the coast), included many people for whom the language of the home was probably some variety of 'Serer'. All the kingdoms had warrior aristocracies to protect themselves from outside incursions.[20] And in Saluum, new waves of Wolof-speaking immigrants from the north were entering the area.

Nevertheless, in regard to relations with Islam, 'Serer' and 'Wolof' contrasted vividly at the time of French expansion in the mid-nineteenth century. The scene of warfare and shifting alliances among Senegalese kingdoms was now reconfigured by an Islamic reformist movement that pitted committed Muslims against those who, whether aristocrats or peasant farmers, were considered unbelievers – a designation that included many Serer in Siin and Saluum as well as people in the 'Serer' enclaves further north, who had remained outside Islamic influence.[21] This identification was reinforced by the fact that the two sets of 'Serer' provided the main source of converts for French Christian missions.

---

[19] In his *Senegambia and the Atlantic Slave Trade* (Cambridge: Cambridge University Press, 1998), Baboucar Barry calls Jolof a 'confederation' rather than an empire; it is not clear how centralised this state, which dissolved into its six constituent provinces in the second half of the sixteenth century, ever was. On the region as a Wolof political sphere, see Martin Klein, *Islam and Imperialism in Senegal: Sine-Saloum 1847–1914* (Stanford, CA: Stanford University Press, 1969), among other sources. That Wolof was the language of 'international' politics even in the southern kingdoms of Siin and Saluum is further evidenced by, for example, the French missionary Alois Kobès's record of his visit to the king of Saloum. Kobès quoted the king's remarks in Wolof. See O. Abiven, *Annales réligieuses de St.-Joseph de Ngasobil, 1849–1929* (Archevêché de Dakar, n.d.).

[20] Despite the use of Wolof as the language of politics, the aristocracies of Siin and Saluum traced some of their genealogies to an early wave of Mande – that is, non-Wolof – invaders, absorbed into the local leadership.

[21] There were actually several reformist movements over the centuries in Senegambia, a region where Islam had been present since at least as far back as the eleventh century. The movement I refer to here is the nineteenth-century jihad led by Pulaar (Fula) marabout Al Hajj Umar Tall and his successor Maba Jaxu Ba from Fouta Toro and Fouta Jalon. For a useful survey of these successive movements see Mamadou Diouf, *Histoire du Sénégal* (Paris: Maisonneuve et Larose, 2001), Chapter 8. Through a combination of conversions, alliances, and military action, this Islamic movement made considerable headway among the Wolof kingdoms until it was opposed on the battlefield only by the French and the 'Serer' kingdom of Siin. In a battle against this jihadist army in 1867 the king of Siin decisively prevailed, allegedly (that is, according to local tradition) by calling upon the Serer *pangol* spirits who sent torrential rains and drenched the jihadists' ammunition (see Barry, *Senegambia*, 199). Given this historical background it is not surprising that the southern Serer were identified by Wolof people as anti-Muslim, as were the enclave populations further north who had also resisted Islam.

It was during the French military campaigns of the 1860s that the first serious linguistic research on 'Serer' was undertaken. Reports of the military expeditions, published in the government journal *Annuaire du Sénégal*, were accompanied by linguistic analyses, ethnographic notices, and a detailed map. The *Annuaire* of 1865 provided grammatical descriptions produced by the army's General Faidherbe.[22] Most of this publication is taken up with a study of 'Kéguem or Serer-Siin', but there is a short note on one of the enclave languages, drawn from a brief interview with a youth picked up in the course of the campaign. Faidherbe's text introduces the languages thus:

The populations that the Wolofs designate by the name of Serers speak two distinct languages: one named *Kéguem* and the other *None*. *Kéguem*, called Serer-Siin by the Wolofs, is spoken in Ndjiégem, in Siin, in Saluum, and in part of Bawol [Senegalese kingdoms and provinces]. *None* [the language] is spoken in the communities of... [enclave communities further north]. The populations who speak the *None* dialects do not at all understand *Kéguem*, and vice versa.[23]

Despite recognising the differences between these languages, and acknowledging that the designation 'Serer' came from Wolof usage, Faidherbe retained the cover term 'Serer' for both of them.[24]

Like his text, Faidherbe's map follows Wolof usage in placing the label 'Serer' on the enclaves and on Siin and Saluum. It also reveals its immersion in French military activity.[25] Besides showing towns and villages, lakes and rivers, and the frontiers between the French colony and the existing African states, the map offers neatly drawn 'lines of separation' between regions labelled Wolof and Serer. Similar lines represent boundaries between each of these and other ethnic groups, 'Mandingues' and

---

[22] A few vocabularies of (southern) Serer had been available earlier. See, for example, Gaspard Mollien, *Travels in the Interior of Africa to the Sources of the Senegal and Gambia... in the Year 1818* (Edinburgh: Bowdich, 1820).

[23] In his note on the enclave languages, Faidherbe again specifies that the speakers of None are 'these inhabitants the Wolofs designate by the name of Serer-Nones'. Louis Faidherbe, 'Étude sur la langue Kuégem ou Sérère-Sine', *Annuaire du Sénégal pour l'année 1865* (Saint-Louis: Imprimerie du Gouvernement, 1865), 244.

[24] He also suggested that they were related to Wolof and, perhaps, to languages just south of the Gambia River. To Faidherbe, the territories in which these languages were found seemed to be too small for really different languages: 'It is impossible to acknowledge that on the small length of coastline which extends from Gorée to Casamance [that is, from the Cap Vert down to the region south of the Gambia], the populations that inhabit these swampy areas could have a large number of entirely different languages.' Faidherbe, 'Étude,' 176.

[25] So do the 'common phrases' in Serer-Siin that Faidherbe offered along with his grammatical sketch and vocabulary: 'They have destroyed the fortifications at Makhana and killed all the inhabitants'; 'Your rifle is good but you are clumsy'; 'I have no more powder or lead'; 'Go tell those people that if they keep following us, we will fire on them'; and so on. Faidherbe, 'Étude', 227–44.

'Peuls'. These populations are accorded distinct blocs in the map's representation of the supposed relationship between language, population, and territory.

To produce this visual representation, Faidherbe and his cartographers had to ignore the multilingualism that characterised indigenous political life among 'Serer' and others. But doing away with indigenous political institutions was part of the French project anyway. Since the colonisers' version of Senegambian history was that the Serer had been enslaved and tyrannised by Wolof and/or Manding aristocrats and Muslim clerics, France (they proposed) was justified in overthrowing those oppressors and substituting French rule. Until these African tyrants were gone and the French *mission civilisatrice* could get properly under way, wrote Colonel Pinet-Laprade, the populations of 'countries like Siin and Saluum... could not attempt any progress, because of the state of stupefaction in which they were held under the regime of the Gelwaar [aristocratic lineages]'.[26] As for 'Serer' further north – the enclave communities – they, Pinet-Laprade claimed, were less thoroughly dominated by the Wolof state of Kajoor in which they were encapsulated. Once the threat of Wolof Kajoor was removed, these Serer, being a simple, childlike people, would be easily led by France.[27]

Evidently, Pinet-Laprade found it ideologically convenient to lump the two kinds of 'Serer' together, although the usage came from Wolof intermediaries. The enclave communities' internal social arrangements fit relatively well with a European notion that black Africans lived in primitive simplicity unless influenced by conquering tyrants, Islam, or white racial infiltration. Their small egalitarian villages, their indigenous religious rituals, their agricultural economy, and their relative lack of interest in military matters except when directly threatened from outside, were characteristics Pinet-Laprade seems to have thought were natural to black Africans. These, then, could be taken to represent Serer society in its basic condition. The Serer further south, in Siin and Saluum, must also (he thought) have been simple egalitarian peasants before they fell under the sway of their northern neighbours.

In keeping with these notions about Serer people, the Catholic missionary Père Lamoise, the author of the first book-length grammar of Serer-Siin, claimed the language was 'simple' compared to Wolof.[28] The

[26] E. Pinet-Laprade, 'Notice sur les Sérères', *Annuaire du Sénégal pour l'année 1865* (Saint-Louis: Imprimerie du Gouvernement, 1865), 147.
[27] '[The enclave populations] are, like all peoples in infancy, very little advanced along the way of social organisation [*association*]; they are generally grouped by families, in the vicinity of their fields. This state of affairs will facilitate the action we are called upon to take on them, because we will not have to overturn established authorities, sever close ties, or combat blind fanaticism.' Pinet-Laprade, 'Notice', 155.
[28] Père Lamoise, *Grammaire de la langue sérère avec des exemples et des exercices renfermant des documents très-utiles* (Saint-Joseph de Ngasobil [Sénégambie]: Imprimerie de la mission, 1873).

claim is not likely to convince a later generation of linguists who notice its complex morphology, among other things. But Lamoise treated complexities and variations as interference and corruption. If Serer now deviated from its original purity and simplicity – the language God must have placed among these simple people – then, Lamoise suggested, the deviations were due to 'errors and vices': either the errors of the fetishism into which the people had fallen, or the vicious influence of Islam and its Wolof perpetrators.[29] The missionary linguist's task was to retrieve as much of the pure language as possible and, he implied, to purge it of error. This was not easy, for, as he commented darkly, 'everywhere, as one can see, the infernal serpent is to be found'.[30]

One solution was to select the regional variety that could be considered the most 'pure' – and to avoid including words and expressions that might come from Wolof. But since linguistic purity was primarily, in his view, a matter of returning to a divinely inspired condition, the purest Serer of all was exemplified in the religious discourse he and his assistants could produce when translating Catholic prayers and religious writings. Actual prayers by Serer-speakers themselves would not do, 'since the rare aspirations that emerge from the mouths of the Serers... are far too incomplete and inadequate'.[31] In Lamoise's works 'Serer' language became, quite literally, what he and his assistants said it was. Meanwhile, other varieties of Serer were not described; and regional varieties that seemed to be mixed or overlapping with Wolof were ignored.[32] The same notions of language purity and ethnic essence that led nineteenth-century linguists to ignore 'mixed' varieties, multilingualism, and expressions they could attribute to linguistic borrowing also discouraged research into African regional dialectology.

Of course there were other factors discouraging dialectology as well: the scarcity of researchers; a positive value placed on language standardisation; and, in the French colonies, a lack of interest in indigenous-language education. But these factors played into one another. Once a variety had been declared to belong to the 'same' language as some already-described variety, there was no reason to investigate it, unless its speakers stubbornly refused to speak anything else. The languages spoken

---

[29] Lamoise, *Grammaire*, 329.
[30] Lamoise, *Grammaire*, 284.
[31] Lamoise, *Grammaire*, 333.
[32] An example would be the variety of Serer spoken in Bawol, which has been reported as a mix. Pinet-Laprade called it a language 'derived from Serer-Siin... and from Wolof' (Pinet-Laprade, 'Notice,' 135). A more recent linguist called it 'Sinsin [i.e., the Siin variety of Serer], penetrated lexically by Wolof'. M. de L. de Tressan, *Inventaire linguistique de l'Afrique Occidentale Française et du Togo* (Dakar: Institut Francais d'Afrique Noire, 1953). As far as I know this variety has never been studied in its own right. For a recent discussion of the Cangin languages, see Gordon Williams, 'Intelligibility and Language Boundaries among the Cangin Peoples of Senegal', *Journal of West African Languages* 24, 1 (1994): 47–67, who focuses on their lack of mutual intelligibility with each other or with the Serer of Siin.

by 'Serers' living north-west of Siin, in enclave communities – languages linguists once called 'Serer-None', or 'Faux-Sérère', and today call the Cangin languages – remained virtually undocumented until the 1950s and 1960s, and have only begun to get full-scale descriptions now in the twenty-first century. Since their speakers have been obligingly mult-ilingual, using Wolof or French in dealings with Europeans and other outsiders, and having little contact with Serer-speakers further south, there was no pressing need for missionaries or administrators to worry about the fact that these ways of speaking failed to resemble the more southerly versions of what they called 'Serer'. Anyway, French colonial policy was assimilationist, emphasising French-language immersion in schools.

'Serer' is still used today as an ethnic label for both populations, and it is only recently that scholars, even linguists, have called the enclave languages anything else. As for the enclave populations themselves, as far as I know they usually refer to themselves by the name of the particular village they inhabit – but sometimes as 'Serer', taking on the Wolof view-point. Recent sources suggest that hyphenated terms are coming into use: thus Serer-Ndut, Serer-Palor, and so on, identifying each enclave language (and village cluster) but retaining 'Serer' as an umbrella term.[33]

While the trend in colonial Senegal was to emphasise distinction and difference between Wolof and Serer, both linguistically and ethnically – and to that end, to downplay differences internal to the 'Serer' category – post-colonial Senegal has seen new political developments and new pictures of the regional scene. A recent trend in Senegalese histori-ography emphasises what the societies and languages of the whole region (Senegal north of the Gambia River, including Wolof and Serer) have in common.[34] In other words, cultural heritage in the region is being rein-terpreted as applicable to a wider grouping than the ethnic distinctions so insisted upon in an earlier time.

Perhaps this trend reflects a new political environment: in a time of new tensions between Senegalese and Mauritanians, and a separatist move-ment in the region south of the Gambia, the other residents of Senegal share a common cause. Meanwhile, all Serer languages are probably losing ground to Wolof.

Comparisons and Conclusions

The two cases discussed in this chapter were chosen because they were located within the domains of different European imperial powers. Yet

---

[33] For example, Fiona McLaughlin, 'Senegal: The Emergence of a National Lingua Franca', in Andrew Simpson (ed.), *Language and National Identity in Africa* (Oxford and New York, NY: Oxford University Press, 2008), 79–97.

[34] See, for example, Makhtar Diouf, *Sénégal: Les ethnies et la nation* (Dakar: Les Nouvelles Editions Africaines du Sénégal, 1998); Barry, *Senegambia*.

they have a great deal in common. In both cases the linguistic and ethnic categorisations that emerged in colonial discourse masked major linguistic differences – cultural differences too, although I have not detailed those. In both south-eastern Nigeria and southern Senegal, ways of speaking were grouped together as if they were variants of a single language, although in fact they differed widely and were mutually unintelligible. In the Senegalese case, Serer-Siin is closer to Wolof – though the two were codified separately, something no modern-day linguist would be likely to challenge – than to the (Cangin) languages spoken by 'Serer' populations in the enclave communities.

A glance at other parts of the continent shows, however, that the experts who classified African languages and 'tribes' did not always create such wide linguistic groupings. In South Africa, for example, Zulu and Xhosa came to be treated as separate languages (and peoples) by investigators in the 1830s and 1840s, even though earlier writings on the languages and peoples of the region had grouped them together as one more or less homogeneous population of 'Kaffirs', speaking one language.[35]

Several factors seem to have combined to produce the codifications that separated Zulu from Xhosa. The missionaries working as language experts came from different backgrounds and different Protestant sects. In the first half of the nineteenth century, it was Methodist missionaries, mainly immigrants from Britain, who worked on linguistic analyses of Xhosa (still often termed 'Kaffir'); meanwhile the American Board of Commissioners for Foreign Missions established a station in the Zulu territory. The American missionaries were mainly Congregationalist; representatives of the Anglican CMS and others followed them to Zululand not long afterwards. The difference in missionary sects would have impeded cooperation among language workers. But what was surely more important was the political scene, with an expanding and centralising Zulu state, on the one hand, and a congerie of looser Xhosa chiefdoms on the other. Although the Zulu king Shaka had died before the missionaries arrived in Zulu-ruled territories, the image of a powerful, aggressive, and uniquely organised Zulu state, led by a despotic king, was already gaining ground in white settler circles. Many aspects of this image have been challenged by some recent historians (including Buthelezi, this volume), but the unity it appeared to offer must have appealed to missionaries eager to work on a language through which they could proselytise to a large population. In this period, moreover, the Khoi and San languages

---

[35] For more detail and discussion on the colonial-era representation of Xhosa and Zulu see Rachael Gilmour, *Grammars of Colonialism: Representing Languages in Colonial South Africa* (Basingstoke and New York, NY: Palgrave Macmillan, 2006). In contrast, in recent years there has been at least one major project investigating the possibility of a new standardisation that would undo the separation of these two languages, unifying them.

were perceptibly in decline, releasing missionary linguists in South Africa to focus their labours among the populations further east.

Many more examples from around the African continent could be brought into this discussion, if space (and attention) permitted. What emerges from a wider look at early African linguistics is that what these projects had in common was not the specific mismatches between their language identifications and what was spoken 'on the ground'. Instead, what these cases share is the ideology about shared language, homogeneous culture, and contiguous territory with which the linguistic research was done – the image of a natural ethnolinguistic heritage that informed the researchers' analyses and publications. What was more variable was whether state-level language policy followed up on the products of these researches, for example in promoting the use of African languages in schools – more common in the British colonies – or forbidding it, as was common in the French colonies.

In conclusion, my purpose in this chapter has been to inquire into the nineteenth-century background of 'ethnolinguistic' groups that are recognised today, to look at how the early colonial-era scholars handled the linguistic and other information they gathered, producing representations of ethnolinguistic groups that became institutionalised in colonial (and even post-colonial) administrations. Like other colonial-era 'experts', these scholars have cast a long shadow.[36]

I do not challenge the importance of African languages in African cultural heritage. Rather, the processes I have described seem to me to have led to a kind of impoverishment of the African linguistic heritage. Languages rich in social deixis were and are often analysed as if they were uniform and flat; yet, variability of style and social positioning is also part of linguistic heritage. Part of linguistic heritage, too, are the longstanding patterns of multilingualism in many parts of the continent. To ignore or override these forms of linguistic richness is to distort what the heritage is. There are political consequences as well. To formulate bounded ethnolinguistic groups, equating language with ethnicity and conceiving of ethnicity as quasi-nation – thus as implying political rivalry – can make the colonial language appear to be the only unifying option for public affairs. Where that happens, the African linguistic heritage is made not to matter.

---

[36] Compare, for example, the work of outside scientific 'experts' discussed by Ciraj Rassool; this volume.

11 The Role of Language in Forging New Identities

Countering a Heritage of Servitude

Mary Esther Kropp Dakubu

There is a very widespread opinion in Ghana, and no doubt elsewhere, that is reflected by Obeng and Adegbija when they say that in sub-Saharan Africa, 'Language is seen as the storehouse of ethnicity: Each ethnic group expresses and identifies itself by the language it speaks....'[1] The popular belief is that there is a simple and indissoluble one-to-one relationship between a people, an 'ethnic group' (the most widespread term in the discourse outside the academy continues to be 'tribe'), and its language. Ghanaian scholars often assume that language and ethnicity define each other; thus Perbi provides what is clearly intended as a basic account of 'the people of Ghana' by summarising the current linguistic classification of the languages considered to be indigenous to the country.[2] Irvine (elsewhere in this volume) attributes the doctrine that a language and a people constitute a fundamental, essentially immutable unity to the ideologies and assumptions that underpinned the linguistic and anthropological activities of the missionary and colonial enterprises of the nineteenth and early twentieth centuries, with their emphasis on classification, ultimately for purposes of control, and their roots in the nationalisms of their times. She is no doubt correct in this, but the practice of giving a name to a group of people, however it may be delimited, plus a language considered to be characteristic of the group, seems to be too convenient a usage for it to be readily abolished. Even Lüpke and Storch, who take a fairly radical view of the unboundedness of a 'language', let alone the mapping of a 'language' to an 'ethnic group', find it inconvenient to discard it altogether and continue to mention 'the Maaka' or 'the Chopi'.[3]

---

[1] Samuel Gyasi Obeng and Efurosibina Adegbija, 'Sub-Saharan Africa', in Joshua A. Fishman (ed.), *Handbook of Language and Ethnic Identity* (Oxford: Oxford University Press, 1999), 353.

[2] Akosua Perbi, 'Who Is a Ghanaian? – A Historical Perspective', in *National Integration: Proceedings of the Ghana Academy of Arts and Sciences* (2003), 29.

[3] Friederike Lüpke and Anne Storch, *Repertoire and Choices in African Languages* (Berlin: Walter de Gruyter Mouton, 2013), 247, 311.

Nevertheless, as Dorian writing in the same volume as Obeng and Adegbija points out, ethnicity is a social construction, and therefore subject to change.[4] When such change occurs, moreover, it often affects the relationship between the ethnic self-identification of the group and the language or languages that this identification may embrace. People individually or in groups may become part of another group, a process that may involve language shift, which in itself may or may not result in a shift in ethnic identity. And as Lüpke and Storch are at pains to point out, in Africa, pervasive multilingualism combined with equally pervasive inter-group kinship and other social ties may make the concepts of both ethnic and linguistic shift very hard to pin down.

With or without language shift, if a group is in some sense or degree assimilated into another the subsumed group may regard itself and be regarded by others as a 'sub-ethnicity', so that ethnic identity becomes even more complex. This is the case for example among the Gã, that is, the people who speak the Gã language and can claim at least two or three generations of forebears who spoke it. Such people have been the 'traditional' inhabitants of Accra since at least the seventeenth century. They recognise that their various named divisions have diverse origins, and that these different origins are manifested in different cultural practices and identifications, but that nevertheless all participate in a Gã 'supra-ethnicity'.[5] Not only is the pairing of language and ethnicity not a simple matter, there is quite obviously no simple pairing of an individual person with an ethnicity, since a person's parents may continue to belong to different groups, and an individual may choose to emphasise one or the other in different circumstances.[6]

Nor is such a situation unique to the Gã – virtually all 'ethnic groups' turn out to include people of diverse origins when examined closely. Note also that the self-identification mentioned by Obeng and Adegbija is not

---

[4] Nancy Dorian, 'Linguistic and Ethnographic Fieldwork', in Joshua A. Fishman (ed.), *Handbook of Language and Ethnic Identity* (New York, NY: Oxford University Press, 1999), 25.

[5] This issue is discussed in M. E. Kropp Dakubu, *One Voice, the Linguistic Culture of an Accra Lineage* (Leiden: African Studies Centre, 1981). The divisions concerned are named political divisions of Accra and other Ga-speaking towns along the coast that seem to have assumed something like their present forms late in the eighteenth century or early in the nineteenth, although they continued to absorb incomers and evolve in their relations with each other at least until the beginning of the twentieth. See John Parker, *Making the Town, Ga State and Society in Early Colonial Accra* (Oxford: James Currey, 2000); also M. E. Kropp Dakubu, *Korle Meets the Sea, a Sociolinguistic History of Accra* (New York, NY: Oxford University Press, 1997). On variations in cultural practices related to different origins see especially Margaret J. Field, *Religion and Medicine of the Gã People.* (London: Oxford University Press, 1937).

[6] In one case personally known to me, a man whose father was Gã and whose academic and professional life revolved around the Gã language became chief of the (Akan) Akuapem town his mother came from. Since such positions devolve matrilineally among the Akan this was perfectly possible, but on assuming the position he had to formally renounce any claim to chiefly position among the (patrilineal) Gã.

simply a personal or group-internal matter. Despite the slipperiness of the language–people nexus, it is a fact that language is very often treated by insiders and outsiders alike as a symbol of a group of people, who in some circumstances may not actually speak it. The status of a language may thus be regarded as a reflex of the status of the people who speak it or otherwise consider it to be 'theirs'. Even where the recent history of a group has not involved political, ethnic, or linguistic shift, members of a linguistically identified group may find it desirable to try to change how they are viewed by others, and this may involve changing the way that others view the language with which they are identified. For many people the fact that a language is written is a major status marker, thought to make the difference between a 'language' and a 'mere dialect'. Efforts at improving its image may therefore take the form of establishing a written version of the language. If the group has been somehow marginalised or denigrated, a successful effort of this kind is likely to also raise its own self-esteem.

The two groups I shall discuss are in most ways entirely different, but they have in common an association with slavery, although that association is now fading into the distant past, and in a subtle way also an involvement in urbanisation. The topic of slavery, particularly indigenous slavery and its implications, is still somewhat sensitive in Ghana. When I first worked in southern Ghana in the mid-1960s, the subject was never discussed. A very rare appearance of the topic in public discourse was Ama Ata Aidoo's play *The Dilemma of a Ghost*, first performed in 1964, which portrays the negative attitudes of at least some Ghanaians to African Americans as the descendants of slaves.[7] Times have changed to some extent, thanks in part to the pioneering work of Akosua A. Perbi.[8] For a long time, the received opinion was that former slaves were incorporated into the extended families and lineages that formerly owned them, and so there was no problem. At the same time, however, it was considered highly improper to mention another's ancestry. It is true that former slaves were incorporated, but it is also true that they were not always incorporated with equal status, or in the same way. After more than a century since the colonial government abolished domestic slavery, institutionalised inequality derived from former slave status can still affect access to local political power and land. Therefore, apart from any lingering social stigma, slave ancestry is a sensitive topic if only for economic reasons.

In this chapter I consider first how the members of a particular Gã lineage, which I have reason to believe is not untypical of a considerable proportion of Gã-speaking society, have used language in forging an

---

[7] Christina Ama Ata Aidoo, *The Dilemma of a Ghost* (Accra and Ikeja: Longmans, 1965).
[8] Akosua Adoma Perbi, *A History of Indigenous Slavery in Ghana from the 15th to the 19th Century* (Accra: Sub-Saharan Publishers, 2004).

identity for themselves that overrides the disadvantage of their historical heritage, in their own eyes at least. My remarks are based on fieldwork carried out during the 1960s and 1970s. The original purpose of that fieldwork was linguistic, to study the phonology and grammar of the Gã language and eventually aspects of its oral literature. I published most of the information to be discussed here in another place (see below), but it is treated here from quite a different point of view.

I shall contrast the story of that lineage with observations from an entirely different group in northern Ghana, the Farefari (or Frafra), whose use of language to validate their heritage and create an acceptable public identity for themselves bears a certain unexpected relationship to that of the Gã group.

Ajorkor Okine We

I began visiting the small Gã villages on which my book *One Voice, the Linguistic Culture of an Accra Lineage* was based, in 1965.[9] These villages belonged to a clan called Ajorkor Okine We, which also had a compound house in Accra, although I did not work with the people, mostly women, who resided there.[10] I had read the standard Gã ethnographies, namely Field on religion and on social organisation, and Pogucki on Gã land tenure,[11] and I assumed that although they did not entirely fit the people I worked with, this was because Field in particular had focused on the coastal towns, and both authors treated the interior villages as appendages of the towns.[12] I quickly realised that these people were not simply the close relatives of members of the lineage based in the 'family house' in

[9] Dakubu, *One Voice*. This section is drawn entirely from the content of that book, which may be referred to for specifics and details.

[10] Since Gã women tend to live with their mothers, many if not most of these women were not members of the patrilineage. *We* is Gã for 'house, lineage'. *Ajɔkɔ* is a woman's name used by some lineages in the Gã-speaking town of Teshie to the east of Accra, so that the name means 'the house of Ajorkor's [son] Okine'. I have used real names throughout, as in Dakubu, *One Voice* (1981), because the people I worked with wanted their house to be famous. Since membership in a Gã lineage and overarching division (*akutso*) is ideally patrilineal, it is slightly odd that it is the founder's mother's name that appears in this name. I have no real explanation. Presumably it served to distinguish him from *another* Okine with a different mother, but it also tends to reinforce the marginalised status of the lineage.

[11] See Margaret J. Field, *Religion and Medicine of the Gã People*; Margaret J. Field, *Social Organization of the Gã People* (London: Crown Agents for the Colonies, 1940); R. J. H. Pogucki, *Gold Coast Land Tenure*, Vol. 3: *Land Tenure in Ga Customary Law* (Accra: Gold Coast Lands Department, 1955).

[12] Kilson's work with a particular group of Gã priestesses, discussed in Marion De B. Kilson, *Kpele Lala, Ga Religious Songs and Symbols* (Cambridge, MA: Harvard University Press, 1971), does not fit, because the songs and practices belong to a tradition essentially alien to the people I worked with – a different 'sub-ethnicity'. Kilson's *African Urban Kinsmen* is explicitly about Gã society in urban Accra. Marion Kilson, *African Urban Kinsmen, the Ga of Central Accra* (London: C. Hurst and Co., 1974).

town who had chosen to live on their farms, but it took several years before the penny decisively dropped, when I started to look closely at names, and discovered that the names of three sons of the founder of the lineage who were always referred to as his 'adopted' sons belonged to the class of names that the Gã call *nyɔŋ gbei* 'slave names'.[13] These names were given by household heads to people acquired through purchase or war, and are invariably in Akan (Twi), not Gã, with a proverb-like internal structure. Even though slave ancestry could not be openly discussed, therefore, to any culturally knowledgeable person it was plainly attested in the very names of the ancestors. Although some of the people I worked with traced their genealogies to other sons with 'normal' Gã names, if they did not directly trace their patrilineal descent to one of the 'adopted' sons they were very frequently descended from them through their mothers. It would appear that it was essentially through these maternal connections that they were resident where they were. This is significant, because Gã society is frequently referred to as patrilineal, although Kilson considered it more accurately described as 'cognatic, with an emphasis on patrilineal affiliation'.[14] The Akan of course are strongly matrilineal.

There are a number of reasons why I should have recognised the situation earlier. During the eighteenth and nineteenth centuries, which saw wars with the (Akan-speaking) Akwamu and later the Asante, the Gã hinterland was not always very secure. Many Gã lineages therefore placed servants on their farmlands, and did not stay there themselves.[15] The custom by which villagers arrive in the coastal town on a particular day at the beginning of the annual Homowo harvest celebrations bearing foodstuffs for the family that owns the lands can be read as presentation of tribute to the landowners. Shortly before slavery was officially abolished by the British in 1874,[16] a report by the Basel Mission indicated that many former slaves had remained on the lands of the Accra hinterland, and that most of them were 'Grunshies', that is, people from the present-day Upper East Region of Ghana, who mainly did not speak Gã but still spoke their original languages or sometimes Twi. If they spoke Twi it was usually because they had lived for some time in Twi-speaking areas before arriving in Accra.[17] There is quite recent anecdotal evidence of remembered 'Grunshie' ancestry, for which the only ready explanation is former slave status.

---

[13] That is, they were referred to as 'adopted' sons in English, by my research assistant who was a member of Ajorkor Okine We. On Gã names, see Dakubu, *One Voice* 82–161.

[14] Kilson, *African Urban Kinsmen*, 20.

[15] See, for example, Parker, *Making the Town*, 7.

[16] David Owusu-Ansah and Daniel Miles McFarland, *Historical Dictionary of Ghana* (Metuchen, NJ: Scarecrow Press, 1995), xxxiv.

[17] J. G. Christaller, 'Sprachproben vom Sudan zwischen Asante und Mittel-Niger', *Zeitschrift für Afrikanische Sprachen* 3 (1889): 10; also Parker, *Making the Town*, 218.

Today, or at least until the 1980s, the Accra rural population (apart from the many relatively recent migrants) speaks Gã.[18] In their customary and linguistic usages there are nevertheless occasional traces of northern origins. Ideologically, or at least this is the impression given by both Field and Kilson and also Gã writers on the topic, Gã ritual life is centred on the major divisions of the main coastal towns.[19] In the case of Ajorkor Okine We, at the time I worked with it there was some ambiguity as to which political division (*akutso*) of Accra the people recognised as 'theirs', a problem to which I will return, but the important fact is that apart from the annual Homowo harvest celebrations it was not true that their ritual life revolved around traditional Accra (Ga Mashie) or their particular division of it. For almost all purposes the main ritual centre for this lineage was not the 'family house' in Atukpai behind Ussher Fort in the area once known as 'Dutch Accra' but their section of the rural town of Mayera, where their cemetery and major shrine were located, and where in the 1970s a stool house was built that also housed the shrine. This shrine was said to have been brought from Moshie country (that is, Burkina Faso) by one of the 'adopted sons' of the founder.[20]

One of the old men whenever he poured libation would invoke *Sankana*. This was thought to be a local deity or *jemawɔŋ*, possibly a hill, but I could not find out where it was, and the only 'Sankana' known to me is a place north of Wa in the Upper West Region, where a famous and disastrous battle was fought in 1896.[21] War disasters of course imply refugees and captives. One man from another branch of the lineage had a joking nickname that was thought to be in the 'Grunshie' language, to which he responded with another word also in 'Grunshie'. These were supposed to be words for different sizes of penis, and the response indeed strongly resembles the word for 'testicles' in Oti-Volta languages such as Dagaare and Farefari.[22] These were the only vestiges of a northern language in actual use that I came across. The lineage members otherwise made no reference at all to any northern heritage. Their own construction of their past and present was entirely centred on the Twi language, which is the focus of interest here.

All the lineage members spoke Gã, which was the language of daily life and also of ritual practices such as pouring libation, but a considerable majority, about 75 per cent, also spoke Twi at least to some degree. It

---

[18] When I worked there, there were many Ewe families settled in the area. See Parker, *Making the Town*, 93 concerning the settlement of Ewe in the nineteenth century.

[19] Two significant works in Gã with an essentially urban orientation are A. A. Amartey, *Omanye Aba* (Accra: Bureau of Ghana Languages, 1969) and E. A. W. Engmann, *Kpawo Kpawo Toi Kpawo* Vol. 2: *Kusumi* (Oxford: Regnum Books International, 2012).

[20] Dakubu, *One Voice*, 50.

[21] Carola Lentz, *Ethnicity and the Making of History in Northern Ghana* (Edinburgh: Edinburgh University Press for the International African Institute, 2006), 30.

[22] Dakubu, *One Voice*, 427, note 16.

should be said, too, that they had strong social and kinship ties with nearby Akuapem (Twi-speaking) villages. The mother of at least one was from Nsakye, and the mothers of several were from Berekuso or Adusa, all within a few miles of Mayera. Even so, it is striking that all their 'state' music, played at funerals and on special occasions, is in Twi. This is the body of artistic performance that they consider symbolises their lineage as a corporate body and encapsulates their unique identity and history. It is supposed to have been created by the eponymous founder of the lineage, and includes a set of verses played on the talking drum known in Gã as *obonu*, a text played on the horn, *bɛlɛ*, with its answering drum *tswɛnshiŋ*, a second horn text that belongs to one sub-section of the lineage, and a group of songs called *akajá* that as far as I know is played only by these people. These Twi texts do not literally recount history, and in fact they seem to be largely composed of proverbial expressions and phrases that occur elsewhere in comparable texts. Inquiry into their meaning never elicited translation into Gã, but immediately led to discussion (in Gã) of the foundation of the lineage after a disagreement between the founder and his relatives. This was what they most wanted to talk about, and they took it very seriously.

It is quite normal among the Gã generally that court music should be in Twi.[23] Several important religious texts, though by no means all, are also in Twi. Thus the songs discussed by Kilson in her *Kpele Lala* were in Twi, and considered the epitome of 'pure Gã' tradition for all that. The talking drums of Gã chiefs are in Twi. The popular songs from their youth that the old men I met in the 1960s still sang were more likely to be in Twi than in Gã. It is not my argument here that this use of Twi within a Gã context is special or peculiar to a certain group, but that its very normality provides an avenue for otherwise marginalised sections of the population to identify themselves as Gã, without danger of confrontation with the power holders.

At the time I began this work I was informed that the lineage had previously been associated with the Gbese division (*akutso*) of Accra, as the location of the family house in Atukpai (a district of old Accra between Ussher Fort and the old central post office) indeed suggests, but that they were in the process of leaving Gbese and joining, or possibly rejoining, the Otublohum division. By the end of the 1970s they had indeed done so. Such shifts in political allegiance to a major Gã division do not seem to be common but they are not unheard of.[24] It seems likely that a land dispute underlies this particular shift. In 1965 I was told

---

[23] On the background to the use of languages other than Gã, especially Akan, among the Gã, see Dakubu, *Korle Meets the Sea*.

[24] In an interview in October 1995 the then *Akwashɔŋ Mantsɛ* (chairman of council of the Asere division of Accra) mentioned a few others in response to a direct question (MEKD field notes).

that Ajorkor Okine We had lost some nearby land through litigation to another group that was also a section of Gbese, but I did not pursue this aspect of the story.

At issue here is the role of the Twi language in the construction, or reconstruction, of the historical identity of the lineage. The Otublohum *akutso* which was founded during the eighteenth century is known to be of Akan origin.[25] In that division, children are named according to the general Gã system of giving names according to patriline, sex, birth order, and alternating generations, but in Otublohum the actual names that realise the system are Akan names common in Akuapem, which is not the case in other Gã *akutsei*. Ajorkor Okine We gives its children (that is, the children of male members of the lineage) names similar to those used in Otublohum, although with slight variation, as is normal between sub-lineages.

To the people I worked with this situation, combined with the fact that the music that symbolised their identity was in Twi, was clear evidence that they themselves were of Akan origin, specifically Akwamu, and belonged properly within Otublohum. They claimed moreover that they constituted the Atifi division of Otublohum (*atífî* being Twi for 'summit' – of a hill, for example). There is indeed an Atifi section of Otublohum, mentioned by both Field and Wilks, but their accounts do not tally with the one I encountered and my informants seemed to have no knowledge of the historical Atifi described by those authors. It is of course not impossible that the two were once associated. According to lineage tradition the relative with whom their ancestor Ajorkor Okine quarrelled was called *Oto Diŋ*, founder of today's *Nii Oto Diŋ We* of Otublohum.

According to the lineage story, then, the founder of Ajorkor Okine We left Otublohum and allied himself with Gbese, and now, apparently after falling out with Gbese, they were realigning themselves with Otublohum. The founder had also changed his name from *Oto* to *Okãi* (anglicised as Okine), a Gbese name. Otherwise the names given to children in this lineage, which definitely resemble Otublohum names more than those given in any Gbese patriline, are consistent with such a history.

The fact that their music is in Twi is at least as salient to their self-image. It is interesting that although it was said to have been composed in defiance of Otublohum generally and the founder's brother Oto Ding in particular, there seemed to be no question of giving it up as part of the reconciliation, for it still symbolised their group identity. The fact that it does not explicitly allude to actual events perhaps facilitates its acceptability in these new circumstances. If it was once confrontational in the manner of the Zulu *izibongo* discussed by Buthelezi elsewhere in this volume, and we may speculate that it probably was, it is not so today.

---

[25] Ivor Wilks, 'Akwamu and Otublohum: An Eighteenth-Century Akan Marriage Arrangement', *Africa* 29, 4 (1959).

It is possible, although not easily verifiable, that the rural Ajorkor Okine We settlements were once mainly Twi-speaking, as noted for the Accra hinterland in the late nineteenth century. If that was the case then there has been language shift from Twi to Gã for normal purposes, but the 'state' music may have been maintained since before the shift. One piece of evidence that may support this is that when giving oral versions of the texts played by the drums and horns, and also in the words of some of the *akaja* songs, the players used a somewhat archaic pronunciation of Twi, which is different from their normal 'everyday' pronunciation of that language. For example the consonant of the modern Twi verb *hyia* 'to meet' is pronounced not as a fricative [ʃ], which is the Gã sound closest to the modern Twi [ɕ], but as the aspirate [h], which is an archaism. Like most Gã they pronounce the Akan place names 'Akyem' [atɕɪm] and 'Nsakye' [nsatɕɪ] as 'Akim' and 'Nsaki'. Comparison of spellings in older writings on the Gold Coast indicates that affrication of these consonants must have occurred in the course of the nineteenth century.

Another suggestive fact is that although the main Gã divisions (*akutsei*) have probably existed since the late eighteenth century, genealogies acquired were in general only about three or four generations deep – meaning that they quite likely go back no further than the late nineteenth century, when the last waves of war captives and also of slaves or recently freed slaves arrived in Accra.[26] Given what is known about the history of the use of Twi in this area, and the close social and kinship ties between neighbouring Gã and Akuapem (Twi-speaking) villages, often involving reciprocal bilingualism, the social and linguistic configuration creates a fuzzy area between being Gã and being Akan, within which those who have little genealogical connection with either, but command or at least identify with both languages, can manoeuvre within the broader Gã context. That is, the point is to connect with other Gã who claim an Akan heritage, not with non-Gã Akans.

I also suggest that although the reconstruction of their past by the members of Ajorkor Okine We whom I met was directed in the first place at explaining their shifting relationship to Otublohum, on another level, perhaps unconscious, it aimed to validate their position within Gã society as a whole, by defining them in relation to a recognised and established

---

[26] Another tradition that was of great interest to the elderly men I spoke to was the story of the Ewe wars, which also brought captives to Accra. The Gã fought the Ewe in both the eighteenth and the nineteenth centuries. It was not possible to determine which wars their accounts referred to, but it is likely that Ewe captives were among their recent ancestors. See Parker, *Making the Town*, 93. I have collected texts from a member of a quite different Accra lineage and division who claimed that the founder of that lineage was a slave trader, himself a former slave, acting for an established Accra lineage early in the twentieth century, after slavery had officially been abolished by the British. The lineage did not want this information published about it, not because of the slave-trading activities of their founder, but because he was from the far north and had been a slave himself.

town-based portion of that essentially urban society. This self-definition is a kind of palimpsest upon their other identity, as disadvantaged descendants of fairly recently unfree immigrants, which is thus obliterated. There is anecdotal evidence that for many similar groups, if not Ajorkor Okine We itself, this other kind of identity is not entirely forgotten, but it will never be mentioned in public.

Farefari

On the surface of it, the situation among the speakers of Farefari, a language of the Upper East Region of Ghana, could not be more different. Apart from being at the opposite end of the country in its far north, the community has been and continues to be relatively monolingual, apart from the use of English in official domains. Akan is not particularly widely known or heard, except perhaps in Bolgatanga, which as the regional capital attracts civil and public servants from all over the country as well as many Akan-speaking traders. Group membership and inheritance are more strictly patrilineal than among the Gã. Although there have been local chiefs since colonial times and perhaps before, socio-political structures are less formal and hierarchical than among the Gã, who adopted a version of the Akan style of chieftaincy well before colonial times. On the other hand, relations within the descent group and the domestic sphere are probably more hierarchical. I should also say that my research experience of the community is different, as I started on it much more recently, have not had a close association with a particular lineage or village, and have worked largely with educated speakers, such as university students and secondary school teachers.

What the two groups have in common is a history of marginalisation, albeit on different levels. If the members of Ajorkor Okine We have had to reconfigure a disadvantaged status within Gã society, members of the Farefari community (as well as their immediate neighbours) have until fairly recently been marginalised within the nation state. The area was for long a source of slaves for raiders from more powerful states, and indeed groups now subsumed under the linguistic label 'Farefari' may well have provided some of the 'Grunshie' ancestors of Gã villagers. Modern education was late in coming to the region, there were very few university graduates until quite recently, and there were extremely few nationally prominent persons from the region until within the past 20 years. Among the generations over 50, highly educated people from the Upper East usually turn out to be the children of public servants, soldiers, or policemen, who got their education mainly in the south. In the 1960s people from the Upper Region, later divided into today's Upper East and Upper West Regions, were known in the south mainly as servants and manual labourers, and held in considerable disdain by many. The

Farefari themselves, or at any rate those who lived in the south, were well aware of this, and the formulation of the name 'Farefari' was intended to avoid the negative social connotations of the commonly used 'Frafra' (originally an anglicised version of a greeting in the language, *farafara*) – which provides another instance of the importance of names in the reification of identity.

For this community there is no need for mediation through another language, even if one were readily available, because internal marginalisation is not the issue. No doubt there are subgroups within the community that have been somehow marginalised with respect to the rest, because virtually every society has such people, but the groups must be small. However on the national level the community as a whole has carried the weight of a generalised heritage of former slavery, 'primitiveness', and underdevelopment, and there is a felt need to assert a positive, modern identity. An indication of the marginalisation of Farefari language and culture is that Bolgatanga, the capital of the Upper East Region, to this day is the only regional capital whose language, which is also the most widely spoken in the region, is not recognised by the Ministry of Education as a medium for primary school teaching and educational publishing. Efforts to have it so recognised by speakers and scholars of the language based at the University of Education in Winneba, where it is possible to do a degree in the language, have so far been unavailing.

It is in this context that the District Assemblies of Bolgatanga and Bongo, the districts where Farefari is spoken, set up Language Development Committees in the 1990s, where 'Language Development' was essentially understood to mean writing in and on the language. I was invited to help develop an orthography for it. The Accra Metropolitan Assembly, which covers virtually the entire Gã-speaking area, so far as I know has never had a comparable committee, presumably because the Gã language has had an established orthography for more than a century. (The most recent revision of this orthography was made by the Gã committee of the Bible Society, in connection with a new translation of the bible, and published by the Bureau of Ghana Languages, an organ of the Ministry of Education, in 1975).

Workshops held in Bolgatanga to discuss the proposed orthography were enthusiastically attended by teachers and others in the area. An orthography had in fact been devised not long before by a GILLBT (Ghana Institute of Linguistics, Literacy and Bible Translation) team of bible translators, but whether because it was unsatisfactory or to signal who owned the language, a new one was desired. Another factor may have been that the GILLBT orthography was based on the language as spoken in Zuarungu, in the eastern part of the territory. The workshop seemed unanimous in preferring the language as spoken in the Bolgatanga area, but with sufficient flexibility to accommodate the many mutually intelligible variants, including especially Booni to the north and Nankani in the west.

Following the workshop a report with a recommended orthography was submitted to the District Assemblies in 1998 and accepted. This was followed by a dictionary development project, funded this time not by the District Assemblies but through a project of the Linguistics Department of the University of Ghana.[27] Again, workshops in Bolgatanga and Legon to develop entries were enthusiastically attended, several people as well as myself put a lot of effort into it, and a dictionary was published in 2007.[28] It was launched with a degree of fanfare in both Bolgatanga and the University of Ghana at Legon, and the community was clearly glad to have it. The fact that the community was eager to launch it not just in the home area but also on the University of Ghana campus, which is more or less a suburb of Accra, is significant. There is a considerable Farefari-speaking community in Accra, which includes a higher proportion of literate and well-educated people than the 'home' community in the north. As a group of urban migrants, moreover, it has a heightened consciousness of both the attitudes of the rest of the country and especially its capital, and of the value of literacy as an indicator of 'modernity'.

This seems to be an exemplary case where the existence of a book validates the language and its speakers – there is a saying, attributed to Max Weinreich, that a language consists of a dialect with an army and a navy,[29] but it can also be a dialect (or in this case a defined group of dialects) with a good-sized book. Bible translations have often filled this role (Lüpke and Storch mention an Africa-oriented revision, 'A language is a dialect with a missionary'),[30] but a dictionary is special because even (or perhaps especially) a bilingual dictionary calls attention to the internal resources of the language itself and the culture it expresses in a way that a translation of a culturally distant text does not.

Concluding Remarks

In this chapter I have tried to show just some of the ways in which language can be used to reify identity and project how a community wishes to be perceived. The two communities examined have by no means the same status: one is a small lineage group within a larger language community, concerned to establish a historically defined niche for itself within that community by calling attention to signifying linguistic traits. The other is an ethnic group broadly defined, attempting to project itself

---

[27] The Legon-Trondheim Linguistics Project, funded by the Norwegian agency NUFU.
[28] M. E. Kropp Dakubu, Samuel A. Atintono, and E. A. Nsoh, *Gurenɛ-English Dictionary with English- Gurenɛ Glossary* (Legon: Linguistics Department, 2007).
[29] Lüpke and Storch, *Repertoires and Choices*, 143.
[30] Ibid.

in a national context by promoting its language as a signifier of modernity. The linguistic situations are also very different; what I have described for the Farefari of the Upper East Region follows most closely what we usually (if inaccurately) think of as a correspondence between a language and a people, with the language functioning as both vehicle and mirror of the culture of the people. The Gã case depends on special circumstances, in which a second language can be used to negotiate the ethnic and social space. What they have in common is the use of the linguistic heritage to redress a heritage of inequality, whether they understand it this way or not.

A final comment on silence. If 'silence' consists in refraining from talk on a particular topic, it seems it can serve at least two opposing functions: commemoration, as discussed by Yankah on Akan oaths elsewhere in this volume, or forgetting, as in the Gã case examined. And yet, both kinds of silence can be broken, paradoxically without negating the reigning silence. The unmentionable historical event that is commemorated by the Akan *ntam* or state oath in fact exists to be voiced out, although under very special circumstances, so that the fact of utterance is made powerful by the taboo, the norm of silence, the fear of utterance that surrounds it. The heritage of servitude that the Gã group has so elaborately manoeuvred to forget is in fact given voice whenever they mention the ancestors, the 'adopted sons' of the eponymous founder of the lineage, to whom they owe their lands. The silence of the Farefari-speaking community is more direct – recognised but unspoken features of the public image are not given voice. Instead the community has given written and therefore 'modern' form to an attribute that is taken to symbolise its inalienable, although hardly immutable, self, namely its language.

12 Folk Opera and the Cultural Politics of Post-Independence Ghana

Saka Acquaye's *The Lost Fishermen*

Moses N. Nii-Dortey

Ghanaian folk opera, which was created by Saka Acquaye[1] in the early 1960s, is fundamentally a work of art; but it was also a political tool. The art form emerged in response to the Nkrumah-led administration's post-colonial cultural re-engineering agenda. As Daniel Herwitz writes of the South African post-apartheid heritage creation experience (Chapter 2, this volume), that agenda was to recover, valorise, and re-contextualise Ghana's authentic cultural heritage. The intent was twofold: first, to wean the citizenry off a colonial cultural mentality caused by many years of colonial political and cultural hegemony; and, second, to nurture a more homogeneous 'national culture' from the diverse array of ethnic-based sectarian cultural forms and interests as a boost to national integration and identity.

This chapter examines how folk opera, created in the nationalistic spirit of the immediate post-independence era, became an integral part of the political and cultural re-engineering efforts of the period, particularly those of the Nkrumah-led Convention People's Party (CPP) Administration and its protégé government – the Acheampong-led Supreme Military Council I.[2]

Folk Opera

The term *folk opera* was introduced into the Ghanaian music and theatre lexicon by Saka Acquaye,[3] who was also the genre's architect and most

---

[1] Saka Acquaye was a multi-talented artist: a neo-traditional and highlife musician, art teacher and administrator, designer, dramatist, carver, and sculptor. He was the architect, most prolific composer, and foremost impresario of folk opera in Ghana.

[2] Colonel I. K. Acheampong (who later became General Acheampong) was Chairman of the National Liberation Council (NLC) military government from 1972 to 1976. He later renamed the Council 'The Supreme Military Council' (SMC) after a referendum in 1976, and ruled for a further two years. He was overthrown by a palace coup in 1978.

[3] Though the earliest known musical drama ever written by a Ghanaian dates back to the 1940s, the composer, one Reverend Robert Danso, called it an operetta, not a folk opera. He titled it *Kokonsa*, which is the Akan word for gossip. Rather unfortunately,

prolific composer.[4] Acquaye defines folk opera as a 'musical form of drama composed of airs, recitatives, and pieces performed by choruses with orchestra, and which makes use of scenery, acting and a blend of poetry and dance'.[5] Richard Wagner's description of Western opera as musical drama or drama set to music underscores the similarities between the two genres beyond their respective designations.[6] These similarities seem to suggest that folk opera is the African version of Western opera – a genre that is over three centuries older. For example, both are composite genres that involve several forms like solo and chorus singing, acting, declamation, and sometimes dance in a staged spectacle.

Of the many art forms that flourished in Ghana's immediate post-independence era, folk opera stands out in two important ways: first, in the manner it was crafted as a blend of several forms (myths, folk tales, dances, drama, mime, songs, poetry, and also visual effects) deliberately drawn from several ethnic-based cultural sources; and, second, because of the immense political patronage it enjoyed, particularly from the Nkrumah-led administration and the pro-Nkrumaist military government led by General I. K. Acheampong. It is this level of political patronage, especially, that set the tone as folk opera became one of Ghana's flagship cultural forms – at least in the first two decades of Ghana's political independence. For example, after Saka Acquaye's first folk opera, *Obadzen*, was launched in 1960 at the Accra Opera Cinema House, President Nkrumah called for a command performance at Flagstaff House, which was then the seat of government. Pleased with the quality of the production, he sent Saka Acquaye and his entire *Obadzen* team on a six-week tour of the Soviet Union ahead of his first official visit to that country in 1961.[7]

In 1975, some nine long years after Kwame Nkrumah's overthrow, Saka Acquaye directed the famous Wulɔmɛi Band to tour the United

no documentary evidence of this first operetta exists for any form of reference to be made except the verbal confirmation from some of the men who took part in its maiden performance. Inferring from an interview Saka Acquaye granted me in August 2002, there is no evidence that he (Saka Acquaye), in his twenties then, ever met Reverend Danso, neither did he see his work.

[4] See Efua Sutherland, 'The National Orchestra in Concert', *Sankofa* 1, 1 (1977); Nana Acheampong, 'Saka Acquaye: The Life and Loves of a Giant', *Uhuru Magazine* 4 (1989): 10–11, 15, 33–6; Kojo Vieta, *The Flag Bearers of Ghana: Profiles of One Hundred Distinguished Ghanaians* (Accra: Ena Publications, 1999); Pietro Deandrao, *Fertile Crossings: Metamorphosis of Genre in Anglophone West African Literature* (Amsterdam: Rodopi, 2001).

[5] See Saka Acquaye, 'Folk Opera in Ghana and Nigeria' (Accra: Institute of African Studies, Legon, 1972).

[6] See Joseph Kerman, *Opera as Drama* (Berkeley, CA: University of California Press, 2005).

[7] See Okai Atukwei, 'Tribute to the Maestro, Saka Acquaye', *The Ghanaian Times* (30 March 2007).

States of America twice with his newest operas, *Sasabonsam* and *The Magic Drum*. The success of that tour is well captured in this observation by one Nana Acheampong (a columnist) in *Uhuru Magazine*: 'Major Tom Bradley of Auckland and Valco workers gave them a red carpet hosting... and the mayor of Detroit, out of appreciation, gave them a plaque to be given to President Acheampong.'[8] Similarly, Saka Acquaye's second folk opera, *The Lost Fishermen* (arguably the most popular of all ten folk operas) was staged as one of Ghana's cultural presentations at the Second Festival of Arts and Culture (FESTAC) in 1977 in Lagos, Nigeria, by the Damas Choir.[9] That performance was commended highly by various critics. For example, a Nigerian journalist described the play as 'the best of the dramas produced during that year's FESTAC because its theme and message transcended the often monotonous colonial exploitation dramas he had watched from other countries'.[10]

Again in 1977, Saka Acquaye's third folk opera *Hintin Hintin* was performed, with the backing of the Ghana National Symphony Orchestra (GNSO), to a packed house including government officials and members of the diplomatic corps. Efua Sutherland,[11] then leader of Ghana's fledgling Theatre Movement, paid a glowing tribute to that performance: 'The concert, which was conducted by Diana Reindorf, attracted the largest audience ever in the history of orchestral concerts in Ghana. Among the audience were senior government officials and members of the Diplomatic Corps.'[12]

As shown in the above account, the unofficial status folk opera enjoyed as one of Ghana's flagship theatre forms far outlived the first President's tenure. Indeed, by 1971 a separate folk opera division of the Arts Council of Ghana had been created, headed by Saka Acquaye himself. It was the only art form to have enjoyed that recognition in post-Kwame Nkrumah Ghana.[13]

There is, therefore, no doubt that folk opera is one of Ghana's most successful literary genres ever. What historical, political, and cultural factors influenced the birth, content, and status of folk opera in post-independence Ghana? And to what extent do the plot and subject matter of *The Lost Fishermen* in particular reflect the nature and form of the political and cultural concerns of the times? I attempt to answer these questions below.

---

[8] Nana Acheampong, 'Saka Acquaye: The Life and Loves of a Giant', 15, 10–11, 33–6.
[9] Damas Choir was a non-denominational mixed choir that was formed by one Ishmael Adams in the late 1950s, in Accra. The fame of the choir was enhanced greatly by its performances of *The Lost Fishermen*.
[10] Willie Bozimo, '*The Lost Fishermen*: Folk Operetta from Ghana', *Lagos Times* (1977).
[11] Efua Sutherland is generally acknowledged as the mother of modern Ghanaian theatre. See Pietro Deandrao, *Fertile Crossings*.
[12] See Efua Sutherland, 'The National Orchestra in Concert'.
[13] Saka Acquaye, 'Modern Folk Opera in Ghana', *African Arts* 4, 2 (1971): 60–3, 80.

Synopsis of *The Lost Fishermen*

The story of *The Lost Fishermen* is based on Gã mythology about the sea and the relevance of its taboos and sacred rituals for peaceful human/cosmos co-existence. Its themes are based on true happenings known to the author and corroborated by a chief priest of his Gã-Mashi community, Nai Wulɔmɔ,[14] in an interview conducted by one Enoch Mensah, stage manager of the Damas Choir.[15]

In the play, a group of ten fishermen, including the chief of the village and his two sons, embark on a fishing venture on a Tuesday – the day fishing in the sea is tabooed in the Gã traditional area. Even though the crew claim to have been misled by Kotey, the crown prince, their ignorance does little to absolve them from the direct consequence of this sacrilegious act. For their punishmernt, they have to battle raging storms for seven continuous days until a mistaken sacrifice to the sea god of Ashie, the chief's own beloved son, gives them a temporary respite. They manage to land on a strange and haunted island, which the playwright sets at a point where the two zero degree lines meet off the coast of Ghana. There the fishermen encounter strange women, who had been stranded there much earlier in the company of their husbands, and mermaids. The husbands of the strange women had all died by the time the lost fishermen encountered them. The lost fishermen and the stranded women suffer further fatalities (losing two more people) before they are, finally, pardoned by the gods and find their way back home.

Politico-Cultural Context

As intimated earlier, one of the factors that influenced the creation of folk opera in Ghana relates to heightened nationalistic agitations for some form of cultural rebirth in the years immediately before and after the country attained political independence. These agitations, which were occasioned by prevailing colonial cultural and political hegemony, came in the form of a clarion call to and support (from the powers that be)

---

[14] Nai Wulɔmɔ is the chief priest of the sea deity of the Ga traditional area. Nai is the name of the sea deity and Wulɔmɔ is the title of its priest. He explained that the injunction became necessary after a series of fishing-related fatalities, most of them happening on Tuesdays. The leadership of the community then divined for a solution and the outcome was that the gods decreed that Tuesdays be set aside as a sacred day in honour of the sea god: hence no native fisherman should go fishing on that day. The priest further catalogued a series of calamities that befell the earlier sceptics: some were drowned, others eaten by sharks, and still others haunted by spirits. Others, as in *The Lost Fishermen*, got lost on the high seas and so were gone forever. It was also a common practice, according to the Wulɔmɔ, for offending fishermen who managed to escape the wrath of the gods to be arrested by his (the priest's) scouts. Heavy fines were imposed on such offenders. The absence of cold storage facilities and the simplicity of the communities then made it easier for such offenders to be tracked, he concluded.

[15] Acquaye, 'Folk Opera'.

for patriotic Ghanaians with interests in the creative arts to venture into creating art works that valorised their indigenous heritage(s).[16] This was intended as the most fitting response to a prevailing cultural malaise in Ghana, and as a show of pride in the people's African cultural heritages. It was, as Daniel Herwitz noted about heritage practice in the rise of the post-colonial state, an exercise of acknowledging and recovering time-honoured values distorted by colonialism, and rescripting those which are 'believed to be of enduring worth and thus to offer the prospect of a unified future' (Herwitz, this volume). The arts, which Nkrumah describes as 'another subtle instrument of ideology',[17] were identified as important tools in the pursuit of that objective. To that end, some performing arts and related educational institutions were set up to research, collate, refashion, and transmit indigenous cultural knowledge, ideas, and values across ethnic, political, religious, and even national boundaries.

For example, in 1955, Kwame Nkrumah, who was then in charge of Government Business of the Gold Coast, set up a ten-man, government-sponsored committee headed by Efua Sutherland. Its mandate was to 'examine how best a national theatre movement could be developed'.[18] The report of the committee asked the government to take the initial steps because 'the people of the colony were too engrossed in other things to realise the threat to their culture'. It was basically this recommendation of the committee that resulted in the formation of the 'National Theatre Movement' by the Nkrumah-led government, in 1956, with the mandate to 'bring into existence a theatre that would derive its vitality and authenticity from roots firmly planted in the true traditions of the people'.[19] The same committee's report led to the formation of the Arts Council of Ghana two years later, in 1958. An Act of Parliament created it to serve as the umbrella body mandated to 'organise the arts and encourage their promotion'.[20]

The establishment of this and other related statutory bodies marked the beginning of Nkrumah's unparalleled engagement with Ghana's creative arts heritage. The National Theatre Movement not only performed extensively across the country but also inspired the formation of several other performing groups throughout the country. Kwabena Nketia, one

---

[16] Moses Nii-Dortey, 'Historical and Cultural Context of Folk Opera Development in Ghana: Saka Acquaye's *The Lost Fishermen* in Perspective,' *Research Review* 27, 2 (2012), 25–58.

[17] Nkrumah, Kwame. *Consciencism: Philosophy and Ideology for Decolonization* (New York, NY: Modern Reader Paperbacks, 1970), 64.

[18] Kofi Agovi, 'The Origin of Literary Theatre in Colonial Ghana 1920–1957' (Legon: Institute of African Studies, 1989), 6.

[19] Agovi, 'The Origin of Literary Theatre', 9.

[20] Kwame Botwe-Asamoah, *Kwame Nkrumah's Politico-Cultural Thought and Policies* (New York, NY: Routledge, 2005), 158.

of the few surviving academics who was directly involved in the implementation of those nationalist initiatives, describes his experiences as follows: 'It was a fast, stimulating new consciousness in theatre based on our own traditional theatre or its resources and concepts. It was called a movement because it suddenly inspired and brought people with certain talents in the arts experimenting and working together. People talked about the arts more than they ever did before. . . . '[21] It was in this spirit and context of revived nationalist consciousness, and of inspiring people with talent to experiment with new art forms, that folk opera was born.

Another factor, and perhaps the most substantive influence on the thematic direction of *The Lost Fishermen* in particular, hinged on prevailing sectarian tribal cultural interests in the country at the time of political independence. These were interests that revolved around traditional chiefs, mainly of the south, and the pre-colonial chiefdoms over which they presided. Such regional political and cultural interests were deemed to be at variance with the collective aspirations of the new nation state presided over by the Nkrumah-led Convention People's Party (CPP) government, and therefore a threat to the new nation state.

The source of those challenges may be traced to the introduction of indirect rule by the British colonial administration in 1925, as a means to circumvent the indigenes' resistance to colonial rule.[22] That initiative resulted in the creation of a local council governance system that revolved essentially around traditional chiefs and the councils over which they presided. The responsibilities imposed on chiefs by this rather obtrusive involvement in mainline colonial politics, together with the coercive political power it conferred on them against their own subjects, corrupted the once sacred office of traditional chiefs. In the eyes of their subjects and the nationalist government, in particular,[23] they came to be seen as mere protégés of the British monarchy, and with that perception came also the ebbing away of the legendary awe that once commanded the allegiance of subjects and shielded the institution from direct opposition. As a direct result, some subjects shifted their allegiances to the nationalist government by enlisting in government-sponsored vigilante groups.

What is more, the period also witnessed the insistence by some of the chiefs of southern Ghana, particularly those of the Akyem and Asante states, on safeguarding the sovereign political and cultural interests of their pre-colonial kingdoms. This obviously provided additional grounds

[21] Nketia, in ibid., 160.
[22] Janet Hess, 'Exhibiting Ghana: Display, Documentary, and "National" Art in the Nkrumah Era', *African Studies Review* 44, 1 (2001), 59–77.
[23] Richard Rathbone, *Nkrumah and the Chiefs: The Politics of Chieftaincy in Ghana, 1951–60* (Athens, OH: Ohio University Press, 2000) and Brempong Arhin, *Transformations in Traditional Rule in Ghana (1951–1996)* (Accra: Institute of African Studies, Legon, 2007).

for conflict with the Nkrumah-led nationalist government. This was because such factional interests, the allegiances they commanded, and the cultural celebrations, exhibitions, and displays that sustained them were in direct opposition to the nationalist agenda of a united and stable nation state.[24]

Seizing upon this self-aggrandising image of chiefs, therefore, the Nkrumah-led (CPP) government and its functionaries adopted both legal and extra-judicial means to suppress chiefs and the chieftaincy institution as a whole. From 1955 through to 1966, when the government was overthrown, the Nkrumah-led administration succeeded in suppressing the regional cultural ambitions of chiefs who did not support his government. At the same time, the government was also encouraging a conscious appropriation of some of their cultural forms for the personal use of the President himself as well as for the creation of a homogeneous national culture. The government appropriated regalia and honorifics as well as the tradition of cultural exhibitions, representations, and displays for which the Asante and Akyem chiefdoms in particular were noted. These were complemented with documentaries and commissioned works by designated artists, most of which were centred on projecting the personality of Nkrumah. It was a two-pronged approach of cultural 'preservation and unification'.[25] The intention was not only to clip the wings of the chiefs, but also to reverse the regional cultural prominence that such chiefdoms had attained and appropriate their regional loyalties to the advantage of the government and the new nation state.[26] Thus it was also the potential threat that such regional interests posed to the new state that further pitted traditional chiefs against the Nkrumah-led administration.

In addition to all the above, the nationalist government encouraged the assemblage of assorted and ethnic-based cultural elements into unified exhibitions and celebrations for national audiences. Such exhibitions were intended not to celebrate the uniqueness and legitimacy of specific regional cultures, but rather their incorporation within a national political context.[27] Such nationalist principles manifested also at the individual level. For example, artists who were inspired by the government's nationalist ideals were encouraged, supported, and sometimes commissioned to create works of art that reflected not only their own respect for indigenous culture but also the relatively superior beauty to be found in synthesising such forms into a homogeneous national heritage.

---

[24] Rathbone, *Nkrumah*, 32.

[25] Carola Lentz, 'Local Culture in the National Arena: The Politics of Festivals in Ghana', *African Studies Review* 44, 3 (2001): 47–72.

[26] Kwame Boafo-Arthur, 'Chieftaincy in Ghana: Challenges and Prospects in the 21st Century', in Odotei Irene and Awedoba Albert (eds), *Chieftaincy in Ghana: Culture, Governance and Development* (Accra: Sub-Saharan Publishers, 2007).

[27] Hess, 'Exhibiting Ghana', 67.

These artists deliberately sought to reflect as many different ethnic and regional groups as possible so as to make the resultant cultural exhibits representative enough of the new and united nation state to provide the desired spectacle for a national audience.[28]

In Ghana, for example, Efua Sutherland's *Anansegoro* series (the 'Spider' plays) blazed the trail in this search for a national identity through the arts.[29] Several other Ghanaian playwrights followed later in this tradition, and prominent among them are Ama Ata Aidoo, Kofi Awoonor, and Ayi Kwei Armah.[30] Other names like Kwabena Nketia, Mawere Opoku, and Kofi Antobam literally became synonymous with the African art music, dance choreography, and sculpture respectively. Indeed, even the Osagyefo (Kwame Nkrumah) himself formed his own drama troupe, called the 'Osagyefo Players'. It was, perhaps, part of his leadership strategy to demonstrate his personal commitment to the burgeoning Cultural Revolution in Ghana more pragmatically.

The development was by no means exclusive to Ghana. From neighbouring Nigeria for example, where the practice seemed more pronounced, writings of people like Duro Ladipo (of *Oba Koso* musical drama fame),[31] Chinua Achebe, and Wole Soyinka are worthy of mention. Similarly, Kenya's Ngugi Wa Thiong'o, whose first play, *Black Hermit*,[32] was performed to commemorate Uganda's independence day celebration in 1962, added to the long list of art works that show how widespread the phenomenon was in Africa's post-independence years.

Saka Acquaye, who was a contemporary of Efua Sutherland, also proceeded on this same principle of creating works of art that valorise indigenous culture and foster national unity and identity. *The Lost Fishermen* in particular exemplifies the culture of strategic appropriation and homogenisation of ethnically based indigenous cultural forms. Kwabena Nketia, mentioned earlier as a rare – perhaps the only – survivor of those pioneers, in an interview refers to that whole cultural re-engineering initiative as a 're-contextualisation of culture'. Saka Aquaye's own attitude to that creative ideology was expressed with great clarity:

Our main objective in the presentation of the first dance-drama was to try to integrate our multi-tribal society in terms of its common reactions, common interests, attitudes, and values of the various classes. It is to create a basis for the formulation of a common destiny and cooperation in pursuing it. To do this,

---

[28] Francis Nii-Yartey, 'The Performing Arts: Identity and the New Social Paradigm', in Helen Leuer et al. (eds), *Identity Meets Nationality: Voices from the Humanities* (Legon-Accra: Sub-Saharan Publishers, 2011).

[29] Efua Sutherland, *The Marriage of Anansewa and Edufa* (London: Longman, 1990).

[30] Charles Angmor, *Contemporary Literature in Ghana 1911–1978: A Critical Evaluation* (Accra: Woeli Publishing Services, 1996).

[31] Duro Ladipo, 'Nigerian Folk Opera and Dance', in Anthony Wysard (ed.), *First Commonwealth Arts Festival Programme Book* (London: Excelads Imprint Ltd., 1965), 96–7.

[32] Ngugi Wa Thiong'o, *The Black Hermit* (London: Heinemann Educational Books, 1968 [Makerere University Press, 1963]).

it was necessary that every section of our society should find itself emotionally involved in the plot.[33]

Indeed, it is reasonable to argue that, apart from the influences from the prevailing political environment, Saka Acquaye may have arrived at this conviction after the poor showing of the original version of his first folk opera, *Obadzen*, earlier in 1960, in Accra. He wrote the entire play (both text and music) in his native Gã language, and attributed that initial failure to prevailing ethnocentric attitudes in the country.

Thus, for those in the performing arts especially, it became the norm for artists deliberately to fuse musical instruments, songs, dances, and costumes of various ethnic backgrounds into one art form in order to project a unified national image.[34] This explains why Saka Acquaye employs several appropriate folk tunes of diverse ethnic backgrounds in his operas. In *The Lost Fishermen*, for example, a good number of the dozens of Gã-dominated folk songs and dances are of Akan and Ewe origins. These two, together with Saka Acquaye's own ethnic Gã of the Accra area, were and still are the dominant languages spoken in the city, representing more than 60 per cent of the entire country's population.

Prominent among the Akan folk tunes in the musical drama is the popular Fante fishermen's song 'Sisir mbom, tabon mbom',[35] which the lost fishermen sing to paddle their canoe ashore. There are also very widely known Asafo songs and dances, as well as their accompanying martial performance tradition. The Ewe infusions include dirges, *Agbekor* drum rhythms and dances, as well as the accompanying performance paraphernalia including costumes and fly-whisks. All these feature prominently in the third and fourth scenes especially of *The Lost Fishermen*. The northern sector of the country is also represented by the inclusion of the famous wooden xylophone (*gyil*) in the performance to accompany some dances that are not of northern origin. Even the overture to the play portrays this nationalist image, as sections of it are written in both Gã and Akan.

It is, therefore, reasonable to argue that the playwright's choices of folk songs, instruments, and all the paraphernalia for the musical drama are guided not only by their artistic/aesthetic appropriateness but also by how popular they were in their respective ethnic areas. The goal, it seems, was to give members of the informed national audience something to identify with and cheer about each time they watch the play being presented.

Beyond valorising indigenous culture in such nationalistic ways, Acquaye's opera goes even further by making specific allusions to the political and cultural challenges that necessitated the re-contextualisation

---

[33] Acquaye, 'Modern Folk Opera', 60.
[34] Nii-Yartey, 'The Performing Arts'.
[35] 'Sisir mbom, tabon mbom' is a Fante fishermen's song performed in strict duple time to accompany synchronised paddling of canoes.

initiative in the first place: the colonial legacy of regionalism and the debased statuses of traditional chiefs due to their open collaboration with the British colonialists. The playwright performs this criticism through the roles he assigns to certain characters including Ataa Amasah – the chief and leader of the fishing crew that violates the sacred day of the sea god. For example, it is difficult to imagine what could make a traditional chief (the principal custodian of the customs and values of his chiefdom) violate these by working on a sacred day. Indeed it is sacrilegious enough for a chief to fail to commemorate such a day, an offence that carries the maximum sentence of destoolment. But it is an even worse offence, tantamount to the desecration of his sacred oath, to lead a section of his subjects, albeit unknowingly, to work on that day.

It can be assumed, therefore, that though the playwright makes no direct reference to the chief's infraction, his characterisation of him could be a subtle allusion to the undue involvement of chiefs in secular political affairs to the perceived neglect of their sacred duties. Similarly, the loss of both his sons, which leaves Chief Ataa Amasa without any legitimate heir to the throne, may also be intended as a metaphor to warn chiefs of the potential danger in involving themselves unduly in the secular politics of the nation, a message that the Nkrumah-led administration was emphasising at the time.

Similarly, the sacrifice of the Chief's beloved son (Ashie) to the sea god is another episode in the play that speaks to the ongoing nation-building efforts of the CPP administration. Contrary to the initial impression of condoning human sacrifice, the author uses that episode to underscore the necessity for individual and communal sacrifices for the survival and unity of the young nation state. This line of argument is implicit in the text of the second stanza of the victim's swan song as well as the chorus's response to it. Below is the text of the song in the Gã language, with an English translation:

Solo (the victim)

Miishɛɛ ji nɔni mi kɛ yaa ei!	I depart willingly and in peace
Kɛji mikɛ mi wala he	If I sacrifice my life
Omanye ha mɛi ni mi sumɔɔ.	To secure peace for those I love.[36]

Chorus

Yaaba ei!	Fare thee well!
kɛ miishɛɛ,	Go with joy,
Mokome gbeɔ shuɔ haa maŋ fɛɛ	It takes one individual to slay an elephant for a whole community

Solo (the victim)

Miiya ei!	I depart,
Nyɛ hia shi, 'jogbaŋŋ.	Stay well

---

[36] Saka Acquaye, *The Lost Fishermen*. See Nii-Dortey, 'Historical and Cultural Context'.

It is evident from the text that Ashie was willing to sacrifice his life for and on behalf of the rest of the crew. It is the chorus's aphorism – 'It takes one individual to slay an elephant for a whole community' – that most accurately reveals the playwright's subtle message: to sacrifice minority interest, no matter how well-placed, for the common good. The intended target, without doubt, was the sectarian tendencies of chiefdoms seeking to advance their own interests, whether this threatened the unity and survival of the larger state or not.

Saka Acquaye, a protégé of Nkrumah, was using the human sacrifice metaphor to lend support to the Nkrumah-led administration's heavy-handedness in checking certain ethnic and regional interests. The playwright also used the same episode to educate his national audience on the higher virtue of sacrifice for the common good, whether offered by an individual, group, or entire ethnicity. The importance of sacrifice to the attainment of liberty is succinctly stated by Gary Minkley and Phindezwa Myaka in their chapter on the commemoration of the Duncan village massacre in apartheid South Africa. During the commemoration, in 2008, the President of South Africa, Thabo Mbeki, is quoted as saying that the victims' 'blood will nourish the tree of liberty'. The statement, which was intended to underscore the importance of such high-level sacrifices for the common good, was an allusion to Thomas Jefferson's famous dictum to William Smith, in 1787, about the need to refresh 'the tree of liberty . . . from time to time with the blood of patriots and tyrants'.[37]

The sea god in the play represents the state of Ghana. Within the leftist ideology – the star by which Nkrumah and most of his post-independence African colleagues steered[38] – the state's interests are supreme and must be respected by all, or resolutely enforced. What this means, therefore, is that the Nkrumah-led administration's policy directive to subdue regional interests in favour of a common national political and cultural identity was binding on all, and would be enforced whatever the cost. The symbolism of Ashie's sacrifice to the sea god by the crew, therefore, represents not only the leftist ideal of people sacrificing willingly for the larger national interest, but also the immense coercive power of the state to whip discordant voices into line.

Conclusion

It is these political inferences that fit the folk opera genre into the postcolonial heritage politics of Ghana. Thus it is plausible to argue that

[37] See Thomas Jefferson, 'Thomas Jefferson to William Smith: Paris Nov. 1787', <http://www.dailykos.com/story/2011/10/29/1031234/--Tree-of-Liberty-letter-Thomas-Jefferson-to-William-Smith-1787>, accessed 13 September 2014.

[38] Steven Mertz, 'In Lieu of Orthodoxy: The Socialist Theories of Nkrumah and Nyerere', *Journal of Modern African Studies* 20, 3 (1982): 377–92.

the extensive public acclaim enjoyed by *The Lost Fishermen*, in particular, during the first two decades of Ghana's post-independence can be attributed not only to its own inherent aesthetic qualities but also to its resonance with the politico-cultural challenges then facing the young nation state.

From the 1980s on, however, the folk opera genre as a whole has lost its popularity on the Ghanaian theatre scene, despite all the efforts we have made in the last ten years to revive the public's interest in it.[39] The loss can be blamed, perhaps superficially, on the genre's long absence from the Ghanaian theatre scene due, in part, to Saka Acquaye's poor health, as well as on obvious sponsorship and marketing lapses in the more recent revival efforts. However, given the factors that influenced the popularity of Ghanaian folk opera, it may be more plausible to attribute the loss to the obsolescence of its nationalistic orientation in particular, and the seasonal nature of popular arts in general.

---

[39] We (the author and four other colleagues) have formed two non-profit-making groups in the last ten years – the 'Accra *Kushite* Production Company' and the 'Saka Acquaye Memorial Theatre group', respectively – dedicated to restaging *The Lost Fishermen* as a first step towards reviving the public's interest in folk opera in Ghana. We have staged three productions so far – in November 2006, February 2007, and in 2011 – with minimal success.

13 Flashes of Modernity
Heritage According to Cinema

Litheko Modisane

The tradition of all dead generations weighs like a nightmare on the brains of the living. And just as they seem to be occupied with revolutionising themselves and things, creating something that did not exist before, precisely in such epochs of revolutionary crisis they anxiously conjure up the spirits of the past to their service, borrowing from them names, battle slogans, and costumes in order to present this new scene in world history in time-honoured disguise and borrowed language.[1]

In *The Eighteenth Brumaire of Louis Bonaparte*, Marx obliquely captures the *raison d'être* of heritage – the 'raiding' of past events, personages, places, or objects for their perceived dignity and value in the present. The inflection of the past with dignity is a highly attractive undertaking in societies emerging from oppression such as in South Africa, and those that are still mired in some kind of systematic repression. In these societies, the imperative of the restoration of dignity is a necessary response to and invalidation of colonial violence. Having been subjected to the epistemic burdens of the French *mission civilisatrice* in his native Martinique, and later Algeria, the psychiatrist and revolutionary writer, Frantz Fanon, famously concluded that 'colonialism is not satisfied merely with hiding a people in its grip and emptying the native's brain of all form and content. By a kind of perverted logic, it turns to the past of the oppressed people, and distorts, disfigures and destroys it. . . . '[2] In colonial and apartheid South Africa, the distortion of the past of the colonised occurred in intricate and often contradictory terms. In the long term, colonial and apartheid 'native' policies tended to espouse a limited understanding of African culture, opting to confine it along with Africans themselves to rural traditionalism. At least from the 1840s, colonial Natal, through the policies of the British statesman, Theophilus Shepstone, championed the recognition and sponsorship of chieftainships and customary law,

---

[1] Karl Marx, *The Eighteenth Brumaire of Louis Bonaparte* (New York, NY: International Publishers, 1963), 15.
[2] Frantz Fanon, *The Wretched of the Earth* (Harmondsworth: Penguin, 1967), 167.

'based upon the assumed need to perpetuate traditionalism'.[3] This legal arrangement contradicted the policies of the Cape Colony, which, at that time, eschewed traditionalism and encouraged assimilation of Africans into the colonial order. However, by the 1880s, and with the ascendancy of Afrikaner nationalism in the 1940s, arguments for a policy of assimilation gave way to increasingly segregationist currents, first in the colonies and Boer Republics, and later in the Union of South Africa. The British colonial 'native' policy, and its motivating rationale – the civilising mission – collapsed under the weight of the ascendant policy of indirect rule. This policy placed the subject populations at the mercy of a purportedly customary rule of 'native' intermediaries such as chiefs, what Mahmood Mamdani calls an 'unmediated decentralised despotism'.[4] The reconstituting of the social and cultural order of the subject populations according to the dictates of the colonial agenda and capitalism built the momentum for colonial authorship of African heritage. Detached from urban modernity and confined to chiefly and customary law, this heritage effectively shored up racial segregation on the grounds of cultural difference. However, the denial of a valuable past to the colonised, and assertions of a false cultural difference between the coloniser and the colonised, ostensibly impervious to any meaningful contact and influences, is untenable.

The observations of Marx and Fanon are instructive pointers to the dynamic relations between a past, which is sometimes disavowed or privileged, and a present which can never be independent of some version of the past. Far from being temporal isolates, the past and the present are connected by actual anxieties of the here and now. In the 'postcolonial' context, state and non-state institutions have set themselves the task of addressing some of these anxieties through the cultural apparatus of heritage. Accordingly, 'heritage offers a language through which to discuss contested issues of culture, identity and citizenship in the postcolony, even as it determines and delimits this discussion in particular ways'.[5]

The ways in which the post-apartheid state mobilises heritage involve and in the main are guided by the imperative of restoration of dignity to the formerly colonised. The preamble of the Heritage Resources Act evinces its guiding vision. The Act charges heritage with a restorative role, which in part must help to 'define our cultural identity and therefore lies

---

[3] D. Welsh, 'The Cultural Dimension of Apartheid', *African Affairs* 71, 282 (1972): 35–53, 35.

[4] Mahmood Mamdani, *Citizen and Subject: Contemporary Africa and the Legacy of Late Colonialism* (Kampala, Cape Town, and London: Fountain, David Philip, and James Currey, 1996), 17.

[5] Nick Shepherd, 'Heritage', in Nick Shepherd and Stephens Robins (eds), *New South African Keywords: A Concise Guide to Public and Political Discourse in Post-Apartheid Society* (Athens, OH and Auckland Park: Ohio University Press and Jacana Media, 2008), 118.

at the heart of our spiritual well- being and has the power to build our nation. It has the potential to affirm our diverse cultures, and in so doing shape our national character. Our heritage celebrates our achievements and contributes to redressing past inequities.'[6]

Clearly then, the state discourse on heritage appropriates the language of decolonisation, and delimits its terms in ways that put emphasis on the post-apartheid government mandate of nation building. As Daniel Herwitz argues in the present volume, the rise of the post-colonial state is defined, in part, by the urgency of reparation and recovery of a past 'partly alienated under the colonial yoke'. This use of heritage coincides, in a very obvious sense, with the theoretical exposition of heritage, primarily as a 'mode of cultural production in the present which has recourse to the past'.[7] Thus, heritage cannot 'exist' prior to the conscious act of giving form and content to the past as inheritance. Heritage is a business of the present; it is '*of* the past *in* the present'.[8] While this chapter proceeds from this basic understanding of heritage, it also recognises that heritage is not problem-free.

One problem that arises out of what appears to be a balancing act in the relationship between the past and the present in heritage discourse is the implication of the doubleness of the notion of heritage. As Nick Shepherd usefully shows, it is in the nature of heritage to be torn between the 'dual valencies of inclusivity and exclusivity . . . the forces of memory and forgetting'.[9] This strongly suggests that for every act of reclamation in the name of heritage, there is a counter-memory. The cohabitation of memories and counter-memories in the heritage discourse of the 'post-colony' further alludes to the complexity of colonial experience, of the intricate encounter of the colonised with modernity. From the perspective of the curators of heritage in post-apartheid South Africa, it appears that the challenge is to draw, out of this complexity, signs of the proper order of things. By this I mean a search and validation of particular objects, biographies, and historical encounters, according to their presumed incarnation of honour and dignity for the formerly colonised, in order to codify them as heritage. Importantly, such objects ought to be germane to the decolonising objective. The compulsion of this approach is to revisit the past in a resolution-oriented manner, which, either inadvertently or by design, excises from the record the generative contexts in which heritage articles subsist – and, with them, the very grounds upon which such articles come to enjoy the status of heritage. This chapter turns the spotlight on how the complexity of colonial relations renders

---

[6] Preamble, National Heritage Resources Act (Republic of South Africa), Act 25 of 1999).
[7] Barbara Kirshenblatt-Gimblett, 'Theorizing Heritage', *Ethnomusicology* 39, 3 (1995): 367–80, 369.
[8] Shepherd 2008: 117.
[9] Ibid.

the practice of sanctifying historical articles as heritage in the 'post-colony' more challenging than the apparent 'search and find' approach may deem it to be. This task is made all the more urgent by the historical conflation of modernity and colonialism in South Africa, conditions which disavowed at the same time as they sanctioned the agency of the oppressed.

If the business of heritage in the 'post-colony' is to re-append virtue where it is deemed to have been desecrated, the chapter puts the accent on heritage as cultural inheritance emanating from and shaped by complex historical relations in the contact zones.[10] How we understand the complexity of colonial experience – in relation to the imperative of the restoration of dignity – underlies the motivation of the present chapter. The point is not to deny the function of heritage as a strategy of affirmation in the present, but to offer a radical rethinking of the terms of such affirmation. In this endeavour, I have begun to consider heritage in relation to that discontinuous, nonlinear, and composite constitution of social and political life called modernity. I reflect on the possibility of a heritage of modernity, and its implications for how we appreciate heritage in the 'post-colony'. I am interested in one site where the problematic of heritage as a restorative strategy of empowerment for the formerly oppressed is more pronounced than may at first appear – the cinema.

The cinema becomes a compelling site for the consideration of heritage in the 'post-colony' because it is a modernising project, and therefore makes possible reflection on how a heritage of modernity for the formerly oppressed can be apprehended.[11] Being an instance and product of modernity *par excellence*, cinema codifies particular palimpsests of the contact zones of modernity in the colonial era. It paints visual instantiations of urban modernity, the fluctuating, unsettled contingencies in the lives of the socially marginalised, as they reach out for modernity's promise of social redemption.

[10] The concept of 'contact zones' was originated by Mary Louise Pratt to refer to the 'social spaces where cultures meet, clash, and grapple with each other, often in contexts of highly asymmetrical relations of power, such as colonialism, slavery, or their aftermaths as they are lived out in many parts of the world today'. See Mary Louise Pratt, 'Arts of the Contact Zones', *Profession 91* (New York, NY: Modern Language Association, 1991), 33–40. See also Mary Louise Pratt, *Imperial Eyes: Travel Writing and Transculturation* (London: Routledge, 1992).

[11] According to Sarah Neely (2005), the twining of heritage and cinema gained currency through Charles Barr's efforts in the mid-1980s. 'Since then, the term "heritage cinema" has gained a certain currency within both circles of criticism and production in Britain.' Sarah Neely, 'Scotland, Heritage and Devolving British Cinema', *Screen* 46, 2 (2005): 241–6. The present chapter is not about the heritage film. Rather, it uses film both to think through heritage and to locate the role of cinema as a possible instance of heritage in the 'post-colony', and not as a part of the heritage cinema genre. For further studies on heritage cinema, see Andrew Higson, 'Re-Presenting the National Past: Nostalgia and Pastiche in the Heritage Film', in Lester Friedman (ed.), *Fires Were Started: British Cinema and Thatcherism* (London: UCL Press, 1993), 109–29.

Cinema or film hardly appears on the radar of the heritage discourse in South Africa, especially as it relates to black South Africans. There isn't much in the heritage literature in South Africa that speaks to the role of cinema in heritage discourse. It can be surmised that, historically, the cursory involvement of black South Africans in cinema at the level of production has something to do with the lack of dialogue between cinema and heritage in contemporary South Africa. Again, during colonialism and later apartheid, local cinema typically availed demeaning or culturally compromised images of blacks. Their lack of access to and control of the cinematic apparatus, because of politically and culturally sanctioned exclusions, made it one of the least available sites for an active engagement and ownership by blacks. Be that as it may, the National Heritage Resources Act (1999) regards film, among other cultural forms, as a heritage resource with potential cultural significance and special value for 'the present community and future generations'. Film, therefore, is considered to be part of the national estate, and as falling 'within the sphere of operations of heritage resources authorities'.[12] The recognition of film in the Act raises the question of how the state imagines it to serve heritage.

Within the 'post-colonial' context, in which heritage has become a significant part of the agenda of the state, corporate bodies, and even traditional authorities, how can the formerly oppressed mobilise the cinema, a modern cultural apparatus, in terms of heritage? Further, we may ask whether and how the inequities and deficits in black cinematic experience from the middle of the twentieth century, when black-centred films were inaugurated, can influence the terms according to which the present discourse on heritage proceeds.[13] In addition to its inequities – shaped, as they were, by material conditions and attendant prejudices of the time – the cinema was always implicated in the representation and construction of cultural difference. Yet this has produced a cultural canon in which even those global populations that were excluded from the cinema's cultural constructions have shaped its history and defined its nature. Cinema's exclusions imply certain levels of inclusion, which call for critical attention in relation to how modernity is understood in terms of the contemporary discourse of heritage, particularly with regard to the formerly oppressed. It becomes imperative, therefore, to understand

[12] Republic of South Africa, National Heritage Resources Act No. 25 of 1999, 3 (1) and 3 (2), (i), (viii).

[13] By black-centred films I refer to films that focus on the social and political experiences of black people. These films are 'black-centred' and not 'black' because blackness is the subject of their focus and not an a priori and hermetically sealed category. Litheko Modisane, *South Africa's Renegade Reels: The Making and Public Lives of Black Centered Films* (New York, NY: Palgrave Macmillan, 2013), 2.

how this has happened, and the purchase of this development on the prevailing discourse on heritage in post-apartheid South Africa.

In this chapter I show that black-centred films, however questionable in their practices and representations, have potential instruction with regard to our reflections on heritage in the 'post-colony'. The chapter reflects on these issues through the lens of an early black-centred film, *African Jim* (1949) or, as it is sometimes called, *Jim Comes to Jo'burg*.[14] The chapter shows that *African Jim* represents black urban modernity ambiguously. The film's simultaneous framing of its discourse in the colonial anthropological register, and signification of politically resonant social relations, evince these ambiguities. As will be shown, this is made possible by *African Jim*'s colonially compatible objective of showing the native's life in the city as stated in its opening scenes, and, as it unfolds, by its disruption of the same. This unsettles the certainty with which early black-centred films have come to be read, until recently, simply as paeans to colonialism or apartheid. Importantly, the effect of this reading is in the unsettling of the neat account of black experiences of modernity as generally subject to a totalising and disabling hegemony. The reading makes possible cinema's contestation of the teleological narrative that seems to underwrite the decolonising motive in the post-apartheid state heritage discourse. This teleology consists in conjuring up the past as a progressive movement from oppression to liberation, without an account of its complexities, and even contestations.

The selection of *African Jim* is based on its focal point, black South African urban life in the 1940s. It is a simple story about a naïve rural man who leaves for the city to look for work. But therein lies its deception. Unlike the later *Come Back, Africa* (1959), *African Jim* did not have an obvious political intention. This makes it seem an unlikely candidate for reflection on cinema and heritage in South Africa. But it is precisely because of its distance from the redemptive telos underlying the post-apartheid state's deployment of the concept of heritage that the film is appropriate for asking difficult questions about the assumptions and limits of heritage in post-repressive societies. Though not interventionist by design, *African Jim*'s claims to simplicity are contradicted by an array of certain representations whose inflections are significant for the appreciation of the social and cultural life of black people in 1940s Johannesburg. *African Jim*'s patronising tone regardless, the film does offer a rare visual record of African cultural practices in the city, a marginal

---

[14] What I have called 'early black-centred' films emerge in the colonial and apartheid periods. The relation of early black-centred films to the contexts of their production and circulation was largely at the mercy of the historical context of apartheid. The early black-centred films tend to be constrained aesthetically and sometimes thematically because of the circumstances influencing their production as well as the people producing and directing them. See Litheko Modisane, ibid., 11.

modernity often elided by the mainstream cinema industry and media of the time. I am intrigued by how it frames black modern life in a manner that makes possible readings that are useful for reflecting critically on the discourse of heritage, particularly the heritage of modernity for the formerly oppressed.

African Jim positions the twenty-first-century viewer to see in it both a piece of entertainment and a trace of the history of cinema, especially the history of black-centred film in South Africa. While it has generated opprobrium, and sometimes indifference, its significance for black South Africans has also been acknowledged.[15] Two interlocking factors have a cumulative effect on the contemporary recognition of the film's role in black cultural modernity in South Africa. First, the passage of time means that *African Jim* can be appreciated anew in conjunction with new objectives and in new contexts. Also, its distinction as the first South African film to feature a predominantly black cast puts it at a defining juncture of modern cultural production among black South Africans in the post-war period.

The focus of this chapter on *African Jim*, an early black-centred film, within the discourse of heritage and the context of colonialism and later apartheid, is a challenging undertaking because it is potentially contradictory. Because of the uneven political and cultural context of its production, and the tacit grammar of power in its narrative diegesis, the status of *African Jim* is not without ambiguity. The film was produced by white expatriates and tells a story about black urban life. Nonetheless, as text, *African Jim* encapsulates both colonial and potentially anti-colonial cultural intimations. This guides the film to resist being framed either as an entirely colonial or a conclusively progressive text. The film escapes easy appropriation or alignment with a neat account of the past and the imperative of restoration of dignity in the post-apartheid state's discourse of heritage. Over and above its ambiguities, and because of them, a retrospective appreciation of the film makes it possible to see in its narrative and history a metaphor of the complexity of cultural heritage. Given the circumstances of its production, and the correspondence of

---

[15] Film scholar Lindiwe Dovey and ethnomusicologist Angela Impey recently contributed a sophisticated reading of the importance of music and language in *African Jim*. See L. Dovey and A. Impey, 'African Jim: Sound, Politics, and Pleasure in Early "Black" South African Cinema', *Journal of African Cultural Studies* 22, 1 (2010): 57–73. The film has also been studied from a historical and 'urban studies' perspective. For this approach to *African Jim* and other early South African films, see Vivian Bickford-Smith, 'How Urban South Africa Life Was Represented in Film and Films Consumed in South African Cities in the 1950s', at <http://www.nottingham.ac.uk/shared/shared_cuc/documents/Paper_2000_Vivian_Bickford_Smith.htm>, accessed 3 October 2009. Consider also Meg Samuelson's discussion of *African Jim*'s links to black urbanity in *Drum* magazine and its iconicity of black urban femininity through the figure of Dolly Rathebe. See Meg Samuelson, 'The Urban Palimpsest: Re-Presenting Sophiatown', *Journal of Postcolonial Writing* 44, 1 (2008): 63–75.

some of its significations to colonial discourse, this might be a sticky point. However, the choice of the concept of metaphor to frame the film is a strategy I have adopted to relate it usefully to the concept of heritage without delinking it from what has become, for the contemporary viewer, its 'pastness'. Its pastness, both as representation and in relation to *African Jim* as a cultural object, serves to locate the grounds for the delineation of some of the ambiguities associated with the concept of heritage as understood and mobilised by the post-apartheid state. Through *African Jim*, the chapter ultimately seeks to provoke reflections on modernity as heritage for the formerly oppressed, whose compromised access to and participation within modernity betrays its cardinal ideals.

The chapter begins by presenting the production background of *African Jim*, and its narrative plot. It proceeds with a discussion of its production of meaning. It examines the film's imaginary of black identity and modernity, as they are mediated through its formal properties – narrative structure and space, as well as music. The discussion surfaces the contrasting elements of *African Jim*, through which its ambiguities become evident. It concludes by affirming the film's fecundity for reflecting on the concept of heritage, especially in relation to the decolonising mandate of the post-apartheid state.

Background

African Jim is a product of two British expatriates to South Africa, Donald Swanson and Eric Rutherford[16] of Warrior Films. Rutherford's fiancée, Gloria Green, and her family financed the film. Swanson would later represent himself in the vein of a colonial adventurer and apologist for colonialism. His patently racist journal, *Assignment Africa* (1965), is replete with gross stereotypes of black people in Southern and Eastern Africa. After splitting from Warrior Films over some differences with Rutherford, Swanson later directed a film called *Mau Mau* (1954), a propaganda documentary film about the Kenyan liberation war. Judging by its credits, which refer to 'South African Native Welfare Departments [sic]', it is evident that *African Jim* received support from the formative apartheid state. It is possible, therefore, that the state considered it as compatible with the strictures of its nascent apartheid programme of partitioning population groups into unequal racial categories. The film stars Daniel Adnewmah and Dolly Rathebe. *African Jim* introduced a new era of black and white collaboration in South African film culture. According to Maingard, the film inaugurated participation of black people at the level

---

[16] Rutherford would later undergo a sex change and adopt the name 'Erica'.

of production. She notes the casting role of one Dan Twala.[17] Maingard suggests that the film and others produced between the 1940s and 1950s 'represent a key "moment" in South Africa's cinema history, a point where black modernity was cinematically represented in feature films for the first time'.[18] Yet, according to Masilela, *African Jim* and others such as *Zonk!* (1950) and *The Magic Garden* (1951) did not elicit responses from African intellectuals because they were made by Europeans, and had a 'superficial coating of blackness'.[19] Lack of responses by the intellectual elite is, however, a partial account of *African Jim*'s publicness because, if Maingard's observation is anything to go by, the 'film's reception was far more complex than might otherwise be thought'.[20] Thus, 'despite the image of Africans as simple-hearted, dogged and irrepressible in the face of hardship that certainly falsified their experience . . . Africans were pleased to see their communities and performers represented in this prestigious medium'.[21] A memorable acknowledgement by one of the film's African audiences, and which Maingard quotes, illustrates this appreciation: 'the fact that Dolly Rathebe was greeted by a crowd shouting the ANC slogan *Mayibuye iAfrika* (Come Back, Africa) at the Durban premiere of the film, reflects something of the film's value to African audiences'.[22] The popularity of *African Jim* can also be gleaned from newspaper reports about the film's premiere in Johannesburg, a historical event in its own right. One newspaper reported how Sam Alcock, black casting co-director of *African Jim*, had trouble dealing with audience congestion outside a capacity-full Rio cinema in Johannesburg.[23] The popularity of the film is itself reflective of black South Africans' hunger for black cinematic images. Commenting on the hold that *African Jim* exercised on black South Africans, Can Themba would write later that 'Black South Africa thrilled at the idea that black faces, black life, black background, could appear on the screen.'[24] Interestingly, the film's footprint widened beyond the cityscape, enabling black countryfolk to share this fascination with black images: 'overnight the name of Dolly Rathebe was flashed across the countryside'.[25]

---

[17] Jacqueline Maingard, *South African National Cinema* (Oxford and New York, NY: Routledge, 2007), 67.

[18] Ibid., 76.

[19] In Isabel Balseiro and Ntongela Masilela (eds), *To Change Reels: Film and Film Culture in South Africa* (Detroit, MI: Wayne State University Press, 2003), 26. *Zonk!* was the name of a pictorial magazine. It was also a variety show adapted to film. *The Magic Garden* is a musical film about the theft of a church donation and the pursuit of the thief who stole it.

[20] Maingard, *South African National Cinema*, 79.

[21] Cited in ibid., 79.

[22] Ibid., 79.

[23] 'They Queue Eight Deep to See Jim Comes to Jo'burg', *Rand Daily Mail*, 2 November 1949, 9.

[24] Can Themba. 'Dolly in Films', *Drum*, February 1957, 49.

[25] Ibid., 49.

Précis

The film, subtitled 'The native in a modern city', launches with a legend that reads: '*the first full length entertainment film in South Africa to be made with an all-native cast. It is a simple film and its quaint mixture of the naïve and the sophisticated is a true reflection of the native in a modern city.*' Against the visual background of an idyllic rural landscape, complete with a herdboy looking after cattle, huts, and traditional dress, a voice-over narration delivered by a patently Nguni accent introduces the story of Jim Jabulani Twala. The young man, we are told, lives a harmonious and simple life in the village, until he feels the need to travel to the city to look for a job.

Arriving in the city by train, Jim is robbed of his belongings. Luckily, a nightwatchman helps him and finds him a job as a gardener. Unfortunately, Jim's childish antics incense his boss, who fires him instantly. Finding another job as a waiter at a local club, he meets Judy, a singer in the resident band, and the daughter of the nightwatchman. Jim impresses the band with his impulsive singing and is invited to perform with them the following evening. Before the appointed time, Jim happens upon the men who had robbed him a few days earlier, and overhears their plan to rob a local factory where the nightwatchman works. As the thieves attempt to carry out their plan, Jim, the nightwatchman, and his colleagues ambush and apprehend them. Jim quickly runs back to the club to fulfil his promise. His singing impresses a recording executive who happens to be his former employer. The executive promises him a recording deal. At the end of the film, Jim and Judy record a song. They eye each other in a manner that suggests potential romance. Judy's father, the nightwatchman, looks on proudly.

Didactic Framing, Intricate Outcomes

In its opening sequence, *African Jim* evinces a preoccupation with the viewers' understanding of the film's background and setting. Guiding the viewer in an instructional manner, the legend and voice-over introduce the story and, in the process, offer subtle perspectives on the rural landscape that it visualises. The instructional voice-over is reminiscent of the film strategies of the colonial film units, and assumes, like them, an omniscient presence – the 'Voice of God'. The voice-over contextualises the protagonist's experiences in terms of a temporal pattern of life, in which young men leave for the cities and return to honour communal obligations. Subsequent to the legend and the voice-over, the narrative unfolds within an effectively musical or variety show template.

In throwing the spotlight on its pioneering status in South African cinema history, the opening legend sets its stamp on time by effectively assigning cultural authority over the present to the film. The legend thus accords the film the status of an authentic record of black South Africans' encounter with cinema, and, with it, *the* true account of their formative experience of modernity. The construction of Africans' encounter with cinema in *African Jim* can be extrapolated from the declaration that this is the first film featuring an 'all-native' cast, a stress on an ostensibly first true collective experience. Interestingly, identity and modernity are key themes in the film, as its titular reference to the 'native in a modern city' reflects. However contrived and biased, the film's focus on black identity and modernity constitute its salience as an instance of the role of cinema in the construction of black urban identity in South Africa.

The voice-over, inflected with the condescending tone of the day, positions the viewer to see in Jim a harmless inferior ('boy'), ill-suited to the city and completely at home in the rural outback. It establishes a problem-free rural background, in whose virginal landscape the innocent and simple protagonist exercises his freedom unhindered. This prelude to the subsequent scenes of the city, and the experiences of the protagonist therein, immediately contrasts the rural and the urban along moral lines: the village equals goodness, and the city is devoid of it. Effectively, then, the problems of the film's 'natives' have a location: the modern city. The legend also distances the viewer, textually imagined as white, from the 'natives', whose conduct in the city, either as rural *naïfs*, petty criminals, or the cultural patrons at the invented Ngoma Club manifests their ostensibly peculiar nature. This distancing automatically assumes a discourse and attitude in keeping with the social discourse of colonialism and the nascent apartheid state.

The documentary film strategies, of voice-over, explanatory subtitle, and intertitles – which are not confined to *African Jim* but are also used in other black-centred films of roughly the same period such as *Song of Africa* (1950) and to a lesser extent the later *Come Back, Africa* (1959) – are decidedly intended to impart assured knowledge about black South Africans' experiences of modernity. They serve what appears to be the film's knowledge-claiming exercise, the course of black people's encounter with modernity. The strategies may appear to be in excess to the film's narrative. However, as rhetorical devices, they guide the viewer to the film's narrative vision, which they reinforce. At the centre of this vision, a colonial perspective on modernity emerges, which is not only restricted to the cinema as such, but also involves black South Africans' experiences of the modern city in general. Jim stands for the film's species of study – the 'native' – and his encounters manifest the ostensible truth about the 'natives' in general that the film purports to know and truthfully represent.

Narrative

The thin narrative structure of the film follows the model of an ostensible cultural reawakening of a rural *naïf* who finds the city an interesting and eye-opening experience. When he departs for Johannesburg, Jim discards his traditional apparel for Western-type trousers and coat. This is a momentous point in the film, as it signifies the beginnings of a transformation from a distinctively traditional past to a decidedly modern future. However, the scene paints a picture of a discrete separation between tradition and modernity, the effect of which is the valorisation of modernity over tradition. The camera's take of the urban landscape is differentiated from the rural space in terms of movement, mediated in the main by the moving train. The rural landscape is static and moribund – emphasising the simplicity of rural life and difference from a modernity bustling with industrial activity. Jim's nonplussed reaction at the sight of modern cityscapes, the quadrangular structures of the houses, busy transportation, and all the associated signs of city life further infantilises him. He can only marvel at the sights and is unable to form any substantive impression of the landscape. Modernity appears to be as marvellous as it is culturally alienating, and tradition, the lens of Jim's cultural make-up, is simply benighted. The value placed on modernity is taken for granted, and in the process silences the dynamics of a pre-modern or traditional setting. Consequently, and in spite of the film's earlier depiction of Jim as naturally tethered to the rural, actually the urban emerges as more attractive.

The simplicity of *African Jim* is potentially misleading. A cursory reading is likely to reproduce the simplicity invested in its storyline. This is bound to lead to a glossing over of the profundities that its setting, characters, and their circumstances register. It is therefore useful to reread *African Jim* with due regard to its textual intricacies. An unscripted scene of a group of labourers lifting a heavy box and chanting offers an opportunity to do so. Latterly, Dovey and Impey have expounded on the scene at some length: 'Struggling under the box's immense weight, the workers chant a song, using its driving call–response recitation to provide rhythmic impetus and to coordinate their movements. The song's lyrics, which have never been subtitled on the film print, are as follows:

Sanibo qhaqhe (Hello/loosen up)
Nansi poyisa (There are the police/supervisor)
They call us Jim!
They call us Jim!
Abelungu goddamn![26] (White people goddamn!)
Abelungu goddamn! (White people goddamn!)
They call us Jim!
Bheka phansi! (Put it down!)
Donsa! (Pull!)
Phansi! (Down!)'[27]

[26] The workers actually say 'Odamn!' but the meaning is the same.
[27] Dovey and Impey, 'Sound, Politics, and Pleasure', 57.

Though it was not a scripted part of the film, the retention of the labourers' scene signals the loose sense of the production values of the film makers, and possibly, as Dovey and Impey speculate, their fascination with its 'dramatic exposition of South Africans at work'. Nevertheless, it is instructive that the film exploits the workers' aesthetic to achieve a number of things. In the main, it 'establishes the subtle, yet multifaceted ways in which music was used in the 1940s by black South Africans to comment on the racial and political oppression of the times'.[28] In the same vein, it is notable that the name the workers are complaining about – 'Jim' – is also the name of the protagonist. Thus the scene coincides with the protagonist's life – highlighting, as it does so, his own subjection to a random identity that many black South Africans were forced to adopt. Historically, the name Jim was one of those generic names, like John, that many white employers reserved for their black servants ostensibly because they could not pronounce their African names. The effect of this practice was the denial of individuality to the oppressed. Thus, the scene subverts the actual social referents to which the name Jim corresponded. With this subversion, the emasculation of the reference to Jim as a boy, a pejorative reserved for African men during colonialism and apartheid, is also contested.

If the labourers' scene is accidental, the codes of social inequality in the film are not. The plotting of Jim's experiences shows the pervasiveness of the film's signification of social inequality, intended or not, which would have been important for the black audiences of the time. In *African Jim*, we can see a city that is as segregated as it is culturally flourishing, and as fantastical as it is dangerous. Though its protagonist, a hopeless *lumpen*, shows no inkling whatsoever of the dangers lurking around every corner, and even more so, the bigger threat of the unseen apartheid hand and the industrial superstructure, his arrival signals the class and racial inequities of the city. First, he happens upon conmen, and then encounters a security guard, his daughter, and other members of the Ngoma Club. In turn, the security guard introduces him to a property-owning white *baas*. The class positions of the conmen, the security guard, the *baas*, and, eventually, of Jim himself immediately expose the viewer to a recognition of the social relations at hand, those of *baaskap* or white supremacy. On its own, this recognition is enough to draw curious questions about the justification for the unequal social structure depicted in the film. The film can be read either as reinforcing racial and class positions of the time, or as making possible a contestation of the depicted class inequalities, and even the cinematic privileging of whiteness. The latter readings constitute a forceful counterintuitive apprehension of the contribution of *African Jim* in particular, and the black-centred cinema

28 Ibid., 58.

in general, to the larger historical narrative of South Africa. Thus, not only does *African Jim* paint knowable, recognisable settings, but its very representation of social identities stretches the viewer's imagination of the social make-up of Johannesburg in the 1940s.

Narrative Space

At the level of the narrative space, the camera briefly renders a visualisation of the domestic spaces in the form of Jim's employer's property and the nightwatchman's house. Scenes of the train station and the streets are also taken in but mostly are concentrated on minimal activity around the main character's experiences. In short, the narrative space is narrowed and can only reach the city's margins. However, the little that is registered on the margins significantly speaks to the larger social problems of the time. Most of the action takes place in the Ngoma Club, a leisure space for those the film, in its opening legend, calls 'sophisticated natives'. The club is a thoroughly racially segregated space, where jazz, acappella, traditional music, and blues intermingle with minstrelsy. The pleasures and pains of city life are played out within the space of the Ngoma Club, which is significantly congruent with the spatial stratification of the then segregationist South Africa. The imaginary of the city's cultural scapes attributed to black people produces something akin to a 'Bantustan' within the city. The stage background, and the space around the auditorium, are adorned with paintings of a wild landscape and isolated huts, the human inhabiting space with fauna and flora. Given that colonial literature and film have used such significations for less than charitable intentions when representing African identities, the use of paintings of the wild landscape in the club is curious. However, *African Jim* goes further than the painting of a simple nostalgia for the countryside – it hybridises the pre-modern with the modern.

In spite of or because of the exclusionary make-up of Johannesburg, the Ngoma Club suggests a site of leisure and the assumption of a certain flair for the modern among the oppressed. It is a necessary and logical outcome of a reality in which the only place for the cultivation of modern sophistication among the oppressed would be racially segregated. The club, therefore, comes to exemplify a physical site for the embrace and practice of modernity. This is a practice or set of practices with a historical pedigree. We can conclude at this point that *African Jim* can be credited with surfacing, cinematically, a modernity of the margins. Ultimately the shortcomings of the spatial limits in the film are tempered by the imaginaries of a liberated modernity in the musical performances and the pleasure derived from it. Here, Judy loses herself in a romantic song and is then joined by Jim. They paint a fantastical picture of freedom even though in the greater scheme of things, the very opposite applies.

Therefore, the musical performances allow a transgression of the spatial restrictions of the city. It is notable that, parallel to transgression by performance, *African Jim* registers transgression at the level of its nature as film, which accentuate its incompatibility with a restrictive regime.

Our taverns and city streets, our offices and furnished rooms, our railroad stations and our factories appeared to have us locked up beyond hope. Then came film and burst this prison-world asunder by the dynamite of the tenth of a second, so that now, in the midst of its far-flung ruins and debris, we calmly and adventurously go travelling.[29]

The travel motif in Benjamin's famous observation surfaces the emancipatory attribute of cinema. Thus – notwithstanding the conservatisms that pervade some of its significations and relations of production – *African Jim* provided an avenue for imaginings of a relatively better life for the oppressed.

Encountering Jo'burg through Song and Dance

It is remarkable that music formed the basis for the early black-centred films' aesthetics. Its use in film suggests that it was the primary artistic vehicle for black urbanites. Thus *African Jim* and other films of the period installed imagery of black identity and culture that was not entirely based on a colonial template, but included and was even driven by the organic culture of the oppressed. Black-centred cinema, in part, depended on the cultural nodal practices of a patently 'ethnic' type, alongside the modern aspirations of the marginalised. Such aspirations can be detected in the musical direction of the black male close-harmony groups, and the adoption of jazz as a genre of choice. Historically, the motivation behind black South Africans' fascination with American, especially African-American musical culture was multifarious. According to Christopher Ballantine, prior to the 1940s, what he calls black South Africans' 'infatuation with African-American culture' had many purposes:

it provided examples for imitation, standards to be striven for, exhortations to achievement, and criteria of success, all of which were premised on the confident assertion of *racial and cultural identity* between blacks in South Africa and those in the United States . . . now in the era after the mid-1940s, this identity took on a new resonance: it became a *political* identification.[30]

---

[29] Walter Benjamin, 'The Work of Art in the Age of Mechanical Reproduction', translated by Harry Zohin, in Leo Baudry and Marshall Cohen (eds), *Film Theory and Criticism: Introductory Readings* (New York, NY and Oxford: Oxford University Press, 2004): 791–811, 806.

[30] Christopher Ballantine. 'Looking to the USA: The Politics of Male Close-Harmony Song Style in South Africa during the 1940s and 1950s', *Popular Music* 18, 1 (1999): 1–17, 3.

On their own, the musical performances and dance routines as represented in *African Jim* did not speak overtly to the political challenges of
the Smuts era. However, some of the musical perfomances at the Ngoma
Club coincided with the referential world of the increasingly politicised
black urbanites.

It is only when we interpolate scenes from Jim's experiences in the city
itself that a rich, perhaps unintended picture of the relations between
tradition and modernity in the film emerges. In this frame, traditional
modes of pleasure now subsist alongside modernised forms. Not only
do traditional songs and artistic renderings of rural scenery make up
the ensemble of Ngoma's offerings, but they also intermingle with
jazz and the petty-bourgeois cultural sensibilities of the black audience. Adapted to the black townships and the predominatly black
spaces in the cities, jazz took an independent route that inadvertently
skidded off the official articulations of African urban culture. Accordingly, the aura of Jazz provided a dimension of modernity in which
black South Africans could imagine themselves outside the contours
of colonial cultural ascription. Consequently, the persistence of traditional modes of song and dance redefines urban modernity by installing
a distinctively new version of it, a version of 'African modernity'. By
African modernity I mean 'the historical cauldron and discursive arena
in which colonialism, neo-colonialism, and various guises of imperialism are played out. Subjection and resistance, negotiation and manoeuvre, as well as appropriations and expropriations of cultural and
political resources to define "new" African worldviews characterise [this]
modernity.'[31]

Though it appears to be a metaphor of black cultural alienation in the
city – and the attempts at surviving it through patently African cultural
forms – the film registers a cultural life that is not altogether in sync with
colonial attitudes. Rather it is more in line with the complex matrix of
colonial reality and African responses to it. Any conviction invested in
the film's documentary strategies and claims to knowledge, founded as
they appear to be on an assumed epistemic authority of cinema, is subsequently destabilised by the unfolding fictional narrative. The narrative
reveals the film's constructedness more so than the legend and the voice-
over. This makes it possible for the film to reveal sites of the cultural
make-up of black urban life that in themselves escape the boundaries of
colonial ideological policing.

---

[31] Litheko Modisane, *Suddenly the Film Scene Is Becoming Our Scene! The Circulation and
Public Lives of Black Centred Films in South Africa: 1959–2001* (PhD thesis, University of
the Witwatersrand, 2010), 40.

Conclusions

As text, *African Jim* brings to light a unique problematic in reflections on heritage. Being a cinematic representation, the film differs from the tangible and sometimes intangible objects that are associated with heritage such as sites (the prison cell, the grave, the house), objects (clothing, books, diaries), and cultural belief systems. It is a thoroughly modern form of representation with a distinctive relation to a particular historical period and condition – the nexus of colonialism and modernity. One cannot take it for the representations it makes without being deluded by its rhetorical designs. Its inventiveness regardless, *African Jim* has a historical 'presence' and even incorporates historical referents in the world it constructs. Such referents may or may not have existed but they represent social relations that are historically verifiable, and culturally resonant. For instance, the Ngoma Club was invented by the film makers, but it indexes a cultural phenomenon of 1940s Johannesburg. Though not 'real', the film's significations of labour migration, and the limited movement of blacks, coincide with the historical restrictions in Johannesburg. The train station, the city streets, and the city's ambience as represented in the film are unquestionably historical. Given the integration of 'real' and 'unreal' objects in the film, how then can its heritage value be appreciated? On the one hand, *African Jim* provides a combing of a particular experience of the past through its own resources as film, and these constitute, in part, its heritage value. Film has a unique ability to signify historical 'reality' and to store it for posterity. Through sound, the viewer is able to gain a sense of the musicality, the speech, and the sounds that are unique to a place. As a visual medium, film also takes in images that are located at a particular time and place, that could not be made available in other forms – save, perhaps, for photography. But the fact that it does this through the illusion of movement adds a great deal of cultural value to the approximation of 'reality' in *African Jim*. Here, the architecture of the city, the liveliness of the streets, and the clubs form an amalgam of a sited experience which corresponds with historical accounts that may be of great value to contemporary heritage work.

As a cultural object, *African Jim* stands out historically as the first film through which black South African urban images were significantly portrayed in a feature film. However, this distinction alone does not carry the weight of its historical baggage, which makes it burdensome to appreciate it as a piece of cultural heritage. Produced by white film makers and featuring black talent, *African Jim* is a product of its time. This poses the question: for whom is *African Jim* heritage? Is it for the white film makers who contributed to black South Africans' entry into the cinematic arts as talent and sometimes as crew? Or does its potential meaningfulness for black South Africans make it a cultural treasure for the latter? Or is the film a shared heritage with split significance for all possible claimants? The film springs from a modernity beset by exclusions and injustices that, at times, percolate into its narrative diegesis. Thus, as regards its possible heritage value as object, *African Jim* poses a problem that reflexively points to black experiences of modernity at a particular historical juncture. It cannot be claimed simply as cultural inheritance without bypassing the contradictions of its provenance. Consequently, *African Jim* problematises any claims of cultural inheritance without a negotiation of the ambiguities that define it as a cultural object caught in the crosscurrents of a messy history, and that the film, in part, also indexes. As a cultural object, the film lucidly demonstrates that there are no ready-made pasts, and that the revisiting and appropriation of the past in the present must necessarily be a reflective exercise on what kinds of instruction we may have for contemporary understanding of heritage. It challenges the understanding of heritage as an exercise in 'raiding' the past for instrumentalist ends.

African Jim did not set out to make heritage. It only claimed to show the experience of the 'native in the modern city', a charged language of another time and place. As one of the few films that managed to seize slices of the cultural make-up of Johannesburg at the close of the 1940s, its images confer on it a capacity to amalgamate some of the historical referents of the time into one composite whole. Through this visual, oral, and aural assemblage, we can fathom something akin to a heritage of the city and its people. *African Jim* is certainly a site for the consideration of the limits of heritage as a discourse of moralising the past through honouring what may be regarded as worthy of praise and preservation. The character of Jim certainly falls outside the imaginary of the decolonising mandate of post-apartheid South Africa and can never command a special place alongside struggle heroes. However, it is through Jim that the viewer is invited to train a critical gaze on the early beginnings of modernity among the oppressed of South Africa. It is also through *African Jim* that the viewer is invited to have a peek at a motion picture record of a cultural phenomenon – the practice of jazz in mid-twentieth-century South African cities. Of course it is not expected that the viewer should treat the film as an indubitable mirror of the past. Rather, looking at some of the elements of the contradictory modernity of the time, as represented in the film, one is led to conclude that *African Jim* occasions possibilities of seeing in it a fragment of heritage *qua* heritage of black urban modernity in South Africa.

14   Conclusion

Carolyn Hamilton

On 28 June 2013, two weeks before his 95th birthday, Nelson Mandela (or Madiba to use his honorific address name), lay in a hospital bed in Pretoria, in a critical condition, while court proceedings in the Eastern Cape became part of a politics of heritage that anticipated his death. Makaziwe, a daughter from his first marriage, and fifteen other members of his extended family, approached the court in Mthatha to force Madiba's grandson, Mandla, to return the remains of three of Madiba's children to the elder statesman's birthplace, Qunu, where they were originally buried. In 2011, Mandla had moved the graves of his father, Makgatho (Madiba's second son, d. 2005), Thembekile (Madiba's eldest son, d. 1969) and Madiba's infant daughter, also called Makaziwe (d. 1948) to Mvezo, where he currently resides as chief. Makaziwe accused Mandla of trying to 'force' the resiting of Madiba's eventual burial place, and the inevitable shrine that would accompany it, from Qunu to Mvezo. The courts ruled in the applicants' favour, ordering Mandla to return the remains by 3 July. When he failed to comply with this order, the sheriff of the high court broke down the gate to Mvezo Great Place in Mandla's absence and the remains were again exhumed and relocated.[1]

The court papers argued that Mandla was motivated by the financial gain that would flow from the burial site. Indeed, Mandla had actively exploited an historic Mandela connection to Mvezo (his great-grandfather, Mphakanyiso, was chief in the area but removed from office in the 1920s) to attract development to the area. The relocated bones would have allowed him to assert Mvezo as the family gravesite and as the appropriate location for Madiba's grave. Pilgrimage tourism would

---

[1] Stuart Graham, 'Mandla Mandela "puzzled" by grave case', *News24* (4 July 2013), <http://www.news24.com/SouthAfrica/News/Mandla-Mandela-puzzled-by-grave-case-20130704>; P. de Wet, *Mail and Guardian*, 9 July 2013, <http://mg.co.za/article/2013-07-09-00-factfile-the-mandela-graves-saga-explained>; Henriëtte Geldenhuys, 'Mandla's grave violation', *IOL News* (11 July 2013), <http://www.iol.co.za/news/crime-courts/mandla-s-grave-violation-1.1545121#.UfKBstI3DeA>; Sarah Evans, 'Mandla Mandela to go back to court over graves debacle', *Mail and Guardian* (18 July 2013), <http://mg.co.za/article/2013-07-18-mandla-mandela-to-go-back-to-court-over-graves-debacle-again>, all accessed 15 September 2014.

follow. But what was at stake was not limited to the potentially lucrative returns of a visitor economy and linked branding opportunities. A high-profile family gravesite of this nature, with multiple burials reaching back in time, would bolster Mandla's claim on the Mvezo chiefship, a position that at the time of writing was being challenged by the beleaguered Thembu king, Buyelekhaya Dalinyebo. Indeed, Mandla's grandfather was not a hereditary chief in the Mvezo area, but had been installed in 1915 on the recommendation of the then Thembu paramount, a position that he only occupied for eleven years, before being dismissed, allegedly for maladministration. The claim on the chiefship is thus far from incontrovertible.[2] Mandla's larger ambitions in the region were revealed in the media statement that he put out on 4 July in response to the sheriff's intervention, in which he was concerned less with where the family remains end up and more with asserting forcefully his position as 'the rightful heir' of the 'Royal House of Mandela'.[3] Referring to Makaziwe by the surname of her husband as 'Mrs Amuah' who 'ought to be focussing on Amuah family [matters]', Mandla explicitly challenged the rights of the applicants to the court to speak on issues pertinent to the Mandela family. 'Many people have been parading as the Mandela family and participating in the day to day decision of the Mandela family,' he noted. With these remarks, Mandla was positioning himself to be more than one among a number of the offspring of a famous man. In terms of a widely held shared understanding of the order of things, in which the well-being of people in the present is linked to the well-being of their ancestors, chiefs and recognised genealogical heirs play an important role in managing ancestral legacies. As the acknowledged rightful descendant of his great-grandfather, Mandla's position as chief is rooted in the discourse of ancestors. Effectively Mandla's claim was that he embodies Madiba's legacy, by hereditary right and with ancestral sanction. In turn, the applicants to the court made their claim to speak for Madiba in the language of the legal system: 'The applicants, as custodians of the last will and testament of Nelson Mandela will have duties to ensure his last wishes are carried out in the event of his demise.... The actions of Mandla Mandela in unlawfully violating the graves of the three deceased would appear to be in furtherance of an agenda to confound the last wishes of Nelson Mandela.'[4] As Madiba's actual ability

---

[2] Philip Bonner, 'The Headman', unpublished paper, 2013. I am grateful to the author for providing me with a copy of the paper.

[3] Mandla Mandela's prepared speech, delivered at a media briefing on Thursday, 4 July 2013. The full text is available on the *City Press* website, <http://www.citypress.co.za/news/full-script-mandla-mandela-slams-family/>, accessed 15 September 2014.

[4] Sarah Evans, *Mail and Guardian* (3 July 2013), <http://mg.co.za/article/2013-07-03-makaziwe-mandla-mandela-trying-to-cash-in-on-madibas-burial>, accessed 15 September 2014.

to enunciate words declined, the battle of who speaks, not just for him, but also potentially with him as an ancestor, and with what authority, escalated.

The sight of ambitious national and international politicians and celebrities pushing for bedside audiences with the aged icon, and making much of the opportunity subsequently to repeat his endorsements, was a regular feature of public life in the years before his death. The Nelson Mandela Foundation has worked actively to protect Madiba and his legacy from opportunistic appropriation and misrepresentation. Its Centre for Memory has curated the Nelson Mandela archive, and furnished materials from the archive to interested parties like the journalists trying to make sense of the family feud. Its work has not been merely reactive, however. The Centre has deployed the record of Madiba's words and actions to drive projects that undertake neglected memory work, harnessing his legacy to the pursuit of social justice and the principle of open access to records.[5] Through the Centre the record of Madiba's life has been positioned to speak truth to power.

The *entanglement* – of ancestral politics, embodied inheritances, graves, custom, political legitimation, struggle legacies, archives, evidence, and legal documents, involving families, politicians, courts, and foundations – around the increasingly frail icon of post-colonial possibility in the last year of his life was emblematic of what distinguishes the field of heritage in post-colonial settings like Ghana and South Africa, both from the prior constitution of the field in those places under colonialism, and in the former imperial metropoles. That kind of entanglement is what underlies heritage's claim on our attention as a distinctive aspect of African modernity. Indeed, its resistance to singular and straightforward specification alerts us to its location in the eye of the storm of post-coloniality, and more specifically, in the latter's characteristic refusal of linear temporality that places the past firmly in the past and outside of the present. The conclusion that follows elaborates on some of these characteristically post-colonial entanglements, expanding on and extending the argument introduced in the opening pages of the volume about the uniquely wide currency of heritage in Africa and the multiple ways in which it operates as a contemporary form of capital and political organisation.[6]

---

[5] Nelson Mandela Centre for Memory, <www.nelsonmandela.org/content/page/vision-and-mission>, accessed 26 July 2013.

[6] Entanglement is used here as a concept that is central to the post-colonial condition, its interlocked pasts, presents, and futures, and a feature of vernacular modernity. See Achille Mbembe, *On the Postcolony* (Berkeley, CA: University of California Press, 2001). Shaped at least in part by the extent of the historical entanglements of indigenous and colonial concepts – see Carolyn Hamilton, *Terrific Majesty: The Powers of Shaka Zulu and the Limits of Historical Invention* (Cambridge, MA: Harvard University Press, 1998), 3–4 – the notion of entanglement allows us to move beyond the many simplifying dualisms on which heritage at first pass seems to depend. See Sarah Nuttall, 'Introduction',

Heritage, Daniel Herwitz tells in his recent book, arose in the eighteenth and nineteenth centuries, 'a central cog in the structure of modernity, a way of framing the past and ongoing traditions into an ensemble... totally caught up in the history of nationalism'.[7] Colonial elites and settlers explored its capacities, creating their own sense of national unity and repressing the pasts of the colonised, and, as Herwitz argues drawing on Achille Mbembe, post-colonial societies seek to rescript much the same material in situations of political improvisation. Herwitz goes on to elucidate his concept of 'live-action heritage' by which he draws attention to what he describes as the logic or grammar of difference that occurs in the way that post-colonial heritage 'games' repeat past heritage 'games' with a difference, accepting and intervening in the rules of the games. Laurajane Smith, another scholar of heritage, marks out the way in which, in the 1960s and 1970s, the discourse of heritage was taken up in relation to particular environmental and social concerns, becoming an explicit and active way of negotiating cultural and social change, as well as the object of dedicated professional disciplines. This move was accompanied by the consolidation of national and international technical processes of management and conservation, and was fed by ideas about indigenous rights and world heritage.[8] Nick Shepherd calls attention to heritage as a site of active cultural construction, a sphere of practice in public life and a point of negotiation of key social rights and entitlements,[9] while Jean and John Comaroff's study, *Ethnicity Inc.*, focuses on its current marketability.[10] There is no shortage of work pointing us to change in relation to heritage as a concept and a practice in the post-colonies. The current volume makes it clear that this is not change already effected, but an ongoing process of concepts and practices in the making.

The volume offers us a history of things and socio-political phenomena that have acquired the label of heritage in public life, or which the volume positions us to think of as forms of heritage making. Derek Peterson's opening comments, and the essays that they introduce, encourage us to see beyond the familiar ideas of heritage as a tendentious, harnessed past. Petersen usefully conceptualises heritage as a mode of political organisation, in operation well outside the confines of the museum. Tracing the

---

Entanglement: Literary and Cultural Reflections on Post Apartheid (Johannesburg: Witwatersrand University Press, 2009) for an extended discussion of the various contributions to a theory of entanglement.

[7] Daniel Herwitz, *Heritage, Culture, and Politics in the Postcolony* (New York, NY: Columbia University Press, 2012), 13.

[8] Laurajane Smith, *Uses of Heritage* (London: Routledge, 2006), 5.

[9] Nick Shepherd, 'Heritage', in Nick Shepherd and Steven Robins (eds), *New South African Keywords* (Johannesburg: Jacana, 2008), 116–28.

[10] Jean Comaroff and John Comaroff, *Ethnicity, Inc.* (Chicago, IL: University of Chicago Press, 2009).

way in which indirect rule and disciplinary interventions categorised and corralled materials about the past, a number of the essays allow us to grasp something of the complexity of how this happens, how it becomes a means of rule and how it has changed over time. They allow us to understand something of the distinctive circumstances of the development of heritage in the colonies and their successor states.

After some three hundred pages of discussion of widely different forms of heritage activity at various times, primarily in two locations on the African continent, the volume has established a strong sense of the socio-political relevance of heritage. As Katharina Schramm's recent monograph on heritage in Ghana shows us, it can be a space of encounter characterised by the existence of shared rhetoric and divergent practices among those involved in the encounter.[11] Increasingly an idea mobilised by ordinary people to think about the meaning of the past in the present, heritage is an idea that has possibilities and consequences in their lives. It does things in the world. It is capable of mobilising or inhibiting people. Sometimes it regulates and authorises; it can be dissonant; and it can itself be a process of engagement.

The changing multiple operations, invocations, and instances of heritage as discourse, phenomenon, and practice raise productive questions about how it is shaped and shifted by the *jostling* of the concepts and practices that it encompasses. A distinctive feature of heritage in both post-colonial Ghana and South Africa is the way in which notions of history, archives, memory, tradition, memorials, monuments, and legacy rub up against one another. The effects of this jostling are one of the ways in which, in Herwitz's terms, post-colonial heritage 'games' intervene in the rules of heritage games. In the rest of this conclusion I wish to draw attention to two features that flow from this jostling in such post-colonial settings, both of which are illustrated in the Mandela family feud: the first concerns the influence on the politics of heritage of ideas about generational inheritances and ancestors; the second has to do with the way in which heritage in the post-colonies is burdened with the responsibilities of archive in a manner that demands of it not to replace the archive, but to negotiate its own position in relation to archive, and which challenges the archive, in turn, to reflect on its own constitution.

In order to bring these features into view it is helpful to think about the relations between the various cognate concepts and practices that make up the field of heritage. To what extent are they mutually unsettling and defining; what improvisations do their interrelations facilitate; what are the limits to which such improvisations are subject; and to what extent is the nature of these interrelations distinctive in a post-colonial

---

[11] Katharina Schramm. *African Homecoming: Pan-African Ideology and Contested Heritage* (Walnut Creek, CA: Left Coast Press, 2010).

setting? These are some of the big questions that flow from this volume. While a conclusion is hardly the place to begin to answer them, it is an appropriate place to draw attention to the pointers generated in the wake of the volume.

As we know well, both heritage and history can promote particular points of view: both can put the past to work in particular ways; both can be poorly or well-researched; both can be used as modes of political organisation. One of the things that distinguishes them, however, is *how* the past and the present are tied together. Where history may provide the bases for forms of inclusion or exclusion much like heritage, it may also allow for voluntary and flexible forms of identification across time, or none at all. Heritage, by way of contrast, *asserts* belonging and connection across time. Heritage has little traction in the recognition of *ambiguity* or *uncertainty* of identity or location.

In the cases of the mobilisation of heritage in the service of the post-colonial nationalism described in certain of these essays, as well as in the history of injustice recalled in the South African Constitutional Court building and the ways in which the past of the struggle is sacralised by the ANC government, the group identities involved are manifestly diverse. The mobilisation of the past that is involved aspires to unite people. In these cases a shared history in the recent past, without any sense of common origin, must translate into a generational inheritance for it to accumulate the force of heritage. Silverman's study of the tourist developments in Manso, centred on African-American diasporic heritage desires, is concerned with whether this will take place in Ghana. Racial discourses that persistently play down the shared history of anti-apartheid struggle by certain black and certain white activists currently militate against the development of a struggle heritage for all South Africans. In all of these cases, ambiguity and uncertainty demand attention in a way that heritage politics does not readily allow for, and that inhibits transformation into a cross-generational inheritance. The matter of generational inheritance is further complicated in situations where the well-being in the present of ancestors intersects with contemporary heritage politics. Added to this is the complexity of the role of chiefs in both South Africa and Ghana, whose claims over the stewardship of tradition are based on lines of descent.[12] In all of these ways we can discern an inclination in heritage discourses and practices towards essentialised ideas about inherited identities. The significance of the tilt is exacerbated by post-colonial epistemological anxieties about the practices of history.

---

[12] cf. Grant McNulty, 'Custodianship on the Periphery: Archives, Power and Identity Politics in Post-Apartheid Umbumbulu, KwaZulu-Natal' (PhD thesis, University of Cape Town, 2014.

A number of the contributions to this volume highlight the role of research in underwriting colonial political rule, drawing our attention to the kinds of political disfavour to which the disciplines of history, archaeology, and physical anthropology are sometimes subject, and the way in which this leads to a valorisation of heritage. In the final essay of this volume, Litheko Modisane quotes Frantz Fanon on how colonialism 'distorts, disfigures and destroys' the past of the oppressed colonial subjects, and notes how post-colonial state and non-state institutions seek to redress this through the contemporary mobilisation of cultural heritage. Heritage is thus positioned as a technology of healing[13] and an alternative source of material about the past. In the face of colonial structuring and determination of the archival record, heritage has been valorised for its capacities to have protected, through time, threatened materials that exist outside of the archives. Anxieties about the biases of the colonial archive drive a turn to heritage practices as an alternative source of materials about the past. Thus heritage today is frequently positioned to do the work of archive, and is burdened with the responsibilities of archive in substantiating claims made about the past. But heritage is often looked on balefully from the position of the historical disciplines and by the law because of its ready adaption to political purpose and its weak commitment to the questions of evidence and rigorous forms of argument. Anxieties about the validity of the inherited archive and concerns about the evidentiary capacities of other materials about the past set the terms of the post-colonial discussion of the past.

In South Africa recourse to heritage forms to do the work of archive is most visible in the way in which land claims take the maintenance of gravesites seriously as a form of evidence. Indeed, gravesites and physical remains are tangible materials with recognisable properties as evidence. Restitution and heritage policies, and linked legislation, attuned to indigenous rights and subaltern perspectives, further take cognisance of forms of 'intangible inheritance', notably cultural repertoires, 'tradition', and a variety of forms of memory in active circulation in society. The manifest *dynamism* of these forms over time demands attention in any situation where they augment or challenge archival records, in order to grapple with how they may have changed over time. By the same token, the apparent *inertia* of materials sequestered in archives – a feature considered central to their testatory capacities – comes under critical scrutiny. The heritage forms thus both test the limits of the notion of archive and challenge its foundational tenets.

[13]   Ferdinand De Jong and Michael Rowlands, 'Postconflict Heritage', *Journal of Material Culture* 13, 2 (2008): 131–4; see also Lynn Meskell and Colette Scheermeyer, 'Heritage as Therapy', *Journal of Material Culture* 13, 2 (2008): 153–74.

Not all attempts to think about the past disfigured by colonialism disavow the inherited archive. Some have a distinctively archival reach, albeit one with post-colonial sensitivities. Elsewhere Modisane has shown how the 1980s worker movement reached into the South African film archive to find testimony and the imagining of a black public sphere denied by apartheid. Modisane is attentive to the dynamism that characterises the archive even at the point where its efforts to immobilise its contents are the most elaborate. He carefully tracks how films enter the archive, subsist there, and re-emerge into public life, curated and re-curated over time in ways that change it significantly.[14] As I have argued elsewhere, for all their preservatory apparatuses, archives themselves shift and change in dynamic relation with the world around them.[15] Not only are the contents of archives dynamic but the notion of archive itself has a history, and is a term with changing and multiple applications, operations, invocations, and instances as discourse, phenomenon, and practice. Like cultural repertoire and memory, archive is positioned within an itself shifting, challenged, and challenging field of related concepts, a point which hoves into view with particular clarity in post-colonial settings. Custodial activity in archives, and in other heritage formations, is, in *all* cases, a process over time involving both change and continuity. A key feature of the wider field is the navigation of understanding what changes and what is continuous within the various practices of these cognate forms.

Heritage, legacy, history, memory, archive, memorials, monuments and so on are all forms in which the past is held in the present. They are all, to adopt and extend Verne Harris's phrase, genres of the trace.[16] Governed by their respective frames, they are all also shaped by past and present practices. Each at its core is quite distinct from the others, even as each may mean different things to different people. While each further involves distinctive practices and forms of valorisation, at their edges they bleed into one another, the nature of their separation unclear. To grasp the politics of heritage is not simply to analyse instances of heritage politics in action but also, and simultaneously, to pay attention to the construal of heritage in relation to these cognate, overlapping domains. It is to investigate the ways in which they collectively give shape

---

[14] Litheko Modisane, 'Outlawed Black Public Spheres: Snapshots of Cinema's Archive', in Carolyn Hamilton and Pippa Skotnes (eds), *Uncertain Curature: In and Out of the Archive* (Johannesburg, Jacana, forthcoming).

[15] Carolyn Hamilton, 'Backstory, Biography and the Life of the James Stuart Archive', *History in Africa* 38, 1 (2011): 319–41; Carolyn Hamilton, 'Forged and Continually Refashioned in the Crucible of Ongoing Social and Political Life: Archives and Custodial Practices as Subjects of Enquiry', *South African Historical Journal* 65, 1 (2013): 1–22.

[16] Verne Harris, 'Genres of the Trace: Memory, Archives and Trouble', *Archives and Manuscripts* 40, 3 (2012): 147–57.

to vernacular modernities forged, and beleaguered, by multiple inheritances, and characterised by a mode of living not only ambitiously but
also, in part, anachronistically – as well as purposefully intransigently –
in relation to late capitalism. Thus Mandla Mandela's act of relocating
bones, which bids for a stake in global tourism, underwrites chiefship,
and defies the law, illustrates key features of the terms of the politics of
heritage in the post-colony.

The challenge is, it seems, to pay attention to the tense-orientation[17]
of each of the jostling forms within the heritage field: to enquire in each
case into a double-story, the account of the past that they support or
offer and the story of their own making and remaking over time. It is
to anticipate that the heritage life of the icon, Madiba, will involve as
much struggle and contest, incarceration and liberation, as the lived life
of the man. It is the cross-field engagements of history, archive, custom,
cultural tradition, memory, memorials, and monuments in Ghana and
South Africa that draw attention to their respective double-storiedness
and disrupt the linear temporal arrangements that place the past firmly
in the past and distinct from the present. But are these features particular
to post-colonial settings, or are they especially starkly visible and more
readily acknowledged in such settings, as in the more general proposi-
tion put forward in the Comaroffs' provocation on 'How Euro-America
is Evolving towards Africa'?[18] Once we give attention to the double-
storiedness that a post-colonial location *demands* of archive as much as of
memory, tradition, and all the other elements that make up the heritage
field, it is hard to imagine that things might be different in the other
locations, other than that the pressure for its recognition might be less
insistent.

Acknowledgements

I am grateful to the many Archive and Public Culture researchers and
associates who offered helpful comments on earlier drafts of this Conclusion.

---

[17] Reinhart Koselleck, *Futures Past: On the Semantics of Historical Time* (New York, NY:
Columbia University Press, 2004 [1974]).
[18] Jean Comaroff and John Comaroff, *Theory from the South: Or How Euro-America is
Evolving toward Africa* (Boulder, CO: Paradigm Press, 2011).

Bibliography

Abiven, O. *Annales réligieuses de St.-Joseph de Ngasobil, 1849–1929.* Archevêché de Dakar, n.d.

Abrahams, Yvette. 'Images of Sara Bartman: Sexuality, Race and Gender in Early Nineteenth-Century Britain.' In *Nation, Empire, Colony: Historicising Gender and Race,* edited by Ruth Roach Pierson and Nupur Chaudhuri, 220–36. Bloomington, IN: Indiana University Press, 1998.

Acheampong, Nana. 'Saka Acquaye: The Life and Loves of a Giant.' *Uhuru Magazine* 4 (1989): 10–15, 33–36.

Achieng, Jane. *Paul Mboya's* Luo Kitgi gi Timbegi. Kisumu: Atai Joint, 2001.

Acquaye, Saka. 'The Lost Fishermen: A Folk Opera.' 1965 (typescript).

———. 'Modern Folk Opera in Ghana.' *African Arts* 4 (2) (1971): 60–63, 80.

———. 'Folk Opera in Ghana and Nigeria.' Accra: Institute of African Studies, Legon, 1972.

Afigbo, A. E. 'The Place of the Igbo Language in Our Schools: A Historical Explanation.' In *Igbo Language and Culture,* vol. 1, edited by F. Chidozie Ogbalu and E. Nolue Emenanjo, 70–84. Ibadan: Oxford University Press, 1975.

———. *The Igbo and Their Neighbours: Intergroup Relations in Southeastern Nigeria to 1953.* Ibadan: University Press, 1987.

African National Congress. *The Reconstruction and Development Programme.* Johannesburg: Umanyano Publications, 1994.

Agovi, Kofi, E. 'The Origin of Literary Theatre in Colonial Ghana 1920–1957.' Institute of African Studies, Legon, 1989. (Typescript).

Agyekum, Kofi. 'Ntam Reminiscential Oath Taboo in Akan.' *Language in Society* 33 (2004): 317–42.

———. 'The Communicative Role of Silence in Akan.' *Pragmatics* 12 (2002): 31–51.

———. *Akan Verbal Taboos in the Context of Ethnography of Communication.* Accra: Ghana Universities Press, 2010.

Ahurwendeire, H. 'Some Aspects of the History of Kinkiizi.' BA thesis, Makerere University, 1973.

Aidoo, Christina Ama Ata. *The Dilemma of a Ghost.* Accra and Ikeja: Longman, 1965.

Allman, Jean. *Quills of the Porcupine: Asante Nationalism in an Emergent Ghana.* Madison, WI: University of Wisconsin Press, 1993.

Amamoo, Joseph G. *The Ghanaian Revolution.* London: Jafint Company, 1988.

Amartey, A. A. *Omanye Aba.* Accra: Bureau of Ghana Languages, 1969.

Angmor, Charles. *Contemporary Literature in Ghana 1911–1978: A Critical Evaluation.* Accra: Woeli Publishing Services, 1996.

261

Anquandah, James Kwesi. *Castles and Forts of Ghana*. Paris: Atalante, 1999.

Anquandah, James. 'An Archaeological Survey of the Takyiman-Wenchi Area.' In *Ashanti and the Northwest*, edited by Jack Goody and Kwame Arhin, 111–34. Legon: Institute of African Studies, University of Ghana, 1965.

Appadurai, Arjun. 'Introduction: Commodities and the Politics of Value.' In *The Social Life of Things: Commodities in Cultural Perspective*, edited by Arjun Appadurai, 3–63. Cambridge: Cambridge University Press, 1986.

Argentine Forensic Anthropology Team/Equipo Argentino de Antropología Forense. 'Annual Report (Covering the Period January to December 2006).' 2007.

Arhin, Brempong. *Transformations in Traditional Rule in Ghana (1951–1996)*. Accra: Institute of African Studies, Legon, 2007.

Arinze, Francis. 'Christianity and Igbo culture.' In *Igbo Language and Culture*, vol. 2, edited by F. Chidozie Ogbalu and E. Nolue Emenanjo, 181–97. Ibadan: University Press, 1982.

Asare, Emmanuel. 'Recounting the Memorial Gardens at Manso.' Techiman, unpublished manuscript, 2008.

Ashworth, G. J. 'From History to Heritage – from Heritage to Identity.' In *Building a New Heritage: Tourism, Culture and Identity in the New Europe*, edited by G. J. Ashworth and P. J. Larkham, 13–30. London: Routledge, 1994.

Askew, Kelly. *Performing the Nation: Swahili Music and Cultural Politics in Tanzania*. Chicago, IL: University of Chicago Press, 2002.

Ballantine, Christopher. 'Looking to the USA: The Politics of Male Close-Harmony Song Style in South Africa during the 1940s and 1950s.' *Popular Music* 18 (1) (1999): 1–17.

Balseiro, Isabel, and Ntongela Masilela, eds. *To Change Reels: Film and Film Culture in South Africa*. Detroit, MI: Wayne State University Press, 2003.

Barry, Baboucar. *Senegambia and the Atlantic Slave Trade*. Translated by Ayi Kwei Armah. Cambridge: Cambridge University Press, 1998.

Bauman, Zygmunt. *Liquid Modernity*. Cambridge: Polity Press, 2012.

Bawa, Ahmed and Daniel Herwitz. 'South African Universities in the Tumult of Change.' *Journal of the International Institute* 15 (2): 1, 12–14.

Bennett, Tony. *The Birth of the Museum: History, Theory, Politics*. London: Routledge, 1995.

Benjamin, Walter. 'The Work of Art in the Age of Mechanical Reproduction.' Translated by Harry Zohin. In *Film theory and Criticism: Introductory Readings*, edited by Leo Baudry and Marshall Cohen, 791–811. New York, NY and Oxford: Oxford University Press, 2004.

Benson, Susan. 'Connecting with the Past, Building the Future: African Americans and Chieftaincy in Southern Ghana.' *Ghana Studies* 6 (2003): 109–33.

Benson, Susan, and T. C. McCaskie. 'Asen Praso in History and Memory.' *Ghana Studies* 7 (2004): 93–113.

Besten, Michael Paul. 'Transformation and the Reconstitution of Khoe-San Identities: AAS le Fleur I, Griqua Identities and Post-Apartheid Khoe-San Revivalism (1894–2004).' PhD thesis, Leiden University, 2006.

Blyden, Edward Wilmont. *Christianity, Islam, and the Negro Race*. Edinburgh: Edinburgh University Press, 1967 (1887).

Boafo-Arthur, Kwame. 'Chieftaincy in Ghana: Challenges and Prospects in the 21st Century.' *African and Asian Affairs* 2 (2) (2003): 126–53.

_____. 'Chieftaincy in Ghana: Challenges and Prospects in the 21st Century.' In *Chieftaincy in Ghana: Culture, Governance and Development*, edited by Odotei Irene and Awedoba Albert. Accra: Sub-Saharan Publishers, 2007.

Bob-Milliar, George M. 'Chieftaincy, Diaspora, and Development: The Institution of Nkosuohene in Ghana.' *African Affairs* 108 (433) (2009): 541–58.

Bonner, Philip. 'The Headman, the Regent and the Long Walk to Freedom.' Paper in preparation for publication, 2013.

Bonner, Philip, Amanda Esterhuysen, and Trefor Jenkins, eds. *A Search for Origins: Science, History and South Africa's 'Cradle of Humankind'*. Johannesburg: Witwatersrand University Press, 2007.

Botwe-Asamoah, Kwame. *Kwame Nkrumah's Politico-Cultural Thought and Policies*. New York, NY: Routledge, 2005.

Bredekamp, Henry C. Jatti. 'Khoisan Revivalism and the Indigenous Peoples Issue in Post-Apartheid South Africa.' In *Africa's Indigenous Peoples: 'First Peoples' or Marginalised Minorities?* edited by Alan Barnard and Justin Kenrick, 191–210. Edinburgh: University of Edinburgh Press, 2001.

Brempong, Arhin. *Transformations in Traditional Rule in Ghana 1951–1996*. Legon: Institute of African Studies, University of Ghana, 2007.

Briggs, Philip. *Ghana*. 5th edn. Chalfont St Peter, Bucks: Bradt Travel Guides, 2010.

Brown, Duncan. *Voicing the Text: South African Oral Poetry and Performance*. Cape Town: Oxford University Press, 1998.

Bruner, Edward M. 'Tourism in Ghana: The Representation of Slavery and the Return of the Black Diaspora.' *American Anthropologist* 98 (2) (1996): 290–304.

Byrd, Alexander X. 'Africans in the Americas. Review of Hall, Gwendoyn Midlo, *Slavery and African Ethnicities in the Americas: Restoring the Links*.' H-Atlantic, H-Net Reviews, August 2006.

Caltex Africa, *South African Heritage: From Van Riebeeck to Nineteenth Century Times*. Cape Town: Human and Rousseau, 1965.

Calvet, Louis-Jean. *Les voix de la ville: Introduction à la sociolinguistique urbaine*. Paris: Payot et Rivages, 1994.

Carton, Benedict, John Laband, and Jabulani Sithole. *Zulu Identities: Being Zulu, Past and Present*. Scottsville: University of Kwa-Zulu Natal Press, 2008.

Chakrabarty, Dipesh. 'Postcoloniality and the Artifice of History: Who Speaks for 'Indian' Pasts?' *Representations* 32 (1992): 1–26.

Chambers, Douglas B. 'Rejoinder – The Significance of Igbo in the Bight of Biafra Slave-Trade: A Rejoinder to Northrup's "Myth Igbo".' *Slavery and Abolition* 23 (1) (2002): 101–20.

Chimhundu, Herbert. 'Early Missionaries and the Ethnolinguistic Factor during the "Invention of Tribalism" in Zimbabwe.' *Journal of African History* 33 (1992): 87–109.

Christaller, J. G. 'Sprachproben vom Sudan zwischen Asante und Mittel-Niger.' *Zeitschrift für Afrikanische Sprachen* 3 (1889): 107–32.

Clarke, Ebun. *Hubert Ogunde: The Making of Nigeria Theatre*. Oxford: Oxford University Press, 1980.

Cole, Catherine. M. *Ghana's Concert Party Theatre*. Bloomington and Indianapolis, IN: Indiana University Press, 2001.

Comaroff, John L. and Jean Comaroff. *Ethnicity, Inc*. Chicago, IL: University of Chicago Press, 2009.

Comaroff, Jean and John Comaroff. *Theory from the South: or, How Euro-America is Evolving toward Africa*. Boulder, CO: Paradigm Press, 2011.

Coombes, Annie F. *History after Apartheid: Visual Culture and Public Memory in a Democratic South Africa*. Durham, NC: Duke University Press, 2003.

Cope, Trevor. *Izibongo: Zulu Oral Literature*. London: Clarendon Press, 1968.

Crais, Clifton and Pamela Scully. *Sara Baartman and the Hottentot Venus: A Ghost Story and a Biography*. Princeton, NJ: Princeton University Press, 2009.

Dakubu, M. E. Kropp. 'City People and the Cultural Heritage.' Paper to African Heritage Initiative Conference, Johannesburg, 8–9 July (2011).

———. *Korle Meets the Sea, a Sociolinguistic History of Accra*. New York, NY and Oxford: Oxford University Press, 1997.

———. *One Voice, the Linguistic Culture of an Accra Lineage*. Leiden: African Studies Center, 1981.

Dakubu, M. E. Kropp, Samuel A. Atintono, and E. A. Nsoh, *Gurenɛ–English Dictionary with English–Gurenɛ Glossary*. Legon: Linguistics Department, 2007.

Danida. *Culture and Development: Strategy and Guidelines*. Copenhagen: Danida, Ministry of Foreign Affairs, 2002.

Dankwa III, Oseadeeyo Addo. *The Institution of Chieftaincy in Ghana–the Future*. Accra: Konrad Adenauer Foundation, 2004.

Davison, Patricia. 'Redressing the Past: Integrating Social History Collections at Iziko.' *South African Museums Association Bulletin* (2005): 101–4.

Deandrao, Pietro. *Fertile Crossings: Metamorphosis of Genre in Anglophone West African Literature*. Amsterdam: Rodopi, 2001.

DeCorse, Christopher R. 'Culture Contact, Continuity and Change on the Gold Coast, AD 1400–1900.' *The African Archaeological Review* 10 (1992): 163–96.

———. 'The Danes on the Gold Coast: Culture Change and the European Presence.' *The African Archaeological Review* 11 (1993): 149–73.

———. 'Introduction.' In *West Africa During the Atlantic Slave Trade*, ed. Christopher R. DeCorse, 1–13. London: Leicester University Press, 2001.

De Jong, Ferdinand, and Michael Rowlands. 'Postconflict Heritage.' *Journal of Material Culture* 13 (2) (2008): 131–34.

Dening, Greg. *Beach Crossings*. Philadelphia, PA: University of Pennsylvania Press, 2004.

Department of Culture, Media and Sport (UK). *Guidance for the Treatment of Human Remains in Museums*. London, October 2005.

Dewhirst, Polly. 'The Establishment of the South African Disappearance Task Team: the Roots for a Regional Network?' *Linking Solidarity Newsletter*, 2005.

Dike, Kenneth Onwuka, and Felicia Ekejiuba. *The Aro of Southeastern Nigeria, 1650–1980: A Study of Socio-Economic Formation and Transformation in Nigeria*. Ibadan (Nigeria): University Press, 1990.

Diouf, Makhtar. *Sénégal: Les ethnies et la nation*. Dakar: Les Nouvelles Editions Africaines du Sénégal, 1998.

Diouf, Mamadou. *Histoire du Sénégal*. Paris: Maisonneuve et Larose, 2001.

Dirks, Nicholas. *Castes of Mind: Colonialism and the Making of Modern India*. Princeton, NJ: Princeton University Press, 2001.

Dlamini, Nsizwa. 'Monuments of Division: Apartheid and Post-Apartheid Struggles over Zulu Nationalist Heritage Sites.' In *Zulu Identities: Being Zulu, Past and Present*, edited by Ben Carton, John Laband, and Jabulani Sithole, 383–94. Pietermaritzburg: University of KwaZulu-Natal Press, 2008.

Dorian, Nancy, 'Linguistic and Ethnographic Fieldwork.' In *Handbook of Language and Ethnic Identity*, edited by Joshua A. Fishman, 25–41. Oxford: Oxford University Press, 1999.

Dovey, Lindiwe and Angela Impey. 'African Jim: Sound, Politics, and Pleasure in Early "Black" South African Cinema.' *Journal of African Cultural Studies* 22 (1) (2010): 57–73.

Drachler, Jacob, ed. *African Heritage: An Anthology of Black African Personality and Culture*. London: Collier, 1963.

Dubow, Saul. *Scientific Racism in Modern South Africa*. Cambridge: Cambridge University Press, 1995.

———. 'White South Africa and the South Africanisation of Science: Humankind or Kinds of Humans?' In *A Search for Origins: Science, History and South Africa's 'Cradle of Humankind,'* edited by Philip Bonner, Amanda Esterhuysen, and Trefor Jenkins, 9–21. Johannesburg: Witwatersrand University Press, 2007.

Duncan, Carol. *Civilizing Rituals: Inside Public Art Museums*. London: Routledge, 1995.

Dunch, Ryan. 'Beyond Cultural Imperialism: Cultural Theory, Christian Missions, and Global Modernity.' *History and Theory* 41 (3) (October 2002): 301–25.

Earle, Jonathon. 'Political Theologies in Late Colonial Buganda.' PhD thesis, Cambridge University, 2012.

Effah-Gyamfi, Emmanuel K. 'Bono-Manso: An Archaeological Investigation into Early Akan Urbanism.' PhD thesis, University of Ghana, 1978.

———. 'Oral Traditions and Archaeology: A Case Study of the Bono State.' MA thesis, University of Ghana, 1974.

Ellis, Bill. 'A Model for Collecting and Interpreting World Trade Centre Disaster Jokes.' *New Directions in Folklore* 5 (October 2001).

Emenanjo, E. Nolue. 'Central Igbo – An Objective Appraisal.' In *Igbo Language and Culture*, vol. 1, edited by F. Chidozie Ogbalu and E. Nolue Emenanjo, 114–37. Ibadan: Oxford University Press, 1975.

Engmann, Osofo E. A. W. *Kpawo Kpawo Toi Kpawo* Vol. 2 *Kusumi (Folklore of the Ga People)*. Oxford and Paternoster: Regnum Africa in association with Regnum Books International, 2012.

Equiano, Olaudah. *The Interesting Narrative of Olaudah Equiano, or Gustavus Vasa, the African*. In *Africa Remembered: Narratives by West Africans from the Era of the Slave Trade*, edited by Philip D. Curtin, 69–98. Madison, WI: University of Wisconsin Press, 1967 [1789].

Faidherbe, Louis. 'Étude sur la langue Kuégem ou Sérère-Sine.' *Annuaire du Sénégal pour l'année 1865*. Saint-Louis: Imprimerie du Gouvernement, 1865, 175–245.

Fanon, Frantz. *Black Skin, White Masks*. New York, NY: Grove, 1967 (1952).

———. 'On National Culture.' In *Colonial and Postcolonial Theory: A Reader*, edited by Patrick Williams and Ian Chrisman, New York, NY: Columbia University Press, 1994.

———. *The Wretched of the Earth*. Harmondsworth: Penguin, 1967.

Feierman, Steven. 'On Socially Composed Knowledge: Reconstructing a Shambaa Royal Ritual.' In *In Search of a Nation: Histories of Authority and Dissidence in Tanzania*, edited by Gregory H. Maddox and James L. Giblin, 14–32. Athens, OH: Ohio University Press, 2005.

Fforde, Cressida, Jane Hubert and Paul Turnbull, eds. *The Dead and Their Possessions: Repatriation in Principle, Policy and Practice*. One World Archaeology 43, London and New York, NY: Routledge, 2002.

Fichte, Johann Gottlieb. *Reden an die deutsche Nation*. Berlin: Realschulbuchhandlung, 1808.

Field, Margaret J. *Religion and Medicine of the Gã People*. London: Oxford University Press, 1937.

Forde, Daryll, and G. I. Jones. *The Ibo and Ibibio-Speaking Peoples of South-Eastern Nigeria*. London: International African Institute, 1950.

Gadzekpo, Audrey. 'The Chief is Dead: Long Live the BBC: Globalization, Culture and Democratization in Ghana.' Unpublished paper, 1999.

Gbagbo, Moses. 'Kristo: A Traditional Opera by Walter Blege. An Analytical Study.' M Phil thesis, University of Ghana, Legon, 1997.

Ghana Statistical Service. *2000 Population and Housing Census: Special Reports on 20 Largest Localities*. Accra: Ghana Statistical Service, 2002.

Ghana Ministry of Tourism. *Guidebook to the Major Pilgrimage Routes in Ghana*. Accra: National Slave Routes Project, Ministry of Tourism and Diasporan Relations, 2008.

Gilman, Sander. 'Black Bodies, White Bodies: Toward an Iconography of Female Sexuality in Late Nineteenth Century Art, Medicine and Literature,' *Critical Enquiry* 12 (1) (1985): 204–42.

Gilmour, Rachael. *Grammars of Colonialism: Representing Languages in Colonial South Africa*. Basingstoke and New York, NY: Palgrave Macmillan, 2006.

Gomez, Michael. 'A Quality of Anguish: The Igbo Response to Enslavement in the Americas.' In *Transatlantic Dimensions of Ethnicity in the African Diaspora*, edited by Paul Lovejoy and David Trotman, 82–95. London and New York, NY: Continuum, 2003.

Gould, Stephen Jay. 'The Hottentot Venus,' *Natural History* 10 (1982): 20–24.

Grundy, Kenneth W. 'Mali: The Prospects of Planned Socialism.' In *African Socialism*, edited by William H. Friedland and Carl G. Rosberg, Jr, 176–93. Stanford, CA: Stanford University Press, 1964.

Grunebaum, Heidi. 'Unburying the Dead in the 'Mother City': Urban Topographies of Erasure', *PMLA* 122 (1) (January 2010): 210–19.

Gunner, Liz and Mafika Gwala. *Musho!: Zulu Popular Praises*. East Lansing, MI: Michigan State University Press, 1991.

Guy, Jeff. *The Destruction of the Zulu Kingdom: The Civil War in Zululand, 1879–1884*. Pietermaritzburg: University of Natal Press, 1994 [1979].

Hagan, George. 'Nkrumah's Cultural Policy,' in *The Life and Work of Kwame Nkrumah*, edited by Kwame Arhin. Trenton, NJ: Africa World Press, Inc., 1993.

Hall, Gwendolyn Midlo. *Slavery and African Ethnicities in the Americas: Restoring the Links*. Chapel Hill, NC: University of North Carolina Press, 2005.

Hamilton, Carolyn. *Terrific Majesty: The Powers of Shaka Zulu and the Limits of Historical Invention*. Cambridge, MA: Harvard University Press, 1998.

———. 'Ideology, Oral Traditions and the Struggle for Power in the Early Zulu Kingdom.' MA thesis, University of the Witwatersrand, 1985.

———. 'Backstory, Biography and the Life of the James Stuart Archive.' *History in Africa* 38 (2011): 319–41.

_____. 'Forged and Continually Refashioned in the Crucible of Ongoing Social and Political Life: Archives and Custodial Practices as Subjects of Enquiry.' *South African Historical Journal* 65 (1) (2013): 1–22.

Hamilton, Carolyn and John Wright. 'The Making of the AmaLala: Ethnicity, Ideology and Relations of Subordination in a Precolonial Context,' *South African Historical Journal* 22 (1990): 3–23.

Harris, Verne. 'Genres of the Trace: Memory, Archives and Trouble.' In *Archives and Manuscripts* 40 (3) (2012): 147–57.

Harries, Patrick. 'The Roots of Ethnicity: Discourse and the Politics of Language Construction in South-East Africa.' *African Affairs* 87 (346) (1998): 25–52.

_____. 'Discovering Languages: The Historical Origins of Standard Tsonga in Southern Africa.' In *Language and Social History: Studies in South African Sociolinguistics*, edited by R. Mesthrie, 154–75. Cape Town: David Philip, 1995.

Hayes, G. D. 'The Museum of Malawi.' *Society of Malawi Journal* 20 (1) (1967): 49–57.

Healy, Chris. ' "Race Portraits" and Vernacular Possibilities: Heritage and Culture.' In *Culture in Australia: Policies, Publics and Programs*, edited by Tony Bennett and David Carter, 278–98. Cambridge: Cambridge University Press, 2001.

Henderson, Richard. *The King in Every Man: Evolutionary Trends in Onitsha Ibo Society and Culture*. New Haven, CT: Yale University Press, 1972.

Herskovits, Frances and Melville. *Dahomean Narrative: A Cross Cultural Analysis*. Evanston, IL: Northwestern University Press, 1958.

Herwitz, Daniel. *Heritage, Culture and Politics in the Postcolony*. New York, NY: Columbia University Press, 2012.

Hess, Janet. 'Exhibiting Ghana: Display, Documentary, and 'National' Art in the Nkrumah Era.' *African Studies Review* 44 (1) (2001): 59–77.

Hess, Janet. *Art and Architecture in Postcolonial Africa*. London: McFarland and Company, 2006.

Higson, Andrew. 'Re-Presenting the National Past: Nostalgia and Pastiche in the Heritage Film.' In *Fires Were Started: British Cinema and Thatcherism*, edited by Lester Friedman, 109–29. London: UCL Press, 1993.

Hildebrand, M. and Thubelisha Homes. 'Case Studies: Successful Energy Efficient Projects in South Africa. Lessons for Thubelisha Homes.' Joe Slovo 3, N2 Gateway Energy Efficiency Project. Pretoria: National Department of Housing, 2008.

Holsey, Bayo. *Routes of Remembrance: Refashioning the Slave Trade in Ghana*. Chicago, IL: University of Chicago Press, 2008.

Horton, James Africanus. *West African Counties and People*. Edinburgh: Edinburgh University Press, 1969 [1868].

Iliffe, John. *Africans: The History of a Continent*. Cambridge: Cambridge University Press, 1995.

_____. 'Breaking the Chain at Its Weakest Link: TANU and the Colonial Office.' In *In Search of a Nation: Histories of Authority and Dissidence in Tanzania*, edited by Gregory H. Maddox and James L. Giblin, 168–97. Oxford: James Currey, 2006.

Irvine, Judith T. 'Subjected Words: African Linguistics and the Colonial Encounter.' *Language and Communication* 28 (2008): 323–43.

———. 'Stance in a Colonial Encounter: How Mr Taylor Lost His Footing.' In *Stance: Sociolinguistic Perspectives*, edited by Alexandra Jaffe, 53–71. Oxford: Oxford University Press, 2009.

Irvine, Judith T., and Susan Gal. 'Language Ideology and Linguistic Differentiation.' In *Regimes of Language: Language Ideologies and the Discursive Construction of Power and Identity*, edited by Paul Kroskrity, 35–83. Santa Fe, NM: School of American Research Press, 2000.

Isichei, Elizabeth. *A History of the Igbo People*. New York, NY: St Martin's Press, 1976.

Ivaska, Andrew. *Cultured States: Youth, Gender, and Modern Style in 1960s Dar es Salaam*. Durham, NC: Duke University Press, 2011.

Jameson, Frederic. Interviewed by Michael Speaks. 'Envelopes and Enclaves: The Space of Post-Civil Society.' *Assemblage* 17 (1990): 30–37.

Jenkins, Trefor. 'Introduction – Fossils and Genes: A New Anthropology of Evolution.' In *A Search for Origins: Science, History and South Africa's 'Cradle of Humankind'*, edited by Philip Bonner, Amanda Esterhuysen, and Trefor Jenkins. Johannesburg: Witwatersrand University Press, 2007.

Jones, Sean. *Assaulting Childhood*. Johannesburg: Witwatersrand University Press, 1993.

Kamugungunu, Joshua. *Abagabe b'Ankole*. Kampala: Fountain, 2005 (1955).

Kankpeyeng, Benjamin W. and Christopher R. DeCorse. 'Ghana's Vanishing Past: Development, Antiquities, and the Destruction of the Archaeological Record.' *African Archaeological Review* 21 (2) (2004): 89–128.

Kasfir, Nelson. 'Guerillas and Civilian Participation: The National Resistance Army in Uganda, 1981–1986.' *Journal of Modern African Studies* 43 (2) (2005): 271–96.

Kea, Ray A. *Settlements, Trade, and Polities in the Seventeenth-Century Gold Coast*. Baltimore, MD: Johns Hopkins University Press, 1982.

Kedem, Kosi. *How Britain Subverted and Betrayed British Togoland*. Accra: Governance and Electoral Systems Agency, 2007.

Kerman, Joseph. *Opera as Drama*. Berkeley, CA: University of California Press, 2005.

Kihumuro-Apuli, David. *A Thousand Years of Bunyoro-Kitara Kingdom: The People and the Rulers*. Kampala: Fountain, 1994.

Kilson, Marion, *African Urban Kinsmen, the Ga of Central Accra*. London: C. Hurst and Co., 1974.

———. *Kpele Lala, Ga Religious Songs and Symbols*. Cambridge: Harvard University Press, 1971.

Kirindi, G. N. P. *History and Culture of the Kingdom of Ankole*. Kampala: Fountain, 2008.

Kirshenblatt-Gimblett, Barbara. *Destination Culture: Tourism, Museums, and Heritage*. Berkeley, CA: University of California Press, 1998.

———. 'Objects of Ethnography.' In *Exhibiting Cultures*, edited by Ivan Karp and Steven D. Lavine, 386–443. Washington, DC: Smithsonian Institution, 1991.

———. 'Theorizing Heritage.' *Ethnomusicology* 39 (3) (1995): 367–80.

Klein, Martin. *Islam and Imperialism in Senegal: Sine-Saloum 1847–1914*. Stanford, CA: Stanford University Press, 1969.

Klopper, Sandra. '"He Is My king, but He Is Also My Child": Inkatha, the African National Congress and the Struggle for Control over Zulu Cultural Symbols,' *Oxford Art Journal* 19 (1) 1990: 53–66.

Kludze, A. Kodzo Paaku. 'The Future of Chieftaincy in Modern Ghana.' In *Chieftaincy in Ghana*, 529–71. Lanham, MD: Austin and Winfield, 2000.

Knierzinger, Johannes. 'Chieftaincy and Development in Ghana: From Political Intermediaries to Neotraditional Development Brokers.' In *Working Papers, Institut für Ethnologie und Afrikastudien*. Mainz: Johannes Gutenberg Universität, 2011.

Koelle, Sigismund W. *Polyglotta Africana*. London: Church Missionary House, 1854.

Kok V, Adam. 'Statement Presented to the Symposium Held to Coincide with the Exhibition, "Miscast: Negotiating Khoisan History and Material Culture" at the Annex to South African National Gallery,' 14 April 1996.

Koselleck, Reinhart. *Futures Past: on the Semantics of Historical Time*. New York, NY: Columbia University Press, 2004 [1979].

Ladipo, Duro. 'Nigerian Folk Opera and Dance.' *First Commonwealth Arts Festival Programme Book*, edited by Anthony Wysard, 96–97. London: Excelads Imprint Ltd., 1965.

Landau, Paul. ' "Religion" and Christian Conversion in African History: A New Model.' *Journal of Religious History* 23 (1) (February 1999): 8–30.

_____. *Popular Politics in the History of South Africa, 1400 to 1948*. Cambridge: Cambridge University Press, 2010.

Langwick, Stacey. *Bodies, Politics, and African Healing: The Matter of Maladies in Tanzania*. Bloomington, IN: Indiana University Press, 2011.

Lamoise, Père. *Grammaire de la langue sérère avec des exemples et des exercices renfermant des documents très-utiles*. Saint-Joseph de Ngasobil (Sénégambie): Imprimerie de la mission, 1873.

Laqueur, Thomas. 'Memory and Naming in the Great War.' In *Commemorations*, edited by John R. Gillis, 150–68. Princeton, NJ: Princeton University Press, 1994.

Legassick, Martin and Ciraj Rassool. *Skeletons in the Cupboard: South African Museums and the Trade in Human Remains, 1907–1917*. Cape Town: South African Museum, 2000.

_____. 'South African Human Remains, Viennese Museums, and the Politics of Repatriation: Reconsidering the Legacy of Rudolf Pöch.' Unpublished paper presented to the Symposium on The Life of the Corpse, WISER, University of Witwatersrand, 25–26 August 2008.

Lentz, Carola. 'Local Culture in the National Arena: The Politics of Cultural Festivals in Ghana.' *African Studies Review* 44 (3) (2001): 47–72.

_____. *Ethnicity and the Making of History in Northern Ghana*. Edinburgh University Press, 2006.

Lounsbury, Carl R. 'Architectural and Cultural History.' In *The Oxford Handbook of Material Culture Studies*, edited by Dan Hicks and Mary C. Beaudry, 484–501. Oxford and New York, NY: Oxford University Press, 2010.

Low, D. A. *Buganda in Modern History*. London: Littlehampton, 1971.

Lüpke, Friederike and Anne Storch. *Repertoire and Choices in African Languages*. Boston, MA and Berlin: Walter de Gruyter Mouton, 2013.

Lwandle Migrant Labour Museum (brochure), *Lwandle Migrant Labour Museum & Arts & Crafts Centre*. Somerset West: Lwandle Museum, circa. 2000.

Mabin, Alan. 'Comprehensive Segregation: The Origins of the Group Areas Act and its Planning Apparatuses.' *Journal of Southern African Studies* 18 (2) (1992): 405–29.

Magezi, M. W., T. E. Nyakango, and M. K. Aganatia. *The People of the Rwenzoris: The Bayira (Bakonzo/Bananade) and Their Culture.* Köln: Rüdiger Köppe Verlag, 2004.

Mahoney, Michael. *The Other Zulus: The Spread of Zulu Ethnicity in Colonial South Africa.* Durham, NC: Duke University Press, 2012.

Maingard, Jacqueline. *South African National Cinema.* Oxford and New York, NY: Routledge, 2007.

Makoni, Sinfree. 'From misinvention to disinvention of language: Multilingualism and the South African constitution.' In *Black Linguistics: Language, Society, and Politics in Africa and the Americas*, edited by Sinfree Makoni, Geneva Smitherman, Arnetha F. Ball, and Arthur K. Spears, 132–51. London and New York: Routledge, 2003.

Makoni, Sinfree, and Alistair Pennycook, eds. *Disinventing and Reconstituting Languages.* Bristol: Multilingual Matters, 2007.

Mamdani, Mahmood. *Citizen and Subject: Contemporary Africa and the Legacy of Late Colonialism.* Kampala, Cape Town, and London: Fountain, David Phillip, and James Currey, 1996.

Manfredi, Victor. 'Àgbọ and Éhụgbò: Ìgbo Linguistic Consciousness, its Origins and Limits.' PhD dissertation, Harvard University, 1991.

Mann, Gregory. 'One Party, Several Socialisms: Mali's US-RDA.' Paper presented at African Studies Association Annual Meeting, 2012.

Marschall, Sabine. 'Commemorating the "Trojan Horse" Massacre in Cape Town: the Tension between Vernacular and Official Expressions of Memory.' *Visual Studies* 25 (2010): 135–48.

Marx, Karl. *The Eighteenth Brumaire of Louis Bonaparte.* New York, NY: International Publishers, 1963.

Maseko, Zola, director. *The Return of Sara Baartman* (film). New York, NY: First Run/Icarus Films, 2003.

Mbeki, Thabo. *Africa: The Time Has Come.* Cape Town: Tafelberg, 1998.

Mbembe, Achille. *On the postcolony.* Berkeley, CA: University of California Press, 2001.

Mbemebe, Achille, Grace Khunou, and Nsizwa Dlamini. 'The Township Now: A Conversation.' *WiSER in Brief* 2 (2) (December 2003): 4–7.

Mboya, Paul. *Luo Kitgi gi Timbegi.* Kisumu: Anyange Press, 1983 [1938].

McCaskie, T. C. 'Asante Origins, Egypt, and the Near East: An Idea and Its Origins.' In *Recasting the Past: History Writing and Political Work in Modern Africa*, edited by Derek R. Peterson and Giacomo Macola, 125–48. Athens, OH: Ohio University Press, 2009.

McClendon, Thomas. *White Chief, Black Lords: Shepstone and the Colonial State in Natal, South Africa, 1845–1878.* Rochester, NY: University of Rochester Press, 2010.

McGregor, JoAnn and Lynn Schumaker. 'Heritage in Southern Africa: Imagining and Marketing Public Culture and History.' *Journal of Southern African Studies* 32 (2006): 649–65.

McLaughlin, Fiona. 'Senegal: The Emergence of a National Lingua Franca.' In *Language and National Identity in Africa*, edited by Andrew Simpson, 79–97. Oxford and New York, NY: Oxford University Press, 2008.

McLeod, Malcolm D. *The Asante*, London: British Museum Publications, 1981.

McNulty, Grant. 'Custodianship on the Periphery: Archives, Power and Identity Politics in Post-Apartheid Umbumbulu, KwaZulu-Natal.' PhD thesis, University of Cape Town, 2014.

Merrington, Peter. 'Cape Dutch Tongaat: A Case Study in "Heritage".' *Journal of Southern African Studies* 32 (4) (December 2006): 683–99.

Meskell, Lynn and Colette Scheermeyer, 'Heritage as Therapy,' *Journal of Material Culture* 13 (2) (2008): 153–74.

Mgijima, Bongani and Vusi Buthelezi. 'Mapping Museum: Community Relations in Lwandle.' *Journal of Southern African Studies* 32 (4) (2006): 795–806.

Miller, Daniel. 'Why Some Things Matter.' In *Material Cultures: Why Some Things Matter*, edited by Daniel Miller, 3–21. London: Routledge, 1998.

Minkley, Gary. 'A Fragile Inheritor': The Post-Apartheid Memorial Complex, A.C. Jordan and the Re-Imagining of Cultural Heritage in the Eastern Cape.' *Kronos: Southern African Histories* 34 (2008): 16–40.

Minkley, Gary, Ciraj Rassool, and Leslie Witz. 'South Africa and the Spectacle of Public Pasts: Heritage, Public Histories and Post Anti-Apartheid South Africa.' Unpublished paper, March 2009.

Minnesota Museum of Art, *African Heritage: Traditional Sculpture and Crafts from the Permanent Collection of the Minnesota Museum of Art*. Saint Paul, MN: The Museum, 1975.

Modisane, Litheko. 'Suddenly the Film Scene Is Becoming Our Scene'! The Circulation and Public Lives of Black Centered Films in South Africa: 1959–2001.' PhD thesis, University of the Witwatersrand, 2010.

_____. *South Africa's Renegade Reels: The Making and Public Lives of Black Centered Films*. New York, NY: Palgrave Macmillan, 2013.

_____. 'Outlawed Black Public Spheres: Snapshots of Cinema's Archive', In *Uncertain Curature: In and Out of the Archive*, edited by Carloyn Hamilton and Pippa Skotnes. Johannesburg: Jacana, forthcoming.

Mollien, Gaspard. *Travels in the Interior of Africa to the Sources of the Senegal and Gambia . . . in the Year 1818*. Edinburgh: Bowdich, 1820.

Morris, Alan G. *Inaugural Lecture: The Politics of Old Bones*. Cape Town: University of Cape Town, 2008.

Msemwa, Paul. *From King George V Memorial Museum to House of Culture: Royalty to Popularity*. Dar es Salaam: National Museum of Tanzania, 2005.

Muravchik, Joshua. *Heaven on Earth: The Rise and Fall of Socialism*. San Francisco, CA: Encounter Books, 2002.

Murray, Martin. *Commemorating and Forgetting: Challenges for the New South Africa*. Minneapolis, MN: University of Minnesota Press, 2013.

Murray, Noëleen. 'Spatial [Re]Imaginings? Contesting Township Development Post-Apartheid.' Paper presented at the Wits Institute for Social and Economic Research Symposium, The Townships Now, 9–11 June 2004.

_____. 'A Campus Apart.' In *Becoming UWC: Reflections, Pathways and Unmaking Apartheid's Legacy*, edited by Premesh Lalu and Noëleen Murray, 58–83. Bellville: University of the Western Cape, 2012.

_____. 'Working with Inconsistencies and Discontinuities: Competing Conceptions of Heritage and Urban Design at the Lwandle Migrant Labour Museum.' *Architecture South Africa* (March/April 2007): 30–33.

Murray, Noëleen and Leslie Witz. 'Dislocation: Making the Lwandle Migrant Labour Museum.' Paper presented at the South African Contemporary History and Humanities Seminar, University of the Western Cape, 10 May 2011.

Murray, Noëleen and Leslie Witz. 'Camp Lwandle: Rehabilitating a Migrant Labour Hostel at the Seaside.' *Social Dynamics: A Journal of African Studies* 39:1 (2013): 51–74.

Mutesa, Edward. *The Desecration of My Kingdom*. London: Constable, 1967.

Mutibwa, Phares. *The Buganda Factor in Uganda Politics*. Kampala: Fountain, 2008.

National Commission on Culture. *The Cultural Policy of Ghana*. Accra: National Commission on Culture, 2004.

National Heritage Council. *The Duncan Village Massacre Memorialization Public Hearing Preliminary Report*. Buffulo [sic] City (24 June 2008): 1–38.

National Heritage Council. 'Position Paper on a Proposed Policy Framework on the Repatriation of Heritage Resources.' Pretoria: National Heritage Council, January 2011.

Neely, Sarah. 'Scotland, Heritage and Devolving British Cinema.' *Screen* 46 (2) (2005): 241–46.

Ngologoza, Paulo. *Kigezi and Its People*. Kampala: Fountain, 1998 [1967].

Ngũgĩ wa Thiong'o. *Decolonising the Mind: The Politics of Language in African Literature*. Portsmouth, NH: Heinemann Educational Publishers, 1981.

Nienaber, Willem C., Natalie Keough, and Maryna Steyn. 'Repatriation of the Mapungubwe Human Remains: An Overview of the Process and Procedure.' Forensic Anthropology Research Centre, University of Pretoria, 2008.

Nii-Dortey, Moses. 'Historical and Cultural Context of Folk Opera Development in Ghana: Saka Acquaye's "The Lost Fishermen" in Perspective.' *Research Review* 27 (2) (2012): 25–58.

Nii-Yartey, Francis. 'The Performing Arts: Identity and the New Social Paradigm.' In *Identity Meets Nationality, Voices from the Humanities*, edited by Helen Leuer et al. Accra: Sub-Saharan Publishers, 2011.

Nkrumah, Kwame. *I Speak of Freedom: A Statement of African Ideology*. Westport, CT: Greenwood, 1976.

———. *Conscienscism: Philosophy and Ideology for Decolonization*. New York, NY: Modern Reader Paperbacks, 1970.

Nora, Pierre. 'Between Memory and History: Les Lieux de Memoire.' *Representations* 26 (1989): 7–25.

Northrup, David. 'Igbo and Myth Igbo: Culture and Ethnicity in the Atlantic World, 1600–1850.' *Slavery and Abolition* 21 (3) (2000): 1–20.

———. 'Becoming African: Identity Formation among Liberated Slaves in Nineteenth-Century Sierra Leone.' *Slavery and Abolition* 27 (1) (2006): 1–21.

Nunoo, Robert B. *Christiansborg Castle – Osu*. Accra: Ministry of Information, 1969.

Nuttall, Sarah. 'Introduction.' In *Entanglement: Literary and Cultural Reflections on Post Apartheid*. Johannesburg: Witwatersrand University Press, 2009.

Nwachukwu, P. Akujuoobi. *Towards an Igbo Literary Standard*. London: Kegan Paul International for the International African Institute, 1983.

Nyakatura, J. W. *Abakama of Bunyoro-Kitara*. Kisubi: Marianum Press, 1998 [1947].

Nyerere, Julius. *Freedom and Unity*. London: Oxford University Press, 1967.

———. *Freedom and Socialism: Uhuru na Ujamaa*. London: Oxford University Press, 1968.

Obeng, Samuel Gyasi and Efurosibina Adegbija. 'Sub-Saharan Africa.' In *Handbook of Language and Ethnic Identity*, edited by Joshua A. Fishman, 353–68. Oxford: Oxford University Press, 1999.

Obote, Apollo Milton. *The Common Man's Charter*. Entebbe: Government Printer, 1969.

Odotei, Irene K., and Albert K. Awedoba, eds. *Chieftaincy in Ghana: Culture, Governance and Development*. Legon: Sub-Saharan Publishers, 2006.

Oldendorp, Christian Georg Andreas. *History of the Mission of the Evangelical Brethren on the Caribbean Islands of St. Thomas, St. Croix, and St. John*, edited by Johann Jakob Bossard and translated by A. R. Highfield and V. Barac. Ann Arbor, MI: Karoma, 1987 [1777].

Owusu, Martin. *Analysis and Interpretation of Ola Rotimi's* The Gods Are Not to Blame. Accra: SEDCO Publishing, 2002.

Owusu-Ansah, David and Daniel Miles McFarland. *Historical Dictionary of Ghana*. Metuchen, NJ and London: The Scarecrow Press, Inc., 1995.

Owusu-Sarpong, Christian. 'Setting the Ghanaian Context of Rural Local Government: Traditional Authority Values.' In *Grassroots Governance? Chiefs in Africa and the Afro-Caribbean*, edited by Donald Iain Ray and P. S. Reddy, 31–67. Calgary: University of Calgary Press, 2003.

Parker, John. *Making the Town, Ga State and Society in Early Colonial Accra*. Oxford: James Currey, 2000.

Parks, Suzan-Lori. *Venus: A Play*. New York, NY: Theatre Communications Group, 1997.

Peers, Laura Lynn and Alison Kay Brown eds. *Museums and Source Communities*. London: Routledge, 2002.

Perbi, Akosua Adoma. *A History of Indigenous Slavery in Ghana from the 15th to the 19th Century*. Legon: Sub-Saharan Publishers, 2004.

———. 'Who Is a Ghanaian? A Historical Perspective.' *National Integration: Proceedings of the Ghana Academy of Arts and Sciences* (2003): 29–37.

Peterson, Derek R. *Ethnic Patriotism and the East African Revival: A History of Dissent, ca. 1935–1972*. Cambridge: Cambridge University Press, 2012.

Peterson, Derek R. and Giacomo Macola. 'Homespun History and the Academic Profession.' In *Recasting the Past: History Writing and Political Work in Modern Africa*, edited by Derek R. Peterson and Giacomo Macola, 1–30. Athens, OH: Ohio University Press, 2009.

Pinet-Laprade, E. 'Notice sur les Sérères.' *Annuaire du Sénégal pour l'année 1865*, 131–71. Saint-Louis: Imprimerie du Gouvernement, 1865.

Pinney, Christopher. *Photos of the Gods: The Printed Image and Political Struggle in India*. New Delhi: Oxford University Press, 2004.

Pitcher, M. Anne and Kelly Askew. 'African Socialisms and Postsocialisms.' *Africa: Journal of the International African Institute* 76 (1) (2006): 1–14.

Pogucki, R. J. H. *Gold Coast Land Tenure*, Vol. 3: *Land Tenure in Ga Customary Law*. Accra: Gold Coast Lands Department, 1955.

Pöch, Hella. 'Beitrag zur Kenntnis des Muskelsystems und einiger Rassenmerkmale der Buschmänner.' *Mitteilungen der Anthropologischen Gesellschaft* 57 (1927): 108–12.

Pratt, Mary-Louise. *Imperial Eyes: Travel Writing and Transculturation*. London, Routledge, 1992.

———. 'Arts of the Contact Zones.' *Profession* 91 (1991): 33–40.

Raath, Mike. 'Human Material in Collections: Airing the Skeletons in the Closet.' Paper presented to the 65th Conference and Annual General Meeting of the South African Museums Association, Port Elizabeth, 5–7 June, 2001.

Ranger, Terence. 'Missionaries, Migrants and the Manyika: The Invention of Ethnicity in Zimbabwe.' In *The Creation of Tribalism in Southern Africa*, edited by Leroy Vail, 151–92. Berkeley and Los Angeles, CA: University of California Press, 1991.

Rassool, Ciraj. 'Community Museums, Memory Politics, and Social Transformation in South Africa: Histories, Possibilities, Limits.' In *Museum Frictions: Public Cultures/Global Transformations*, edited by Ivan Karp, Corinne Kratz, Lynn Szwaja, and Tomás Ybarra-Frausto, 286–321. Durham, NC: Duke University Press, 2006.

———. 'Rethinking Documentary History and South African Political Biography.' *South African Review of Sociology* 41 (2010): 28–55.

———. 'Beyond the Cult of "Salvation" and "Remarkable Equality": A New Paradigm for the Bleek-Lloyd Collection.' *Kronos* 32 (2006): 244–51.

———. 'Ethnographic Elaborations, Indigenous Contestations, and the Cultural Politics of Imagining Community: A View from the District Six Museum in South Africa.' In *Contesting Knowledge: Museums and Indigenous Perspectives*, edited by Susan Sleeper-Smith, 106–26. Lincoln, NE: University of Nebraska Press, 2009.

———. 'The Rise of Heritage and the Reconstruction of History in South Africa.' *Kronos* 26 (2000): 1–21.

Rassool, Ciraj and Patricia Hayes. 'Science and the Spectacle:/Khanako's South Africa, 1936–1937.' In *Deep hiStories: Gender and Colonialism in Southern Africa*, edited by Wendy Woodward, Patricia Hayes, and Gary Minkley, 117–61. Amsterdam: Rodopi, 2002.

Rassool, Ciraj, Leslie Witz, and Gary Minkley. 'Burying and Memorialising the Body of Truth: The TRC and National Heritage.' In *After the TRC: Reflections on Truth and Reconciliation in South Africa*, edited by Wilmot James and Linda van de Vijver, 115–27. Cape Town: David Philip, 2000.

Rassool, Ciraj and Leslie Witz. '"South Africa: A World in One Country": Moments in International Tourist Encounters with Wildlife, the Primitive and the Modern.' *Cahiers d'Etudes Africaines* 143 (XXXVI-3) (1996): 335–71.

Rassool, Ciraj and Leslie Witz. 'Transforming Heritage Education in South Africa: A Partnership between the Academy and the Museum.' Paper presented at SAMP 2001: Strengthening the Network: A Meeting of African Museums of the Swedish African Museum Programme, 22–27 August 1999.

Rathbone, Richard. *Nkrumah and the Chiefs: The Politics of Chieftaincy in Ghana, 1951–1960*. Athens, OH: Ohio University Press, 2000.

Ray, Donald Iain. 'Chiefs in Their Millennium Sandals: Traditional Authority in Ghana – Relevance, Challenges and Prospects.' In *Critical Perspectives in Politics and Socio-Economic Development in Ghana*, edited by Wisdom Tettey, Korbla P. Puplampu, and Bruce Berman, 241–71. Leiden: Brill, 2003.

Ross, Fiona. *Women and the TRC*. London: Pluto Press, 2003.

Rubongoya, L. T. *Naaho Nubo: The Ways of our Ancestors*. Köln: Rüdiger Köppe Verlag, 2003.

Samuelson, Meg. 'The Urban Palimpsest: Re-presenting Sophiatown.' *Journal of Postcolonial Writing* 44 (1) (2008): 63–75.

Saville-Troike, Muriel. 'The Place of Silence in an Integrated Theory of Communication.' In *Perspectives on Silence*, edited by D. Tannen and M. Saville-Troike, 3–18. Norwood, NJ: Ablex, 1983.

Sauer, Walter. 'Österreich – Südafrika: Die Geschichte von Klaas und Trooi Pienaar.' *Indaba: Das SADOCC-Magazin für Südliche Afrika* 74 (2012).

Schramm, Katharina. 'The Politics of Dance: Changing Representations of the Nation in Ghana.' *African Spectrum* 35 (3) (2000): 339–58.

_____. 'Senses of Authenticity: Chieftaincy and the Politics of Heritage in Ghana.' *Ethnofor* 17 (1/2) (2004): 156–77.

Schramm, Katharina. 'Slave Route Projects: Tracing the Heritage of Slavery in Ghana.' In *Reclaiming Heritage: Alternative Imaginaries of Memory in West Africa*, edited by Ferdinand de Jong and Michael Rowlands, 71–98. Walnut Creek, CA: Left Coast Press, 2007.

_____. *African Homecoming: Pan-African Ideology and Contested Heritage.* Walnut Creek, CA: Left Coast Press, 2010.

Scully, Tony. 'Online Anthropology Draws Protest from Aboriginal Group,' *Nature* 453 (1155) (2008).

Sealy, Judith C. 'Managing Collections of Human Remains in South African Museums and Universities: Ethical Policy-Making and Scientific Value,' *South African Journal of Science* 99 (2003): 238–39.

Segbefia, Alexander Yao. 'Community Approach to Tourism Development in Ghana.' In *Tourism in Ghana: A Modern Synthesis*, edited by Oheneba Akyeampong and Alex Boakye Asiedu, 54–68. Accra: Assemblies of God Literature Centre Ltd., 2008.

Seleti, Yonah. 'Letter from Yonah Seleti, Heritage Manager, Freedom Park Trust to History Advisory Panel Members,' 21 October 2005.

Shepherd, Nick. 'Heritage.' In *New South African Keywords*, edited by Nick Shepherd and Steven Robins. Athens, OH: Ohio University Press, 2008.

Shepherd, Nick and Christian Ernsten. 'The World Below: Post-Apartheid Urban Imaginaries and the Bones of the Prestwich Street Dead.' In *Desire Lines: Space, Memory and Identity in the Post-Apartheid City*, edited by Noëleen Murray, Nick Shepherd, and Martin Hall, 215–32. London and New York, NY: Routledge 2007.

Shepperson, George. 'The African Abroad or the African Diaspora.' In *Emerging Themes in African History*, edited by T. O. Ranger, 152–76. Nairobi: East African Publishing House, 1968.

Silverman, Raymond. 'Locating Culture with/in a Ghanaian Community.' In *Translating Knowledge: Global Perspectives on Museum and Community*, edited by Raymond Silverman. London: Routledge, forthcoming.

Sithole, Jabulani. 2008. 'Preface – Zuluness in South Africa: from 'Struggle' Debate to Democratic Transformation.' In *Zulu Identities: Being Zulu, Past and Present*, edited by Ben Carton, John Laband, and Jabulani Sithole. Pietermaritzburg: University of KwaZulu-Natal Press, 2008.

Skotnes, Pippa. 'The Politics of Bushman Representations.' In *Images and Empires: Visuality in Colonial and Postcolonial Africa*, edited by Paul S. Landau and Deborah D. Kaspin, 253–74. Berkeley, CA: University of California Press, 2002.

Sloth-Nielsen, Julia, Desiree Hanson, and Colleen Richardson. *Chickens in a Box: A Progressive Participatory Study of Lwandle Hostel Residents' Perceptions of Personal Safety.* Pretoria: HSRC, 1992.

Spring, Christopher, Nigel Barley, and Julie Hudson. 'The Sainsbury African Galleries at the British Museum.' *African Arts* 34 (3) (Autumn 2001): 18–37.

Ssebalija, Yohana. 'Memories of Rukiga and Other Places.' In *A History of Kigezi in South-West Uganda*, edited by Donald Denoon. Kampala: The National Trust, 1972.

Steinhart, Edward. *Conflict and Collaboration in the Kingdoms of Western Uganda.* Princeton, NJ: Princeton University Press, 1977.

Strother, Z. S. 'Display of the Body Hottentot.' In *Africans on Stage: Studies in Ethnological Show Business*, edited by Bernth Lindfors, 1–61. Bloomington, IN: Indiana University Press, 1999.

Sutherland, Efua. 'The National Orchestra in Concert.' *Sankofa* 1 (1) (1977).

———. *The Marriage of Anansewa and Edufa*. London: Longman, 1990.

Suttner, Raymond. 'Talking to the Ancestors: National Heritage, the Freedom Charter and Nation Building in South Africa in 2005.' *Development Southern Africa* 23 (2006): 3–27.

Swanson, Donald. *Assignment Africa*. Cape Town: Simondium Publishers, 1965.

Symonds, James. 'Historical Archaeology and the Recent Urban Past.' *International Journal of Heritage Studies* 10 (1) (2004): 33–48.

Szuchewyez, Bohdan. 'Silence in Ritual Communication.' In *Silence: Interdisciplinary Perspectives*. Studies in Linguistics 10, edited by Adam Jaworski, 63–84. Berlin: Mouton de Gruyter, 1997.

Thurman, Sarah. 'Umzamo: Improving Hostel Dwellers' Accommodation in South Africa.' *Environment and Urbanization* 9 (2) (1997): 43–62.

Tilley, Helen, ed. *Ordering Africa: Anthropology, European Imperialism, and the Politics of Knowledge*. Manchester: Manchester University Press, 2007.

Tobias, Phillip V. with Goran Štrkalj and Jane Dugard 2008. *Tobias in Conversation: Genes, Fossils and Anthropology*. Johannesburg: Witwatersrand University Press.

Tomlinson, John. *Cultural Imperialism*. London: Continuum, 1991.

de Tressan, M. de L. *Inventaire linguistique de l'Afrique Occidentale Française et du Togo*. Mémoires 30. Dakar: Institut Français d'Afrique Noire, 1953.

Trowell, Margaret, and K. P. Wachsmann. *Tribal Crafts of Uganda*. London: Oxford University Press, 1953.

Ubahakwe, Ebo. 'The Language and Dialects of Igbo.' In *A Survey of the Igbo Nation*, edited by G. E. K. Ofomata, 252–71. Onitsha: Africana First Publishers, 2002.

Urban Design Services. 'Lwandle: Investigation into the Potential for Black Housing.' Cape Town: Urban Foundation, 1987.

van Dantzig, Albert. *Forts and Castles in Ghana*. Accra: Sedco Publishing Limited, 1980.

van Dugteren, William Ruijsch. 'Lwandle Hostels-to-Homes Project: Retrofitting for Sustainability.' Paper presented at City Energy Strategies Conference, Cape Town International Convention Centre, 19–21 November 2003.

van Duuren, David with Mischa ten Kate, Micaela Pereira, Steven Vink, and Susan Legêne. *Physical Anthropology Reconsidered: Human Remains at the Tropenmuseum*. Amsterdam: KIT Publishers, 2007.

Vieta, Kojo. *The Flag Bearers of Ghana: Profiles of One Hundred Distinguished Ghanaians*. Accra: Ena Publications, 1999.

Vowles, Valerie. 'Uganda in the Fifties.' *Newsletter (Museum Ethnographers Group)* 12 (October 1981).

Ward, Sarah. *The Energy Book for Urban Development in South Africa*. Noordhoek: Sustainable Energy Africa, 2003.

Webb, Colin and John Wright. *The James Stuart Archive of Recorded Oral Evidence Relating to the History of the Zulu and Neighbouring Peoples*, Volume 4. Durban: Killie Campbell Africana Library and University of Natal Press, 1986.

Welbourn, F. B. 'Kibuuka Comes Home.' *Transition* 5 (July–August 1962): 15–17; 20.

Wellington, Nii-Adziri H. *Stones Tell Stories at Osu: Memories of a Host Community of the Danish Trans-Atlantic Slave Trade*. Accra: Sub-Saharan Publishers, 2011.

Welsh, D. 'The Cultural Dimension of Apartheid.' *African Affairs* 71 (282) (1972): 35–53.

Werbner, Richard. 'Smoke from the Barrel of a Gun: Postwars of the Dead, Memory and Reinscription in Zimbabwe.' In *Memory and the Postcolony: African Anthropology and the Critique of Power*, edited by Richard Werbner, 71–102. London and New York, NY: Zed Books, 1998.

Wilks, Ivor. *Asante in the Nineteenth Century: The Structure and Evolution of a Political Order*. Cambridge: Cambridge University Press, 1975.

———. 'The State of the Akan and the Akan States: A Discursion.' *Cahiers d'Études Africaines* 22 (3–4) (1982): 231–49.

———. 'Akwamu and Otublohum: an Eighteenth Century Akan Marriage Arrangement.' *Africa* 29 (4) (1959): 391–404.

Williams, Gordon. 'Intelligibility and Language Boundaries among the Cangin Peoples of Senegal.' *Journal of West African Languages* 24 (1) (1994): 47–67.

Winter, Edward. *Bwamba: A Structure-Functional Analysis of a Patrilineal Society*. Cambridge: Heffer and Sons, 1952.

Witz, Leslie. 'Transforming Museums on Postaparthied Tourist Routes.' In *Museum Frictions: Public Cultures/Global Transformations*, edited by Ivan Karp, Corrine A. Kratz, Lynn Szwaja, and Tomás Ybarra-Frausto, 107–34. Durham, NC: Duke University Press, 2007.

———. 'Making Museums as Heritage in Post-Apartheid South Africa.' Unpublished paper, June 2012.

———. 'Revisualizing Township Tourism in the Western Cape: The Migrant Labour Museum and the Re-Construction of Lwandle.' *Journal of Contemporary African Studies* 29, 4 (2011): 371–88.

———. 'Observing and Disobeying the Signs: The Lwandle Migrant Labour Museum, a Heritage Park in Cape Town.' Paper Presented at Norms in the Margins and Margins of the Norm conference, 25–27 October 2012, Royal Museum for Central Africa, Tervuren.

Witz, Leslie and Noëleen Murray. 'Writing Museum Biography: Displacing Development and Community in Lwandle.' Paper presented at The Politics of Heritage conference, University of Michigan/University of the Witwatersrand, Johannesburg, 8–9 July 2011.

Witz, Leslie and Ciraj Rassool. 'Making Histories.' *Kronos: Southern African Histories*, 34 (2008): 6–15.

Wright, John. 'Reconstituting Shaka Zulu for the Twenty-First Century.' *Southern African Humanities* 18 (2) (2006): 139–53.

———. 'Rediscovering the Ndwandwe Kingdom.' In *Five Hundred Years Rediscovered: Southern African Precedents and Prospects*, edited by Natalie Swanepoel, Amanda Esterhuysen, and Phil Bonner. Johannesburg: Witwatersrand University Press, 2008.

———. 'Reflections on the Politics of Being 'Zulu'.' In *Zulu Identities: Being Zulu, Past and Present*, edited by Benedict Carton, John Laband, and Jabulani Sithole, 35–43. New York, NY: Columbia University Press, 2009.

Wright, John and Carolyn Hamilton. 'Traditions and Transformations: the Phongolo-Mzimkhulu Region in the Late Eighteenth and Early Nineteenth Centuries.' In *Natal and Zululand from Earliest Times to 1910: A New History*, edited by Andrew Duminy and Bill Guest, Pietermaritzburg: University of Natal Press, 1989.

Wylie, Dan. *Myth of Iron: Shaka in History*. Pietermaritzburg: University Kwa-Zulu Natal Press, 2006.

Yahaya, Ahmad. 'The Scope and Definitions of Heritage: From Tangible to Intangible.' *International Journal of Heritage Studies* 12 (3) (2006): 292–300.

Yankah, Kwesi. *Speaking for the Chief: Okyeame and the Politics of Akan Royal Oratory*. Bloomington, IN: Indiana University Press, 1995.

_____. *Free Speech in Traditional Society: The Cultural Foundations of Communication in Contemporary Ghana*. Accra: Ghana Universities Press, 1998.

_____. *The Proverb in the Context of Akan Rhetoric*. New York, NY: Diasporic Africa Press, 2012.

Zeitlyn, David, and Bruce Connell. 'Ethnogenesis and Fractal History on an African Frontier: Mambila – Njerep – Mandulu.' *Journal of African History* 44 (2003): 117–38.

Index

TITLES IN THE SERIES

Lightning Source UK Ltd.
Milton Keynes UK
UKHW01f0502030518
322044UK00001B/29/P